9

2000

2000

2

1

A MANUAL OF ALPINE AND ROCK
GARDEN PLANTS / EDITED BY
CHRISTOPHER GREY-WILSON .

40-190379

D0279615

A Manual of Alpine and Rock Garden Plants

Rock Gardener's Library
Series editor: Richard Bird

Forthcoming titles include:

An introduction to Rock Gardening
Richard Bird

The Propagation of Alpine Plants and Dwarf Bulbs
Brian Halliwell

Gardening with Raised Beds and Tufa
Paul Ingwersen

The Alpine House
Robert Rolfe

Other gardening books published by Christopher Helm

An Anthology of Garden Writing
Edited by Ursula Buchan

Bonsai: Its Art, Science and Philosophy
Deborah Koreshoff

Conifers
Keith D. Rushforth

The Conservatory Handbook
Ann Bonar

The Cottage Garden Year
Roy Genders

Creating a Chinese Garden
David H. Engel

The Flower Show
E.D. Wearn

Gardening with Dwarf Trees and Shrubs
Andreas Bärtels

Gardening with Trees
Sonia Kinahan

Growing Begonias
E. Catterall

Growing Bulbs
Martyn Rix

Growing Chrysanthemums
Harold Randall and Alan Wren

Growing Cyclamen
Gay Nightingale

Growing Dahlias
Philip Damp

Growing Fuchsias
K. Jennings and V. Miller

Growing Hardy Perennials
Kenneth A. Beckett

Growing Irises
G.E. Cassidy and S. Linnegar

Growing Lilies
Derek Fox

A Handbook of Annuals and Bedding Plants
Graham Rice

A Handbook of Greenhouse and Conservatory Plants
Anne Swithinbank

The Handbook of Soft Fruit Growing
Ken Muir and David Turner

Hardy Geraniums
Peter F. Yeo

Hebes and Parahebes
Douglas Chalk

The History of Gardens
Christopher Thacker

The Hosta Book
Paul Aden (ed.)

Maidenhair Ferns in Cultivation
Christopher Goudy

Miniature and Dwarf Geraniums
Harold Bagust

Laissez-faire Gardening
Nigel Colborn

Plants for Problem Places
Graham Rice

The Rock Gardener's Handbook
Alan Titchmarsh

The Winter Flower Garden
Sonia Kinahan

A Manual of Alpine and Rock Garden Plants

General Editor:
Christopher Grey-Wilson

Contributors:

Susyn Andrews
Richard Bird
Brian Burrow
Martin Gardner
Christopher Grey-Wilson
Pat Halliday
Sabina Knees
Gwilym Lewis
Brian Mathew
Victoria Matthews
George F. Smith

Illustrations by

Christine Grey-Wilson

CHRISTOPHER HELM
London

TIMBER PRESS
Portland, Oregon

© 1989 Christopher Grey-Wilson
Line illustrations by Christine Grey-Wilson
Christopher Helm (Publishers) Ltd, Imperial House,
21–25 North Street, Bromley BR1 1SD

ISBN 0-7470-1224-5

A CIP catalogue record for this book
is available from the British Library

All rights reserved. No reproduction, copy or transmission
of this publication may be made without prior permission.

No paragraph of this publication may be reproduced, copied
or transmitted save with written permission or in accordance
with the provisions of the Copyright Act 1956 (as amended),
or under the terms of any licence permitting limited copying
issued by the Copyright Licensing Agency, 7 Ridgmount Street,
London WC1E 7AE.

Any person who does any unauthorised act in relation to
this publication may be liable to criminal prosecution and
civil claims for damages.

First published in North America in 1989 by
Timber Press
9999 SW Wilshire
Portland, Oregon, 97225
USA

ISBN 0-88192-146-7

Essex County Library

Typeset by Paston Press, Loddon, Norfolk
Printed and bound in Great Britain by The Bath Press

FV 86585

Contents

Colour Plates

Figures

Introduction

Alpine plants have never been more popular than they are today. Most gardens have room for a rockery, a raised bed or a simple trough or sink. Indeed, alpine plants are ideally suited to today's gardens; many are small, easily grown and colourful, providing interest, with careful selection, throughout the year. So it is not surprising that more and more people are being bitten by the 'alpine plant bug'. It has also become easier to take one's holidays in the Alps and the Pyrenees, or on mountain ranges in more exotic parts of the world, and to see for oneself, in their natural habitats, many of the delightful mountain plants that can be grown in our gardens. A wide range of these are fairly easy to obtain, being listed in the catalogues of specialist nurseries. Many species are very adaptable, so it is quite possible to have species from distant lands, from say Nepal, North America and New Zealand, all growing side by side in the rock garden.

This book is primarily intended for the beginner, but it is also a compendium of the large majority of alpines listed in nurserymen's catalogues. From the onset, the aim was to include, above all, those species that could be grown in the open garden, sometimes with winter protection, as well as some which really thrive better within the confines of the alpine house or cold frame.

Some rare and more difficult species are included in the hope that the newcomer, having tried the easier ones, will move on to growing more challenging species after a year or two. The scope for growing a large collection of mixed species, or a specialized collection of say Gentians or Saxifrages, is almost limitless, providing a hobby that will last a lifetime.

As many cultivars as possible have been included although in some groups, like the dwarf Rhododendrons or Sempervivums, only a selection has been offered, otherwise the task would have become impossibly complicated.

The full range of alpine flowering plants has been included with the exception of the many bulbous species, which alone would fill a similarly sized volume. Dwarf bulbs mix very well with many alpine plants and are well covered by the various books available on the market.

In order to help the reader understand the requirements of the many species described, a simple system of symbols has been employed as follows:

○—plants require full sun
◑—plants require shade or half-shade
▥—plants require an acid soil
☆—easy and especially recommended to the beginner
▲—difficult species to cultivate successfully

The genera are listed alphabetically. Within each genus similar species are grouped together for easy comparison in most instances—see the comprehensive

1

index for a complete alphabetical list of accepted names and synonyms. Cultivar names are included under relevant species, or, if their origin is unknown, at the end of each genus.

Alpine gardening can be great fun. Nowhere else in the garden is it so easy to create special conditions for different groups of plants simply by adding the right amount of grit or peat to the compost, by selecting an acid or alkaline compost or by establishing a wall or crevices for the cliff dwellers. During the winter months, when gardening becomes impossible, this volume, in conjunction with a selection of nurserymen's catalogues, can be browsed through to select new plants to grow the following season.

CONSERVATION

All the species included in this book are available in the horticultural trade and the reader is implored not to dig them up in the wild. The collection of a little seed from wild plants does very little harm, except when the species is rare, but digging up of wild specimens simply to enhance one's own collection is intolerable. Many countries have laws forbidding the removal of wild plants from their habitats and it is an offence to do so. These laws are there to protect a wide range of habitats and the plants and animals that they harbour. Left alone they will remain for many of us to enjoy for years to come.

SOCIETIES TO JOIN

The Alpine Garden Society
The Scottish Rock Garden Club
The American Rock Garden Society

Cultivation of Alpines

ALPINES IN THE WILD

When considering any form of gardening, with the possible exception of vegetables, it is often important to consider the native habitat of the plants involved in order that they may be given the best growing conditions. With alpine plants this is particularly relevant.

The term 'alpines', at first sight, would appear to state the habitat of the plants that fall into that category; however, not only is the definition used very loosely, but there is also a wide variation of conditions in alpine regions. Botanically, alpines are those mountain plants growing above the tree-line, although this may include species growing in the treeless regions beyond the Arctic Circle, or occasionally in coastal areas where similar conditions may prevail. Most alpine plants are small, but alpine gardeners include in their collections a vast range of small plants from other habitats, often away from the mountains—hence the terms rock-garden plant and alpine plant are frequently, if not rather loosely, used and definitions start to involve other criteria. In many respects the actual definition of alpines is irrelevant—as far as cultivation is concerned, it is the habitat of each plant that is important, whether it comes from the high peaks, wooded hillsides, lush meadows or barren hillsides, or the rocky shores of the Mediterranean.

The plants of the peaks above the tree-line are highly specialized to cope with the harsh conditions; generally speaking, the higher one goes the more specialized and more difficult to grow the native plants become. Some of them grow in crevices and cracks in the rock, others in fixed or moving collections of stone known as screes, or on moraines left by retreating glaciers. A common feature of these positions is that the roots have to delve deep for moisture and nutrients, since there is very little soil available. The conditions are harsh, often swinging from hot days to freezing nights. In winter the plants have to put up with very cold conditions, but are often blanketed with snow which affords them some insulation, especially from winds. They have a very short growing season and as soon as the snow retreats,they put on growth and flower. This means that the best place in which to search for the flowers of many mountain plants is close to the retreating edges of the snow.

As one moves down the mountain so the condtions become less harsh and the plants easier to grow, with longer growing and flowering seasons. The woods and forests below the tree-line provide a shady habitat, but one which is still quick-draining. Further down are the alpine meadows full of colourful flowers that thrive in a soil rich in humus and minerals which are washed down from above, dissolved in the water from the melting snows. Even this humus-rich soil is quick draining.

At lower levels, right down to sea level, it is still possible to find plants growing in crevices and fissures of rock, but these often have more soil and detritus in which to grow. Also, at the lower levels, many of the plants in the hotter regions, such as

3

around the Mediterranean, are subject to intense heat and drought during the summer months. Although not alpines, many of these plants, particularly bulbs, are grown by alpine growers on account of their compactness and suitability for rock gardens or alpine houses.

Another aspect of a plant's habitat which must be considered is the acidity of the soil. Some plants can be found on a variety of soils, whilst others prefer a limy, alkaline medium. Yet others will not tolerate even a trace of lime and require acid soils if they are to thrive.

ALPINES IN THE GARDEN

Although many of the plants grown on rock gardens are tolerant of a wide range of conditions, many others are more exacting and it is essential to try and match the growing habitats in the garden with those in the wild as closely as possible. In essence this means that attention must be given to drainage, soil, and the amount of sun or shade that a plant requires. To grow the largest possible collection of plants it is necessary to provide a wide range of habitats, but this is not precluded by the size of the garden. In the past, alpines used to be grown almost exclusively on a rock garden; today it is perfectly feasible to grow them on a balcony in a trough or in pots.

Rock gardens

The traditional way of growing alpine plants was on a rock garden. Although there are still very many people who prefer to grow their plants this way, few aspire to recreate complete mountains or whole ranges in minature as once was the case! The modern attitude to rock gardens is that, if built correctly, they should not only look good in themselves but also provide a foil for the plants and, more importantly, provide a range of habitats in which the plants will flourish.

The essence of a good rock garden is that it should look natural, as if it were an outcrop of a local rock formation. For this reason, and also because it will probably be cheaper, local stone should be used as far as it is possible. Care must be taken not to mix different types of stone; as this would look very odd and out of place!

The rocks are a very important element; they are not there just to look pretty. They hold warmth and transmit it back to the plants, they give protection against the winds, whilst underneath they provide cool and moist root runs. Furthermore they can be positioned to form crevices for plants that need such conditions and they can provide shade.

The soil will be discussed in more detail later under cultivation, but for the rock garden a good loam with added leafmould or peat is ideal. Drainage is vital in most instances, and this must be provided by the addition of grit.

The site should be chosen carefully. It should be as open as possible, away from over-hanging trees which not only cause shade and drip from rain, but also have very hungry roots which can soon impoverish the bed without the grower realizing what is happening. It is possible to build rock gardens in light shade, but then the number of plants will be restricted to those that grow in, or will tolerate, shade. The site should be thoroughly cleansed of perennial weeds before any construction work starts, as once constructed and planted, it is very difficult to purge a rock garden of these tiresome plants. Adequate drainage away from the site is also essential.

This is not the place to go into the details of construction or the aesthetics of a rock garden. The shape, size and general appearance is up to the individual, but it must be said that the rockwork should look as natural as possible. The strata in the rock should all go the same way, preferably horizontally, and the blocks should all have a slight incline back into the soil, giving the appearance of a natural outcrop of rock. They should be part buried in the soil and not just strewn around on the surface. In many respects, it is easier to construct it on a natural slope or bank, but if the site is flat then one can choose the orientation and general slope of the whole bed. A gravel mulch, 25–50mm (1–2in) deep, should be applied. This helps to keep the necks of the plants dry, to conserve moisture round the roots and to prevent panning of the soil. It also helps to make weeding easier by keeping the weeds down.

The overall aim, as already stated, is to provide as large a varity of habitats as possible. So within the rock garden use can be made of the warm protected south sides of the rocks for those plants that love the sun and need its warmth, while the north sides provide shade and cool root runs for plants that grow in that type of situation in the wild. Many plants like to grow on their sides so that water does not collect in their crown. These, and other plants that prefer acute drainage, can be planted in crevices between the rocks where they can get maximum drainage. Some plants will prefer to be planted in pockets containing a higher percentage of leafmould or peat, which will be more moisture retentive. A pool can be included to give yet another type of specialized habitat. Before planting out any specimen check in the A–Z to ascertain what are its natural requirements and then try to satisfy them as closely as you can.

Raised beds

For a wide variety of reasons many people prefer to grow alpines in artificial, raised beds rather than the more natural-looking rock gardens. One advantage of these beds is that they can be of any size and in any position. Small rock gardens can look ridiculous and positioning them sympathetically within the overall scheme of the garden can be difficult. Another big advantage is drainage. Since the whole bed is above ground level it is possible to make it very free draining. Depending on the height and size of the bed, the plants grow nearer to the hand, eyes and nose; so weeding, examining and smelling them is relatively easy—a factor of particular advantage to the elderly or handicapped gardener.

The siting of the raised bed is not so crucial as with a rock garden, but it should still be in an open position, unless it is intended to grow shade-loving species. The raised bed need not be in the main part of the garden but can be in the utilities part, near a greenhouse or against a garden fence. A well constructed and well-planted raised bed can be most attractive. As with the rock garden, it is important to clear the site of perennial weeds.

The construction can be of virtually any rot-proof material. If it is to be placed in the main garden then some attempt should be made to harmonize it with its surroundings and here stone or soft-coloured brick could be a natural choice; but in an area tucked away from general site it could be built of concrete blocks or paving slabs embedded on their sides. Wood can be used in the form of old railway sleepers or simply logs. Thin softwood, even if painted does not last very long.

An advantage of using stone or brick is that gaps can be left to imitate crevices so that plants can be planted on the vertical face.

The soil should again be a good loam with plenty of grit added, plus leafmould or peat. The base of the bed should be filled with a layer of rubble or other drainage material.

The size and shape is of little relevance and can be built to personal preference or dictates of the site. It should be at least 30cm (1ft) high to allow adequate drainage, but a single 25cm (10in) railway sleeper on its side should give adequate depth providing the site is well drained. For elderly and handicapped growers extra height will prevent the need to stoop. In their case the beds should not be too wide, so that the centre can be comfortably reached, but more agile growers can have it any width as long as there are stepping stones strategically placed throughout the bed so that all parts can be tended. Some of the larger beds have a series of terraced inner walls to raise the plants in the centre so that they may be better seen, whilst at the same time providing little nooks and crannies for vertical and shade plantings. A gravel top dressing of 25–50mm (1–2in), besides looking attractive, is beneficial to many alpines and stops birds and other animals messing up the soil.

Some rectangular beds can be constructed so as to be covered during the winter by one or more coldframe lights—not so much for protection from the cold, but more to keep out the winter wet. The lights should be held on a framework without sides, as it is important that air circulates freely. Keep an eye out that the beds do not become too dry as many plants start their growth during this time of the year and can suffer just as badly from too little as too much moisture.

Peat beds

There are two reasons for using peat beds. First, to be able to grow calcifuges (i.e. plants that dislike chalk) in areas where they would not normally grow; and, second, to provide a habitat which is always moist and resembles the conditions that many woodland plants enjoy.

The siting of the bed should ensure that it is in light shade as most of the plants that are likely to be grown in it will prefer this. It is, however, a good idea to have at least part of it, or a separate bed, which is in full sun to accommodate those moisture-loving plants that thrive only in a sunny position. If you are not too worried about appearance, then shading can be provided by plastic netting; otherwise shade from trees or a northerly aspect can be utilized. If the bed is large enough it is often possible to use shrubs on the bed itself to provide the shade.

The soil should consist of about three parts of peat, one part of loam and one part of grit. If it is woodland conditions that are being imitated, then sieved leafmould can be substituted for the peat. The grit allows surplus water to drain away and, should the bed dry out, it helps the water percolate into the peat.

The walls of the bed should be constructed of peat blocks or logs. The former is preferable particularly as it gives a vertical planting face which many of the plants will enjoy. The peat blocks and the peat for the infill should be thoroughly soaked before they are used. The height of the walls should be at least a foot and height can be gained towards the centre or back of the bed by having successive walls forming terraces. Stepping stones should be incorporated in the design to give easy access and prevent soil compaction.

Troughs and sinks

Alpines can be grown in any size of garden and the use of troughs or other containers allows even the smallest garden consisting of no more than a patio, or even just a balcony, to be employed.

Original stone troughs are often difficult and expensive to come by. It is possible to make adequate substitutes out of 'hypertufa' (a mixture of one part cement, one part sand and one part sieved peat). This can either be applied to the outside of a glazed ceramic sink which has previously been coated with a contact adhesive or used to cast a trough from a wooden or even cardboard mould. Ready-made troughs can be bought in a variety of materials and shapes, but the majority look too slick to be used for alpines; choose with care. Whatever is used must have adequate drainage holes.

The soil should be a mixture of three parts sterilized loam plus two parts of grit and two parts of peat with the addition of bone meal or a suitable base fertilizer.

The trough can be positioned anywhere, but an open sunny site is to be preferred. It is probably better if it is raised from the ground, so that it can be seen and attended all the better, but the supports must be strong and secure, with no hint of instability. It should be placed in its final resting place before the soil is added otherwise the weight may make it impossible to move. The bottom should be well crocked and a layer of coarse peat or inverted turves put on top of this before the compost is added. This should be well firmed down, particularly in the corners. If possible allow the soil to settle for a few days before planting, so that the level can be topped up if necessary.

The landscaping on the top is up to individual taste, but, again, if possible, create different types of habitat by careful positioning of the rocks. Top dressing with grit is an adantage both from the aesthetic and practical point of view.

Tufa rocks

An interesting way of growing alpines is in lumps of tufa. Tufa is a very soft porous stone made up of natural deposits of calcium carbonate precipitated in limestone regions where the water becomes saturated with soluble calcium. A wide range of plants will grow in tufa and many of the more difficult species that are normally only grown in an alpine house will also be quite happy in this medium.

Tufa is normally bought by weight and should be purchased after a dry spell otherwise one can pay for several hundredweight of expensive water which has been absorbed by the stone.

It should be bedded into earth or damp sand so that it can constantly suck up water from below the surface. Holes of about 30mm (1.5in) or so can be drilled or scooped out in its surface. They can then be filled with potting compost. Plants can be introduced to these holes either as seed, cuttings or young specimens. They need to be carefully inserted by first removing sufficient compost, then positioning the plant and trickling compost round its roots firming them well in; do not try to ram a plant from a 7.5cm (3in) pot into a 2.5cm (1in) hole. Holes drilled into vertical faces should have a slight slope down into the tufa to prevent both compost and plant being washed out. Once planted, the tufa should be well-watered and lightly shaded for several weeks until the plants have settled in. Spring and early autumn are the ideal time for establishing plants in tufa blocks, troughs or raised beds.

Alpine houses

Although the majority of plants described in this manual can be grown in the open garden, there are several reasons why alpine houses are used. Although most alpines can stand any amount of cold, many are susceptible to damp, particularly during the winter. The alpine house, then, is used as a protection against rain rather than frost. Many growers exhibit plants at Alpine Garden Society or other shows and feel they can give their specimens more individual attention if they are in pots at a comfortable height in an alpine house. In pots, plants have no competition from other individuals, composts can be compounded to each individual requirement and watering can be adjusted likewise. As well as growing plants in pots, many enthusiasts construct raised beds or miniature rock gardens under glass, where the plants are placed directly into the compost. Again the emphasis is on protection from the elements. However, this is a specialist activity, and rewarding as it is, the beginner is recommended to start in the open with the earlier alpine species.

If some protection is needed then a cold frame will prove more than adequate. Frames are also useful for propagation and growing plants on (see p. 10).

Other sites

There are many other possible sites for growing alpines, some needing hardly any preparation. Old stone or brick walls, particularly retaining walls, that have crevices make a good habitat. Trailing and tufted plants as well as some dwarf shrubs look particularly good here. Another possibility is in paving, planting in gaps in the paving or in the cracks between adjacent slabs. This is particularly good for aromatic plants that smell when crushed such as thymes and camomiles.

Alpine lawns are often advocated, but these are difficult to manage satisfactorily and can soon end up looking like a badly overgrown weed patch. To start with, it is better to grow plants under controlled conditions. Pools can be very useful and pleasant adjunct to a rock garden or peat bed. They not only help keep the roots cool, but provide the air with a certain amount of moisture which many plants from damper climes appreciate. The pool environment also extends the range of plants that can be grown.

CULTIVATION

Soil

The soil, or the compost in which the plants grow, is all important and, in turn, the most important aspect of the soil is the drainage. Few alpine plants will tolerate stagnant water round their roots, yet most will not survive without water. Although it seems contradictory, what they require is a free-draining, moisture-retentive soil. Peat holds sufficient water for the plants' needs and grit allows excess water to drain away to prevent stagnation.

The exact composition of the soil varies, as plants growing in scree conditions need a sharper drainage than those, say, native to an alpine meadow. A good grower will note these different requirements and try to provide for them. The standard mix that most people use consists of three parts of John Innes No. 2 or 3 (or any good loam), with an extra one part each of grit, peat and leafmould. Buying prepared compost such as John Innes is fine for small areas and troughs or pots, but can get expensive when dealing with large rock gardens and raised beds. Good garden soil can be used as a basis, adding extra grit and peat to bring it to roughly the same composition as given above. There is not much that can be done for heavy clay, unless years can be spent in working it before the beds are constructed. Under these circumstances good top-soil should be purchased. It is impractical to sterilize soil on a large scale, but if there are facilities to treat soil and leafmould before planting on a smaller scale then it is advantageous to do so. In some areas it is possible to buy pre-sterilized loam. The basic mixture can be varied according to whether more grit or more peat is required.

8

Obtaining plants

An increasing number of garden centres are stocking alpine plants, but it is to the specialist nurseries that one must turn for quality and variety as well as expert knowledge. Many issue mail-order catalogues which also give invaluable advice regarding the various conditions the plants require. A personal visit to these nurseries can be most rewarding.

As well as buying plants most growers propagate their own. Seed is readily available from nurseries, specialist seed merchants or from the seed exhanges run by societies sich as the Alpine Garden Society, whose seed list has some 4,500 items each year. Many of the local alpine garden groups have plant sales and swap plants amongst themselves.

There is no shortage of material, and it can prove a most satisfying and rewarding experience to exchange plants with friends and fellow alpine enthusiasts.

Planting

The success of a rock garden can be judged by the quality of its planting. This is reflected aesthetically in how the plants relate to each other and practically in whether the plants are happy in the position chosen for them. Notice must always be taken of the natural habitat, although it should also be remembered that some plants are far less exacting than others. Information regarding this can be found in this manual, nursery catalogues, society journals and other periodicals. Trial and error also play an important part, and ultimately this is how experience is gained.

The aesthetic aspect of planting depends on personal taste and is really outside the scope of this introduction, but colour, shape, texture and the way the plants relate to each other and to their situation is important. Although some plantsmen grow plants for their own sake rather than for any general design, the overall effect of good associations can greatly enhance individual plants, besides being very pleasing.

The ultimate size of a plant must be taken into consideration for small plants can be easily swamped if placed too close to more vigorous neighbours. Care must be taken over labelling, giving precise details of the name and source of supply, and the date when raised and planted out. Some gardeners make this their only record, others keep details of plants in a notebook or card index. Such records can be an invaluable source of information for many years to come.

Do not plant in hot weather or in strong drying winds. Plants should be watered before being removed from their pots and then again when in position. If the plant's roots have spiralled tightly around the inside of the pot, gently tease them loose before planting. Plants should be well firmed into the ground.

Weather conditions

The weather conditions that plants have to contend with in lowland regions are obviously different from those found in the Alps, Himalayas, or other mountain areas. Surprisingly, winter conditions can be harsher where the plants do not have a snug blanket of snow under which they can hide from the winter. In the open they have to face freezing winds and, probably worse still, mild wet winds. In the main, most of the plants we grow in the open can take all that is thrown at them, but some people like to give some species the protection of a cloche or sheet of glass placed overhead to keep off the worst of the winter wet; these should be put in place at the onset of winter and removed in early spring. The more tender subjects can be protected to a certain extent by being planted on the south side of rocks. Others are helped by deeper planting.

Some plants, particularly bulbs, normally experience a period of drought and sunny baking during the height of summer, and these need a covering of glass to keep off the summer rains. The more demanding species can be grown in permanent frames where a summer dry period is easier to regulate.

Watering

Watering can be a source of worry to some people. If the beds have adequate drainage then overwatering should not be a problem. Beds of all sorts should be regularly watered in dry weather, and particular attention should be given to troughs and tufa which can dry out rapidly. Peat beds should never be allowed to dry out and some form of sprinkler system should be devised—at its simplest this can be a hose, but a variety of more sophisticated devices are available.

Feeding

Alpine beds should not be over fed. Initial preparation with John Innes composts should provide sufficient nutrition for the first year or so; after that, an annual light dusting of a general fertilizer can be applied in late January or February, when the beds are given their annual top-dressing of stone chippings or gravel. As the beds are not rebuilt for many years, the initial quantity of humus gradually breaks down, so it is also a good idea to scatter a small quantity of peat on the bed before covering with gravel mulch.

Pests and diseases

Alpines are prone to the same range of pests and diseases as other garden plants and should be treated accordingly. Slugs and snails can wreak havoc on tender young shoots and seedlings of a whole range of different plants. Aphids (greenfly) and vine weevils can be particularly bothersome. Birds can also prove a menace in some gardens, wrecking choice cushion plants and pecking at flower buds—some form of protection such as black cotton or netting can help to keep these attacks to a minimum.

Maintenance

Weeds are the biggest maintenance problem. Once weeds become established in a rock garden they can be difficult to clear without reconstructing the bed. Perennials should be thoroughly cleared from the site before beds are built and any introduced soil should be as weed-free as possible. Regular weeding is essential, and provides an opportunity to look closely at and examine all the plants. General tidying up and removal of dead material will keep the beds neat and help prevent the spread of diseases. Other regular maintenance has already been covered: watering in dry weather, top dressing with fertilizer and grit, and checking for pests and diseases.

PROPAGATION

Raising one's own plants from seeds or cuttings can be a most rewarding experience. It is not essential to have any expensive equipment for undertaking routine propagation. However, it is useful to have a cold frame in which newly potted plants can be kept for a few days or weeks before they are hardened off. Frames should be in an open sunny position, but should have some form of shading available for use during hot, dry periods. The frame lights will rarely be on during the summer months except when it is essential to keep a close shady atmosphere for newly potted plants. Frames can also be invaluable for overwintering young plants and seedlings.

Seed

Seed is the cheapest way of increasing plants. Many gardeners save their plants' seed; alternatively, many different types are listed in nursery and society catalogues and seed lists. Most plant come true from seed, but some hybrids and cultivars produce variable offspring—this in itself can be a fascinating aspect with the chance of producing some novel form or colour.

It is advisable to sow the seed when it is fresh; if it has been obtained through exchanges or from nurseries, it should be sown as soon as possible after receipt.

A sterilized loam- or peat-based seed compost is best used, as ordinary garden soil is weedy and generally unsuitable. Some people prefer a soil-less compost, but others find that the plants dislike the transition to a loam-based compost or to garden soil when planted out. Unless a large quantity of plants is required it is only necessary to sow in 8cm (3in) pots.

Firm the compost down into the pot and then sow the seed thinly, unless you know that it has a low viability. Cover the seed with a layer of fine chick grit (not sand) and water from beneath by standing it in a pan of water. Ensure that the pot is clearly labelled and then stand it outside in a shady spot where it is exposed to all weathers. Some seed needs frost to break its dormancy, so no protection is required in winter except during periods of excessive rain.

Some seed will germinate in a matter of days and others in weeks, but some, sown in the spring, will not germinate until the following year. So do not throw away seed pots for at least a year; indeed most growers keep them at least three as seed can lay dormant for a couple of seasons and then suddenly germinate. Seedlings should be potted up as soon as they are large enough to handle and be kept in a cool, closed environment for a few days before hardening off. They can then be left in open frames or in plunge beds, although some protection may be required during periods of inclement weather—heavy rain for instance can wreck pots of seedlings.

Cuttings

Seed cannot always be relied on to produce a complete replica of its parent. All kinds of variation in colour, size, shape and vigour can occur. In the main this is not a problem (sometimes it can be exciting), but occasionally we want to reproduce a particular variety exactly. There are also plants that do not produce seed; those with double flowers and sterile hybrids for example. To reproduce these plants, cuttings provide an easy alternative.

Some form of propagation frame is needed. One can buy a plastic one or make a box with a glass lid. A plastic pot covered with a plastic bag can be often used successfully—indeed this is the most basic type of propagator. The best potting medium for a propagator is a moist mixture of one part of sharp sand and one part of peat.

Half-ripened cuttings can be taken in June or early July. These should be non-flowering stems of about 15–40mm ($\frac{1}{2}$–1$\frac{1}{2}$in) long and cut off just below a leaf node. The bottom leaves are cut off, the lower part of the stem dipped in a suitable hormone rooting powder and then dibbed firmly into the sand/peat mixture. The cover is put on and the frame placed in the shade. Length of rooting time varies, but signs of new growth on the cuttings usually indicate that they have taken. They are potted up when roots have been established and are placed in a closed frame for a few days before hardening off.

Mature, or hardwood, cuttings are taken later in the year and treated in the same fashion, except that they are left in the frame before potting up.

Division

Yet another way of faithfully reproducing a particular specimen is by division. Plants are dug up and broken into a number of pieces. Each piece is then potted up separately. Not all plants can be divided: for instance those with a single central rooting system, such as tap-rooted plants, cannot be treated this way.

Many plants benefit from being split up occasionally, particularly if flowering has dwindled or the plant is spreading outwards and the centre is dying. Always use the newer growth from the outer parts of the plant for divisions; the worn-out centre should be discarded.

Growing alpine and rock plants is a vast subject and cannot easily be covered in one chapter. The best way of learning is undoubtedly by growing one's own plants and practising with them. However, a lot can be learnt by reading books and magazines and meeting people with a like interest. Much can also be gained by joining one of the specialist societies such as the Alpine Garden Society, the Scottish Rock Garden Club or the American Rock Garden Society.

A–Z

ACAENA (Rosaceae)

A curious genus native primarily to New Zealand, but with a few species scattered in South America and Polynesia. Most are mat-forming perennials, with neat pinnate leaves reminiscent of Salad Burnet, *Sanguisorba*, or a miniature briar rose. The flowers are insignificant, but borne in dense globose heads followed by more showy spiny burr-fruits. Those generally grown are good for ground cover, along pathways or between paving slabs. Being low growing they are a good foil for small bulbs which can be allowed to grow through the mat of foliage.

Acaena buchananii ○◗
Mat of grey-green foliage with yellowish brown burrs in the late summer, 30–60mm (1⅕–2⅖in) tall. New Zealand—South Island. June–August.

Acaena glauca ○◗☆
One of the most striking with carpets of neat blue-grey silky foliage. New Zealand. July–August.

Acaena microphylla ○◗☆
Perhaps the best with mats of bronzed leaves which are greyish to begin with. The pretty burrs are crimson and produced in quantity giving a very pleasing effect, 30–60mm (1⅕–2⅖in) tall. New Zealand. June–July.

Acaena novae-zealandae ○◗
Forms laxer mats than the preceding species, the foliage green and silky, the burrs reddish- or purplish-brown when mature; to 60mm (2⅖in) tall. New Zealand. June–August.

ACANTHOLIMON (Plumbaginaceae)

Although this large genus has over 120 species, only one or two are commonly grown in gardens. This is because they mostly come from the hot dry deserts of the E Mediterranean through to C Asia and would not be hardy enough to survive harsh wet winters. They are closely allied to *Armeria*, the thrifts or sea pinks, and really need the shelter of a hot dry corner of the garden, preferably facing south, and a freely drained substrate. A scree or raised bed is ideal. Plants are best raised from seeds; cuttings root with difficulty.

Acantholimon glumaceum ○
A compact rosette-forming plant with spiny, evergreen, needle-like leaves which eventually form domes as the plant ages. The flowers are borne in clusters on arching stems, to 15cm (6in) long, and are a rich pink. Armenia. May–July.

Acantholimon venustum ○
Another spiny-leaved plant forming loose silvery-grey tufts. The spikes of clear pink flowers rise above the leaves to 18cm (7⅛in), though often less. S Turkey. June–July. More difficult to cultivate than *A. glumaceum*, but well worth a try when obtainable.

ACHILLEA (Compositae)

An attractive genus of perennials with over 200 species scattered throughout the north temperate zone and mostly referred to as yarrows or milfoils. Many are too tall for the rock garden, but some make excellent compact plants and have the advantage of a long flowering season, especially towards the end of the summer. All have finely divided, often aromatic, leaves and dense heads of tiny flowers which vary in colour from white, cream, lemon, golden-yellow to pale pink. All can be grown in a sunny or semi-shaded position in almost any type of soil. Propagation by cuttings or division.

Achillea ageratifolia ○☆
As the specific name suggests, this species has leaves not unlike those of *Ageratum*, being spoon-shaped, greyish-white, toothed at the tip and borne in close basal rosettes. The flower-stems are 15–25cm (6–10in) tall and have white flowers in solitary heads. N Greece. July–August. One of the finest rock garden species.

Achillea argentea ○
There is some confusion between this species and *A. clavennae* in catalogues and other literature and the two names probably refer to the same species. An attractive plant with silver-grey divided leaves and tightly packed heads of white flowers on stems 15–20cm (6–8in) tall. E Alps. July–August.

Achillea aurea ○☆
One of the more spectacular species, with emerald-green leaves and heads of rich golden-yellow flowers borne on stems 18–23cm (7–9in) tall. June–August. A selected clone with larger heads is sometimes seen under the cultivar name 'Grandiflora'.

Achillea chrysocoma ○
An interesting species from S Yugoslavia and Albania with highly aromatic foliage and bright yellow flowers on 15–25cm (6–10in) stems. It is distinguished from closely related species by having blackish-brown markings on the floral bracts. June–July. Like the previous species it thrives best in a sunny well-drained gritty soil.

Achillea huteri ○
An unusual shrubby species eventually producing mounds of aromatic foliage with greyish-green leaves. In comparison with other species in the genus the flowers of this one are a pure white, whilst others tend to be greyish or creamy white. May–June. Worth growing for its foliage alone.

Achillea × jaborneggii ○◖
This is a hybrid between *A. clavennae* and *A. moschata* in which the flowers are carried in loose heads on short stems. The foliage is not as silvery as in *A. clavennae*. May–July.

Achillea × kolbiana ○
This is another hybrid involving *A. clavennae* in its parentage; the other parent is *A. umbellata*. The white flower-heads are carried on 10–15cm (4–6in) stems. May–June.

Achillea rupestris ○☆
Like many of the other cultivated species this also hails from S Europe and is considered by some to be just a subspecies of *A. erba-rotta*. Plants have entire leaves borne in compact tufts and pure white flower-heads on short stems, 8–15cm (3–6in) tall. S Italy. May–June. A pretty plant often flowering in profusion.

Achillea tomentosa ○☆
This is probably one of the most widely grown species in which the stems and leaves are finely divided and covered with soft white hairs. The flowers are an attractive deep golden-yellow in colour, borne in tight heads on stems up to 25cm (10in) high. May–June.

ACINOS (Labiatae)

Formerly included in *Calamintha*, the species of *Acinos* are small, rather thyme-like plants of great charm, although surprisingly seldom seen on rock gardens.

Acinos alpinus (syn. *Calamintha alpina*) ○
A widespread alpine species in the mountains of C and S Europe. Plants form spreading or prostrate tufts of slender shoots bearing small, oval, untoothed leaves. The small flowers are violet with white markings and are borne in profusion in leafy spikes throughout the summer months. Easily raised from seeds or cuttings. A plant of rocky meadows, pathsides and screes in the wild.

ACONITUM (Ranunculaceae)

A relatively large genus distributed throughout temperate regions of the northern hemisphere. They range from coarse perennial herbs to dwarf alpine species. Most are too gross for the rock garden, but several are worthy of attention. The flowers have a characteristic hooded shape designed for pollination by various types of bee. All the species are extremely poisonous.

Aconitum vulparia ◑☆
The wolfsbane is widely distributed in the mountains of C and S Europe as well as temperate Asia, growing usually in semi-shaded woodland. Plants have erect stems to 1m (3ft) bearing numerous palmately cut leaves. The slender, often branched, racemes of pale yellow, narrowly hooded flowers are very characteristic. June–August. A charming, though scarcely showy, plant for the back of the rock garden, particularly beneath trees.

Aconitum napellus ◑
The common monkshood is native to damp meadows and open woodland throughout the mountains of C and S Europe (the British plant is the closely related *A. anglicum*). Plants form tufts of stiffly erect stems to 80cm (2ft 8in), bearing numerous finely cut palmately lobed leaves and rather dense racemes of deep purplish-blue broadly hooded flowers. July–September. Unsuitable for the smaller rock garden.

15

Aconitum hookeri ○

A real gem from the high Himalaya: only 15–20cm (6–8in) tall with narrowly divided leaves and wiry stems carrrying several intensely deep blue flowers. August–September. Well worth growing though not widely available in cultivation. Suitable for a scree or a well-drained trough.

There are a number of other fine, small, Himalayan species though these are rarely available outside botanic gardens and specialist collections. *A. uncinatum* with lilac flowers, the plants only 10–16cm (4–6in) tall, is also worth keeping an eye open for.

ADONIS (Ranunculaceae)

The genus includes several species of great distinction. The perennial species mostly have glistening yellow flowers whilst the annual ones have deep red, occasionally yellow, flowers. All have finely divided bright green leaves. Those included here flower early in the spring, pushing their fat buds above the soil surface quickly once the weather begins to warm up, the foliage maturing after the flowers have faded. They thrive best in an open sunny site in a well-drained loamy soil and are not always easy to please, but well worth every effort.

Adonis vernalis ○☆

The Spring Pheasant's-eye is perhaps the finest species forming bold clumps with large shiny golden-yellow flowers 50–70mm (2–2⅔in) across, each with 12 or more narrow petals. Plants may eventually reach 40cm (16in) tall, though often less; the stems have a characteristic scale at the base distinguishing it from the next species. Mountains of Europe. April–May.

Adonis pyrenaica ○

The Pyrenean Pheasant's-eye is superficially similar to the previous species, but has more finely cut leaves and smaller flowers. E Pyrenees and Maritime Alps. June–July. Far less common in cultivation than the previous species.

Adonis amurensis ◐

This delightful species is native to Japan, and is very like a small *A. vernalis*; the flowers, like large winter aconites, are often bronzed or green on the outside and unfurl in the early spring. There is also a double-flowered form. February–early March. Requires a more peaty soil than the preceding species.

Adonis brevistyla ◐

Another striking species with deep green leaves whorled below the silky buds which often have a bluish or greyish tint. The buds open into white cups of great beauty. Himalaya. May. Requires a cool leafy or peaty soil.

AETHIONEMA (Cruciferae)

An attractive little genus with about 70 species scattered in the Mediterranean region and western Asia. They are mostly perennials or small subshrubs of neat habit with rather succulent small leaves. The small flowers are borne in narrow racemes or heads at the shoot tips. Those cultivated thrive best in a sunny position in well-drained gritty soils, especially calcareous ones. Propagation from seed which is usually produced in abundance.

Adonis vernalis

Aethionema armenum ○
A neat, compact, mat-forming species to 10cm (4in) tall with blue-grey leaves and clusters of pink flowers. Armenia. Late May–July.

Aethionema cordifolium ○☆
Very similar to the previous species but the flowers are paler and borne in more rounded clusters. W. Asia. June–July. Very similar in flower to *A. grandiflorum*, but more distinctive in fruit—the fruits are boat-shaped and borne in very lax racemes. 'Warley Rose' (syn. *A.* × *warleyense* 'Warley Rose')—the most beautiful of Aethionemas grown in gardens, believed to be a hybrid of *A. cordifolium* and *A. grandiflorum*; the flowers are deep pink; 'Warley Ruber'—flowers deep rich red, only 10cm (4in) tall.

Aethionema grandiflorum ○☆
A handsome tufted species to 30cm (12in) tall with simple unbranched stems and blue-green, rather blunt, oblong leaves. The rose-pink flowers are relatively large and borne in crowded racemes at the stem-tips. Middle East. May–July. Well worth growing—a very floriferous plant when well grown.

17

Aethionema 'Warley Rose'

Aethionema pulchellum ○☆
A laxly tufted species forming rounded mounds to 20cm (8in) with attractive grey-green foliage. The bright pink flowers are borne in condensed racemes which slowly elongate. W Asia. June–July, occasionally later. Perhaps only a form of *A. grandiflorum*.

Aethionema iberideum ○
Another tufted subshrub, to 15cm (6in) and distinguished by its linear leaves and white, fragrant flowers. Greece and Turkey. June–July. Quite distinct and not easily confused with any other species of *Aethionema*.

Aethionema saxatile ○
A pretty, little, few-stemmed biennial or short-lived perennial, to 12cm (4¾in) tall, with narrow-lanceolate blue-green foliage. The flowers are white or pink, small, but borne in dense, rounded heads which slowly elongate in fruit. Greece and Turkey. May–June. A charming species, but not always easy to keep going in gardens, often tending to die after flowering.

Two other species sometimes offered by nurseries are *A. schistosum* and *A. thomasianum*. The former, from Turkey, is allied to *A. grandiflorum*, but with linear leaves and smaller flowers. The latter is a native of Italy and is sometimes considered to be a variant of *A. saxatile*, differing mainly in its congested racemes of closely overlapping fruits and its more compact habit.

AJUGA (Labiatae)

The ajugas or bugles are a small group of species widespread in Europe and Asia. Several are native to Britain and those commonly grown are easy and accommodating plants thriving on a wide variety of soils. The species listed below are mat-forming, with rooting stolons and can prove invasive on rock gardens—not plants to place close to more choice alpines.

Ajuga reptans ○◐
The Common Bugle is a vigorous stoloniferous perennial forming mats of lustrous deep-green leaves. The spike of deep blue, pink or white flowers are interspersed with purplish leaf-like bracts. The whole plant is seldom more than 12cm (5in) tall in cultivated forms. Throughout much of Europe and W Asia where it grows in damp, often shaded habitats. April–August. 'Atropurpurea'—purple leaves and deep blue flowers; 'Burgundy Glow'—green leaves variegated with pink and wine-red; 'Multicolor'—leaves flushed with bronze and red; 'Variegata'—green leaves variegated with silver.

Ajuga pyramidalis ○◐
The Pyramidal Bugle is similar to the preceding, but generally taller, the stems hairy all round (not just on two opposing sides as in *A. reptans*). The hairy leaves are oval and slightly toothed and form a regular pyramid up the stem. The flowers are violet-blue, deep violet, pink or white and are interspersed with purple leaf-like bracts. C and S Europe, where it grows in meadows, scrub and in stony places, frequently on acid soils. April–August.

Ajuga genevensis ○◐
Essentially like *A. pyramidalis*, but the leaves more deeply toothed and bright blue flowers. Similar distribution and flowering time.

ALCHEMILLA (Rosaceae)

The Lady's Mantles are a large and complex genus widely distributed in temperate areas of both the northern and southern hemispheres, particularly in mountain regions. A few are grown in gardens. They are mostly low-tufted perennials with attractive lobed leaves, which are one of their loveliest features. The flowers are small but are produced in billowy masses, giving a haze of green or greenish-yellow, each flower like a tiny 8-pointed star, borne in branched clusters just above the foliage. They are particularly good close to water and in semi-shaded parts of the rock garden and are very easy to grow.

Alchemilla alpina ○☆
The Alpine Lady's Mantle grows widely in the mountains of Europe. The leaves have 5–7 deep lobes, dark green above, but strikingly silvery with hairs beneath. The pale greenish-yellow flowers are in small clusters held above foliage. June–August. Best for its handsome and rather neat foliage.

Alchemilla pentaphylla ○□
A laxer habit than the previous species with small deeply cut, plain green leaves, not more than 30mm (1⅛in) across. The small clusters of greenish-yellow flowers are borne just clear of the foliage. Alps. July–August. Good in screes and generally preferring acid soils.

Alchemilla mollis ○◗
This is the Common Lady's Mantle of gardens, which name disguises a range of similar looking plants including *A. vulgaris*. Plants form large mounds, up to 30cm (12in) tall, of soft grey-green leaves, beautifully and symmetrically cut into rounded, toothed lobes. The mass of yellowish-green flowers are borne in broad, branched clusters, erect at first, but soon tending to sprawl. Mountains of Europe and W Asia. June–August. Generally too coarse in the average rock garden, but excellent in or along paving and by water.

Alchemilla ellenbeckii ○◗☆
An African species only fairly recent in cultivation. Different from the preceding in its long trailing stems and carpeting habit. The small daintily scalloped leaves make good ground cover, although the greenish flower clusters are of little significance. Mountains of E and NE Africa. July–August.

ALYSSOIDES (Cruciferae)

A small genus of 4 species closely allied to *Alyssum* from Europe and W Asia. Propagation best from seed.

Alyssoides utriculata ○
An erect perennial to 40cm (16in) with leafy rosettes borne on a woody stock. The leaves are greyish-green, oblong or spoon-shaped. The bright yellow flowers, each 8–14mm (⅓–⅝in) are borne in elongating heads, succeeded by characteristic inflated fruit-pods. Mountains of C and S Europe. April–June. A plant of rocks and rock crevices to 1,500m (4,950ft) altitude, in the wild.

ALYSSUM (Cruciferae)

A well-known genus which contains some 150 species, mainly natives of Europe or W Asia. They are mostly annuals or perennials, though a few are subshrubby. Many have attractive grey, or silver, hairy leaves and heads or racemes of usually yellow flowers. The fruits are characteristically small, rather flat and rounded. Those listed below are generally easy to grow, succeeding well in sunny positions on the rock gardens, scree or raised bed. Propagation by seed is the easiest method to increase stock, though early summer cuttings can also be successful.

Alyssum saxatile (including *A. petraeum*) ○☆
This familiar and widely grown garden plant in often called Gold Dust, owing to its bright display of yellow flowers. The plant is subshrubby, to about 20cm (8in) tall, forming a mound of large silvery-grey leaves. S Europe. April–August or later. One of the very easiest of alpines to grow, indeed it may often become too gross and invasive on a small rock garden or scree; however, few plants can compare with its brightness. The more compact forms are worth seeking out. 'Citrinum'—a very

pleasing form with pale lemon flowers; 'Compactum'—a dwarfer form with bright yellow flowers; 'Dudley Neville'—a curious form with orange-buff flowers (there is also a form of this with variegated foliage—'Variegata'); 'Gold Ball'—more compact with rich golden flowers; 'Nanum'—a dwarfer form of the type; 'Plenum'— has double yellow flowers.

Alyssum arduinii ○

Very similar to *A. saxatile*, but with denser, flatter flower clusters and smaller fruits. C Europe.

Alyssum montanum ○☆

The Mountain Alyssum is a widespread species in the mountains of C and S Europe. It forms a spreading mat with greyish-green or whitish, elliptical or spoon-shaped leaves and elongated clusters of fragrant yellow 5mm (⅕in) flowers. The petals are notched. June–July. An easy and floriferous plant found in the wild in rocky and gravelly habitats to 2,500m (8,250ft). 'Berggold'—a cultivar occasionally offered.

Alyssum alpestre ○

Similar to the previous, but with more numerous and smaller flowers. W and C Alps. June–July.

Alyssum cuneifolium ○

Also similar, but with grey leaves and more elongated flower clusters. Forms a more tufted, less spreading plant. C and S Apennines.

Alyssum argenteum ○

Another species frequently offered by nurseries. A more upright plant than the previous species, often reaching 40cm (16in). The elliptical leaves are green above, but greyish beneath, and the small flowers bright yellow. S Alps—Italian. June– July.

Alyssum wulfenianum ○

A low spreading greyish or whitish perennial to 20cm (8in) tall, though often less, with small oval leaves and yellow flowers borne in rounded clusters. The small fruits are characteristically inflated and with a long 'beak'. SE Alps. June–July, occasion- ally later. A plant of dry rocky habitats in the wild, to 2,000m (6,600ft) altitude.

Alyssum serpyllifolium ○☆

A charming little mat-former closely allied to *A. alpestre* and possibly only a form of it, the stems becoming woody in time. The leaves are smaller and grey hoary and the flowers only 2–3mm (⅛in), borne in tight heads. Pyrenees and N Spain. June–August or later. One of the best—an easy and long-lived plant.

Alyssum moellendorffiana ○

This dreadful name belongs to a species sometimes seen in gardens which hails from W Yugoslavia. It is a small tufted plant to 15cm (6in) tall with spatula-shaped, silvery-grey, scurfy leaves. The yellow flowers are borne in long racemes. June– July.

Alyssum spinosum see *Ptilotrichum spinosum*, p. 187

Other species occasionally offered by nurserymen are *A. longifolia*, *A. murale*, *A. stribryni* and *A. troodii*.

ANACYCLUS (Compositae)

There are about 25 species in this attractive genus of daisy-like plants and all are found in countries bordering the Mediterranean. Most are fairly low growing, but some have a tendency towards weedyness. Only one species is widely available.

Anacyclus depressus (syn. *A. moroccanus*) ○☆
This delightful species is very hardy, which is not entirely surprising, since it originates from the High Atlas mountains of Morocco. Indeed it is often referred to as the Mount Atlas Daisy. Unlike our familiar daisy, this plant has finely divided, carrot-like leaves that are greenish-grey and red-backed heads of yellow and white flowers. May–August. Thrives best in a sunny position in a gritty, well-drained soil.

ANAGALLIS (Primulaceae)

A genus of 28 or so species of small herbs distributed worldwide and related to *Lysimachia*. Most are pretty annuals with axillary red, blue or white flowers with rotate or shallow bell-shaped corollas. Most of them like a sunny position and a light well-drained soil. *A. arvensis*, the Scarlet Pimpernel or Poor Man's Weather Grass, is a well-known European native of arable land and waysides.

Anagallis tenella ○◗
This is the Bog Pimpernel, a charming and floriferous small perennial carpeter. Plants form a mat of slender, prostrate, rooting stems, 5–15cm (2–6in), bearing pairs of small opposite roundish leaves. The single flowers are borne on slender erect stalks. The bell-shaped corolla is 5-lobed and is of a delicate pink with deeper veins, 6–10mm ($\frac{1}{4}$–$\frac{2}{5}$in) across. Widespread in Europe where it thrives in bogs and marshy habitats. June. Plants tend to be short-lived in cultivation and may be killed in a severe winter. They need a moist soil. 'Studland', the finest form, deeper pink than the usual wild one.

Anagillis linifolia var. *monellii* (syn. *A. collina, A. monellii*) ○
A very fine plant which forms a low, 15–30cm (6–12in), mound of branching stems with elliptic leaves, 10–15mm ($\frac{2}{5}$–$\frac{3}{5}$in) long and usually in threes. The deep blue, 5-lobed flowers often have a red eye and are borne on long stalks from upper leaf axils. Spain. Flowers profusely over a long period, May–October. Does best in light well-drained soil in full sun, and heartily dislikes wet conditions.

ANAPHALIS (Compositae)

A genus with over 35 species in Europe, America and Asia, but only one is offered for sale with any regularity. This genus contains plants with simple leaves and small papery flower-heads in which the male flowers are tubular and the female flowers are long and thread-like.

Anaphalis nubigenus ○
A delicate species with silver-grey leaves and stems reaching up to 20cm (8in). The flower-heads are a dull yellowish-white, but none the less attractive and the common name 'Pearly Everlasting' is sometimes applied to this species and its allies. The flowers can be removed and used for dried flower arrangements. Although Himalayan in origin this species does require a well-drained soil and a sunny position. August–September. Propagation by division of the parent plant.

ANCHUSA (Boraginaceae)

A familiar group of garden plants which can be annual, biennial or perennial. There are about 50 species which are predominantly native to the Mediterranean region where they enjoy dry, well-drained soils in full sun. The flower colour is usually blue, which characteristically becomes purplish on maturity, a state often referred to as 'blushing'. A few species have white or even yellow flowers. Their leaves, stems and inflorescences are usually covered in rough, bristle-like hairs which are often white, giving some species a silvery appearance.

Anchusa caespitosa ○▲

This is the only true alpine species in the genus. It is well known to the alpine enthusiast for its neat, compact habit of radiating, deep green leaves, which rarely exceed 50mm (2in) in length. Nestled within this stemless rosette of leaves is a dense cluster of stalkless flowers which are of a gentian blue. Crete. March–April. Like so many alpines, this species has a long fleshy tap-root which requires a deep well-drained, gritty soil; however, it is not particularly easy in cultivation. Propagation by cuttings, when available, or from seed.

ANDROMEDA (Ericaceae)

This genus originally included many species, but in recent years most of these have been transferred to other genera in the family. As a result only two species remain, *A. polifolia*, described here, and *A. glaucophylla* from North America. They are dwarf evergreen shrubs occurring in Arctic and temperate regions of the northern hemisphere. The small, nodding, urn-shaped flowers are borne in small terminal clusters. As the fruits begin to develop the flower-stalks turn upwards putting the fruits into an erect position.

Andromeda polifolia ○◑▢

The Bog Rosemary is a familiar and commonly grown species. Plants form hummocks of tangled wiry stems up to 45cm (18in) tall and spreading by underground stolons. The narrow, elliptical, leathery leaves are deep green above, greyish and often rather felted beneath, the margins characteristically rolled under. The flowers are white or pale pink, 5–6mm (¼in) long and borne on slender red stalks. May–July. Various forms exist in cultivation, although only two are worthy of mention. 'Compacta'—a lower more compact form than the type, barely reaching 20cm (8in) in height, with longer and narrower leaves, grey-green above and silvery beneath; 'Compacta Alba'—a fine white-flowered form.

ANDROSACE (Primulaceae)

Commonly called rock jasmines, this genus contains many delightful species popular among enthusiasts. There are some 150 species widely distributed in the northern hemisphere; most of them are cushion plants made up of tight globular leaf rosettes. From each leaf rosette arises one or several single flowers or stalked umbels. The simple and well-formed flowers are flat-faced and have a marked 'eye'. Most of the larger species are mat-forming. In general most species require a well-drained sunny position where the soil is never allowed to dry out. Most do well in the alpine house and also in the open garden in scree, where many benefit from overhead protection in winter, particularly those species with woolly leaves. If grown in pots, an open gritty compost with plenty of moisture during the summer is

23

ideal. Aphids are the main enemy and an attack is often not seen until too late; another frequent pest is the slug. Precautions should be taken to protect plants from these pests. Propagation is easy from seed or from cuttings taken in the summer. Flowering is April–May unless otherwise stated.

Androsace carnea ○☆

The Pink Rock Jasmine is a very popular species with pink flowers 5–8mm ($\frac{1}{4}$–$\frac{1}{3}$in) across borne in tight umbels on long stalks. The rosettes of stiff, narrow, straight to outcurved pointed leaves form mats or low cushions. Alps and Pyrenees, 1,400–3,000m (4,600–9,900ft). The species is divided into various subspecies. Subsp. *brigantiaca*, from the SW Alps, is the tallest, with pink or white flowers on scapes to 15cm (6in) tall. The largish toothed leaves are up to 30mm (1$\frac{1}{8}$in) long. Subsp. *laggeri*, from the Pyrenees, is arguably the prettiest, with bright magenta pink flowers and needle-like leaves about 10mm ($\frac{2}{5}$in) long. Subsp. *rosea* (syn. *halleri*), from the French Massif Central, is the easiest to keep and seeds itself freely once established. The leaves, 15–25mm ($\frac{3}{5}$–1in) long, are relatively broad at the base and outcurving. All are quite easily grown in a raised bed and are winter hardy. They benefit from a collar of chippings placed around the leaf rosettes.

Androsace hedraeantha ○

This species is similar to *A. carnea* subsp. *rosea*, but differs in the leaves which are broadest above the middle (in *A. carnea* they are broadest at the base). Another difference is that the umbel has on average more (5–10) and smaller flowers than that of *A. carnea* (3–8). Balkans. An easily grown species which does well in the open garden if provided with a raised bed.

Androsace ciliata ○

This pretty species forms largish rosettes of hairy-edged leaves to 35mm (1$\frac{1}{4}$in) across and can grow to quite a sizeable cushion. The numerous bright pink flowers, 5–8mm ($\frac{1}{5}$–$\frac{1}{3}$in) across, are borne singly from the leaf axils and are held clear of the leaves. Pyrenees. Does well in a raised bed but needs some form of winter protection and is particularly prone to aphid and slug attacks. Recent introductions have larger, deeper pink, flowers on shorter stalks and are much more attractive than those formerly cultivated.

Androsace cylindrica ○

This species is extremely rare in the wild, but is offered by many nurseries. Plants form tight rounded cushions of dark green rosettes, each 15–20mm ($\frac{3}{5}$–$\frac{3}{4}$in) wide. The somewhat shiny firm leaves are hairy on the margins. The white flowers, 7–9mm ($\frac{1}{4}$–$\frac{2}{5}$in) across are borne singly, several per rosette, on tall stalks to 20mm ($\frac{3}{4}$in) long. Pyrenees. Plants are best given alpine house treatment, but will do well outside in tufa or scree with winter protection. A healthy plant will cover itself with bloom. A species of limestone rocks and cliffs in the wild, from 2,000–3,500m (6,600–11,550ft) altitude. Many plants in cultivation prove to be hybrids between *A. cylindrica* and *A. hirtella*, so specimens should be selected with care.

Androsace hirtella ○☆

One of the easiest and most rewarding of the cushion Androsaces in cultivation. Plants form tight round cushions of rosettes made up of soft green linear to oblong leaves covered on both surfaces with small upright hairs (*hirtella* means shaggy). The charming, almond-scented, white flowers, 7–9mm ($\frac{1}{4}$–$\frac{2}{5}$in) across, are held close to the cushion. The flower size is variable, so select good forms, and beware of hybrids with *A. cylindrica*. Best grown in the alpine house, but it does well enough in scree if given winter protection.

Androsace delavayi ○▲
A lovely species which forms rounded cushions of soft green rosettes, each 7–10mm ($\frac{1}{4}$–$\frac{2}{5}$in) across, bearing stemless fragrant white flowers with a yellow throat, each 6–7mm ($\frac{1}{4}$in) across. The criss-crossing of relatively long marginal hairs on the overlapping incurved leaf tips gives the rosette a unique appearance. Himalaya and SW China. Leaf rosettes root very easily in the summer. It is usually a short-lived plant and best grown in the alpine house. Plants can be killed by frost when in growth. Pale pink-flowered forms are found in SW China.

Androsace globifera ○▲
Another splendid Himalayan species. The grey-green woolly leaf-rosettes, 5–10mm ($\frac{1}{5}$–$\frac{2}{5}$in) across, form deep rounded cushions. The leaves are covered on both surfaces with small silky hairs, densest on the undersurface and at the tip. The form with pale lilac-pink flowers with a yellow eye is fairly easy to grow, but can be shy flowering; the white-flowered form is much more difficult to keep. Both are prone to winter die-back but are easily propagated from cuttings. Best confined to the alpine house.

Androsace lanuginosa ○◐☆
One of the finest and showiest of species; it grows vigorously to form a dense mat of grey-green, hairy leaves to 20mm ($\frac{4}{5}$in) long, which, unlike all the other species, are placed alternately on longish stems or runners growing from the parent rosettes. The lovely soft lilac-pink flowers are held in a tight globular umbel on erect stems to 8cm ($3\frac{1}{5}$in) long. Himalaya. A later flowerer, at its best in July. Easily propagated by rooted fragments. No winter protection is usually needed. Plants can prove rather invasive and can swamp more delicate neighbours on a rock garden. Var. *leichtlinii* is a particularly fine form worth seeking out.

Androsace sarmentosa ○☆
This species and *A. primuloides* are very similar. The latter occurs in the W Himalaya eastward to Kumaon, and *A. sarmentosa* from Kumaon eastward to W China. They are among the larger Androsaces and are the easiest to grow. They are quite beautiful when well grown and form loose mats by means of rooting runners which make plants easy to propagate. The woolly leaf-rosettes, 20–40mm ($\frac{3}{4}$–$1\frac{3}{5}$in) across, bear relatively large flowers of a bright pink to mauve-red, borne in a tight umbel on 4–10cm ($1\frac{1}{2}$–4in) tall stalks. Plants thrive in a sunny raised bed, and flower in May–June. *A. sarmentosa* is offered in several varieties, such as var. *watkinsii*, var. *yunnanensis*, var. *chumbyi* and 'Galmont's Variety'. These may once have been distinct types, but now all varietal names yield virtually the same form. Recent introductions from Nepal are frequently much less woolly in general appearance.

Androsace mathildae ○☆
This species forms small cushions up to 30–40mm ($1\frac{1}{5}$–$1\frac{3}{5}$in) across. The bright green, fairly open, rosettes are made up of shiny stiff leaves which are hairless except for a few small cilia near the tip. The white or occasionally pale pink flowers, 5mm ($\frac{1}{5}$in) across, are borne 3–6 to a rosette—each with long slender stalks.

C Apennines, where it is a plant of rock crevices above 2,000m (6,600ft). Plants grow well in an open sunny scree, and, though not very long-lived, they set seed freely.

Androsace muscoidea ○▲

A very variable species, most forms of which are generally difficult to keep in cultivation. Plants are floriferous and very pretty, and resemble a much reduced, very short-stemmed *A. villosa*. It forms woolly grey-green cushions with white, virtually stemless flowers borne singly or in umbels of 2–3. Himalaya. Plants do well in the open in scree with winter protection. There is one commercially available form which appears to be hardier than its cousins and worth seeking out. Forma *longiscapa*, also from the Himalaya, is of uncertain status and may prove to be a new species. It is a variable and attractive plant close to *A. villosa* var. *jacquemontii*. From the woolly grey-green rosettes rise 5–10cm (2–4in) long stalks bearing a tight umbel of mauve-pink to lilac-blue flowers with a yellow or orange eye which turn red on fading. Though offered by only a couple of nurseries, it will probably become more widely available. It is best grown in the alpine house, although it also does well in scree outdoors, given winter protection.

Androsace pyrenaica ○

The Pyrenean Rock Jasmine is another delightful species which forms deep rounded cushions of small, tight, greyish-green leaf-rosettes; the stiff outcurving leaves bear very small hairs on the margins. The single white flowers, solitary or paired and 4–5mm ($\frac{1}{8}$in) across, are held just clear of the cushion surface. Pyrenees, where it grows on granite rocks and screes. Easily propagated from cuttings or seed. Hybridises readily with *A. carnea*. Best grown in the alpine house, but it will do well outside in scree with some winter protection.

Androsace pubescens ○

This high altitude species from the Alps makes a soft, green downy cushion which can cover itself with single stemless white flowers. The leaf-rosettes, about 10mm ($\frac{2}{5}$in) across, have an open appearance because the outer leaves are outcurving. A high proportion of the fine leaf hairs are forked. Usually a short-lived plant in cultivation and not too easy to please; it is best grown in an alpine house, but can be grown in scree if given adequate winter protection.

Androsace primuloides see *A. sarmentosa*, p. 25

Androsace sempervivoides ○☆

This easily grown and popular mat-forming species is very stoloniferous and hence easily propagated. The flattish 10–30mm ($\frac{2}{5}$–1$\frac{1}{5}$in) rosettes are made up of relatively broad, oblong, ciliate-margined leaves of a leathery texture. The pink to pinkish-mauve flowers have a yellow eye which turns bright red as the flowers fade and are borne in a tight umbel on a 1–7cm ($\frac{2}{5}$–2$\frac{3}{5}$in) stalk. This species does best in a scree in full sun. W Himalaya.

Androsace mucronifolia ○

This lovely tight, mat-forming species is reappearing in our gardens after an absence. It has often been confused with *A. sempervivoides*, from which it differs by being very sparsely stoloniferous and by its smallish globular rosettes of incurving ciliate-edged leaves. The pink flowers are borne 2–6 in a tight umbel just above the leafy mat. W Himalaya and E Hindu Kush. May–June. Some forms are shy flowering, but it does well in the open garden on a scree or raised bed and has proved quite hardy.

Androsace strigillosa ○
This large and rather coarse species, when well grown, can be quite elegant. It forms loose clumps of open-leaf rosettes and spreads by means of stolons. The downy elliptic leaves are up to 10cm (4in) long. The flowers are borne in a very open umbel on 30cm (12in) long peduncles, each flower with a long slender stalk; the colour varies from white to pink, often in the striking combination of white on the upper surface and purplish-red on the reverse. Himalaya. May–June. Plants grow well in a raised bed, best among small shrubs, and need some winter protection.

Androsace vandellii (Syn. **A. imbricata, A. argentea**) ○
This super little cushion-forming species is a popular exhibit at alpine flower shows in the spring. The small, tight leaf-rosettes are silvery owing to a dense covering of star-shaped hairs. The white flowers are solitary or several to each rosette, borne on very short stalks; in a well-flowered plant the leaf-cushions are totally covered in bloom. Flower size varies considerably from 3mm to 6mm ($\frac{1}{8}$–$\frac{1}{4}$in) across, and it pays to look for a good clone. Pyrenees and Alps from 2,000m to 3,000m (6,600–9,900ft). A fairly easy plant which does best in the alpine house, but it can be grown in scree or on tufa block, with winter protection—a sheet of glass placed overhead is ideal.

Androsace villosa ○
One of the favourites, but it requires care and attention to get the best results from it in cultivation. Plants form a more or less tight mat, in some clones a cushion of densely silky-hairy leaf-rosettes. The flowers are white and particularly pretty; they are held in a tight umbel of 3–7 on relatively short stalks. Mountains of C and S Europe eastwards to Afghanistan. There are forms which have significantly larger flowers 8–10mm (c. $\frac{2}{5}$in) across and more densely silky-hairy than average, and these are sold as var. *arachnoidea* 'Superba'. Var. *taurica* from the Crimea has markedly less hairy and somewhat longer umbel stalks and flowers that regularly turn pink with a red eye before fading. This variety does well in the alpine house, where it can grow to a large size; it also grows happily in a raised bed if given winter protection. Var. *jacquemontii* from the W. Himalaya is a quite delightful plant. It forms a more or less tight mat of very silky woolly rosettes which, at flowering time, have two distinct types of leaf. The flowers are borne 4–10 in a very tight umbel carried on 1–4cm ($\frac{2}{5}$–1$\frac{2}{5}$in) stalks subtended by longish silky bracts. The corolla is a bright purple red, which can vary in intensity in different clones. It is essentially an alpine house plant. Being stoloniferous, its propagation presents no problems.

Androsace carnea × **A. pyrenaica** ○☆
At its best a very nice hybrid which combines the cushion habit of *A. pyrenaica* with the ease of cultivation and pink flower colour of *A. carnea*. The flowers range from solitary white to pink umbels. One clone named 'Pink Gin' falls into the latter category.

Androsace hirtella × **A. cylindrica** ○☆
This is the most widely grown hybrid and is really rewarding and beautiful in nearly all its forms. At its best it rapidly forms a sizeable cushion with relatively large, fragrant, stemless, single white flowers. It will do reasonably well outdoors in scree or on a tufa block, but a perfect mound of flowers is only obtained under alpine house conditions.

27

ANEMONE (Ranunculaceae)

The anemones or wind-flowers are a group popular in gardens, with many species being cultivated. The smaller ones are ideal rock garden plants, showy and mostly easy to grow. The flowers are solitary, though clustered in several species; they are without true petals, their place being taken by coloured sepals. There is usually a whorl of leaves below the flowers. The genus contains some 150 species distributed in both the northern and southern hemispheres, but particularly the Mediterranean region and in mountain habitats. The Pasque flowers, *Pulsatilla*, are sometimes included in *Anemone*, but differ in their pinnately rather than palmately cut leaves and in the long feathery tails to the fruits.

Anemone nemorosa ○◐☆

The Wood Anemone is a widespread plant of woodland and mountain pastures in Britain and much of Europe. The wild form normally has white flowers, often flushed with pink or mauve on the outside. They are 25–30mm (1–1¼in) across and with 6 sepals. The leaves have 3–lobed, toothed segments. March–April. 'Allenii'—large lavender-blue flowers, the finest cultivar; 'Alba Flore-plena'—double, white flowers; 'Blue Bonnet'—mid-blue flowers flushed with crimson on the outside; 'Robinsoniana'—pale lavender-blue flowers, with a greyish reverse; 'Royal Blue'—has the deepest blue flowers; 'Vestal'—the best of the pure white cultivars.

Anemone trifolia ○◐

Like the previous, but the leaves have simply toothed, not lobed, segments. The flowers are slightly larger, with white rather than yellowish anthers. Replaces *A. nemorosa* in much of SE Europe. March–April. Far less common in cultivation.

Anemone ranunculoides ○◐☆

The so-called Wood Ginger is not unlike a Wood Anemone, but the leaves are a brighter green and the flowers bright yellow, buttercup-like, 15–20mm (⅗–⅘in) across. There are sometimes 2–3 flowers to a stem. C Europe to W Asia. April–May. There is also a fine double-flowered form. Very good in semi-shaded positions and on peat banks.

Anemone sylvestris ○◐☆

The Snowdrop Wind-flower can be likened to a giant Wood Anemone, although it may also recall an Alpine Pasque-flower, *Pulsatilla alpina*. The satiny-white, cupped flowers are 30–50mm (1⅕–2in) across, with a central boss of yellow stamens. The leaves are lobed to the centre and deeply toothed. Mountains of C Europe, E to W Asia. April–May. Easy and forming clumps in time.

Anemone baldensis ○

Essentially like a small version of the preceding species, but with more finely divided leaves and flowers, 25–40mm (1–1⅜in), with 8–10 pointed (not 5 rounded) sepals, often with a purplish reverse. A local plant of the Alps—named after Mt Baldo. June–July. Less often seen than *A. sylvestris* in cultivation, not difficult to grow, but seldom flowering freely.

Anemone magellanica ○☆

A native of Chile rather resembling a taller *A. sylvestris*. However, the flowers are rather smaller and creamy-white and the leaves hairy and more finely divided. Plants form tufts to 15cm (6in) tall, the stems lengthening considerably in fruit. May–June. A free-flowering and handsome plant. 'Major'—the finest form.

Anemone multifida ○

A larger plant than the previous (the two are sometimes included in the same species), the flower often suffused with yellow or pink. To 30cm (12in) tall. North America. June–July.

Anemone narcissiflora ◑

Plants form tufts to 30cm (12in) tall with bright green, softly hairy, palmately lobed leaves. The flowers are borne in distinctive umbels of 3–8, each 20–30mm ($\frac{4}{5}$–1$\frac{1}{5}$in), white, often with a soft pink reverse. Widely distributed from the Alps and Pyrenees to Asia and North America. June–July. Not particularly difficult to grow, but a shy flowerer, well worthwhile perservering with, for this is a delightful species. Plants succeed best in a cool, moist, leafy or peaty soil. The Himalayan *A. demissa* is very similar, but rare in cultivation.

Anemone apennina ◑☆

The Blue Wood Anemone is a feature of scrub and open woodland throughout much of S Europe, but has become naturalized in English woodlands. It is a low plant like *A. nemorosa*, seldom exceeding 15cm (6in) in height. The flowers are deep sky blue, 32–38mm (1$\frac{1}{4}$–1$\frac{1}{2}$in) across with 10–18 narrow sepals. The leaves have narrow, deeply cut segments. White, pink and double-flowered forms are also known, but those with deep blue flowers really are the finest. March–April.

Anemone blanda ○◑☆

This is deservedly the most popular and widely grown of the smaller anemones. Plants have a stouter and more substantial rhizome that the previous species, and can be purchased and planted as dried 'corms'. Those of *A. nemorosa* and *A. apennina* cannot withstand drying and plants are best divided and replanted soon after flowering. *A. blanda* is superficially like *A. apennina* and often confused with it; however, the flowers are larger, 35–50mm (1$\frac{3}{5}$–2in), with only 9–14, broader, sepals, deep blue in the wild form. E Europe and Turkey. February–April. Easy to grow, often forming extensive patches once established. Particularly good beneath shrubs and trees. 'Atrocaerulea'—intense deep blue flowers; 'Radar'—fine pinkish-red flowers with a white centre; 'White Splendour'—exceptionally large, glistening white flowers.

Anemone obtusiloba ○

An exceptionally beautiful species from the Himalaya. The basal leaves form a rather spreading rosette from the centre of which rise one or two large buttercup-flowers, 20–30mm ($\frac{4}{5}$–1$\frac{1}{5}$in), deep blue in the best forms, but yellow and white ones are also known. June. Requires a well-drained, but moist, peaty soil.

Anemone lesseri ○☆

A clump-forming plant with erect stems to 30cm (12in) tall, with rather coarse, stiffly hairy foliage. The bright, deep-pink flowers have a darker eye, giving the plant a striking appearance. North America. June–July. Easy to grow and readily available.

ANEMONELLA (Ranunculaceae)

The genus contains a species native to North American woodland.

Anemonella thalictroides ◑

The Rue Anemone is a delightful little plant which bears small tuberous roots. The leaves are finely divided like those of a *Thalictrum*. The stems are thin and rather

29

Anemone blanda

fragile, bearing small white, or sometimes pale pink blooms. The whole plant rarely exceeds 12cm (5in) in height. March–April. A double-flowered form is also known. Plants thrive best in semi-shaded places.

ANTENNARIA (Compositae)

Although this widespread genus has over 100 species only one is grown with any regularity. The genus is closely related to the group of genera which include the so-called everlasting flowers, such as *Anaphalis*. The leaves of many of the species are grey or silver and eventually form mats which make good ground cover if left unattended. Propagation by division of the parent plant.

Antennaria dioica (syn. *Gnaphalium dioicum, Omalotheca dioica*) ○☆
Also known under its old name of *A. tomentosa,* this species is characterized by its spreading habit and is sometimes used for making herb lawns, as its dense mats of creeping stems can stand a certain amount of trampling without damage. These stems become erect for 5–10cm (2–4in) when ready to flower and bear heads of rayless flowers which vary from white to pink. Mountains of Europe, N Asia and North America. May–June. A common species of European mountain meadows, heaths and dry open places. The cultivars 'Nyewoods Variety' and 'Rosea' are among the best pink-flowered forms; 'Minima'—slightly smaller than the typical form.

ANTHEMIS (Compositae)

This genus is named after the Greek word for the Chamomile, a group to which it is closely related. There are more than 80 species occurring throughout Europe, Asia and North America. Many are rather weedy, and not worthy of cultivation, but several do make good rock garden plants, requiring a position in full sun. Most are readily propagated by division or by summer cuttings of vegetative shoots.

Anthemis biebersteinii ○☆
Formerly known as *A. rudolphiana*, this pretty species hails from the Caucasus Mountains, where it occurs in stony gritty soils. The leaves are finely pinnately divided and silver-green in colour and these contrast well with the rich golden-yellow flower-heads, carried on 15–20cm (6–8in) stems. June–August.

Anthemis punctata ○☆
A semi-woody perennial with whitish grey foliage forming intricately branched mounds, from which the daisy-like heads of yellow and white flowers arise on stems 15–25cm (6–10in) long. The Italian subspecies *cupaniana* (syn. *A. cupaniana*) is commonly offered for sale, while the typical form is native of North Africa and is less widely grown. June–October. The plant generally sold under the name *A. cupaniana* is a fine plant, though often too vigorous for the smaller rock garden.

Anthemis nobilis ○
Recently transferred to the genus *Chamaemelum*, this species is the true Chamomile, which is often used for making herb lawns. It is also an attractive plant quite suitable for growing on the rock garden. One of the most appealing features of this plant is the highly aromatic foliage, so it is a good idea to plant it close to a path, where its fragrance can be more readily appreciated. The inflorescences have characteristic dome-like heads of tiny pale yellow flowers surrounded by a ring of large white ray-florets. They are borne on stems 5–20cm (2–8in) long throughout most of the summer. 'Flore-pleno' has flowers with many white ray florets; 'Treneague'—the non-flowering clone used for lawns, forming dense carpets no more than about 5–8cm (2–3in) in height.

ANTHYLLIS (Leguminosae)
Species of *Anthyllis*, or the kidney vetches, range in stature from prostrate perennial herbs to small shrubs. The genus contains 20–25 species, with a centre of diversity in Mediterranean Europe, a few species extending into mainland Europe, the Atlantic Islands and NE Africa. The leaves are usually pinnate, rarely single or trifoliate. The flower colour ranges from white to yellow, red, pink and purple and the small pea-like flowers are usually aggregated into dense heads or short racemes. The calyx varies in shape, but is frequently inflated near the base, and the small ovoid fruits with their 1–2 seeds are usually completely included within it. In general, species of *Anthyllis* thrive on poor well-drained soils, and are readily propagated from seed.

Anthyllis hermanniae ○
A subshrub to about 1m (3ft) tall, although often less, with tortuous woody branches, the branchlet tops becoming spiny. The leaves have 1 or 3 oblong leaflets which are silvery-hairy beneath. The yellow flowers are aggregated into an interrupted raceme. Corsica. April–June. This species particularly favours dry stony sites. 'Compacta'—a shorter more rounded cultivar.

Anthyllis montana ○
A woody-based perennial to 10cm (4in) in height often forming large clumps and occasionally becoming rather shrubby. The greyish-hairy pinnate leaves are mostly

clustered at the base of the plant. The flower stems are erect with the pink flowers clustered into dense heads. A native of the Alps and mountains of SE Europe, preferring limestone soils. May–July. 'Rubra'—deep red flowers, the only cultivar generally available. Subsp. *jacquinii*, from the E Alps and mountains of the Balkan peninsula, is ideally suited to cultivation in rock gardens being more compact and with attractive bright yellow flowers.

Anthyllis vulneraria ○☆
The Common Kidney Vetch is a biennial or perennial plant to 30cm (12in) tall. The lowermost leaves are sometimes reduced to one large leaflet or, if more typically pinnate, then the terminal leaflet is the largest. The flowers are normally yellow, ageing to orange, and borne in dense long-stalked clusters; the calyces are inflated when the flowers open, being constricted at the apex. Throughout much of Europe, especially in mountain habitats. May–August. The species is tolerant of various soil types, but thrives on sandy and calcareous composts. An extremely variable species which includes some 24 subspecies in Europe ranging in colour from yellow and white to pink and red. Surprisingly few of these are in cultivation. 'Coccinea'—red flowers.

ANTIRRHINUM (Scrophulariaceae)

In the wild, snapdragons are found in the W Mediterranean as well as Pacific North America; there are about 42 species in all. Of these the most widely cultivated species is the Common Snapdragon, *A. majus*, from which much breeding has been done. Antirrhinums require a well-drained, sunny and somewhat sheltered position. The pouched flowers, 2-lipped, usually covered in glandular hairs, are solitary or borne in terminal racemes and are characterized by having a prominently coloured palate on the lower lip.

Antirrhinum molle ◐
The Soft Snapdragon is a delicate, short-lived perennial with stems becoming woody at the base. Its fragile, trailing or semi-erect stems are covered in sticky hairs and clothed in soft, mid-green, oval leaves. Flowers white with a yellow boss on the lower lip. A Pyrenean endemic, where it grows in rock crevices in semi-shade. June–July.

Antirrhinum sempervirens ○◐
Similar to the preceding, but with tougher, greener leaves and smaller flowers which are often marked with red or purple on the lower lip. N Spain and the Pyrenees. June–July.

APHYLLANTHES (Aphyllanthaceae)

A genus of species native to the Mediterranean region. The species is hardy, but hates disturbance and is best planted out when young. A well-drained gritty soil and plenty of sunshine are its chief requirements. Propagation is easiest from seed.

Aphyllanthes monspeliensis ○☆
A tough rush-like plant forming erect tufts to 20cm (8in) tall with deep green stems. The flowers are 6–petalled, opening widely to 20–25mm ($\frac{4}{5}$–1in) across, deep blue, borne near the stalk tips. June–July.

AQUILEGIA (Ranunculaceae)

A very popular genus in gardens with many species scattered across the northern hemisphere, particularly in mountain regions. Plants are generally short-lived perennials, the ternately divided leaves mostly basal, generally with numerous neat, lobed, leaflets. The nodding flowers have a characteristic appearance with their 5 straight or hooked spurs.

Most species thrive on ordinary, well-drained soils, but some of the smaller high-alpine types are better on screes or in troughs. Most produce seed readily, but—beware—many have a weakness to hybridization with neighbouring species. To maintain a pure stock plants should be isolated. Mature plants greatly resent disturbance. The common Columbine of gardens, *A. vulgaris*, is generally too coarse and invasive for the average rock garden.

Aquilegia flabellata ○☆
One of the finest species which hails from Japan. The form usually seen in gardens is a dwarf version, 'Nana'. Plants grow to 15cm (6in) tall with bluish-green leaves. The flowers are relatively sturdy, bluish-mauve, the petals, usually white-tipped. June–July. 'Nana Alba'—white flowered.

Aquilegia nivalis ○
Like the preceding species one of the real gems in the genus. Plants are of similar proportions, but the solitary flowers are a handsome deep purple-blue, the protruding stamens almost black. W Himalaya. June–July. A delightful species for scree or troughs or in the alpine house. Becoming more widely available and well worth seeking out.

Aquilegia alpina ○
A large columbine to 60cm (2ft) tall with grey-green foliage and large bright blue flowers, 50–80mm (2–3¼in) across, of great beauty. The spurs are straight or slightly curved. Alps and Apennines. June–July. One of the most handsome species, the Alpine Columbine is less often seen in gardens than it should. Unfortunately it crosses readily with *A. vulgaris*, as well as others, and it is difficult to maintain a pure species. In the wild it inhabits meadows, woods and damp rock crevices, reaching altitudes up to 2,600m (8,580ft).

Aquilegia pyrenaica ○
Rather like a delicate and shorter version of *A. alpina*; flowers few and bright blue or violet-blue with curved spurs. Plants seldom more than 25cm (10in) tall. Pyrenees. June–July. A plant of rock and stony habitats at high altitudes, in its native haunts, sometime growing on grassy cliff ledges.

Aquilegia caerulea ○
Rather like the *A. alpina,* but a shorter plant with pale blue and white flowers, with long straight spurs. North America. June–July. Best grown as a scree plant.

Aquilegia atrata ○
Not unlike the common Columbine, *A. vulgaris*, in general proportions, but flowers a sombre dusky purple-red, 30–50mm (1⅕–2in) across. The stamens protrude well beyond the petals, a characteristic feature of this species, allowing for easy identification. Alps and Apennines. June–July.

Aquilegia bertolonii ○☆
A delightful little species, rarely more than 15cm (6in) tall. The leaves are dark green and the violet-blue flowers, 25–35mm (1–1⅜in) across, have incurved spurs and characteristically downturned sepals. SW Alps and N Italy. June–July.

Aquilegia discolor ○
A small Spanish species seldom more than 10cm (4in) tall, with a dense tuft of grey-green leaves and stems bearing several, or sometimes one, pale blue flowers with contrasting cream centre. June–July. Another gem, perhaps seen at its best in a trough, or in a pan in the alpine house.

Aquilegia jonesii ○▲
Another much sought-after species which hails from the Rocky Mountains of North America. Plants are scarcely as tall as the previous species, the foliage even neater and a striking blue-grey. The flowers turn upwards, unlike most other species, blue with white or pale blue sepals. June–July. Not nearly as easy in cultivation as the previous species and certainly a plant for protected environments.

Aquilegia laramiensis ○
This is another Rocky Mountain species, being perhaps the tiniest of all Columbines. In the wild it is a scree plant forming small tufts of deep green leaves to 50mm (2in). The creamy-white flowers, 14–16mm (½–¾in) nestle amongst the leaves. June–July. Scarce in cultivation, but highly desirable.

Aquilegia canadense ○◑☆
A very striking plant reaching 50cm (18in) in height, sometimes more. Leaves lax and rather sparse, deep grey-green. The flowers are rather narrow, brilliant scarlet, the petals tipped with yellow and produced in lax sprays which wave nicely in the wind. North America. June–early August. Short-lived in cultivation, but readily raised from seed. The flowers are pollinated in the wild by both bees and humming-birds. Var. *flavescens* has yellow flowers.

Aquilegia formosa ○
Like a laxer-flowered *A. canadense*; the flowers vary from red to yellow, often bicoloured, and have widely spreading sepals; those of the previous species are short and forward pointing. North America. June–July.

Aquilegia viridiflora ○
Not unlike the previous species, but unusual in its dark greenish-black flowers with straight spurs. More a curiosity than of any ornamental value. Siberia and neighbouring parts of China. June–July.

ARABIS (Cruciferae)

One of the most popular of rock garden groups, including some easy and accommodating species. The genus contains about 120 species native to Europe, North America and Asia as well as the mountains of tropical Africa. Many are weedy annuals of little garden merit but those that are grown are generally compact plants with toothed leaves and flowers of white, pink or purple. The fruit-pods are elongated, often very long and slender thus readily distinguishing them from similar-looking genera such as *Aubrieta*.

Arabis caucasica (syn. *A. albida*) ○☆
The Common Arabis of gardens belongs to this species. It is an easy and most accommodating plant forming a low spreading mat of scalloped-edged leaves borne in rosettes. The flowers are white or pale pink, borne in racemes clear of the foliage. E Europe and SW Asia. March–June. Generally too invasive for the small rock garden, but an ideal path edger or as a subject for a dry or retaining wall. 'Flore-plena' (probably the same as 'Alba plena')—double, white flowers; 'Rosea'—rose-pink flowers; 'Variegata'—attractively variegated leaves—there are both single and double-flowered forms, the latter often named 'Plena Variegata'. Various other cultivars are available including 'Coccinea', 'Pink Pearl' and 'Rosabella'.

Arabis alpina ○◗
The Alpine Rockcress is very similar to the previous, but with a rather laxer habit and smaller flowers. Mountains of Europe and W Asia. April–June. A plant of damp rocks, gravelly places and streamsides to 3,000m (9,900ft) in the wild. 'Variegata'—variegated leaves. *A. rosea* is probably only a pink-flowered form of this species.

Arabis androsacea ○
A charming little plant with numerous small rosettes of elliptical leaves, sometimes mistaken for a species of *Androsace*, hence the specific name. The small flowers are white on stems only 20mm (⅜in) high. Turkey—Cilician Taurus. April–May. A good trough plant, but easily overlooked on the rock garden.

Arabis blepharophylla ○☆
Far more Arabis-like than the previous species, forming rosettes of grey-green elliptical toothed leaves. The flowers vary from white to deep rose-pink, borne in racemes up to 10cm (4in) tall. California. April–May, occasionally later. Perhaps the best Arabis for the rock garden though not particularly long-lived. The best forms have rich rose-pink flowers.

Arabis caerulea ○
Another charming little alpine species native to the European Alps where it occurs on limestone rocks and moraines. Plants seldom exceed 80mm (3in) tall. The tiny flowers occur in various shades of bluish-purple and pale blue. April–May. Short-lived and not always easy in cultivation. It will sometimes seed around on a scree garden.

Arabis bryoides ○
Forms cushions of small silvery-hairy leaf-rosettes each only about 20mm (⅜in) across. The small flowers are white. The whole plant is scarcely 60mm (2⅜in) tall. Greece. May–July. Best as a trough or pan plant. 'Olympica'—a fine compact stemless form.

Arabis ferdinandi-coburghii ○◗☆
Plants form rather flat rosettes of green, narrow and rather fleshy leaves. The flowers are white or pale pink. SE Europe. May–June 'Variegata'—leaves variegated with yellow or cream, by far the best form cultivated.

Several other species of *Arabis* are cultivated, including 3 European species, *A. halleri*, *A. pumila* and *A. soyeri*, but they are hardly worth cultivating, except as curiosities.

ARCTERICA (Ericacae)

A genus containing a single species native to Japan, the adjacent region of Kamtchatka, as well as the Bering Islands. However, not everyone is agreed on the position of this species in the family so that it will sometimes be found in catalogues listed as a species of *Andromeda* or *Pieris*.

Arcterica nana ○◑□

An evergreen, mat-forming subshrub spreading by underground runners, its wiry stems rarely exceeding 40mm (1½in) in height. The leaves, dark and glossy green and leathery, are in pairs or threes. The urn-shaped flowers, nodding and waxy, creamy-white, are borne in short terminal clusters. April–May.

ARCTOSTAPHYLOS (Ericaceae)

This genus contains the bearberries characteristic of heaths or open rocky woodland and native to many parts of N Europe, Asia and North America. They are plants of acid soils like many members of the heath family, *Ericaceae*. Three species, *A. alpinus, A. nevadensis* and *A. uva-ursi*, are commonly offered by nurserymen; although several others are grown, they are rarely available commercially. The flowers superficially resemble those of *Arbutus*, the strawbery tree, being urn-shaped and nodding, with five reflexed teeth. The leaves are often rather leathery, generally untoothed, but toothed in *A. alpinus*. The edible fruits of *Arctostaphylos* are fleshy and berry-like, and like the flowers are borne in clusters.

Arctostaphylos uva-ursi ◑□

The Bearberry is found in many parts of Europe, except the extreme south, as well as N Asia and North America. A trailing and mat-forming evergreen shrub, rarely more than 15cm (6in) tall, but often making extensive patches with its long prostrate branches. The leaves are bright shiny-green with the margins rolled neatly under. The white flowers are tinged with pink, 4–6mm (¼in) long, and borne on short stalks. The berries are shiny bright red when they ripen in the late summer, 6–8mm (¼–⅜in) across, and with rather dry flesh. April–June. A vigorous grower useful as ground cover or when grown over an old tree stump which it will soon hide. Generally too large for the small rock garden.

Arctostaphylos nevadensis ○□

This species strongly resembles *A. uva-ursi* and is a native of North America. 'Ouray', the most notable cultivar, is named after an Ute Amerindian chief, and is occasionally listed in catalogues.

Arctostaphylos alpinus (syn. *Arctous alpinus*) ○◑□

The Alpine Bearberry is readily distinguished from the other two species by its bright green, clearly toothed leaves which wither in the autumn, but are not shed until the following spring. In contrast, those of *A. uva-ursi* are held for three years. Plants form prostrate mats, seldom more than 50mm (2in) high and with long reddish stems that root down as they grow, often breaking away from the parent to establish new plants. The leaves have a silvery lustre due to a layer of air trapped beneath the skin. The white flowers are sometimes tinged with pink or green, 5–6mm (¼in) long, with crimson or chocolate coloured anthers. The berries are succulent, purplish-black when ripe, generally ripening in the autumn. April–June. A native species found in Europe, except the south, N Asia and North America.

ARENARIA (Caryophyllaceae)

The Sandworts constitute a large group, most of which are of little garden value since their flowers are very small and starry. There are, however, a few good cushion-forming or carpeting species in the genus, some with relatively large flowers, which make good rock garden subjects. There are about 250 species scattered throughout the temperate zones of the northern hemisphere.

They are annual, biennial or perennial plants with opposite leaves which are very small or needle like. The flowers are usually white with 4 or 5 petals and sepals, all free from each other, the petals usually entire, not notched or bilobed at the apex as in many of the members of this family. Usually there are 10 stamens and 3 styles, and the capsules open to reveal 6 teeth.

Arenaria balearica ◐☆
A minute carpet-forming plant producing dense green flat mats of tiny oval or orbicular leaves only 2–4mm ($\frac{1}{12}$–$\frac{1}{8}$in) long on thread-like stems. The solitary white flowers are about 5–7mm ($\frac{1}{4}$in) across and are carried on slender erect stalks well above the mat of leaves. Balearic Is., Corsica and Sardinia. May–June. Can be invasive.

Arenaria tetraquetra ○
A cushion-forming plant consisting of densely packed rosettes of small triangular leaves only 1–4 mm ($\frac{1}{25}$–$\frac{1}{6}$in) long, which completely hide the stems; viewed from above the individual leaf-rosettes are like 4-pointed stars. The solitary white flowers are 5–10mm ($\frac{1}{5}$–$\frac{2}{5}$in) across, stemless or on very short stems so that they are almost resting on the leaf-cushions; they usually have 4 petals. Spain including the Pyrenees. June–August.

Var. granatensis makes extremely dense cushions and usually has flowers with 5 petals and 5 sepals. S Spain.

Arenaria purpurascens ○◐
The Pink Sandwort is one of the prettiest species which forms rather loose cushions with lanceolate, pointed leaves up to 10mm ($\frac{2}{5}$in) long and borne in small rosettes; from these appear the erect flower-stems, reaching 30–60mm ($1\frac{1}{4}$–$2\frac{1}{2}$in) in height. These have a few widely-spaced pairs of leaves and carry tight clusters of 2–4 (rarely solitary) pale purple or whitish flowers about 10mm ($\frac{2}{5}$in) across. Pyrenees. June–August. A plant of damp rocky habitats from 1,800–2,800m (5,900–9,200ft) in its native haunts.

'Elliot's Variety'—deeper coloured, pinkish-lilac flowers and a rather more compact habit.

Arenaria montana ○
A sprawling perennial forming loose mats of wiry stems carrying pairs of narrowly lanceolate or linear, hairy, grey-green leaves 10–20mm ($\frac{2}{5}$–$\frac{4}{5}$in) long. The white flowers may be solitary or sometimes several in a loose head, borne on a stem 10–20cm (4–8in) tall, each flower about 15–20mm ($\frac{3}{5}$–$\frac{4}{5}$in) across. After flowering the stalks of the individual flowers bend downwards. Spain, Portugal and W France. May–June. 'Grandiflora'—a large-flowered selection well worth seeking out.

Arenaria caespitosa ○
This is occasionally offered by nurseries. Plants have prostrate stems forming mats covered with tiny, rather fleshy leaves. 1–3 white flowers are produced at the tips of each shoot, and these are 5–10mm ($\frac{1}{5}$–$\frac{2}{5}$in) across. Chile. July–August.

ARMERIA (Plumbaginaceae)

A genus of 80 species, mostly native to the northern temperate zones of the earth, but with a few in the Andes. Most species form compact and rather dense tufts of linear basal leaves; rosette-leaf formation is common in the more herbaceous species. The flowers are borne in dense globular heads on slender stems sheathed at the top by papery bracts. The smaller species are most attractive, developing into neat plants which remain compact throughout the year. Propagation from seed or by division of the parent plant.

Armeria maritima ○☆
Probably the best-known species, commonly found on cliffs around the coasts of W Europe. Plants have the characteristic clumps of tightly arranged dark green linear leaves and flower stems which vary in length from 10cm to 60cm (4–24in), although most cultivated forms do not exceed 25cm (10in) tall. Flowers vary also in colour from white to deep reddish-pink. May–July. There are several cultivated clones including subsp. *alba* with large white flowers on short stalks; 'Birch Pink'—rose-pink flowers; 'Laucheana'—bright red flowers; 'Merlin'—rich pink flowers; 'Vindictive'—clusters of reddish-pink or pink flowers.

Armeria corsica (syn. *Armeria maritima* var. *corsica*) ○
This name has no botanical standing, but refers to a form of *Armeria maritima* with brick-red flowers. It is found for sale under this name and is therefore included. May–June.

Armeria girardii ○
Also sold under the names *A. setacea* and *A. juncea*, this slender species is characterized by having two types of leaves in the rosette: the outer ones are broadly linear to triangular, whilst the inner ones are much narrower, being almost thread-like. The flower-heads are pink, borne on stalks 10–15cm (4–6in) long. May–June.

Armeria juniperifolia (syn. *A. caespitosa*) ○☆
A small, but attractive, species with basal rosettes of linear leaves and pale lilac pink flowers borne on 25cm (10in) stems. Spain. May–June. Two varieties are grown: var. *alba*—white flowers; var. *rubra*—ruby-red flowers. 'Bevan's Variety'—one of the best known cultivars, has deep rose coloured flowers; 'Beechwood'—large heads of bright pink flowers.

Armeria welwitschii ○
An attractive and variable species from Portugal where it forms a compact dwarf shrub with many stems. The narrow lanceolate leaves are 5–10cm (2–4in) long and 2–7mm ($\frac{1}{12}$–$\frac{1}{4}$in) wide. The flower-heads are pink or white and borne on stalks 15–25cm (6–10in) long. May–July.

ARNICA (Compositae)

A small genus of herbaceous rhizomatous perennials with simple leaves which usually form basal rosettes. The flower-stems often have a pair of leaf-like bracts about half-way along their length. The flower-heads are solitary and bear both ray- and disc-florets of a rich golden-yellow. Only 2 species are regularly grown as alpines.

Arnica montana ○

A very colourful alpine with a wide distribution throughout the mountainous areas of Europe, where it inhabits meadows and open woods. It forms leafy rosettes of elliptical leaves which are glandular-hairy. The stems, 15–25cm (6–10in) tall, carry a solitary large, golden-yellow daisy flower, 45–60mm ($1\frac{3}{4}$–$2\frac{2}{5}$) across. May–June. Prefers a slightly alkaline soil.

Arnica alpina ○☐

Very similar but a lower plant with flower-heads only 35–45mm ($1\frac{2}{5}$–$1\frac{3}{4}$in) across. Scandinavia. May–July. Prefers a slightly acid soil.

ARTEMISIA (Compositae)

A large genus of herbaceous perennials, annuals and shrubs which are well known for their aromatic qualities. Although most have tiny dull flowers which form clustered racemes, they are quite often grown for the beauty of their grey or silvery foliage. All are natives of the northern hemisphere and in cultivation require full sun. Most are too large for the rock garden being more suitable for the herbaceous border. However, the following are often cultivated.

Artemisia eriantha ○

A tufted perennial up to 25cm (10in) tall, with silver, downy leaves which are deeply divided. Flower-heads 8mm ($\frac{1}{3}$in) wide, covered with white hairs and arranged in dense racemes which become nodding when fully mature. Native of mountain rocks in southern and central Europe. July–August.

Artemisia pedemontana (syn. *A. lanata*) ○

Often sold under various names including *A. assoana* and *A. lanata*. A delightful neat-foliaged subshrub only 40–60mm ($1\frac{1}{2}$–$2\frac{3}{8}$in) tall with flower-spikes up to 10–20cm (4–8in). Foliage finely divided into thin segments and covered with white hairs. Flowers densely hairy, yellow, crowded in 8mm ($\frac{1}{3}$in) wide heads. Limestone rocks, S and C Europe. July–August.

Artemisia brachyloba ○☆

A very small tufted perennial only 80mm ($3\frac{2}{8}$in) tall in flower, forming tight bunches of narrowly divided silvery-grey leaves. Flowers tiny, yellow, forming globe-shaped terminal heads. Mongolia. August–September. Another delightful foliage species forming mats scarcely exceeding 20mm ($\frac{3}{8}$in).

Artemisia schmidtiana ○☆

This Japanese species is too large for the rock garden and therefore the cultivar 'Nana' is usually grown. It forms rounded rosettes of finely divided silvery leaves which eventually grow into prostrate mats. 15cm (6in). July–August. A very beautiful foliage plant, delightful in young growth.

ASARINA (Scrophulariacea)

A genus closely related to and sometimes included in *Antirrhinum*. It contains a single species from S France and NE Spain.

Asarina procumbens (syn. *Antirrhinum asarina*) ○☆

A sticky, trailing perennial only 20cm (8in) tall. Its velvety leaves are 5-lobed and heart-shaped at the base. The flowers are borne singly at the leaf axils, and are whitish with faintly purple veins and a prominent golden-yellow palate on the lower

Asarina procumbens

lip. June–September. Prefers a shady site in a well-drained, lime-free soil, either amongst rocks or beneath trees. Once established, plants often seed around freely.

ASPERULA (Rubiaceae)

A genus of about 80 species from Europe, Asia and Australia, many of which are weak-stemmed and weedy; however, several are suited to the rock garden. The branches are usually square with leaves in whorls of 4 or 8. The individual flowers are very small, and borne in terminal or axillary clusters, usually pink, although in some species they can be white or yellow. Most flower in the spring or early summer and prefer an exposed position, but not too hot, and a gritty well-drained soil. Most can be readily propagated by division of the parent plant.

Asperula gussonii ○ ☆
A perennial up to 90mm (3½in) tall with slender stems which arise from a woody base and form a dense dwarf tuft. Flowers stalkless, 9–12 to a 'head', flesh-pink. Endemic to northern Sicily. June. Requires a well-drained open position; ideal for the scree garden or planted in a piece of tufa.

Asperula lilaciflora ○
A recent introduction from the E Mediterranean. Plants form very neat cushions of deep green glossy foliage, which is almost heath-like. Flowers 20mm (⅘in), rich pink, smothering the foliage in June and July. Often represented in cultivation by the variety *caespitosa* which is more prostrate. Most often seen as a pan plant in the alpine house, or as a trough plant.

Asperula suberosa ○
A well-known alpine from the mountains of Greece and Bulgaria, which makes a tufted, many-stemmed cushion only 80mm (*c.* 3in) tall, the leaves crowded in whorls of four and covered with silvery wool. Flowers in clusters of 2–3 on 50mm (2in) spikes, each flower tubular, 8mm (⅓in) long, pink. June. A well-drained soil is essential for this truly delightful little plant, which is most often seen as a pan plant in the alpine house.

ASTER (Compositae)

This huge genus contains over 500 species which are distributed throughout the temperate world of America, Africa and Eurasia. It is well known for its large herbaceous perennials, but also contains several species suitable for the trough or rock garden. The leaves are simple and basal, although sometimes they are alternately arranged throughout the length of the stem. The flowers are borne in daisy-like heads. The inner florets are always yellow and tubular while the outer florets are ray-like and vary in colour from white, to lilac, pink and purple. They mostly thrive in a well-drained, gritty soil in full sun. Propagation by seed or division of the parent plant.

Aster ericoides ○
This North American species is occasionally found naturalized in Europe alongside its close relative *A. pilosus*, also from North America. It is a herbaceous perennial reaching 25–35cm (10–14in), with linear leaves. The flower-heads are arranged in broad panicles and the rays are white at first, but become purplish with age. July–September. Rather too tall for smaller rock gardens.

Aster alpinus ○☆
The Alpine Aster is native to the mountains of Europe and Asia where it inhabits dry meadows and rocky places. Plants rise to 15cm (6in) tall, the leaves arranged in basal rosettes and along the lower part of the stems; they are covered with soft whitish hairs. The flower-heads are solitary, 25–40mm (1–1⅝in) across, and usually have rich purplish ray florets, although the colour may vary to include shades of pink or rarely white. May–July. A charming plant, rather neat and rarely invasive. The rich blue-flowered forms are the best. 'Albus'—a good white-flowered form; 'Beechwood'—has exceptionally large violet-blue flowers.

Aster likiangensis ○
This is probably just the eastern form of *A. alpinus*, coming from Yunnan in China and resembling it in almost every way except for its smaller stature; flower-stems rarely exceed 80mm (3in) tall.

Aster natalensis ○
A South African species forming dense mats of rich green spoon-shaped leaves up to 80mm (3in) long. The flowers are borne in solitary heads up to 40mm (1⅝in) across on stems 10–15cm (4–6in) tall. The ray-florets are a good deep blue in colour, contrasting well with the rich yellow disc florets. June–August.

Aster pygmaea ○◗☆
This attractive species forms low, creeping mats of densely hairy leaves, both features designed to protect the plant in its native habitat, in the Canadian Arctic. The flower-heads are borne on short stems up to 10cm (4in) tall and have lilac coloured ray-florets. Three cultivars are sometimes offered, though there is little

Aster alpinus

real difference between them. 'Blue Baby'—slightly bluer ray-florets than the type; 'Snow cushion'—has dense woolly hairs surrounding the flower-head; 'Peter Pan'—of uncertain distinction.

ASTILBE (Saxifragaceae)

A genus of 25 species from Eastern Asia and North America. Most are subjects for the herbaceous border, but a few of the smaller ones can be grown on the rock garden. The ferny leaves are usually 2–3-ternate, often with toothed leaflets and the white or pink flowers are borne in panicles. They are often confused with *Aruncus* or *Filipendula* (both in the Rosaceae), but the flowers of *Astilbe* differ in having many stamens. Propagation is easiest by division of the parent plants or from seed.

Astilbe chinensis ◐☆
Plants grow up to 22cm (9in) tall, and have 2–3 parted leaves and dense spikes of rosy-mauve flowers on stems up to about 22cm (9in). China. July. The form usually offered in catalogues is 'Pumila' which is more compact than the wild form.

Astilbe glaberrima ◐
Another clump-former which produces neat, 3-parted leaves of a bronzy green colour above which are carried branched racemes of pink flowers on stems 15cm (6in) tall. Japan. July–August. 'Saxatilis'—the best cultivar.

Astilbe simplicifolia ◐
Plants have distinctive leaves which are simple, ovate, but much lobed. The flower-spikes are white. Japan. July–August. 'Rosea'—the smallest cultivar, with flowers of a rich pink; 'Willy Buchanan'—reddish leaves and creamy-white flowers on stems about 20cm (8in) tall.

Astilbe crispa 'Perkeo' ◑
Plants have feathery, rather crinkled leaves and pink flowers on stems only 7–8cm (3in) tall. Japan. July.

ASTRAGALUS (Leguminosae)

A vast genus of about 2,000 species mainly of northern temperate regions, the most numerous being in W Asia and in W North America. Some species are very wide ranging, geographically, whilst others are narrowly restricted endemics known from only a single locality. Plants are herbs or subshrubs, very diverse in form, some being very spiny. The leaves are mostly pinnate. The pea-like flowers are white, yellow, pink, purplish or greenish, being clustered into racemes or spikes. Often confused with *Oxytropis*, which differs in the clearly beaked keel-petal. Most species, like many legumes, are intolerant of root disturbance and prefer light, gritty or sandy soils and full sun. They are best propagated from seed.

Astragalus alpinus ○☆
A procumbent or ascending herb, 15–40cm (6–16in) in height. The leaves have numerous small elliptical leaflets. The flowers are up to 15mm (⅗in) long, whitish to pale mauve with darker keel-petals, borne in relatively long-stalked clusters. The fruit is an oblong pod covered with blackish hairs when young. European Mountains. July–August. In the wild a plant of rocky and stony habitats up to 2,850m (9,400ft) altitude. Cultivated forms are generally quite prostrate.

Astragalus angustifolius ○
A compact woody-based subshrub forming dense spiny tussocks to 30cm (12in) tall. The pinnate leaves have up to 20 greyish-green, hairy leaflets. The flowers are 13–25mm (½–1in) long, usually white with the keel petals sometimes tinged purplish at the tips, borne just clear of the foliage in small oval clusters. Balkan Peninsula and some Mediterranean Islands. May–June.

Astragalus monspessulanus ○
The so-called False Vetch is widespread in the mountains of C and S Europe. It is generally trailing, but to 15cm (6in) in height. The leaves are usually in rosettes at the plant base. The slender flowers, 20–30mm (⅘–1⅕in) long, are purplish, reddish, or, rarely, white, borne in long-stalked clusters. April–August. The species has a preference for calcareous soils, growing usually on limestone, in meadows or rocky places in the wild.

Two other species occasionally seen in cultivation are *A. sempervirens* from the Alps and E Pyrenees, with its white or pale greyish purple flowers, and the North American *A. utahensis* (syn. *A. halleri*), a prostrate bushy species with purple flowers.

ASTRANTIA (Umbelliferae)

A small genus of about 10 species, native to Europe and Asia. Most are hardy perennials, usually too tall for the rock or scree garden. Astrantias are characterized by the striking collar of bracts surrounding the small pin-cushion heads of flowers. These bracts are often very ornamental, either because of their colour and veining or as a result of highly modified sculpturing with toothed or spiny margins. Easily propagated by division of the parent plant or from seed.

Astrantia minor ○❶

A slender tufted perennial, 20–40cm (8–16in) tall, often with branched stems. The basal leaves have 7 toothed lobes and the flower-stems sometimes have reduced leaves with only 3 or 5 lobes. The delicate collar of saw-toothed bracts which surrounds the cluster of tiny white flowers is one of the most endearing features of this species; the flower-heads, including the bracts, are about 20–30mm ($\frac{4}{5}$–1$\frac{1}{5}$in) across. Native of the mountains of C and S Europe. May–July.

ATHAMANTA (Umbelliferae)

A genus of about 10 species which have the cow-parsley appearance typical of the family *Umbelliferae*, with umbels of white flowers and delicate fern-like foliage. Only one species is small enough for the rock garden or trough, where it will benefit from a position in full sun and a very freely drained compost. Propagation is easiest from seed.

Athamanta cretensis ○

A delicate, softly hairy perennial with basal rosettes of grey-green, finely divided leaves which give rise to reddish flowering stems 15–25cm (6–10in) tall. The pleasantly fragrant umbels of tiny white flowers appear in the early summer. Crete. July–July. Well suited to pan culture since long periods of winter wet can cause rotting of the tap root.

AUBRIETA (Cruciferae)

Such a well-known genus scarcely needs any introduction. The species most widely grown in gardens is *A. deltoidea*, which exists in numerous cultivars. The genus contains some species primarily native to S Europe and W Asia. The finest, such as *A. intermedia* and *A. gracilis*, are inexplicably rare in cultivation for they are the most beautiful mat-formers, brightly flowered. Perhaps the modern hybrids of *A. deltoidea* are so splendid and diverse that the species themselves have been overlooked and forgotten. The garden forms are easily raised from seed and the best, named, ones can be increased from cuttings. Large plants can be clipped back after flowering to promote new and more compact growth.

Aubrieta deltoidea ○☆

A dense mat-former with numerous rosettes of grey-green, toothed leaves, smothered in mauve or purple flower racemes in the spring. S and SE Europe, W Asia. March–May. There are numerous named cultivars of which only a few are listed here. 'Astolate Blue'; 'Aureovariegata'—yellow leaf variegations and pale mauve-blue flowers; 'Belisha Beacon'—bright rose-red; 'Blue Beauty'; 'Bressingham Pink'—double deep pink; 'Bressingham Red'—red, particularly fine, large-flowered; 'Bridesmaid'—pale pink, darker in centre; 'Crimson Bedder'; 'Dream'—pale blue; 'Doctor Mules'—violet-blue; 'Gloriosa'—rose-pink; 'Greencourt Purple'; 'Gurgedyke'—deep purple; 'Hartswood'—rich purple, large flowers; 'Joan Allen'—crimson, double; 'Joy'—pale mauve, double; 'Mrs Rodewald'—rich red, large-flowered; 'Red Carpet'; 'Riverslea'—mauve, late flowering; 'Variegata'—white or cream leaf variegations and pale blue flowers; 'Wanda'—pale red, double.

AZORELLA (Umbelliferae)

A large genus of about 70 species from temperate South America and some Atlantic Islands, closely related to the pennyworts, *Hydrocotyle*, and therefore perhaps not immediately recognisable as members of the carrot family. Only one or two are sufficiently ornamental to be worthy of cultivation and these may often be found under their old generic name of *Bolax*.

Azorella glebaria (syn. *A. gummifera, Bolax glebaria, B. gummifera*) ◗

A wiry perennial forming hard green cushions up to 30cm (12in) high with closely arranged 3-lobed leaves, rather ericoid in appearance. The greenish-white umbels are surrounded by leafy bracts and are composed of 3–20 flowers. Azores. April–August. The attractive cushions of leaves are the most decorative feature of this plant.

Azorella trifurcata ◗

A perennial plant forming dense mats or hard cushions up to 11cm (5in) high and 45cm (18in) in diameter, with prostrate or ascending, branched stems. The leaves are shiny, apple-green in colour and leathery in texture, divided into 3 more or less equal lobes, each ending with 3 coarse teeth. The rather dirty-yellow flowers are grouped into somewhat irregular umbels on very short stems, so that they sit very close to the foliage. South America. June–August.

BAECKIA (Myrtaceae)

This genus was named in honour of Abraham Baeck, a Swedish physician and friend of Linnaeus. There are some 70 species which occur mainly in Australia, but one is found in New Caledonia and another in Asia. All are evergreen shrubs with opposite leaves which are untoothed or slightly lobed. The small pink or white flowers are borne solitarily or in clusters, with 5–10 or up to 20 stamens in a single row. The fruit is a small woody capsule. Most species require greenhouse conditions and prefer a soil of sandy peat, leaf-mould or lumpy peat.

Baeckia camphorosmae ◗

A compact or spreading small shrub up to 70cm (2ft 4in) in height. The leaves are small, camphor-scented, crowded on the many small branches. The white to pink flowers, 10–15mm ($\frac{2}{5}$–$\frac{3}{5}$in) in diameter, are solitary or in clusters of up to 4, borne in the leaf axils. June. An eye-catching plant when in flower. It needs a warm protected site in the garden and does well in well-drained light to heavy soils; also useful in the alpine house. Best in dappled shade or partial sun.

BALUSTION (Myrtaceae)

A small genus of two species endemic to SW Australia. They are prostrate to low growing evergreen shrubs with small untoothed leaves and orange-red flowers borne on the new growths, the corolla with five spreading lobes. The fruit is a woody capsule. Propagation by seed or summer cuttings.

Balustion pulcherrimum ○

A dwarf shrub to 80cm (2ft 8in), often less in cultivation, with numerous branchlets. The grey-green leaves are covered in glands. The beautiful and spectacular waxy-red, bell-shaped, flowers are borne singly at the leaf axils, each up to 25mm (1in) long. April–May. Still rather unusual in cultivation, this splendid shrub needs some care—a warm sheltered site and a light to medium well-drained soil, preferably in full sun. In less mild regions plants are best confined to the alpine house.

45

BARBAREA (Cruciferae)

A small genus of little appeal to the gardener. There are some 20 species scattered in Europe and W Asia as well as North America. Very easy to cultivate.

Barbarea vulgaris ○

An erect perennial rocket to 35cm (14in) with pinnate leaves with a large end leaflet. The small yellow flowers are borne in branched racemes. Europe, including Britain. 'Flore-pleno'—double flowers; 'Variegata'—leaves variegated with yellow.

BETULA (Betulaceae)

The Birch genus contains mostly large deciduous bushes and trees; however, one is small enough to be included here.

Betula nana ○◑☆

The Dwarf Birch is a charming plant, a dwarf shrub to 1m (3ft) tall with thin branches and tiny rounded, shiny, deeply toothed leaves. The catkins are small and yellowish, borne with the young leaves; male and female catkins are borne separately, but on the same plant. N Europe (including Britain) and N Asia, March–April. A plant of bogs and moors in its native habitats. Plants require a cool moist soil; they also make good pot plants for the alpine house. The recently introduced *B. calcicola* from SW China may also prove to be a valuable small Birch for the rock garden.

BRUCKENTHALIA (Ericaceae)

A genus containing a single species native to the mountains of SE Europe and Asia Minor, where it inhabits woods and subalpine pastures. It can scarcely be described as a showy plant, but it has an elegance which attracts it to the heather enthusiasts, especially as it fills the gap in flowering time between the heaths, *Erica*, and heather, *Calluna*.

Bruckenthalia spiculifolia ○□

The Spike Heath is a dwarf evergreen shrub, closely resembling the heathers, with slender erect stems to 25cm (10in) tall. The narrow leaves are congested along the stems, being borne in whorls of 4 or 5, with rolled-under margins and a white undersurface. The rosy-pink flowers are bell-shaped, each 3mm (⅛in) long and forming a dense erect raceme up to 20mm (⅘in) long. May–July.

CALAMINTHA (Labiatae)

An attractive genus of perennials and subshrubs, rather thyme-like in general appearance, but generally larger. They are not particularly fussy in cultivation, but relish sunny well-drained soils. Most flower during the late summer.

Calamintha grandiflora ○☆

A rather bushy perennial to 40cm (16in) tall with pleasantly aromatic, paired oval or oblong, toothed leaves. The flowers are large for the genus, 25–40mm (1–1⅜in) long, pink, borne in lax leafy heads. Pyrenees and Alps. July–September.

CALANDRINIA (Portulacaceae)

Fleshy plants related to the well-known Lewisias, but differing in having capsules which split open by valves; in *Lewisia* they open like a small lid. Although some species have very showy flowers, few are cultivated by rock gardeners since they are mostly unsuitable for this purpose, being either annual or not frost hardy. There are, however, a large number of attractive dwarf species in temperate South America which are untried in cultivation and the genus probably has great potential in this respect.

Calandrinia caespitosa ○▲
A rare species in cultivation. It has a fleshy taproot and compact tufts of linear, grey-green leaves less than 50mm (2in) high, looking rather Armeria- (thrift) like. The short-stemmed, 5-petalled flowers are carried amid the leaves and are white or cream, about 10mm (⅖in) across. Chile and Argentina. May–July.

CALCEOLARIA (Scrophulariceae)
A large genus of over 200 species, natives of New Zealand and the Americas. Most are either biennial or perennial and many are tender, but the hardier ones require a cool moist position in a humus-rich soil. The flowers are in shades of yellow, orange or red and consist of a 2-lipped corolla, the lower lip inflated and slipper-like, the upper often smaller and ascending. Propagation by seed or by division of the parent plant.

Calceolaria biflora ◐
A perennial with a basal rosette of downy leaves from which arises a 25cm (10in) tall flowering stem bearing yellow flowers 25mm (1in) wide. Chile. June–August. Requires a humus-rich soil.

Calceolaria darwinii ◐☐▲
One of the most enchanting of all alpine plants. A short-lived perennial, with toothed, dark green, basal leaves which support a solitary yellowish-brown flower 20–25mm (⅘–1in) across. Each flower has a striking horizontal white bar across its lower, pouched lip. Chile. June–August. A difficult plant to cultivate as it needs exacting conditions: a sheltered and shady position in a gritty humus-rich soil is best. Plants heartily dislike lime in the soil. Particularly fine as a pan-plant in the alpine house.

Calceolaria tenella ◐
A tight-forming perennial from Chile, bearing 50mm (2in) tall stems with tiny, delicate, yellow flowers only 10mm (⅖in) across. June–August. Will thrive in a cool moist soil.

CALLIANTHEMUM (Ranunculaceae)
Buttercup-like plants of great charm thriving in deep, moist, but well-drained soils. The genus contains a handful of species scattered in the mountains of Europe and Asia. Only one species is in general cultivation.

Callianthemum anemonoides ○
A native of the NE Alps. The bluish-green foliage is reminiscent of an *Aquilegia*, being divided into a number of lobed and cut leaflets. The solitary flowers, 30–35mm (1⅕–1⅖in) across, are white with an orange central ring, each flower with up to 20 narrow petals. The whole plant is rarely more than 10cm (4in) tall. March–April. In the wild this species inhabits open coniferous woodland on calcareous soils, to 2,100m (6,900ft). Shy flowering in cultivation

CALLUNA (Ericaceae)

Although the genus contains only a single species, *C. vulgaris* (Heather or Ling), it is an important plant in gardens with many varied forms and hybrids. The species itself is native to N Europe, Asia Minor and E North Africa where it often forms extensive heaths and moorland. In catalogues it is often, and wrongly, included in the genus *Erica*. Although a selection of cultivars is included here, they represent only a few of the many hundreds available; the only sensible course is to recommend heather-specialist catalogues to anyone wishing to grow them.

Calluna vulgaris ○▯

Plants form a dwarf, much-branched evergreen shrub, rarely more than 60cm (2ft) tall, the stems bearing minute grey-green, scale-like leaves in 4 neat rows, giving the stem a square appearance. The pinkish-lilac flowers are borne during the summer months and form dense spike-like racemes or panicles. The petal-like flower parts are separate from one another, in contrast to those of *Erica* in which they are fused together into a bell- or urn-shape. The flowers are persistent and the plant is much used in dried flower arrangements. A popular plant with beekeepers as the flowers produce abundant nectar for bees. June–October. On large rock gardens a selection of *Calluna* cultivars can add interest for much of the summer and autumn. Like Ericas they need to be clipped over after flowering to keep them compact and bushy. Frequently recommended cultivars are: 'Alba Plena'—prostrate with double white flowers, very free flowering; 'Alportii'—dark green foliage and red-purple flowers, an old, popular and vigorous cultivar; 'Darkness'—compact and dense growth and bright crimson flowers; 'H. E. Beale'—grey-green foliage, double pink flowers, vigorous and good for cutting; 'J. H. Hamilton'—compact growth and large clear pink flowers, a good plant for heavy soils; 'Peter Sparkes'—dark grey-green foliage, double deep pink flowers; 'Robert Chapman'—orange-gold foliage and mauve-pink flowers; 'Ruth Sparkes'—golden foliage and double white flowers; 'Silver Queen'—silvery-green hairy foliage, lavender-pink flowers; 'Sir John Carrington'—yellow foliage and crimson flowers; 'Variegata'—foliage variegated with white.

CALTHA (Ranunculaceae)

The genus contains the familiar and widely grown Marsh Marigold or Kingcup and as the name suggests they are plants for moist boggy soils, looking at their best along the edge of, or growing in, shallow water.

Caltha palustris ○◑

The common Marsh Marigold is an extremely variable plant in the wild. The wide shiny heart-shaped leaves are familiar as are the large glossy golden-yellow flowers like giant buttercups, 30–50mm (1⅕–2in) across. Europe and Asia. March–May. The larger forms are too gross for the average rock garden; however, there is a lower more spreading form, var. *minor*, as well as a very fine double-flowered form, 'Flore-plena', and a white-flowered one, 'Alba'. All these are easy to grow and very floriferous.

CAMPANULA (Campanulaceae)

A genus of almost 300 species confined to the northern hemisphere. The genus contains, besides annual species and coarse herbaceous ones, numerous small

Campanula carpatica

mountain plants very suitable for rock garden cultivation. They range from those with simple needs to those demanding every gardening skill. The flowers are always bell-shaped, but range from narrow tubular bells to broad salver shapes in the different species. Most have blue flowers though some are white or occasionally pink or lilac. They usually require free drainage, but adequate moisture during the summer months. Most can be readily propagated by division of the parent plant or from seed. The coarser species are described first.

Campanula portenschlagiana (syn. **C. muralis**) ○◑☆
A vigourous tufted perennial to 30cm (12in) across with spreading stems. The deep green leaves are coarsely toothed, broad, kidney shaped. The starry bellflowers are erect and pale purple, borne in masses. S Europe. July–September. A very easy plant for the larger rock garden, gravel drives and the base of walls. Seeds around once established.

Campanula poscharskyana ○◑☆
Very like the preceding, but even more vigorous, with long trailing stems. The lavender-blue flowers are borne in profusion in narrow panicles. Dalmatia. July–September. Another rampant and easy species in cultivation. 'Lilacina', has attractive lilac flowers.

Campanula carpatica (including **C. turbinata**) ○☆
One of the commonest species seen in our gardens. Plants form rather coarse bright green, spreading tufts with stems sometimes up to 20cm (8in) tall. The leaves are heart-shaped or oval and toothed. The large flowers form broad, open cup-like bells with shallow lobes, typically purple-blue, but varying in the named cultivars.

49

Carpathian Mountains. July–early September. A fine species though rather too vigorous for small rock gardens, seeding itself around once established. 'Bressingham White'—a large pure white saucer-shaped flower; 'Ditton Blue'—mid-violet-blue flowers; 'White Star'—another good white form. The plant sold under the name *C. turbinata* has exceptionally large deep violet flowers.

Campanula pseudo-raineri ○
Possibly a form of *C. carpatica,* but it may be a hybrid between this species and *C. raineri.*

Campanula × *pulloides* ○☆
A hybrid between *C. carpatica* and *C. pulla*. Plants are tufted, to 15cm (6in) tall, with shorter, wider bellflowers than *C. pulla*. 'G. F. Wilson' is possibly of similar origin—a very floriferous plant.

Campanula garganica ○●
Another easy species. Plants form a rosette of long-stalked leaves which are heart-shaped and coarsely toothed. The wide erect starry bells are borne in numerous sprays up to 16cm (6in) long. The flower colour is a clear blue, often almost white in the centre. July–October. Italy and Cephalonia. A useful and floriferous species looking fine on a dry wall, but often rather invasive on the rock garden, seeding itself about freely. 'Blue Diamond'—a fine free-flowering form.

Campanula fenestrellata ○
A finer and denser plant than *C. garganica* with smaller shiny leaves and deeper blue flowers, forming attractive low mounds. July–August. Yugoslavia.

Campanula arvatica
Like a very small compact version of *C. garganica*, only 5cm (2in) high and smothered with small starry blue flowers. N Spain. July–August.

Campanula waldsteiniana ○
Similar to the previous, but a laxer growth to 10cm (4in) high, forming neat, rounded tufts bearing numerous mid-blue starry flowers. Yugoslavian mountains. August–October. Valuable for its late flowering. This and the previous species thrive in a gritty, well-drained compost in a sunny position—they are fine scree or trough plants.

Campanula elatines ○☆
Like a smaller and more refined version of *C. garganica* with more rounded leaves and a mass of small starry blue flowers on stems up to 8cm (3in). Piedmont. July–August. A useful and easy plant for a pan in the alpine house, but succeeding equally well out of doors.

Campanula cochleariifolia (syn. *C. pusilla*) ○☆
The Fairy's Thimble is one of the most delightful and easily grown species. Plants form spreading mats of bright green leaves, rounded, heart-shaped, somewhat toothed. From these arise numerous delicate stems up to 10cm (4in) tall bearing several perfect little pendant blue bells of great charm, the stem leaves few and narrower than the basal ones. Mountains of C and S Europe, including the Pyrenees, where it inhabits rocky places and screes, generally on limestone to an altitude of 3,400m (11,200ft). An often invasive plant in cultivation which should not be placed too close to more delicate neighbours—perhaps best confined

between large rocks for this reason. 'Alba'—pure white flowers; 'Flore-plena'—see *C. × haylodgensis.*

Campanula pulla ○
Not unlike a rich-purple form of *C. cochleariifolia*, but with leafier stems and rather longer bells, 18–24mm (up to 1in) long. NE Alps. July–August. Free flowering, but often dying out in patches from the centre in older plants—frequent division and replanting will help to prevent this.

Campanula × haylodgensis ○
Very like *C. cochleariifolia*, but rather larger. The usual form found in catalogues, 'Flore-plena' has double flowers.

Campanula scheuchzeri ○☆
Like a taller version of *C. cochleariifolia* but all the leaves narrow lanceolate or linear. Flowers large, blue, 12–18mm (up to ¾in) long. Europe. July–August.

Campanula × hallii ○
A hybrid between *C. cochlearifolia* and *C. portenschlagiana*, intermediate in characters, about 80mm (3in) tall and with white flowers.

Campanula isophylla ○
Most commonly known as a pot plant or as a subject for hanging baskets, this species is hardier than is generally supposed, succeeding in a very well-drained, sunny, sheltered part of the garden; the top of a raised bed sheltered by a large rock being ideal. The stems are rather straggly, but are hidden by the large blue saucer-shaped flowers. N Italy. July–September. 'Alba'—has white flowers. In less mild districts plants are best moved indoors in the autumn when frosts threaten.

Campanula mollis ○
Somewhat like a more compact form of *C. isophylla*, but with stiffer stems and more cupped flowers. C and S Spain and North Africa. July–October.

Campanula rapunculoides ○◗
The Creeping Bellflower, as its name implies, is a spreading species, often invasive, forming a mat of tufted oval or heart-shaped leaves, only the lowermost stalked. The flower spikes are erect, to 50cm (28in) or more, bearing a series of drooping purplish-blue bells, each 20–30mm (⅘–1⅕in) long. Europe. June–August. Nice, but not for the small rock garden—plants spread rapidly by thread-like underground stolons.

Campanula barbata ○☆
The Bearded Bellflower is a familiar species of meadows and open woods in mountainous Europe. Plants are tufted, to 30cm (12in) tall, though often less, with a coarse rosette of pale green, slightly bristly oblong leaves. The erect one-sided racemes carry mid to pale blue or white bellflowers, each flower 20–30mm (⅘–1⅕in) long and containing a beard of silvery hairs. June–August. A charming plant, often short-lived and sometimes biennial, but easily raised from seed. 'Alba'—a good white-flowered form.

Campanula excisa ○▢
A little oddity, but delightful all the same. A tufted creeping perennial, only 60–80mm (2½–3in) tall, like a delicate little harebell, the basal leaves heart-shaped, but the stem leaves very narrow. The narrow, nodding, lilac-blue flowers, 10–16mm

51

($\frac{2}{5}$–$\frac{3}{4}$in) long, have a strange rounded perforation at the junction of each pair of petal-lobes. S and C Switzerland. June–August. A plant of acid rocks and screes in the wild from 1,400 to 2,350m (4,600–7,750ft) altitude. In cultivation a plant for the scree garden, which seems to suit it best and where it can creep about as it pleases.

Campanula zoysii ○▲
Another curious species but one of the gems of the genus. The so-called Crimped Bellflower forms small tufts only 30–50mm (1$\frac{1}{5}$–2in) tall with small rosettes of shiny spoon-shaped leaves. The blue flowers are borne almost horizontally, each a narrow bell 15–20mm ($\frac{3}{5}$–$\frac{4}{5}$in) long; unlike any other Bellflower, the corolla is curiously crimped or puckered at the apex. SE Alps where it inhabits high limestone rock crevices and screes. July–September. Often thought to be difficult, although it will succeed well enough in a well-drained gritty compost. Plants should not be allowed to dry out during the summer months and die down completely at the onset of winter. An ideal plant for a tufa block. Slugs can prove troublesome.

Campanula cenisia ◐▲
A high alpine of great charm forming small tufts scarcely 50mm (2in) tall. Plants form tight rosettes of oval blue-green leaves and send out short leafy runners at intervals. The flowers are open, rather starry upright bells in a shade of greyish-blue, each 10–15mm (up to $\frac{3}{5}$in) across. European Alps. July–September. In the wild, this delightful little species inhabits acid rock crevices, ledges and screes above 2,000m (6,600ft). An awkward plant in cultivation, sometimes thriving, sometimes sulking, but worth every effort, like the preceding species. Hot sunshine can easily ruin a fine plant.

Campanula raineri ○▲
Another low tufted species, with greyish green, oval, toothed leaves. The outsized pale to mid-blue erect bells are 30–40mm (1$\frac{1}{5}$–1$\frac{3}{5}$in) long and are generally solitary on stalks up to 70mm (2$\frac{3}{4}$in) tall. S Alps and Dolomites. August–September. Not very common in cultivation, but highly desirable. It thrives best in a limestone scree.

Campanula morettiana ○▲
Like the previous species, but with more heart-shaped leaves and beautifully formed, smaller but still apparently oversized bells of deep blue. The whole plant is scarcely 40–50mm (1$\frac{1}{2}$–2in) high. S and SE Alps. August–September. Difficult but well worth a try—best in a tufa block or in a pan in the alpine house. 'Alba'—a white-flowered form.

Campanula alpestris (syn. *C. allionii*) ○▲
A tufted species to 90mm (3$\frac{1}{2}$in) tall. Plants bear tufts of narrow-elliptical, silvery-hairy, scarcely toothed, leaves. The large, usually solitary, upright flowers are deep, 30–45mm (1$\frac{1}{4}$–1$\frac{7}{8}$in) long, dark purple, like solitary Canterbury Bells. French Alps, where it inhabits limestone rocks and screes above 1,400m (4,600ft). Not always easy; like some of the other small species with large flowers, this often does well for a time but then sulks or declines; frequent splitting and planting in new places may be the answer.

Campanula tridentata ○◐
An attractive crevice dweller which forms dense tufts of rather narrow oblong, slightly toothed leaves. The flowers, generally a few to each stem, are relatively large, purple-blue with deep lobes. The whole plant is 10–15cm (4–6in) high.

Turkey and the Caucasus. July–September. Generally grown as a pan plant in the alpine house, but it will also make a fine trough plant wedged between suitable rocks. *C. saxifraga* from the same region is very similar and may only be a form of *C. tridentata*.

Campanula oreadum ○◗

Native to the mountains of mainland Greece, this is a fine plant of the *C. tridentata* persuasion, but smaller, with more leathery leaves and narrower bells.

Campanula cashmeriana ○☆

Another charming Bellflower. Plants grow to about 10–15cm (4–6in) tall, but spread sideways by a system of delicate thread-like stems. The grey-green leaves are oval or elliptical, somewhat toothed, but almost stalkless. The small rather narrow blue bells, 10–12mm (½in) long, are borne in airy profusion. W Himalaya. July–September. A short-lived perennial, but well worth having in a collection, being readily grown from seed. Most often seen in the alpine house, but fine on a scree or in a large trough.

Campanula piperi ○

One of the very few American bellflowers in cultivation. Plants form creeping tufts with numerous glossy-green, sharply toothed leaves. The flowers are deep blue and relatively large for the plant which only reaches 30–50mm (1⅕–2in) high. Rocky Mountains. July–August.

Campanula pilosa ○◗

A handsome Japanese species to 8cm (3in) tall, but variable in height and form. The tufts of lanceolate leaves are a bright mid-green and the erect blue bellflowers are borne on relatively short stalks. June–July. Rather rare in cultivation. The form normally obtainable is usually sold under the name 'Superba'.

Campanula punctata (syn. *C. nobilis*) ○◗▲

A large species, to 30cm (12in) tall in flower. Plants form a fairly large rosette of long-stalked, heart-shaped leaves. Several large creamy-white bellflowers are borne on erect or arching stems, each flower 40–50mm (1¾–2in) long. E Siberia and N Japan. July–August. A highly desirable species but rare in cultivation and considered difficult. It requires a very well-drained gritty compost.

Campanula bellidifolia (syn. *C. adamii*) ○

A tufted perennial with small oval, blunt-toothed leaves; stem leaves narrower than basal. The bellflowers are violet. Caucasus. June-July.

Campanula raddeana ○

Another Caucasian species, forming a tuft to about 24cm (10in) tall, the stems practically leafless. The basal leaves are heart-shaped, pointed and toothed. The large nodding bellflowers are violet-blue. July.

Several cultivated species are monocarpic, that is, they form a rosette of leaves for a year to two, then flower, seed and die. It is therefore essential to collect seed and carry out repeated sowings in order to ensure a stock of plants. Three are worth including here.

Campanula formanekiana ○

An exceedingly handsome plant to 35cm (14in) tall in flower. The leaf-rosettes consist of numerous lyre-shaped hoary leaves. The inflorescence forms a pyramid of large white bells of great distinction, each bloom borne on a long stalk. S Yugoslavia and Greece. June–July. Often flowers in the second season.

Campanula rupestris ○◑

A name covering a complex of species centred on the Balkans. The rather flat leaf-rosettes are grey or white-hairy, oval, irregularly toothed and long-stalked. The deep blue or lilac-blue bellflowers arise on stalks radiating from the rosette. Greece. July–August. A well-flowered plant is a beautiful sight. Plants sometimes prove unreliably hardy, so some form of winter protection is advisable. A good pan-plant in the alpine house.

Campanula thyrsoides ○◑

One of the most distinctive bellflowers, forming a rosette of oblong, bristly, rather wavy leaves, in the first season. In the second or third season an erect inflorescence pushes upwards to 30–40cm (12–16in) bearing numerous, densely packed, sulphur yellow bellflowers, the whole forming a dense blunt spike. European Alps and Cevennes. July–September. A plant of moist meadows and stony places in its native haunts between 1,500 and 2,700m (4,950–8,900ft) altitude.

CARDAMINE (Cruciferae)

A widespread genus with some 160 species scattered in many parts of the world, but especially in temperate regions. They are annual or perennial species, mostly of little consequence as garden ornamentals (a few have become invasive and unpopular weeds); however, there are some worthy of inclusion here. The genus, as here defined, includes *Dentaria*, sometimes listed as a genus in its own right. Easy in most leafy, moist, but not waterlogged, soils.

Cardamine pratensis ○◑

The familiar Cuckoo Flower or Lady's Smock, with its clumps of pinnate leaves and racemes of pink or white flowers, is perhaps too commonplace for the smaller rock garden. The double-flowered form 'Flore-pleno' is, however, rather rare in cultivation and worth seeking out. It grows about 25cm (10in) tall. The species is native to Europe and W Asia. June–July. 'Flore-pleno' is a useful plant for a damp semi-shaded site. It is often sterile and produces no seed. However, the leaves often produce new plantlets which will root down into the soil.

Cardamine trifolia (sometimes incorrectly *trifoliata*) ◑☆

Perhaps the best rock garden species forming small dense mats of fairly large deep green trifoliate leaves. In spring a profusion of small white flowers are carried in racemes above the foliage. Alps and Apennines. March–April. Easily increased by division of the parent plant. A native of moist woods and shady habitats to 1,400m (4,600ft).

Cardamine raphanifolia (syn. *C. latifolia*) ◑

A large Cuckoo Flower, to 30cm (12in) with broad deep green leaflets and relatively large bold racemes of rich purple flowers. Mountains of S Europe. May–July. Requires a moist site.

Cardamine pentaphyllos (syn. *C. digitata, Dentaria pentaphylla*) ◑

A rhizomatous perennial to 30–40cm (12–16in) tall with a solitary stem and several palm-like leaves, each with 3–5 toothed leaflets. The relatively large flowers are pink or purple, borne in terminal racemes. Pyrenees and Alps, to 2,200m (7,200ft). May–June.

CARLINA (Compositae)

This genus includes several of the very attractive low, often stemless, thistles, commonly seen in the Alpine meadows, but also one species which is native of the English chalk downs. They are characterized by their sharply pointed, hard prickly leaves and flower-heads which persist for several months after flowering has finished. They also produce copious quantities of seed carried in large disks and these may remain nestled in the old flower-heads until a strong gust of wind removes them from the plant. The outer floral bracts are needle-like and shiny, opening widely in dry sunny weather. They are plants for well-drained rather poor soils and sunny positions. Propagation is simplest from seed.

Carlina acaulis ○☆
The Stemless Carlina Thistle has been cultivated in Britain since the seventeenth century. It is most attractive, bearing rosettes of large acanthus-like leaves up to 30cm (12in) long. The flowers are creamy-white, 5–10cm (2–4in), and the total height of the plant rarely exceeds 50–80mm (2–3in). Mountains of C and S Europe. Although named the 'stemless thistle', plants are rarely truly stemless in cultivation. The flower-heads are ideal as dried decoration for the winter. Two further species, *C. acanthifolia* and *C. vulgaris*, are cultivated, but are too gross for the average rock garden.

CARMICHAELIA (Leguminosae)

A genus of small shrubs named after the Scottish botanist Captain Dugald Carmichael. The genus contains about 40 species from New Zealand, with one on Lord Howe Island; most are little known in cultivation. Plants are usually leafless or become so; when present the leaves have 1, 3 or 5 leaflets. The small, pea-like flowers are aggregated into racemes. The sole species included here requires a light well-drained soil, a sheltered site and full sunshine, and dislikes lime.

Carmichaelia enysii ○▢
A little-known dwarf, woody shrublet, 5–10cm (2–4in) in height, with a spread of 25cm (10in). Young stems green and rather flattened and grass-like, generally leafless as the leaves are shed very early. The flowers, up to 4mm (⅛in) long, are creamish white, the standard petal blotched violet-purple, borne in clusters of 1–3. Fruit a rounded, 1–(2)-seeded pod. New Zealand. November–January.

CASSIOPE (Ericaceae)

A charming small genus of hardy low-growing evergreen subshrubs native to N Europe, E Asia and NW North America. The stems resemble whipcord due to the arrangement of the small, alternate or paired, scale-like leaves. The nodding, generally solitary, bell-shaped flowers are borne on slender stalks, each bell with 5 short teeth. As the fruits develop the stalks turn to assume an erect posture. Cassiopes are not easy plants to grow in warmer regions, preferring the cooler moisture regime of more northerly latitudes. The following species are those most likely to be found in nurserymen's catalogues.

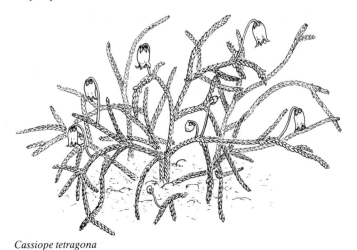

Cassiope tetragona

Cassiope fastigiata ◑☐

A Himalayan species forming a dwarf subshrub with erect stems up to 30cm (12in) tall. The closely-set scale-like leaves are set in 4 ranks, giving the stems a characteristic 4-angled appearance. Flowers relatively large, 6–8mm ($\frac{1}{4}$–$\frac{1}{3}$in) long, white, solitary on thread-like stalks. April–May.

Cassiope hypnoides (syn. *Harrimanella hypnoides*) ◑☐

The Matted Cassiope is a tough little Arctic species forming prostrate mats, with alternate overlapping scale-leaves. The white flowers, 4–5mm ($\frac{1}{5}$in) long, are rather rounded and bell-shaped, nodding on arched stalks and contrasting with the crimson sepals. July–August. A delightful species, but a fickle plant in cultivation, perhaps best avoided by all but the most expert and dedicated of growers.

Cassiope lycopodioides ◑☐☆

Another prostrate, mat-forming species, rarely reaching 70mm (2$\frac{3}{4}$in) tall. The slender, thread-like branches are furnished with small glossy-green, scale-like, overlapping leaves. The small flowers, 4–5mm ($\frac{1}{5}$in) long, are white with contrasting red sepals and borne on red stalks. A native of NE Asia, including Japan, and NW North America. One of the easiest species to cultivate and much to be recommended.

Cassiope mertensiana ◑☐

Another species from North America, occurring in the western mountains from Alaska to California. Plants are 15–30cm (6–12in) tall with erect or spreading stems. The leaves are thick and characteristically keeled beneath; the flowers cup-shaped, white or tinged with pink. April–May.

Cassiope tetragona ◑☐☆

The Common Cassiope with a circumpolar distribution in the northern hemisphere. It is the tallest species in cultivation; an erect shrub 30–45cm (12–18in) in height with tiny deep green, opposite leaves forming 4 distinct ranks. The creamy-white flowers, occasionally tinged with pink, are open bells, 6–8mm ($\frac{1}{4}$–$\frac{1}{3}$in) long, clustered towards the stem tips. April–May.

There are several hybrids and cultivars of *Cassiope* readily available from nurserymen. They are admittedly rather alike, differing mainly in height and density of growth. 'Badenoch' (probably *C. fastigiata* × *C. lycopodioides*)—slender loose growth to 10cm (4in) and white flowers; 'Bearsden'—a vigorous, free-flowering form to 20cm (8in); 'Edinburgh'—a dense erect bushy plant to 25cm (10in) with congested white-edged leaves and white flowers contrasting with the red-bordered sepals: the finest and perhaps the easiest Cassiope in cultivation which arose as a chance seedling at Edinburgh Botanic Garden; 'Muirhead' (*C. lycopodioides* × *C. wardii*)—semi-erect to 15cm (6in) with pale green leaves and white flowers borne on delicate pink stalks: an easy hybrid raised by R. B. Cooke of Northumberland.

CELMISIA (Compositae)

A large daisy genus of 65 species from Australia, Tasmania and New Zealand, few of which are commonly cultivated. Most are perennial herbs with a short thick rhizome and a rosette of closely overlapping leaves which narrow to a sheathing base and are covered beneath with silvery, woolly hairs. The solitary, stalked flower-heads consist of white ray florets and a yellow disk of tubular florets. Most species have proved to be difficult to cultivate and have a tendency to either rot off from the base or to suffer from winter frosts. They are best grown in a rich, well-drained soil in a warm position that is well sheltered.

Celmisia bellidioides ◑☆
One of the easiest and therefore most commonly grown. Plants form an attractive prostrate mat of dark green leaves, slightly woody at the base. Leaves glossy green above, but paler beneath and with a prominent midrib. The white daisy flowers arise on 50mm (2in) tall stalks and are produced in abundance. Native of New Zealand where it favours subalpine, wet, gravelly places by streams. May–July. A plant for a moist position.

Celmisia 'Inshriach Hybrids' ○
A group of attractive plants which were raised at Inshriach Nurseries near Aviemore in Scotland. All have rosettes of large leaves which vary in colour from being bronze to silver-green. The flowers are borne in large, white, daisy heads carried on 45cm (18in) stalks. June–July.

Other species worth trying are *C. coriacea* with rosettes of stiff silvery leaves; *C. glandulosa*, a prostrate sticky-leaved species ideal in scree conditions; *C. sessiliflora* with stiff silvery leaves and almost stalkless flower-heads.

CENTAUREA (Compositae)

This large genus contains over 600 species of hardy annual, biennial and perennial herbaceous plants, including the cornflowers and knapweeds, many of which are suitable candidates for the rock garden. However, few are widely available in cultivation and the best known species are those grown as herbaceous border plants. Centaureas are sometimes called 'hardheads', a reference to the solid globular base of the inflorescence. The leaves in most species are alternately arranged along the stem as well as forming basal rosettes. In some species they are hard, leathery and spine-tipped, whilst in others they are soft or covered in fine hairs; they may be entire or coarsely divided. The flowers are tubular and arise from a receptacle surrounded by variously ornamented bracts; they vary in colour from white, yellow, blue, pink and purple to shades of red and orange. All require a position in full sun and most prefer a well-drained soil.

Centaurea simplicicaulis ○
This attractive perennial produces a much-branched rootstock, which forms tufts of pale greyish-green, finely divided leaves. Many of these tufted shoots are sterile, but none the less make an attractive display of foliage. Some shoots do produce slender flower-stems about 15cm (6in) tall, topped with solitary heads of pale lilac-pink flowers in compact heads about 20mm ($\frac{3}{8}$in) across. May–July.

Centaurea montana ○◗
The Mountain Cornflower is perhaps the best-known species, often grown in the herbaceous border, but equally suitable for the larger rock garden. The splendid flower-heads may reach 80mm (3in) across and are usually found in rich shades of blue and purple; these are borne on stems 20–30cm (8–12in) tall. C and S Europe. May–June. The cultivars 'Alba', 'Rosea' and 'Violetta' have white, pink and deep bluish-purple flowers respectively. A vigorous spreading plant that needs to be sited with care.

Centaurea cana ○◗
Although now thought to be just a subspecies of the above, this plant is often found under its old name. It is a native of the Balkan peninsula, where it occurs in dry rocky situations and is characterized by the densely hairy, greyish-white leaves and flower-stems varying from 3–20cm (1¼–8in) in height. The flowers are a little paler than *C. montana*. May–June. 'Rosea'—a form with pink flowers.

Centaurea triumfetii ○☆
A small plant related to the *C. montana* complex, with greyish-white leaves that are covered in woolly hairs. The outer florets are a rich deep blue and the inner, lilac-purple. The stems rarely exceed 20cm (8in) and are often much shorter. Like the above-mentioned species, this one also comes from S Europe, and is especially common in the S Alps. June–July.

CENTAURIUM (Gentianaceae)
The centaurys are a genus of 40–50 species worldwide in distribution, except for the Tropics and South Africa. They form basal rosettes of leaves with leafy stems bearing a terminal inflorescence in pink, yellow, or sometimes white. The flowers, like small gentians, have a slender tube and 5 spreading petal-lobes.

Centaurium scilloides (syn. Erythraea diffusa) ○
A pretty mat-forming species, resembling a small pink *Gentiana verna*. Prostrate stems bear opposite roundish leaves in a cluster, each to 10mm ($\frac{3}{8}$in) long. The stems rise 60–80mm ($2\frac{2}{5}$–3in) tall and bear a solitary terminal flower or a few flowers in a cluster. The rich pink corolla has a narrow tube and a flat limb, 15–18mm ($\frac{3}{5}$–$\frac{3}{4}$in) across, with protruding stamens. Atlantic coastal Europe and the Azores. June–July. It is not usually long-lived in cultivation, but is very floriferous and easily propagated from seed. Does well in light soil in full sun.

CERASTIUM (Caryophyllaceae)
Some of the Mouse-ear Chickweeds are to be avoided by the gardener, being either weedy or rather insignificant in flower, but a few of the species are well

worth growing. There are approximately 60 species distributed almost worldwide.

Cerastiums have white flowers, solitary or in loose clusters, and these have 5 petals, notched or bilobed at the apex. There are 5 or 10 stamens and usually 5 (rarely 3, 4 or 6) styles. When the capsule splits open it normally has 10 teeth at the apex.

Cerastium alpinum ○

The Alpine Mouse-ear is a compact woolly-leaved, low growing plant, forming dense mats or clumps to 5–10cm (2–4in) when in flower. The oval leaves are broadest above the middle, 10mm (⅖in) long. The 1–5 shiny white flowers are carried on short stems and are 15–20mm (⅗–⅘in) across. N Europe and on mountains of C and S Europe. May–June. Subsp. *alpinum* is greyish-green with long soft hairs, while subsp. *lanatum* has all its parts covered with a felt of whitish-grey hairs.

Cerastium tomentosum ○

Snow-in-Summer is a very rampant plant, suitable only for very large areas or on rock walls. It makes loose mats of whitish-hairy, linear-lanceolate, leaves 10–30mm (⅖–1⅕in) long which have slightly rolled margins. The loose infloresences may reach 45cm (18in) in height, but are often rather sprawling, and carry 3–15 white flowers, each 10–20mm (⅖–⅘in) in diameter. Italy (incl. Sicily), but widely cultivated and often seen as a garden escape. May–July.

Cerastium biebersteinii ○

Very like *C. tomentosum* but with longer leaves, 20–50mm (¾–2in) in length. Endemic to Crimea, but often cultivated.

CHAENORRHINUM (Scrophulariaceae)

A genus very closely allied to *Linaria* and often included under that name. There are about 20 species found throughout Europe where they grow amongst mountain rocks and stony slopes. Their flowers are typical of the toadflaxes, having a 2-lipped corolla, differing from *Linaria* in their wide-open mouth. The lower lip is 3-lobed with a long spur protruding from the back.

Chaenorrhinum origanifolium (syn. *Linaria origanifolia*) ○☆

A leafy perennial up to 20cm (8in) with racemes of rich purple flowers that have a paler throat. The green lanceolate leaves are opposite below, but alternate above. Pyrenees. July–August. A pretty little alpine worth cultivating; it requires a well-drained soil in a sunny position. In the wild it inhabits stony places and screes to 1,500m (4,950ft).

Chaenorrhinum glareosum ○

A beautiful Spanish endemic with perennial prostrate stems ascending to 25cm (10in). These carry racemes of large violet and yellow flowers. June to August. Requires a very well-drained stony soil in a sun-drenched part of the rock garden. June–August.

CHAMAECYTISUS (Leguminosae)

A genus of generally thornless shrubs, similar to the brooms, *Cytisus*, with yellow, white, pinkish or purple flowers. Like *Cytisus*, the species require light well-drained soils and a sunny aspect. Propagation by cuttings or seed.

Chamaecytisus purpureus (syn. *Cytisus purpureus*) ○
An almost totally hairless procumbent or erect subshrub to about 30cm (12in) in height. Leaves trifoliate, long-stalked. Flowers 15–25mm ($\frac{2}{5}$–1in) long, solitary or in clusters of 2–3, forming leafy racemes, pinkish-lilac to purplish, the standard-petal with a darker central blotch. S and SE Alps, where it occurs in scrubby and rocky places. May–June. The wild form is generally too lax and spreading for all but a large rock garden. However, the following cultivars are worth consideration. 'Albus'—a white-flowered form; 'Atropurpureus'—darker purple flowers; 'Redwings'—purple flowers with red wing petals.

Chamaecytisus hirsutus (syn. *Cytisus hirsutus*) ○□☆
An erect or rarely procumbent subshrub to 1m (3ft) in height, but usually smaller, the branchlets with spreading hairs. Leaves trifoliate, the leaflets hairy, especially on the lower face. Flowers in clusters of 1–4, each 20–25mm ($\frac{4}{5}$–1in) long, yellow or pinkish-yellow. Alps. April–June. Prefers an acid soil unlike *C. purpureus* which thrives best on a calcareous soil. The prostrate form more generally grown in cultivation is distinguished as var. *demissus,* but often found in catalogues as *Cytisus hirsutus* or *C. demissus.*

CHAMAEDAPHNE (Ericaceae)

This genus is closely related to *Gaultheria*, but is distinguished by its capsular rather than fleshy fruits. It has been included in both *Cassandra* and *Andromeda* in the past and is sometimes offered in catalogues under those names, but the current opinion is that it is sufficiently distinct to form its own genus with a single species.

Chamaedaphne calyculata (syn. *Andromeda calyculata, Cassandra calyculata*) ○◖□
The Leatherleaf makes an erect, evergreen shrub 60–90cm (2–3ft) in height, occasionally more, with slender wiry stems and gaunt habit. The scaly, narrowly oblong leaves are tough, 10–40mm ($\frac{2}{5}$–1$\frac{1}{2}$in) long. The 5–20 urn-shaped flowers are produced in leafy, arching racemes, the corollas hanging beneath the stems like small white lanterns. March–April. A plant for a cool peaty soil. 'Nana'—a similar but smaller plant up to 30cm (12in) in height, sometimes listed in catalogues.

CHAMAEPERICLYMENUM (Cornaceae)

The only herbaceous genus of the dogwood family contains two species which occur on the mountains of North America, Europe and Asia. Both are rhizomatous herbs with annual flowering stems. They are deciduous and have opposite, sessile leaves. The inconspicuous clusters of flowers are surrounded by 4 conspicuous bracts which look remarkably like petals. The berry-like red fruits are produced in dense clusters. Propagation by seed (when available) or by division of the parent plant.

Chamaepericlymenum canadense ◖□☆
The Creeping Dogwood of North America and Asia runs underground to form dense carpets up to 20cm (8in) in height. The oval leaves are dark green and borne in clustered whorls of 4–6, each leaf up to 70mm (3in) long; in autumn they turn a bronzy colour. The tiny greenish purple or violet flowers are surrounded by 4 white bracts, the whole head 30–40mm (1$\frac{1}{5}$–1$\frac{3}{5}$in) across. May–June. The scarlet fruits are only occasionally borne in cultivation. This species can become invasive. It prefers a lime-free soil and cool conditions. Excellent as ground cover for the peat garden or shady corners of a large rock garden.

Chamaepericlymenum canadense

Chamaepericlymenum suecicum

This is the Dwarf Cornel which is a rare native of N England and Scotland, but is widespread in Europe, N Asia and North America. It differs from *C. canadense* in that its leaves are not whorled, and its flowers and bracts are smaller. The flowers are violet. June–July. This species is said to be difficult to establish, but spreads nicely once it has settled in. As with *C. canadense,* two distinct clones are generally required in order to get a regular and reliable set of fruit—one of the chief attractions of the genus.

CHEIRANTHUS (Cruciferae)

A small genus best known for the Wallflower, *Cheiranthus cheiri*. Most modern authorities would place the genus in the very similar genus *Erysimum*, and under this latter genus will be found the species.

CHIASTOPHYLLUM (Crassulaceae)

The genus contains a single species from the Caucasus, hardy enough in gardens. Plants thrive in sun or partial shade in a well-drained sheltered site. They can be readily propagated by cuttings or division of the parent plant.

Chiastophyllum oppositifolium (syn. *Cotyledon oppositifolia, C. simplicifolia*) ○◑☆

A tufted succulent plant with thick stems and rounded, toothed, succulent leaves, mostly in a basal rosette. The small, bright yellow, starry flowers are borne in characteristic slender dangling racemes, catkin-like. The whole plant seldom exceeds 14cm (5½in) tall. June–August.

CLAYTONIA (Portulacaceae)

A relative of *Lewisia*, but on the whole the species have less showy flowers. The main botanical difference is that in *Lewisia* the capsules open by splitting off horizontally at the base (circumscissile) while in *Claytonia* they open by longitudinal valves. They are fleshy plants, little-cultivated by rock gardeners since most of the species are either unattractive or not hardy. There are about 10 species native to North America, one of which is cultivated to a small extent by specialists.

Claytonia megarhiza ○
The thick, fleshy, branched rootstocks give rise to many oval or spoon-shaped basal leaves, arranged in a flattish rosette. Several flower stems are produced, shorter than or equalling the leaves and each carries a raceme of up to 10 white to pinkish-rose, 5-petalled flowers, each 10-20mm ($\frac{2}{5}$-$\frac{4}{5}$in) across. Widespread in W USA. May–July. Var. *nivalis* (syn. *C. nivalis*) is the most attractive variant with the largest flowers, which are usually a rich pink colour.

CLEMATIS (Ranunculaceae)

A large genus mostly of vigorous climbers scattered in many parts of the world, more especially in temperate regions. Most are far too gross for the rock garden but several are worthy of attention.

Clematis alpina (syn. *Atragene alpina*) ◑☆
The most popular species for the rock garden, and an ideal plant for trailing over shrubs and small trees or rocks. Plants have climbing stems with opposite, ternately-divided leaves. The elegant drooping flowers are violet or purplish, 25–40mm (1–1½in) long, with a cluster of prominent whitish 'stamens'. These are followed by typical fluffy seed heads common to many species of *Clematis*. Mountains of Europe and W Asia. June–July. A very variable species—the more vigorous forms can be trimmed back after flowering if they become too invasive. Like most *Clematis*, plants prefer to have their roots in a cool, shaded position. A number of named cultivars are sold such as 'Markham Pink' and 'Francis Rivis', though the best of the wild forms with rich blue-purple flowers are difficult to better. The closely related *C. sibirica* has cream-coloured flowers.

Clematis hirsutissima ○
An herbaceous perennial to 40cm (16in), often less, very like a species of *Pulsatilla*, but with opposite pinnate leaves. The solitary drooping, dusky mauve-purple flowers are bell-shaped. North America. June–July. Not common in cultivation and rather temperamental, though succeeding well in some gardens.

Clematis marmoraria ○
This delightful little species, perhaps the smallest in the genus, was only recently discovered in the S Alps of New Zealand. Plants form small cushions of leathery, neatly-cut foliage. The small creamy-white flowers, 10–15mm ($\frac{2}{5}$-$\frac{3}{5}$in) across, rise on short stems. May–July. Still rather rare in cultivation, but becoming more widely available and readily raised from seed. Plants are either male or female, so several are required to ensure seed set. In the wild *C. marmoraria* is a plant of screes; it is a fine subject for a pan or trough. Perhaps hardy in the open with the protection of a sheet of glass during the winter.

CODONOPSIS (Campanulaceae)

A charming genus native to central Asia, the Himalaya and W China. Many have rather straggling stems which often twine around convenient supports. The flowers are narrow or broad bells; in the less exciting species they are green, but in the best they are various shades of blue or purple, often beautifully marked inside. All the species have a rather foxy odour emanating from both the flowers and the leaves. The cultivated species die down to a tuberous stock each season and succeed best in a moist but freely-drained, gritty compost. New plants are readily raised from seed,

Clematis alpina

except for *C. meleagris* which is now very rare in cultivation. The twining species are best when allowed to clamber amongst low bushes as they do in the wild. Young shoots should be protected from slugs. The flowers of most species are attractive to wasps.

Codonopsis clematidea ○
This is the commonest species in cultivation and has rather straggling, though not twining, stems, to 30cm (12in), sometimes more. The pale green, heart-shaped leaves are borne in pairs along the stems and the large pendent bellflowers, 15–25mm ($\frac{3}{5}$–1in) long, are pale blue, beautifully marked on the inside and borne at the stem-tips. Central Asia and W Himalaya. July–August. Often grown at the front of the herbaceous border, but equally deserving of a place in the larger rock garden where it will seed itself around once established.

Codonopsis ovata ○☆

Less commonly seen in cultivation than the previous species, but more beautiful. The plants have a slender habit, smaller leaves and the deeper blue flowers have a more flared bell-shape, wonderfully marked with orange within. Plants grow to about 20cm (8in) tall. W Himalaya. July–August. Plants under this name should be selected with care as they often turn out to be *C. clematidea*.

Codonopsis meleagris ○▲

Perhaps the finest jewel in the genus, but sadly rare in cultivation. The species comes from the mountains of Yunnan in SW China. Plants grow 18–30cm (7–12in) tall. The broad, pendant bellflowers are a faint blue or greenish, heavily veined with chocolate which forms a distinctive network over the corolla. Within, the flowers are sometimes spotted with yellow. August. A plant for the connoisseur, but well worth a try if the genuine species can be obtained—all too often seed grown under this name turns out to be one of several green-flowered species which really have little value in the rock garden.

Codonopsis vincaeflora ◑☆

A charming species with delicate thread-like stems and small oval leaves. The stems eventually coil around adjacent supports and terminate in a mid-blue salver-shaped flower, often about 20mm ($\frac{4}{5}$in) across. Plants rarely clamber more than 40cm (16in) and are often content to sprawl close to the ground. Asia. July–September. Best grown in a peat border where it relishes the cool moisture; elsewhere it tends to desiccate too readily in hot weather.

Codonopsis convolvulacea ◑☆

A more rampant species twining like a bindweed and often reaching more than 1.5m (5ft). The heart-shaped leaves diminish in size up the stem; the large salver-shaped flowers may reach 40mm ($1\frac{1}{2}$in) in diameter with broad triangular lobes, the whole a good clear blue, sometimes with a hint of violet. Himalaya and SW China, where it inhabits woodland fringes or scrub. August–early October. A very fine plant for growing amongst rock garden shrubs though just as much at home in the peat border. However, this species is more often seen as a pot plant in the alpine house, though it does not require such confined conditions. 'Alba' is a particularly good white-flowered form sometimes obtainable.

Codonopsis forrestii ◑

Very like *C. convolvulacea*, and is sometimes included in that species as a variety, but the flowers have a dark centre. Very rare in cultivation. SW China.

CONVOLVULUS (Convolvulaceae)

The bindweeds are of course mostly despised in the garden because of their invasive habits and there is no worse weed in the rock garden than the common Bindweed, *C. arvensis*, which spreads far and wide underground. However, *Convolvulus* is a large genus of some 250 species, distributed worldwide, and some of them are very attractive and well-behaved in the garden, even difficult to grow in certain cases.

They vary in their habit from low-growing herbs to shrubs and even small trees, quite a high percentage being climbers or trailers. They have alternate leaves which are often heart-shaped at the base, sometimes deeply lobed into finger-like segments; the stems and leaves frequently have rather silky hairs. The flowers have

5 petals, all united to make a regular rounded funnel-shaped flower, usually quite large and showy.

Convolvulus boissieri (syn. ***C. nitidus***) ○
A cushion or mat-forming species only 50–80mm (2–3in) in height in flower, with small, oval, silky-silvery leaves carried on woody stems which may be completely hidden by the foliage. Short stems carry 1–4 large pale pink flowers 20–25mm ($\frac{4}{5}$–1in) across, held just above the leaves. S Spain and Balkans. May–June.

Convolvulus lineatus ○
This attractive species makes tufts of erect, pointed, lanceolate leaves, 4–10cm ($1\frac{3}{5}$–4in) long and covered in silky hairs. The flower stems are 10–15cm (4–6in) tall, bearing solitary or small clusters of pale pinkish-purple flowers in the leaf axils and at the apex of the stem; each flower is about 25–30mm (1–$1\frac{1}{5}$in) across. S Europe. May–July.

Convolvulus cneorum ○☆
A shrubby species, rather tender, but well worth trying in a sheltered sunny spot on a large rock garden. It makes a compact leafy bush to about 50cm (20in) in height with attractive silvery-hairy lanceolate leaves, the stems bearing dense terminal clusters of pink woolly buds opening to white, pink-flushed flowers about 35–40mm ($1\frac{2}{5}$–$1\frac{1}{2}$in) across. W and C Mediterranean region. June–September. A super little shrub admired as much for its foliage as for its flowers. Cuttings should be over-wintered in a frost-free place in case the parent plant succumbs to winter frosts.

Convolvulus althaeoides ○☆
A trailing, rather rampant, but very attractive species for a sunny position on the larger rock garden. The long stems have two kinds of silver-grey leaves, the lower ones heart-shaped and toothed, the upper ones deeply cut into narrow finger-like lobes. It has long-stalked, large pink flowers 4–5cm ($1\frac{1}{2}$–2in) in diameter. S Europe and Turkey. June–July.

Subsp. tenuissimus is a more slender plant, densely silvery-hairy with very narrow lobes to the leaves.

Convolvulus sabatius (syn. ***C. mauritanicus***) ○
A trailing, but fairly compact plant with prostrate stems carrying many small broadly oval to almost rounded, softly hairy, leaves. The beautiful bright blue flowers are borne in abundance at the leaf-axils, each 20–25mm ($\frac{4}{5}$–1in) across. NW Italy, Sicily and N Africa. June–October. A beautiful species only fully hardy in the mildest districts. Sometimes seen in hanging baskets or as a pot plant.

Convolvulus cantabricus ○
This has trailing or ascending stems and may reach 15–25cm (6–10in) in height, bearing long narrow-linear or narrow-oblong, pointed, greyish-hairy leaves. The large pink or reddish flowers, 25–35mm (1–$1\frac{2}{5}$in) across, are borne in clusters of 2–3 at the apex of the stems and at the upper leaf axils. S and SC Europe. June–August.

Convolvulus incanus ○
A trailing species, almost prostrate, but spreading to 30cm (12in) or more across. The silvery-grey leaves are lanceolate or arrow-shaped, often wavy-margined and distinctly lobed near the base. Long-stalked pink or white flowers are produced in the leaf axils, usually solitary and about 20–25mm ($\frac{4}{5}$–1in) across. North America. April–September.

COPTIS (Ranunculaceae)

A genus of small, rather fragile woodland plants from North America and Japan with delicately cut leaves and small buttercup- or anemone-like flowers. The species thrive in moist soils in semi-shaded places in the garden.

Coptis trifolia ◑

A widespread species in N Asia and North America with 3-parted leaves and small white flowers. The smallest of those grown, rarely reaching 10cm (4in) tall. April.

Coptis asplenifolia ◑

More finely divided foliage than the previous species and white flowers. To 20cm (8in) tall. North America and Japan. April–May.

Coptis quinquefolia ◑☆

As the name implies, this charming species has 5-lobed leaves, the plant up to 15cm (6in) tall. The shiny white flowers are borne on short stalks. Japan. April.

Coptis anemonifolia ◑

Not unlike the previous but with smaller flowers and more cut foliage. North America. March–April.

CORONILLA (Leguminosae)

A genus of annual or perennial herbs or subshrubs, taking its name from the Latin word for little crown in allusion to the arrangement of the flowers in a crown-like head; they are commonly referred to as the Crown Vetches. The genus contains about 20 species in Mediterranean Europe, the Canary Islands, NE Africa and W Asia. The leaves are usually pinnate, and the flowers pea-like. The 2 alpine species are easy to cultivate, readily propagated from seed, and both relish a well-drained soil and sunny aspect.

Coronilla minima ○☆

A woody-based procumbent herb 5–10cm (2–4in) tall. The foliage is flat, soft, grey-green and hairless. Flowers golden-yellow, sweetly scented, rarely over 10mm (⅜in) long, clustered in small umbels. Fruit oblong, breaking up into 1-seeded segments. SW Europe. May–July. A charming plant which thrives best in rather dry sandy soils.

Coronilla varia ○

A trailing or straggling diffuse perennial herb, 25–30cm (10–12in) tall. The pinnate leaves are stalkless. The flowers are in dense, 10–20-flowered clusters held clear of the foliage, varying in colour from pinkish-white through mauvish-white to purple. Like the previous species the fruit pod breaks up into 1-seeded pieces. June–October. Rather too gross for the smaller rock garden, but none the less an attractive and floriferous species.

CORTUSA (Primulaceae)

A genus of some 10 species distributed from C Europe to Japan. They are hairy woodland plants with rounded leaves and tall scapes with umbels of yellow or red drooping flowers. Most are plants for cool moist shaded spots in the garden.

Cortusa matthiolia ◑☆
This lovely woodland species has softly hairy, long-stalked leaves rounded in outline, palmately 7–9-lobed, and coarsely toothed. The drooping flowers are held in an umbel well above the leaves, on stalks 15–35cm (6–14in) high. The funnel- to bell-shaped corolla is of a rich reddish-purple, 9–11mm (*c* $\frac{2}{5}$in) across and 5-lobed. Europe and temperate Asia. April–June. Commonly called Alpine Bells, this species is well worth growing. It does best in a moist rich loam in half shade and can be propagated by division of the parent plant. There is a var. *pekinensis* which scarcely differs from the type, as well as a white-flowered form.

CORYDALIS (Papaveraceae)

A group of delightful perennials with neat ferny foliage and clusters or racemes of narrow spurred flowers. *Corydalis* is related to the fumitories, *Fumariia*, which are annual species with rounded rather than linear fruit-capsules. From the alpine gardener's point of view, *Corydalis* can be divided into two main groups, those with fibrous and those with a tuberous rootstock. *Corydalis* is distributed throughout the temperate regions of the northern hemisphere.

Tuberous-rooted species

Plants die down in early summer—except *C. cashmeriana*.

Corydalis bulbosa ○◑☆
The Bulbous Corydalis has a rough hollow tuber and an erect stem to 15cm (6in), without a scale below the lowest leaf. The grey-green leaves are neatly lobed and mature at the same time as the flowers. The flowers themselves are dull purple in the common form but white in subsp. *cava*. Each flower is 18–30mm ($\frac{3}{4}$–1$\frac{1}{5}$in) long with a down-curved spur and is subtended by a scale-like, unlobed bract. Mountains of C and S Europe. February–March.

Corydalis solida ◑☆
Superficially very similar to the preceding, but distinguished readily by its solid tuber, by the presence of a scale below the lowest leaf and also by the lobed bract below each flower. Mountains of Europe and W Asia. February–April. Like *C. bulbosa* an attractive plant for semi-shaded places on the rock gardens and beneath deciduous trees and shrubs.

Corydalis rutifolia ○
A W Asian species more usually seen in alpine houses or frames though it will succeed outdoors given a sheltered niche. Plants are 15cm (6in) tall, often more, with rather fleshy rue-like foliage with rounded lobes. The flowers vary in colour, but in the best forms are a good rose-pink, 18–30mm ($\frac{3}{4}$–1$\frac{1}{5}$in) long. April–May.

Corydalis cashmeriana ◑◫
One of the most beautiful of all alpine plants, but, like many a beauty, fickle to the extreme. The species demands a cool, moist, lime-free soil and does particularly well in wet northerly latitudes, but even there it will grow for some, fail for others. The ferny blue-green foliage is a perfect foil to the stunning bright blue flowers, 12–20mm ($\frac{1}{2}$–$\frac{4}{5}$in) long, held in clusters on delicate stalks above the foliage. The whole plant is rarely more than 12cm (5in) tall. W and C Himalaya. April–June, occasionally later. Although not an easy plant everyone will want to give it a try.

Corydalis lutea

Fibrous-rooted species

Corydalis lutea ◑☆

The Yellow Corydalis is a familiar plant, relishing corners of the garden, half-shielded from the sun, particularly in the cracks of paving and walls, where it seeds around prolifically. Plants form a mound of rather fragile green foliage, grey beneath, to about 15–18cm (6–7in) tall. The flower racemes are golden-yellow, each flower 12–20mm ($\frac{1}{2}$–$\frac{4}{5}$in) long and produced in profusion. C and E Alps. One of the easiest alpines to grow and a rewarding one with a very prolonged flowering season, March–November.

Corydalis cheilanthifolia ○◑

Occasionally mistaken for the previous, but quite distinct on close examination. The leaves form a spreading grey-green rosette from the centre of which rise a number of bright yellow racemes borne on long stalks. China. May–July. Less easy than *C. lutea* and requiring a moister and sunnier position.

Corydalis wilsonii ○◑☆

The finest in this group and a native of W China. The grey- or bluish-green foliage is rather fleshy and more substantial than the other species, forming a lax spreading rosette. The spike-like racemes of deep yellow flowers ascend from the centre of the leaf-rosettes, to 12cm (5in), sometimes more. May–July, occasionally later. A good plant for a sheltered crevice, scree or trough, though greatly disliking winter wet. A sheet of glass placed above the plant will help to see it safely through the winter.

Corydalis glauca ○◑

An annual North American species with a quiet charm, but scarcely as striking as the other species mentioned. A rather fragile plant with slender erect stems to 18cm (7in) tall. The small flowers are pink and white. June–July.

68

COTULA (Compositae)

A genus of 75 species of carpet-forming annuals and perennials, native to South Africa, Australasia and America, though the vast majority of cultivated species come from New Zealand. The leaves are arranged alternately along the creeping stems and can be entire or finely divided. The flower-heads are borne on long stems, either at the ends of branches or else in the axils of the leaves. The flower-heads vary betweeen 3–10mm (⅛–⅖in) in diameter and contain only disc florets. This group of plants is useful for ground covering and is sometimes used for planting between paving stones, as the plants are well adapted to trampling. Although generally too vigorous for the smaller rock garden, they none the less have a quiet charm of their own and are worth considering where space allows.

Cotula striata ○◗☆

The creeping stems of this species are noticeably grooved, about 20cm (8in) in length. The leaves are narrowly oblong and occur in basal clusters and along the branches, being covered in glandular hairs. The most striking feature of this species is the dense cluster of reddish-black florets within the flower-heads. May–July.

Cotula potentillina ○◗

Another species with creeping stems, which root at the nodes, where the leaves are clustered together. The frilled *Potentilla*-like leaves are pinnately-divided and broadly egg-shaped in outline. The purplish flower-heads are 8–10mm (⅖in) across. June–July.

Cotula pyrethrifolia ○◗

This species is characterized by its highly aromatic foliage and has creeping stems which root at the nodes and become erect at the tips. Old plants may form circular patches up to 1m (3ft) across. Like the preceding species this also has divided leaves. The purplish flower-heads are larger though, 10–18mm (⅖–¾in) across. July.

Cotula sericea ○◗

The leaves of this species are well covered with silky hairs and are grouped in clusters at the rooting nodes. The branches are stiff and terminate in small flower-heads, 5–8mm (⅕–⅓in) across. July–August.

Cotula squalida ○◗

The wiry stems of this species are well-branched and form slow-growing bronze-tinged mats up to 40cm (16in) across. As with the preceding species the leaves are grouped at the nodes and pinnately divided. The flower-heads are small and rather inconspicuous, only 6–9mm (¼–⅜in) across and purplish. July.

COTYLEDON (Crassulaceae)

A genus of primarily South African succulent plants. Most of the species, about 40 in all, are not hardy and those generally grown in our gardens have, in recent years, been transferred to other genera. The most important of these are the following:

Cotyledon chrysantha—now *Rosularia pallida*
Cotyledon oppositifolia—now *Chiastophyllum oppositifolium*
Cotyledon spinosa—now *Orostachys spinosus*
Cotyledon simplicifolia—now *Chiastophyllum oppositifolium*

CRASSULA (Crassulaceae)

A genus of 300 species of succulent herbs and shrubs mostly native to Africa. Most are too tender for outdoor culture; however, two are worth considering as suitable for the rock garden or as a pan plant in the alpine house.

Crassula milfordiae (syn. *C. sediformis*) ○
Plants form low dense rosettes to 50mm (2in) high, green in summer, becoming attractively bronzed during the autumn and winter. The tiny white flowers are crimson in bud and borne in dense clusters. South Africa. July–August. Not always hardy, but surviving most average winters.

Crassula sarcocaulis ○
A subshrub, the stems becoming much branched, woody and gnarled with age, to 25cm (10in) tall eventually. The deciduous leaves are oval, pointed and the tiny pale pink flowers are borne in dense clusters, being red or crimson in bud. South Africa. July–August. The hardiest species, surviving outdoors in all but the most severe winters. A hybrid between this and the previous species is sometimes available, being rather like *C. sarcocaulis*, but more compact and smaller in all its parts.

CREPIS (Compositae)

Commonly referred to as hawkweeds, *Crepis* is a large genus of annual, biennial and perennial herbs, with over 200 species distributed throughout the temperate world. Their dandelion-like flower-heads vary in colour from pink, orange, yellow to white, though the vast majority are yellow. Most species tend to be far too weedy for the gardener and only two are commonly grown in the rock garden.

Crepis aurea ○
This variable species occurs in the mountains of S Europe where it displays great variation in form. The leaves are either toothed or deeply divided and borne in basal rosettes. They can be hairless or covered in soft downy hair. Flower-stems vary from 3 to 25cm (1–10in) tall bearing heads of orange-bronze flowers; the rays are often red or purple on the underside. June–August. The form usually supplied by alpine nurseries rarely exceeds 80mm (3in) tall; others are too weedy and must be removed before they become invasive.

Crepis incana (syn. *C. rosea*) ○☆
Similar to the preceding species, but with soft, grey, hairy leaves and 1–5 branching stems 10–15cm (4–6in) tall. Basal leaves vary from 3 to 13cm (1¼–5in) and are coarsely divided. The pale pink flower-heads are 10–12mm ($\frac{2}{5}$–$\frac{1}{2}$in) across. Native of S Greece, where it occurs amongst mountain rocks. June–August. A charming and pretty species.

CYANANTHUS (Campanulaceae)

A small genus of perennials, occasionally annuals from the Himalaya, Tibet and SW China. Most of those grown in gardens have spreading stems with small leaves and solitary terminal flowers, often resembling a periwinkle, with a tube and five spreading lobes. All those described below require a damp leafy or peaty soil which is well-drained. They can be propagated from cuttings taken in the late spring or early summer, or fairly readily from seed when available.

Cyananthus lobatus

Cyananthus lobatus ◑☆
A prostrate plant with radiating stems bearing short-lobed oval leaves. The large flowers, up to 30mm (1⅛in) across, have rounded lobes and large hairy calyces. In the best forms the flowers are a deep purple-blue, but they can vary through various shades of pale and mid-blue, lilac, as well as white ('Albus'). Seed mixtures generally produce a range of colours. Himalaya. July–September. This and the following species are probably the easiest to cultivate and deserve a place in any garden; however, they thrive best in wetter regions, greatly disliking hot dry summers. In the wild, it is a plant of low scrub and grassy meadows.

Cyananthus microphyllus ◑
A smaller plant than the previous species, more compact in habit and with narrow-elliptical unlobed leaves. The flowers are a clear blue, often whitish in the throat, and with narrow, spreading lobes. Himalaya and Tibet. August–October. Thrives on moist screes and in the peat garden in an open position. Often found in gardens under the name *C. integer*, a distinct species which is doubtfully in cultivation.

Several other species are rare in cultivation, but are well worth seeking out. Of these, the finest are *C. delavayi*, from SW China, which has downy foliage and flowers with a tuft of hairs in the throat; *C. longiflorus*, from the same region, with exceptionally long flowers (up to 50mm (2in)) of an intense purple-blue; and *C.*

sherriffii which hails from the remote regions of the high Himalaya and the Tibet plateau.

CYATHODES (Epacridaceae)

A genus of small Australian and New Zealand shrubs which are, as might be expected, mostly too tender for temperate gardens. However, 2 are reasonably hardy, though they can be cut back by severe winters and late spring frost. They require a moist, lime-free soil and greatly resent summer droughts. At the same time they should be kept relatively dry during the winter. Given these conditions and a sheltered site, they will succeed on the rock garden, although more often seen as a pan plant in the alpine house.

Cyathodes colensoi ◐☐

Forms a rounded bush to 30cm (12in) with numerous narrow, blunt, bluish-grey leaves. The urn-shaped flowers are white, borne in short racemes and followed by striking fleshy berries, white or rose-pink. New Zealand. July.

Cyathodes empetrifolia ◐☐

A smaller, creeping plant only 15cm (6in) tall at the most, rather heath-like, with small linear leaves and fragrant white flowers. The berries are red or purple. New Zealand. May–June.

CYCLAMEN (Primulaceae)

The genus *Cyclamen* needs no introduction. There are 19 species distributed in C and S Europe, W Asia and N Africa. All the species are cultivated and most are extremely desirable. Most can be readily grown in pans and frames, thriving best in a gritty compost with plenty of leaf-mould; added pine-needle compost can also be beneficial. A number are good and floriferous garden plants, which, once established, will seed themselves around. They will thrive on a variety of soils, but dislike heavy clays and poor drainage. A place below shrubs, beneath a wall or between rocks is ideal. Only the hardiest are listed here. All can be readily propagated from fresh seed, sown as soon as it is ripe.

Cyclamen hederifolium (syn. *C. neapolitanum*) ◐☆

Probably the commonest and certainly the easiest species to grow in our gardens. The tubers may eventually be very large and plate-like, rooting all over the surface. The ivy-like leaves may be lobed or unlobed and are usually attractively variegated with grey-green, grey or silver. The pale pink, auricled flowers are solitary, the stalks coiling in fruit. S Europe. August–October. A very accommodating plant. 'Album'—a white flowered form.

Cyclamen repandum ◐☆

Like the previous species, to 12cm (5in) tall and with brighter green, ivy-like leaves. The fragrant flowers are without auricles and are a deep magenta-purple, with slender twisted petals. SE France to Greece. April–May. Subsp. *rhodense* from Rhodes has white flowers with a pink snout—less hardy than the type; 'Peloponnesiacum'—has attractively speckled leaves and pale pink flowers with a darker snout, also less hardy than the type.

Cyclamen coum (syn. *C. orbiculatum*) ☽☆
The lovely little winter cyclamen is a must for every alpine garden. The rounded or kidney-shaped leaves are a deep green, plain or attractively patterned with grey, white or silver. The stumpy little flowers come in various shades of pink with darker markings around the snout. The tubers never grow very large. Turkey, Caucasus and Lebanon. January–April. This delightful plant does equally well in the garden, a frame or pan. 'Album'—white flowers; 'Roseum'—large flowers, rose-pink. There are also various forms with distinctive leaf markings, well worth seeking out. Subsp. *caucasicum*, from the Caucasus and N Iran, has distinctive heart-shaped leaves, but is less hardy.

Cyclamen parviflorum ☽
Like a miniature version of the previous, scarcely 30–40mm ($1\frac{1}{5}$–$1\frac{1}{2}$in) tall with unmarked leaves. NE Turkey. February–April. Hardy, but best in a pan or trough because it is so small—dislikes drought.

Cyclamen trochopteranthum ☽
Similar to *C. coum*, but the petals, instead of twisting backwards, spread sideways into a propeller shape. The flowers range in colour from pale to deep pink. W Central Turkey. February–April. Less common in cultivation, but just as hardy.

Cyclamen purpurascens (syn. *C. europaeum*) ☽
A widespread species of woodland in C and E Europe. The large shiny green orbicular leaves may be mottled or plain. The sweetly scented flowers are pale to deep carmine-pink, sometimes rather dumpy, but in some forms with longer, more elegant petals. July–September. Not always easy to please. The tubers should be deeply buried in a semi-shaded sheltered spot—heartily dislikes drought.

Cyclamen cilicium ☽☆
A dainty little species with oval, prettily patterned leaves, often marked with silver. The pale pink flowers have a narrow snout with deep rose markings, but no auricles, and delicately twisted petals. WC Turkey. September–November. Thrives with annual top-dressings of pine needles.

Cyclamen mirabile ☽
Like *C. cilicium*, but the leaves are often flushed with red, especially when young, and the petals are distinctly toothed. SW Turkey. September–November. Less common in cultivation, but almost as hardy. The forms with pronounced red blushes on the leaves are worth seeking out.

Cyclamen intaminatum (syn. *C. cilicium* var. *'alpinum'*) ☽
Like a small and slender version of *C. cilicium*, but with white flowers veined with grey, otherwise unmarked. W Turkey. September–October. Particularly suited to pan or trough culture, as it is often overlooked on the rock garden.

Other species that can be tried outdoors in milder districts are *C. balearicum*, *C. creticum*, *C. graecum*, *C libanoticum* and *C. pseudibericum*. Plants can survive a reasonable amount of frost, but the tubers should be deeply planted (except *C. graecum*); a rock placed directly overhead then covered with soil will add extra protection.

Cyclamen intaminatum

Cyclamen libanoticum

CYTISUS (Leguminosae)

The brooms are popular garden shrubs. The genus contains 33 species native to Europe, N Africa, the Canary Islands and just extending to W Asia. Most have solitary or trifoliate leaves and the small pea-like flowers are axillary and usually clustered into leafy, terminal heads or racemes. They range in colour from white to yellow and, although rarely, to reddish. Planting them in pots retains their dwarf habit and permits occasional movement to a new site, otherwise older plants do not respond well to transplanting, being intolerant of major root disturbance. The plants are ideally suited to well-drained gravelly soils in sunny positions. Propagation from cuttings or seed. See also *Chamaecytisus*.

Cytisus ardoinii ○☆
The Ardoin Broom is a dwarf shrublet up to about 20cm (8in) in height (reaching a maximum of 60cm (24in) in the wild), with arching stems. The young branchlets are strongly grooved with a downy pubescence and bear trifoliate leaves. The golden yellow flowers, each 8–12mm ($\frac{1}{3}$–$\frac{1}{2}$in) long, are solitary or in clusters of 2–3. The hairy pod is 20–25mm ($\frac{4}{5}$–1in) long. French Maritime Alps, where it inhabits calcareous rocks to 1,500m (4,950ft) altitude. April–May. 'Cottage'—a particularly fine dwarf form.

Cytisus × *beanii (C. ardoinii* × *C. purgans)* ○☆
A dwarf hybrid to 60cm (24in) in height but spreading up to 1m (3ft). The golden yellow flowers are borne on the previous year's growth. May–June. An elegant rock garden plant with neat growth.

Cytisus × *kewensis (C. ardoinii* × *C. multiflorus)* ○
A spreading shrub 30–60cm (12–24in) tall, but often over 1m (3ft) across. It is similar to *C. ardoinii*, but its flowers are creamish or pale yellow. April–May. A profusely flowering hybrid suitable for sunny positions; fine at the back of a large rock garden.

Cytisus × *praecox (C. multiflorus* × *C. purgans)* ○
One of the most prolific flowering brooms, with creamish flowers, but usually forming a large shrub 2–3m (6–9ft) in height. Dwarf forms are available and are sometimes given varietal names commercially: var. *albus*—white flowers in pendulous sprays; var. *luteus*—yellow flowers. All April–May.

Cytisus procumbens (syn. *Genista procumbens*) ○
A prostrate or somewhat ascending shrublet up to about 40cm (16in) tall, with interwoven stems. The young branchlets are strongly ribbed, with simple grey-green leaves. The golden-yellow flowers, 12–15mm ($\frac{1}{2}$–$\frac{3}{5}$in) long, are solitary or in clusters of 2–3 along the younger stems. May–July.

Cytisus decumbens (syn. *C. prostratus*) ○☆
A prostrate, ground-hugging shrublet, up to 10–15cm (4–6in) in height, with wiry stems and simple oblong leaves. The bright yellow flowers, 10–14mm ($\frac{2}{5}$–$\frac{1}{2}$in) long, are clustered 1–3 in the axils of the previous year's growth. S Alps and Apennines. May–June.

Cytisus albus (syn. *C. leucanthus*) ○
An erect shrub 30cm–1m (1–3ft) tall, with hairy branches and trifoliate leaves. The flowers, white to cream, are borne in small clusters usually of 3–6. June–July.

DABOECIA (Ericaceae)

This attractive genus of dwarf, bushy, evergreen shrubs has only 2 species native to W Europe. Both species are in cultivation, but several cultivars also exist and are to be found in lists. They should be treated in the same way as the hardy heathers, *Erica*; they are lime-haters requiring a peaty-sandy soil.

Daboecia cantabrica ○☐

St Daboec's Heath grows 30–70cm (12–28in) in height and is at first dense and compact, but can become straggly after flowering if not trimmed. The leaves are dark, glossy green above but white-felted beneath, about 10mm (⅖in) long, lanceolate with downrolled margins. The rosy-purple pendent flowers are egg-shaped, 9–14mm (⅖–½in) long, with 4 tiny lobes at the constricted mouth, and are borne in terminal racemes. NW Europe including Ireland. June–November. The following cultivars are generally commercially available: 'Alba'—a white flowered form originating in the wild in Connemara, floriferous and hardier than the type, with vivid green leaves; 'Atropurpurea'—flowers a darker, richer colour than those of the type; 'Bicolor'—white, rose-purple and striped corollas, often all in the same inflorescence; 'Nana'—dwarf form with smaller leaves and flowers; 'Praegerae'— also originated in Connemara, this cultivar has clear deep pink flowers, and the plant is less robust than the type.

Daboecia azorica ○☐

This species is sometimes offered in catalogues. It is a smaller plant with glabrous, pink to crimson flowers, but is less hardy than *D. cantabrica*. Doubtfully hardy in exposed places and cold districts.

DAPHNE (Thymelaeaceae)

This large group of shrubs has many species which are too tall for the rock garden, but at the same time there are some which are among the best of all dwarf flowering shrubs, and they are often deliciously fragrant. There are over 100 species distributed throughout Europe and temperate Asia to Japan, but it is mainly the European ones which are cultivated to any extent.

They are evergreen or deciduous shrubs with alternate, often leathery leaves and tough stringy bark which makes them almost impossible to pick without a knife or secateurs. The usually scented flowers are carried in terminal or axillary clusters and have no petals, the showy rather fleshy perianth consisting of a calyx tube with four spreading lobes which may be pointed or rounded; the 8 stamens are carried in fours at two different levels within the tube. The fruit is a fleshy berry containing one seed; it is brightly coloured, usually reddish or orange, and is attractive to birds, but extremely poisonous to humans. Plants can be increased by cuttings, layerings or by seed when available; however, some are very tricky to propagate and specialist growers often resort to grafting onto a suitable stock—often *D. mezereum*.

Daphne mezereum ○◑

The lovely Mezereon is a rare British native but reaches alpine altitudes in C and S Europe. However, it is really only suitable for large rock gardens. Plants form a much-branched erect shrub to 1m (3ft), rarely to 2.5m (7½ft), flowering before the leaves appear. The fragrant flowers are produced in lateral clusters all the way along the shoots and are reddish-purple or pinkish (or white in *forma alba*) about 8–10mm (⅖in) across. The leaves appear just after the flowers and are elliptical, generally broadest above the middle, about 5–10cm (2–4in) long. The berries are bright red, ripening in summer. Widespread in Europe. February–March. Worth a place in every garden.

Daphne blagayana ◖

An excellent evergreen species, unusual in the genus in being a shade-loving plant. It has a prostrate habit branching to form spreading clumps. The oval leathery leaves, which have rounded tips are clustered towards the ends of the shoots so that plants often become bare in the centre. The creamy-white, strongly fragrant, flowers are produced in a dense head of 20–30, each about 10mm (⅜in) across. Plants do not normally fruit in cultivation. SE Europe. March–April. Often grows amongst other shrubs in the wild thus disguising the rather open habit of the species.

Daphne laureola ○

The Spurge Laurel is not really suitable for rock gardens, being rather tall, but subsp. *philippi* is an attractive low evergreen, forming compact dark green mounds of growth, usually 40cm (18in) or less in height. The oval leaves, broadest above the middle, are leathery and glossy-green, and carry in their axils clusters of yellowish-green flowers; these are not fragrant but often have a rather sickly scent. The black berries are produced freely on *D. laureola*, but not very frequently on subsp. *philippi*. Pyrenees. February–March.

Daphne oleioides ○

This is a slow-growing much-branched evergreen shrub, eventually making compact bushes to about 45cm (20in). The rather small, tough leathery leaves are grey-green, usually 10–30mm (⅖–1½in) long and up to 10mm (⅜in) wide. Clusters of 2–8 fragrant flowers are produced at the ends of the shoots and these are each about 10cm (4in) across, creamy-white with narrow, pointed lobes, and beautifully fragrant. The berries are orange when ripe. Widespread in S Europe and E Asia. April–June.

Daphne alpina ○

Like *D. oleioides*, but deciduous and not so compact, eventually making a loose open shrub to 70cm (28in). S Europe. May–June. A delightful species that deserves to be more widely grown.

Daphne jasminea ○

This attractive species is related to *D. oleioides*, but is much more compact. There are two forms in cultivation, one prostrate and one a dwarf upright shrub to 15cm (6in). It is evergreen with tiny greyish to bluish leaves to 10mm (⅜in) long. The fragrant flowers are white, flushed pink in the prostrate form, and have narrow, pointed, slightly recurved lobes. Plants do not fruit in cultivation. Greece. April–May.

Daphne arbuscula ○☆

An excellent and very beautiful rock garden plant making a dwarf, dense, evergreen shrub, usually 10–20cm (4–8in) in height. The tough leathery leaves are narrowly linear, deep shiny green and crowded towards the ends of the shoots where the terminal clusters of up to 30 flowers are produced; these are very fragrant, deep pink with a long tube and each about 8–10mm (⅜in) across. Berries are rarely produced in gardens. Czechoslovakia. April–June. A superb subject for a well-drained trough or sink garden, slow-growing and long-lived.

Daphne cneorum

Daphne petraea ○▲
This rare species is like an extremely compact *D. arbuscula,* making mounds of dark shiny green foliage only 5–10cm (2–4in) in height. The leaves are linear, oblanceolate, up to 10mm ($\frac{2}{5}$in) long. There are 3–5 bright pink, fragrant flowers in each cluster and they are 5–10mm ($\frac{1}{5}$–$\frac{2}{5}$in) across. 'Grandiflora' is the form usually cultivated by specialist rock gardeners; a superb plant for the alpine house with larger flowers in a bright glowing pink. Berries are not produced in cultivation. N Italy, near Lake Garda. April–June.

Daphne cneorum ○☆
This is perhaps the best of all Daphnes, commonly known as the Garland Flower. It is a trailing evergreen shrub, much-branched to form patches up to 2m ($6\frac{1}{2}$ft) across, but never more than about 15cm (6in) high. The dark green narrowly oblong leaves, broadest above the middle, clothe the stems, not just at the apex. About 6–10 flowers are produced in a cluster at the tip of each shoot, very fragrant and deep rose pink, about 10mm ($\frac{2}{5}$in) across and sometimes so numerous that the whole plant is a mound of pink; the tube is downy on the outside. It does not normally fruit in cultivation. Widespread in the mountains of Europe. April–May. 'Eximia'—the most widely cultivated form, very vigorous with larger flowers; 'Variegata'—the leaves are margined with yellow and has paler pink flowers. Var. *pygmaea* is a very compact slow-growing form of the species, completely prostrate. Var. *verlotii* has very narrow pointed leaves and the flowers have narrower more acute lobes. There are white-flowered forms of *D. cneorum* and of var. *pygmaea*.

Daphne striata ○
A closely related species to *D. cneorum*, but a difficult plant to cultivate. It differs from the latter in the tube of the flower being hairless, and in having narrower leaves. A native of the Alps. April–May.

Daphne collina ○
A very neat plant forming domed evergreen bushes, usually about 30–40cm (12–16in) in height and as much across, but sometimes much larger in old specimens. The shiny mid-green leaves are oval and rather rounded at the apex, about 20–40mm ($\frac{4}{5}$–$1\frac{1}{2}$in) long and 10mm ($\frac{2}{5}$in) wide. The flowers are borne in terminal clusters of 5–15, deep rose and highly fragrant, each 8–10mm ($\frac{2}{5}$in) across, with a silky-hairy tube. It does not fruit in gardens. S Italy. April–May.

Daphne sericea ○
A related species from the E Mediterranean, taller and looser in its growth and less hardy. *D.* × *neapolitana* is clearly related to *D. collina* and is possibly of hybrid origin. It also makes dense bushes, but the leaves are darker green, narrower (7mm (⅓in) or less wide) and the flowers are produced in the upper leaf axils as well as in terminal clusters. Of unknown origin.

Daphne retusa ○☆
A very hardy rather stiff upright evergreen shrub 30–60cm (12–24in) high with deep shiny green leathery leaves 15–35mm (⅗–1⅖in) long and 5–12mm (⅕–½in) wide; they have a notched apex and slightly rolled margins. The flowers are in large terminal clusters, very fragrant, white with purple backs to the lobes and a purple tube; they are large compared with the species given above, 8–10mm (⅖in) across. Bright red berries are freely produced in cultivation. W China and E Himalaya. April–May.

Daphne tangutica ○
Also from China, is similar to *D. retusa*, but is of larger, more open habit. The larger leaves (to 6cm (2½in) long) are rather dull green, flat with the margins not rolled under, the apex is usually acute, not notched. April–May.

Daphne giraldii ○
A deciduous shrub, upright in habit, usually reaching about 50–60cm (20–40in) eventually. The oblong leaves are broader above the middle, 35–60mm (1¼–2½in) long and pale bluish-green. It is unusual in that the fragrant flowers are bright yellow, produced in clusters of 4–8. Orange berries are produced freely. China. May–July.
   Daphne jezoensis (and nearly identical *D. kamtschatica*) is also an upright shrub with yellow flowers, but they are produced in winter between November and March. Although deciduous, it loses its leaves rather unexpectedly in summer and develops a new set in autumn. Unfortunately it is not as hardy as *D. giraldii*.

DEINANTHE (Saxifragaceae)

A small genus with only two species, both from E Asia. One species (*D. coerulea*) is cultivated and is useful for a shady, cool position on soil which is peaty and free from lime. The inflorescence is a corymb (branched but forming a spreading flattish head) composed of sterile flowers around the edge and fertile flowers in the centre. Propagation is by division of the rhizome in spring, or by seed.

Deinanthe coerulea ○□
A laxly tufted plant up to 30cm (12in) tall with opposite, coarsely toothed leaves. The flowers are bluish-violet: the sterile ones, 10–12mm (⅖–½in) across, consist of 2 or 3 enlarged calyx-lobes; the fertile ones, up to 30mm (1⅕in) across, have 5 petals and a central boss of white or pale blue stamens. China. July–August. A beautiful plant that deserves to be more widely known.

DELPHINIUM (Ranunculaceae)

This large genus is widely scattered across Europe and Asia as well as North America and the mountains of N and E Africa. The large spiked border delphinium is a well known and popular garden plant, but the genus contains some delightful small alpine species. Several are widely cultivated, but many of the finest are not.

79

Most require a well-drained soil and the young shoots should be guarded against slug attacks. Propagation by seed, cuttings or division.

Delphinium chinense ○☆
A small perennial to 30cm (12in) tall with branched stems and deeply lobed and cut leaves. The bright blue flowers have a slender spur and are produced in succession over a long season. W China. June–early August. Plants tend to be short-lived, but are easily raised from seed which should be collected as the fruits ripen.

Delphinium caeruleum ○
Similar to the previous species, but laxer in habit and with more finely cut foliage. The flowers are a deeper blue. Himalaya and S Tibet. June–July.

Delphinium menziesii ○
A variable species 10–40cm (4–16in) tall with deep blue flowers. A native of NE North America. June–July. The dwarfer forms are worth seeking out. Rather rare in cultivation.

Delphinium muscosum ○
The most delightful of the alpine species in cultivation. Plants form a low tuft up to 12cm (5in) tall, with hairy, deeply cut basal leaves. The blue, furry flowers, 18–22mm ($\frac{3}{4}$–$\frac{7}{8}$in), have an inflated appearance and seem large for the size of the plant; they are quite different in shape from the preceding species, which have open blooms with wide-spreading petals. C and E Himalaya. June–July. Rather a rare species in cultivation, but well worth seeking out if seed is available. Plants require a well-drained scree or pan-culture.

Delphinium nudicaule ○☆
A variable species with slender stems 15–30cm (6–12in) tall, sometimes more. The deeply lobed leaves are mostly basal and the well spaced, long-spurred flowers are a distinctive mixture of red and yellow. There is also a form with all yellow flowers. Mountains of W North America. June–July. Most often seen grown in pans in the alpine house, but it will succeed outdoors in a well-drained site.

DIANTHUS (Caryophyllaceae)
This very large and popular group of garden plants, to which the pinks, carnations and sweet williams belong, contains many excellent alpine species (and hybrids derived from them) and are among the most important of summer-flowering rock garden plants. There are about 300 species widely distributed in Europe, Asia and Africa. Most of those cultivated are readily propagated from cuttings or seed.

Dianthus are mainly tufted perennials, often with narrow, pointed, rather stiff, grey-green leaves overtopped by wiry flower stems bearing well-spaced pairs of leaves and upward-facing terminal flowers, either solitary or in loosely-branched to very tight heads. The individual flowers are often delightfully fragrant and large, most frequently in shades of pinkish-purple with the 5 petals toothed to deeply cut at the apex and narrowed abruptly into a claw at the base. A distinctive feature of *Dianthus* is that the fairly long tubular calyx is surrounded in the lower half by several shorter scale-like lobes known as the epicalyx scales; these are usually rather broad at the base and narrowed to a point at the apex. There are usually 2 styles, protruding from the throat of the flower.

Dianthus alpinus ○☆
The Alpine Pink is one of the most attractive species for rock gardens, reaching up to 10cm (4in) tall. It forms loose cushions of narrowly oblong, blunt-tipped leaves up to 30mm ($1\frac{1}{5}$in) long and 3–5mm ($\frac{1}{5}$in) wide. The stems carry widely spaced pairs of narrow leaves and large solitary flowers which are about 25–40mm (1–$1\frac{1}{2}$in) across, with bearded petals, toothed at the apex; the colour is a purplish shade of red with paler spotting. SE Alps of Austria, Italy and Yugoslavia, where it inhabits limestone rocks to an altitude of 2,500m (7,250ft). June–August. 'Joan's Blood'—bronze-tinted leaves and blood red flowers with blackish centres.

D × boydii is a hybrid of *D. alpinus*, with large pink flowers with fringed petals. *Dianthus nitidus* is related to *D. alpinus*, but has smaller deep pink flowers 15–20mm ($\frac{3}{5}$–$\frac{4}{5}$in) across, carried in pairs on longer stems. Czechoslovakia and Poland, in the Carpathian Mts. June–July.

Dianthus callizonus ○
A most attractive species, not unlike *D. alpinus*, which makes loose tufts of narrow linear-lanceolate leaves 20–40mm ($\frac{4}{5}$–$1\frac{3}{5}$in) long and only 2–3mm ($\frac{1}{10}$in) wide. The 5–10cm (2–4in) flower stems have a few pairs of leaves and solitary carmine flowers, 20–30mm ($\frac{4}{5}$–$1\frac{1}{5}$in) in diameter, which have a central zone of whitish spots on a darker background. The calyx is stained with dark purple at the top. Romania. July–August.

Dianthus glacialis ○
Like a very compact *D. alpinus*, only 20–50mm ($\frac{3}{4}$–2in) in height with solitary, short-stemmed, bright rose-red flowers, 10–15mm ($\frac{2}{5}$–$\frac{3}{5}$in) in diameter, carried amongst tufts of linear leaves which are only 1–2mm ($\frac{1}{16}$in) wide. E Alps, east to Carpathians. June–August. In the wild *D. glacialis* inhabits rocky meadows and stony places, over acid rocks.

Subsp. *gelidus* (syn. *D. gelidus*) is very similar to subsp. *glacialis*, but has the leaf margins hairy near the base and the flowers are larger, 20–25mm ($\frac{3}{4}$–1in) across. Carpathians. June–July.

Dianthus freynii ○
Similar to *D. glacialis*, but has leaves less than 1mm ($\frac{1}{16}$in) wide. The flowers 10–20mm ($\frac{2}{5}$–$\frac{3}{4}$in) across, are overtopped by the leaves. Yugoslavia, Bulgaria. June–August.

Dianthus petraeus (syn. ***D. kitaibelii, D. strictus***) ○☆
An excellent alpine plant forming loose spiky cushions of many linear, often greyish, sharply pointed leaves 20–40mm ($\frac{4}{5}$–$1\frac{3}{5}$in) long and 1–2mm ($\frac{1}{16}$in) wide. Slender flower stems reach 10–20cm (4–8in) bearing widely spaced pairs of narrow leaves and solitary, fragrant, white flowers 10–20mm ($\frac{2}{5}$–$\frac{4}{5}$in) across, which have their petals toothed or fringed at the apex. Widespread in the Balkan Peninsula. June–July. 'Albus Plenus' is sometimes offered in catalogues. This is a double white form, but since it has several flowers per stem it may not be referable to this species.

Dianthus noeanus ○
This plant is sometimes treated as a subspecies of *D. petraeus*; it has 2–3 flowers per stem and these have deeply cut petals and a longer calyx 25–30mm (1–$1\frac{1}{5}$in) long (not 20–25mm, $\frac{4}{5}$–1in). Bulgaria. June–July.

Dianthus gratianopolitanus (syn. *D. caesius*) ○
The Cheddar Pink is a rare British native and an excellent dwarf *Dianthus* for rock gardens. It is a clump-forming plant to 15cm (6in) tall with grey-green leaves 1–2mm ($\frac{1}{16}$in) wide. The stems carry 2–3 pairs of leaves and solitary pink flowers 15–30mm ($\frac{3}{8}$–1$\frac{1}{8}$in) across; the petals are bearded near the base and coarsely toothed at the apex. Widespread in S Europe. June–August. 'Plenus' is a garden selection with double flowers.

Dianthus deltoides ○☆
The Maiden Pink is one of the most popular of all rock garden plants. It is a slender species producing mats of narrow linear leaves and wiry stems 15–45cm (6–18in) in height, bearing up to 10 widely spaced pairs of sharply pointed leaves. The flowers are solitary or in loosely branched heads and are about 15mm ($\frac{3}{8}$in) across, pink or reddish with a darker zone in the centre, the petals irregularly toothed at the apex. Widespread in Europe including Britain. June–August. Once established, plants seed themselves around freely.

The following cultivars may be found in gardens; some may well be identical plants under different names: 'Albus'—dark green leaves and white flowers; 'Balkan Scarlet'—purple-tinted leaves and vivid crimson flowers; 'Brilliance'—carmine flowers; 'Broughty Blaze'—dark green foliage and magenta-crimson flowers; 'Flashing Light'—crimson-red flowers; 'Samos'—carmine-red flowers; 'Steriker'—crimson-scarlet flowers; 'Wisley'—bronze-tinted leaves and deep crimson flowers.

Dianthus myrtinervius ○
Although probably closely related to *D. deltoides* this is a much more compact plant. It forms prostrate mats of tiny, narrowly elliptical, leaves only 2–5mm ($\frac{1}{12}$–$\frac{1}{5}$in) long. The solitary pink flowers, 5–10mm ($\frac{1}{5}$–$\frac{2}{5}$in) across, are almost stemless at the apex of each leafy shoot; they have a bell-shaped calyx about 5–10mm ($\frac{1}{5}$–$\frac{2}{5}$in) long. N Greece, S Yugoslavia. June.

Dianthus erinaceus ○
A prickly, cushion-forming species to 50mm (2in) tall with spiny leaves up to 20mm (⁶ in) long and 1–3mm ($\frac{1}{16}$in) wide at the base, long-tapering to the sharp point. The stems carry solitary (rarely two) pink flowers, each about 10–15mm ($\frac{2}{5}$–$\frac{3}{5}$in) across. The calyx is surrounded by 8–10 sharply pointed epicalyx scales. Turkey. July.

Dianthus squarrosus ○
A distinctive species forming loose cushions or clumps, the very narrow leaves not clustered at the base, but distributed along the stems; they are rather spiny and distinctly curved, about 10–20mm ($\frac{2}{5}$–$\frac{4}{5}$in) long. The branched flower-stems are 15–30mm (6–12in) tall and carry several fragrant white flowers, each about 15–20mm ($\frac{3}{5}$–$\frac{4}{5}$in) across; they have deeply cut petals. USSR, in the Ukraine and Kazakhstan. June–July. Well worth acquiring, like the previous species.

Dianthus knappii ○
An unusual species with yellow flowers, perhaps rather tall for the average rock garden, being up to 40cm (16in) when in flower, with pairs of long linear-lanceolate leaves scattered up the stems. The flowers, about 10–15mm ($\frac{2}{5}$–$\frac{3}{5}$in) across, are produced in tight head-like clusters and have toothed petals, and the calyx is surrounded by very long, pointed, green epicalyx scales which equal or overtop the flowers. Yugoslavia. July–August.

Dianthus microlepis ○
A very compact species with many narrow, linear, basal leaves only 1–2mm ($\frac{1}{16}$in) wide and up to 20mm ($\frac{4}{5}$in) long, forming dense rounded cushions. The solitary pink flowers are carried just above the leaves on very short stems and are about 10–15mm ($\frac{2}{5}$–$\frac{3}{5}$in) across, with smooth or only slightly toothed petals; the calyx is stained with purple and rather funnel-shaped. Bulgaria. June–August.

Dianthus monspessulanus ○◑
The Fringed Pink is a widespread species in the mountains of C and S Europe. It is a loosely tufted plant with rather soft linear leaves 1–3mm ($\frac{1}{25}$–$\frac{1}{8}$in) wide, often greyish-green. The flower stems are 15–30cm (6–12in) (sometimes up to 50cm, 20in) in height with widely spaced pairs of long, linear, leaves and bearing up to 5 fragrant pink or white flowers in a lax cluster; these are each about 20–30mm ($\frac{3}{4}$–1$\frac{1}{5}$in) across, with the petals deeply cut to the middle into many narrow lobes. The flowers are delightfully fragrant. June–August. In its native haunts a plant of meadows, stony places and open woodland to 2,000m (6,600ft) altitude.

Dianthus sternbergii (syn. ***D. monspessulanus*** subsp. ***sternbergii***) ○
This is very like *D. monspessulanus*, but is more compact and thus of more interest to alpine gardeners. It has solitary flowers, is only 10–20cm (4–8in) in height, the individual flowers being 30–40mm (1$\frac{1}{5}$–1$\frac{3}{5}$in) across. Alps of Italy, Austria and N Yugoslavia. June–August.

Dianthus × arvernensis ○
This is a hybrid between *D. monspessulanus* and *D. sylvaticus* with grey leaves forming a mat of growth, and stems 30–45cm (12–18in) high, bearing 1–3 large purplish flowers. Rather a tall plant for the average rock garden. June–July.

Dianthus subacaulis ○
A compact cushion-forming species, usually only 20–30mm (1$\frac{1}{5}$–1$\frac{3}{5}$in) in height when in flower, looking almost like a thrift in its habit of growth. Leaves linear-lanceolate, only about 1mm ($\frac{1}{25}$in) wide and up to 10mm ($\frac{2}{5}$in) long. It usually has solitary flowers on short stems, each 5–10mm ($\frac{1}{5}$–$\frac{2}{5}$in) across, pale pink with the rounded petals scarcely toothed at all at the apex. SW France, Spain and Portugal. May–July.

Subsp. brachyanthus is a very tightly compact version, very similar, but with the calyx teeth blunt rather than pointed. Pyrenees, Spain, Portugal. June–July.

Dianthus minutiflorus (syn. ***D. strictus*** var. ***brachyanthus***) ○
This is related to *D. subacaulis*, but is less densely cushion-forming and has solitary white flowers with entire or shallowly toothed petals. Greece, S Yugoslavia. Albania. June–July.

Dianthus sylvestris ○◑
The Wood Pink is a slender species with dense green tufts of rather long, erect leaves only 1mm ($\frac{1}{25}$in) wide sometimes less. the wiry stems, 10–30cm (4–12in) tall, have one or more pink flowers, each 15–25mm ($\frac{3}{5}$–1in) across, and these have toothed petals. A distinctive feature is the size of the epicalyx scales, very short compared with the calyx and broad, cut off abruptly at the apex, or sometimes with a very sharp point. Alps and Balkans. June–July.

Dianthus carthusianorum ○◑☆
The Carthusian Pink is extremely variable and usually rather tall for the rock garden, although there are some fairly short forms. Plants make clumps of long,

linear, basal leaves up to 5mm ($\frac{1}{5}$in) wide, overtopped by the flower stems, which
may be 15–60cm (6–24in) in height and bear dense heads of pink or purple flowers
10–20mm ($\frac{2}{5}$–$\frac{4}{5}$in) in diameter, with toothed petals. Widespread in the mountains of
SW and C Europe. June–July. A plant of meadows, stony places and open woods
in its native haunts. 'Nanus'—an attractive compact form representing the lower
end of the height range at about 15cm (6in).

In addition to the above species there are a great many hybrid cultivars which are
suitable for rock gardens. The following is a selection of those generally available
from the leading alpine nurseries in Britain: 'Fanal'—single crimson-rose flowers
with deeply fringed petals; 'Garland'—prostrate growth and small pink flowers with
neatly toothed petals; 'Hidcote'—mats of silver-grey leaves and small double
crimson flowers, several per stem; 'Inshriach Dazzler'—compact growth with deep
crimson flowers with a buff colour on the exterior; 'Inshriach Startler'—silver-grey
foliage and bright cherry-red flowers; 'La Bourbrille'—compact habit with single
pink flowers; 'La Bourbrille Albus'—a white-flowered form of the previous one;
'Little Jock'—stocky growth and large double pale pink flowers; 'London Poppet'—
a laced Pink, with pink flowers with a contrasting red eye; 'Nyewoods Cream'—
grey-green mats and cream flowers; 'Oakington Hybrid'—fairly compact growth
and deep rose-pink double flowers; 'Pikes Pink'—compact blue-grey leaves and
semi-double rose-pink flowers with a dark zone in the centre; 'The Dubarry'—
compact growth; small rose-pink double flowers. All ○☆

DIASCIA (Scrophulariaceae)

A genus of about 25 pretty annuals and perennials from southern Africa. Most are
either too tall for the rock garden or not winter hardy. The flowers are borne in
terminal racemes and consist of 5 flat lobes with 2 distinct spurs. All require a hot
sunny position in a light well-drained soil.

Diascia cordifolia ○
A relatively new introduction which has proved to be reasonably hardy. Plants form
loose, leafy mats to 20cm (8in) tall, which become smothered in pretty rose-red
flowers. South Africa. A long flowering season from June through to late August.

Diascia 'Ruby Fields' ○☆
A delightful hybrid between *D. barbarae* and *D. cordifolia*, which forms low mats
of glossy green leaves. The 20cm (8in) high stems bear flowers of tangerine-rose.
June–August.

DICENTRA (Papaveraceae)

A popular group in gardens generally, excellent for pockets in the rock garden, and
often known as Bleeding Hearts. The Dicentras are closely related to *Corydalis*
with rather similar ferny, finely cut foliage, but two-spurred, rather than one-
spurred, flowers, nodding in lax racemes. The foliage dies down shortly after
flowering. The common Bleeding Heart, *Dicentra spectabilis*, is generally too gross
for the rock garden.

Dicentra cucullaria ◑
Dutchman's Breeches is a native of the USA and one of the most delightful species.
The rootstock is thick and fleshy and covered in brittle scales. The grey-green

foliage provides a soft foil to the creamy, yellow-tipped flowers held in flights above the leaves, to 15cm (6in) tall. Each flower has two blunt spurs. USA. April–May.

Dicentra canadensis ○◑
The plant gets its common name, Squirrel Corn, from its small rounded corn-like tubers. The foliage is similar to the previous species, and the whitish tubular flowers are noticeably constricted at the mouth. North America. April–May.

Dicentra oregana ○◑
A dwarf species similar to *D. cucullaria*, bearing handsome blue-green foliage and white flowers tipped with purple. W USA—Oregon. June–July. A striking species less often seen than it deserves.

Dicentra eximia ○◑
A taller plant than *D. cucullaria*, often reaching 20cm (8in) or more. The leaves are grey- or bluish-green and rather compact. The pendent flowers rise slightly above the foliage and are a rich reddish-purple, less prominently spurred than the previous species. SE USA. May–July. There is a good white flowered form, 'Alba', available.

Dicentra peregrina ▲
The gem of the genus and like many gems one of the most difficult to obtain and cultivate successfully. The neatly cut silvery-grey foliage forms small tufts, often less than 80mm (3in) tall. The pretty bleeding hearts are a clear pink and appearing large against the foliage. E Asia and Japan. May–June. A difficult plant and perhaps best left alone, if indeed one can obtain it, until one has had more experience with increasingly tricky alpines. Seldom succeeds unprotected.

Several hybrid cultivars are available. They are generally vigorous and floriferous plants prized for their foliage as much as their flowers. The finest are 'Bountiful'—red flowers on stems to 40cm (16in); 'Rokujo Hybrids'—similar height and flowers in a range of pinks and reds; 'Stuart Boothman'—attractive bronze foliage and pink flowers, 40cm (16in). All ○◑☆

DIONYSIA (Primulaceae)
The 40 or so species of *Dionysia* are native to the hot dry mountains of C Asia, particularly Iran and Afghanistan. Most grow in shaded cliff crevices and in cultivation are demanding and temperamental. However, there are several that have proved amenable and long-lived. They require the very best of drainage and a gritty compost with rocks placed around the leaf cushions. Plants can be grown on lumps of tufa, but few have succeeded with them outdoors. Root aphids, summer scorch and winter rot are their chief enemies. Without doubt they are well worth trying, but only after one has had some experience growing other, easier, alpines. The flowers are Primrose-like with a long tube and spreading lobes. As with *Primula*, plants produce either pin- or thrum-eyed flowers. One of each type are required in order to get viable seed.

Dionysia aretioides ○
Plant form soft grey-green cushions with numerous rosettes of oval leaves, rolled under along the toothed margins. The solitary bright yellow flowers, 9–10mm ($\frac{2}{5}$in) in diameter, have notched petals. The whole plant has a pleasing aromatic fragrance. N Iran. April–May. One of the easiest species in cultivation, fairly easily

raised from seed or summer cuttings. 'Paul Furse' and 'Gravetye'—the finest and most floriferous cultivars.

Dionysia tapetodes ○▲

Forms tight green or grey-green, often mealy, rosettes of tiny oval, untoothed leaves. The solitary yellow flowers, 6–7mm (¼in) in diameter, have oval un-notched petals. NE Iran and Afghanistan. March–May. Plants are slow growing, eventually forming a rather flat cushion to 20cm (8in) across, sometimes more. Several forms are in cultivation.

Dionysia curviflora ○

Like the previous species forms dense grey-green rosettes, hairy at the tip. The solitary flowers, 7–8mm (¼in), are violet-pink with a whitish eye and with notched petals. W Iran. March–April. Perhaps the most charming species, long established in cultivation. Several forms are available, some very much more floriferous than others, and well worth seeking out.

Dionysia involucrata ○

This fine species from the Pamir Mountains of the S USSR has been in cultivation for only a few years. The small cushions of rather large rosettes are held closely together, the broad leaves shallowly toothed towards the apex. The violet flowers have a deep eye, several being held on a distinct scape, the petals notched. March–May, sometimes later. Sets seed readily and this has proved one of the easiest species in cultivation.

Dionysia mira ○

A rather coarse *Primula*-like species forming large lax rosettes of bright green elliptical, toothed leaves. Scapes up to 20cm (8in) high carry several whorls of small yellow flowers, the petals unnotched. The stems become woody below as they age. N Oman. April–August. Perhaps the easiest species in cultivation; it can easily be mistaken for a *Primula*. Plants require a well-drained gritty compost with very little water during the winter. They are readily raised from seed or by summer cuttings.

Several other species are cultivated although often difficult to obtain and certainly not easy to grow. These include *D. archibaldii*, *D. bryoides*, *D. freitagii*, *D. janthina* and *D. michauxii*.

DODECATHEON (Primulaceae)

Popularly known as Shooting Stars, these natives of W North America favour cool shady environments. Plants have branching rhizomes and produce leaf-rosettes from which rise tall stems bearing umbels of drooping flowers. They are characterized by the sharply reflexed cyclamen-like petals, and the protruding, bunched, stamens and style. The species differ mainly in corolla colour and in overall size. They are generally easy to cultivate and prefer a partially shaded, moist spot. Propagation is easy from seed and from roots broken off at the point of attachment to the rhizome.

Dodecatheon dentatum subsp. *ellisiae* (syn. *D. ellisiae*) ◑

Easily recognized by its pale green, oval and heart-shaped, toothed leaves and few-flowered umbel of white flowers with purple spots at the centre. A smaller version of the type species. W USA. May–June.

Dodecatheon jeffreyi ◑

This species has long, narrow, erect, long-stalked leaves, and up to 30cm (12in) long stalks, The scapes bear a many-flowered umbel of deep reddish-purple flowers, each 20–25mm ($\frac{4}{5}$–1in) long. The deep purple stamens are an additional feature. California. May–June.

Dodecatheon media ◑☆

Perhaps the most widely cultivated species. Plants have rosettes of oblong, pointed, somewhat toothed leaves, to 15cm (6in) long. The flower-stems, up to 60cm (24in) long, bear umbels of 10–20 flowers; the colours range from white to lilac and glowing magenta. Flower size varies, but they are usually 15–20mm ($\frac{3}{5}$–$\frac{4}{5}$in) long. NW USA. May–June.

Dodecatheon radicatum ◑☆

A beautiful and hearty species which flowers profusely. From oblong 10cm (4in) long leaves rise stems bearing rose to red flowers in umbels of 3–5; the stamens are purple. USA—Colorado. May–June.

DORONICUM (Compositae)

A small genus of herbaceous perennials with tubers or stolons and simple alternate leaves. The daisy flower-heads contain both ray and disc florets and are generally golden-yellow in colour. The 35 species occur throughout temperate Eurasia and North Africa. Most species are too rampant for inclusion in the rock garden and only one is commonly grown as an alpine.

Doronicum columnae ○◑☆

Often referred to under its old name, *D. cordatum*, this species has been grown for many years as a rock garden plant. The leaves, mostly arranged in a basal rosette, are heart-shaped and up to 70mm (2$\frac{2}{3}$in) long; the stem-leaves are similar, but unstalked. The golden flower-heads are solitary, 50–60mm (2–2$\frac{2}{3}$in) in diameter. Native of SE Europe where it grows amongst shady mountain rocks. May–June.

DORYCNIUM (Leguminosae)

A small genus of about 12 species native to Mediterranean Europe and W Asia. The white or pinkish flowers are aggregated into heads. Modern authorities generally include the genus within *Lotus*.

Dorycnium hirsutum ○

A perennial herb or small shrublet, 20–50cm (8–20in) in height. The stems and leaves have long, spreading hairs, and the silvery leaves usually have 5 crowded leaflets. The flowers, 10–20mm ($\frac{2}{5}$–$\frac{4}{5}$in) long, are white or pink with a dark reddish-black keel borne in small, stalked clusters. S Europe. May–June.

DOUGLASIA (Primulaceae)

Very close to *Androsace*, indeed some authorities include it in *Androsace*. The genus contains 6 species, all native to NW North America, several of them also occurring in NE Siberia. They form tight cushions or mats of small leaf-rosettes which bear single or stalked umbels of pink to red flowers. The European *Vitaliana primuliflora* used to be known as *Douglasia vitaliana*.

Douglasia laevigata ○☆

Plants form domed mats of rosettes of dark green shiny lanceolate leaves, 5–20mm ($\frac{1}{5}$–$\frac{4}{5}$in) long. Up to 10 flowers are held in a tight umbel on a 20–70mm ($\frac{4}{5}$–$2\frac{3}{4}$in) long stalk. The corolla is deep pink to bright rose red, 10–18mm ($\frac{2}{5}$–$\frac{3}{4}$in) across; the lobes do not overlap. NW USA. June–July. This lovely species thrives in a well-drained gritty soil in a sunny position and comes readily from seed. Var. *aliolata* is somewhat larger and more vigorous.

DRABA (Cruciferae)

A large genus containing about 300 species widely scattered in the Northern Hemisphere, especially in temperate and Arctic regions, as well as on the mountains of South America. Whereas some are weedy annuals, the genus contains a number of delightful, cushion-forming perennials: some are easy to cultivate, others, like the choice grey-cushioned *D. mollissima*, are more difficult. These cushion species form cramped rosettes of leaves and generally bear small racemes of yellow or white flowers above the cushion. Most are grown in pans in the alpine house or in troughs or raised beds; they are quite hardy and there is no reason why more should not be tried on a scree in a well-drained sunny site. Those with woolly foliage require protection from winter rain—a sheet of glass or cloche placed overhead will do admirably. Propagation is easiest from seed.

Draba aizoides ○☆

This familiar yellow Whitlow Grass is a widespread species in the mountains of Europe. It forms small dense tufts or cushions of deep green, bristle-edged, lanceolate leaves. The bright lemon-yellow flowers are borne on leafless scapes 5–15cm (2–6in) long. April–May. Native of rocky and stony mountain habitats, generally on limestone, to 3,600m (11,800ft). One of the finest and easiest species for the beginner to try, even though variable.

Draba lasiocarpa (syn. *D. aizoon*) ○

Similar to the previous, but more robust, to 20cm (8in), with smaller deeper yellow flowers. The leaves are also rather broader. E and SE Alps. April–May.

Draba sauteri ○

Similar to *D. aizoides*, but smaller, rarely more than 50mm (2in) tall and laxly rosetted. E Alps. May.

Draba scardica ○

Like the previous, but flowers rather smaller, the fruits with a 3–7mm ($\frac{1}{8}$–$\frac{1}{4}$in) long point. Balkan mountains. April–May.

Draba athoa ○

Like a robust form of *D. aizoides*, but leaves bristly all over, not just along the margins. The fruits are also hairy (hairless in the latter). SE Europe, particularly Greece. Late March–April.

Draba rigida ○

Forms larger cushions than *D. aizoides*, bristly-margined leaves and dense heads of golden flowers on stems to 12cm ($4\frac{3}{4}$in) tall. E Turkey and neighbouring area. April–May.

Draba bryoides ○
A fine Caucasian species forming dense 50mm (2in) cushions, with slender-scaped racemes bearing a few small yellow flowers. April. Var. *impricata* (syn. *D. impricata*) has smaller and denser cushions, rarely exceeding 25mm (1in).

Draba polytricha ○
Another Armenian species. This one forms dense greyish or whitish, soft woolly cushions; the leaf-rosettes are tiny and cramped. The bright yellow flowers are borne above the cushion on wiry stalks, the whole plant often about 50mm (2in) tall. Late March–April. Good on a block of tufa or in a pan in the alpine house.

Draba mollissima ○▲
Another very attractive species forming domed mossy cushions up to 10cm (4in) across. The small flowers are lemon yellow, borne on long slender scapes. Caucasus. April–May. A connoisseur's plant, but worth trying out of doors on a raised bed or on a tufa block, providing plants are protected from winter wet.

Draba dedeana ○
Another dense cushion-forming species with grey-green leaves and small white flowers, 4–6mm ($\frac{1}{6}$–$\frac{1}{4}$in), borne on hairy, leafless scapes. N and E Spain. April–early May.

Draba hispanica ○
Rather like the previous, but flowers rather larger and yellow. E and S Spain. April.

Other species found occasionally in catalogues are *D. brunifolia, D. cossoniana, D. glacialis, D. haynaldii, D. longisiliqua, D. rosularis, D. stellata, D. norvegica* (syn. *D. rupestris*) and *D. repens*. None have any particular merits over those described, although they are useful additions to a specialist collection.

DRACOCEPHALUM (Labiatae)

A small genus of striking perennials widely distributed from Europe to Asia. They have upright stems with paired, generally aromatic leaves and flowers borne in dense whorls, forming stiff erect spikes. The flowers, like those of most labiates, have 2 lips. Those mentioned below are fairly amenable plants useful for their summer flowering. They can be propagated from seed or cuttings, or by division of the parent plant.

Dracocephalum grandiflorum ○☆
The Large-flowered Dragon-head hails from Siberia. It forms a neat tuft to 24cm (9½in) tall, though often less. The basal, heart-shaped leaves form a lax rosette, those on the stem are smaller and well spaced. The violet-blue flowers are large, 44–48mm (*c*. 2in) long, forming a rather dense spike. July–August.

Dracocephalum purdomii ○
A Chinese species not unlike the previous, but with smaller, purple, flowers borne during July and August.

Dracocephalum tanguticum ○☆
Another Chinese species, rather taller than *D. grandiflorum*, but distinguished by its neatly cut leaves and spikes of deep blue flowers. July–early September. Perhaps the finest species, with the added bonus of a pleasing fragrance.

Dryas octopetala

Dracocephalum austriacum ○
The Austrian Dragonhead is rare in cultivation, but it is a fine species with large violet-blue flowers. The leaves are divided into 3–5 narrow segments. A plant of grassy and rocky places in the W and C Alps. May–July.

DRYAS (Rosaceae)
The Mountain Avens are well-known carpeting subshrubs with leathery leaves, 8-petalled flowers and feathery fruit heads reminiscent of *Pulsatilla* and *Geum*. They are valuable plants for large rocks and ledges in the rock garden, hardy and easy to grow. They can be clipped back with care during the summer to keep them in check.

Dryas octopetala ○☆
The common Mountain Avens is a familiar plant on many European mountains, including Britain. The mats of deep green oval leaves (whitish beneath) can be extensive, the stems rooting down at intervals so that new plants are easy to

procure. The solitary white flowers are 30–40mm (1⅕–1⅗in) across with a central boss of yellow stamens. May–July, occasionally later. An easy and obliging alpine for sunny exposed places. 'Minor'—a finer plant for smaller rock gardens, being more compact.

Dryas drummondii ○
The North American equivalent of the previous species, similar in general appearance, but the flowers more nodding, and cream rather than white. The flowers tend not to open widely as they do in its European cousin. June–July. Less often seen in cultivation.

Dryas tomentosa ○
Similar to the previous species, but with rather hairy leaves and yellow flowers. North America—Rocky Mountains. June–July. Rare in cultivation.

ECHINOSPARTUM (Leguminosae)
Small spiny shrubs with trifoliate leaves and yellow flowers with inflated calyces which are 2-lipped. The genus contains only 3 species, native to SW Europe.

Echinospartum horridum (syn. *Genista horrida*) ○☆
A densely spiny shrublet, 25–40cm (10–16in) tall with grey-green silkily-hairy leaflets. The bright yellow flowers, 12–16mm (½–⅝in) long, are usually borne in pairs at the stem tips. Pyrenees and N Spain. In the wild a native of limestone rocks and stony meadows, to 1,800m (5,940ft).

EDRAIANTHUS (Campanulaceae)
A small primarily Mediterranean genus often mistaken for *Campanula*, but more closely allied to *Wahlenbergia* from which the species differ principally in their clustered, rather than solitary, flowers. Indeed the species are sometimes found in catalogues under both, or either, generic names. They thrive in sunny parts of the rock garden in well-drained gritty soils and can be propagated from seed or cuttings of short vegetative shoots struck in mid-summer.

Edraianthus graminifolius (syn. *E. ternifolius*) ○☆
A small tufted plant to 10cm (4in) tall, though often less, with slender grass-like leaves and clusters of blue-purple, narrow, erect bells on stems held just clear of the foliage. Yugoslavia, Albania and Greece. May–July. Probably the most widely grown species. In the wild, it is a plant of rocky mountain meadows and rock clefts; occasional white-flowered forms can be found. Wild seed produces varying offspring.

Subsp. *niveus* (syn. *E. niveus*) with deep green, grassy leaves and pure white flowers is very rare in cultivation, but well worth seeking out. Yugoslavia. July–August.

Edraianthus dalmaticus ○
About the same size as *E. graminifolius*, but with tufts of greyish-green leaves and purple flowers. W Yugoslavia. June–August.

Edraianthus pumilio (syn. *Wahlenbergia pumilio*) ○☆
The gem of the genus for all alpine enthusiasts. Plants are low, rarely more than 60mm (2½in) tall and forming a compact tuft of slender silvery-grey leaves. The violet flower clusters practically hide the foliage. Yugoslavia. June–August.

EMPETRUM (Empetraceae)

A small genus of some 10 species distributed in temperate and arctic regions of the northern hemisphere and South America. Only one is generally cultivated, thriving best on an acid moist soil. Propagation by cuttings is the usual means of increase.

Empetrum nigrum ○◑□
The Crowberry is a familiar plant of northern moors and bogs—a small heath-like plant to 15cm (6in) forming a congested mat of wiry stems covered in small dark green narrow-oblong leaves. The small flowers are pink or purplish, 1–2mm ($\frac{1}{16}$in) across, solitary or in small lateral clusters. The fruit is a small, juicy, black berry, only occasionally produced in cultivation. Widely distributed in the northern hemisphere. May–June. Some forms have hermaphrodite flowers, others have male and female flowers on separate plants.

EPIGAEA (Ericaceae)

A genus of 3 prostrate, creeping, evergreen shrubs, 2 from Asia, 1 from North America. They have alternate leaves and 5-parted flowers. The fruit is a fleshy, hairy, 5-valved capsule. All the species in this genus have a reputation for being difficult to keep going in cultivation. However, they are delightful plants worth persisting with; a cool peaty soil with added leaf-mould suits them admirably, but they must be shielded from strong sunlight and positively hate any trace of lime. Propagation generally by layering, or seed when available.

Epigaea asiatica ◑□
The easiest of the species is mat-forming and only a few centimetres in height, with leathery leaves and 3–6 flowered terminal and axillary racemes of narrow bell-shaped, fragrant, pink flowers on 10–20mm ($\frac{2}{5}$–$\frac{4}{5}$in) long stalks. Japan. April. The most suitable species for the novice to attempt to grow.

Epigaea repens ◑□▲
The Trailing Arbutus, or Mayflower, has large glossy-green, bristly leaves and dense clusters of pink or white funnel-shaped flowers. North America. May. It is more demanding in cultivation than *E. asiatica* and is not reliably hardy, but is very free-flowering once established. Only occasionally offered in catalogues.

   Epigaea × *intertexta* is a hybrid between *E. asiatica* and *E. repens*, rather resembling the former, but with larger flowers; 'Aurora'—the only cultivar.

Epigaea gaultherioides ◑□▲
This species is occasionally offered in catalogues, often under the name *Orphanidesia gaultherioides*, once separated as a monotypic genus, now considered to be synonymous with *Epigaea*. It is a fine evergreen, mat-former with large oval leaves and large pale rose flowers to 25mm (1in) across with 5 widely flaring lobes. E Turkey and adjoining region. March–April. It is not fully hardy except in mild moist areas.

EPILOBIUM (Onagraceae)

Most gardeners spend a great deal of time ridding their borders of various noxious weedy willowherbs, so it is often difficult to persuade them that one or two well deserve a place on the rock garden. This genus contains over 200 species scattered in temperate and arctic regions of both hemispheres. They all have 4-petalled flowers and characteristic fruits with silky-plumed seeds which are carried by the wind. Propagation by division, cuttings, or from seed.

Epilobium obcordatum ○◐☆
Perhaps the finest for the rock garden, forming an entanglement of spreading wiry stems to 12cm (5in) tall. The bright green leaves are oval and the relatively large rose-pink flowers have a protruding deep red style. SW USA. Late June–August.

Epilobium glabellum ○
Plants to 15cm (6in) tall, the stems with scattered pairs of oval leaves. The creamy-white, occasionally pink, flowers are borne in succession throughout the summer. New Zealand. Late June–September. 'Sulphureum'—unusual with its soft yellow flowers.

Epilobium kai-koense ○◐
Another dwarf species, up to 12cm (5in) tall with erect stems bearing pairs of small rounded or oval leaves. The flowers are rose-pink. Japan. July–September.

Epilobium dodonaei ○◐
A larger species, patch-forming, with spreading stems 30cm (8in) tall, bearing numerous narrow-lanceolate, grey-green, slightly hairy leaves. The flowers are large, 20–25mm ($\frac{4}{5}$–1in) across, deep rose-pink and borne in long racemes. Alps and Apennines. June–July. An attractive plant once established, but not always easy to please. In the wild it is an inhabitant of rocky places, gravels and moraines, to 1,500m (4,950ft) altitude.

ERANTHIS (Ranunculaceae)
The Winter Aconites are familiar harbingers of spring, unfurling their cheerful bright yellow flowers the moment temperatures begin to rise at the end of the winter. The genus contains a handful of species distributed from Europe to Asia. Those commonly cultivated tend to look very similar, indeed some botanists place the two common species in a single one. They are easy garden plants succeeding on most garden soils, but best in a moist, well-drained loam in partial shade. They are generally bought as dried tubers, but can be transplanted the moment the flowers fade.

Eranthis hyemalis ○◐☆
The common Winter Aconite bears flowers 20–30mm ($\frac{4}{5}$–1$\frac{1}{5}$in) across, each with 5–7 yellow sepals and surrounded by a ruff of cut shiny green leaves. The basal leaves arise on long stalks after the flowers are over. C and W Europe, but widely naturalized elsewhere. February–March. Plants seed around prolifically once they have become established.

Eranthus cilicicus ○◐☆
The E European and W Asian equivalent of the previous species which differs primarily in having more finely cut foliage and flowers usually with more sepals. The flowers are often tinged with bronze on the outside as are the leaves. Like *E. hyemalis*, plants reach 8–10cm (3–4in) tall. February–March. There is a widely grown hybrid between the two species, *E* × *tubergenii*, distinguished by its rather larger, deep yellow flowers. The finest cultivar is 'Guinea Gold', which, unfortunately is rather difficult to obtain.

ERICA (Ericaceae)

The heathers comprise a genus of over 500 species with 2 centres of distribution, one being the Cape Province of South Africa, where the vast majority of the species occur, the other being Europe. Ericas are all dwarf to medium-sized evergreen shrubs or subshrubs, of which only comparatively few species are grown out-of-doors in temperate regions. However, this paucity of hardy species is more than made up for by the diversity of form and colour in the innumerable cultivars and hybrids which are commercially available. A small selection of easily obtainable forms is given after each description. Ericas have whorls of 3–6 needle-like leaves and 4–5 parted flowers in few- to many-flowered, axillary or terminal umbels, racemes or panicles. The corollas are white, pink, or rarely yellowish, cylindrical, bell or urn-shaped, generally with short lobes. Most are readily grown, requiring peaty or sandy acid soil, although the forms of *E. herbacea* (*E. carnea*) are lime tolerant. Propagation from cuttings.

Erica ciliaris ○□

The Dorset Heath is not confined to that county of England, but also occurs in France, Spain and Portugal. It forms a straggly, glandular shrub 30–80cm (1–2¾ft) in height with the leaves soft in texture and whitish beneath. The long, rosy-purple, pitcher-shaped flowers, 8–12mm (⅓–½in) long, are borne in terminal racemes. July–October. Crosses between *E. ciliaris* and *E. tetralix* have resulted in some very attractive hybrids which are well worth trying: 'Corfe Castle'—clear salmon-pink flowers and mid-green leaves; 'Mrs C. H. Gill'—small, but abundant reddish-purple flowers and dark green leaves; 'Stoborough'—a vigorous grower with long racemes of large white flowers and pale green leaves; 'White Wings'— a fine form with pure white flowers and deep green leaves.

Erica tetralix ○□

The Cross-leaved Heath grows to 30cm (12in) tall. The silvery-grey leaves are in whorls of 4; the flowers are soft pink, urn-shaped, borne in dense terminal clusters on the current season's growth. Europe. June–October. Choice forms are: 'Alba Mollis'—an erect, compact plant with silver leaves, greener with age, and pure white flowers; 'Con Underwood'—neat, erect and free-flowering with grey-green leaves and crimson flowers; 'Hookstone Pink'—erect, loose growth becoming denser as plants mature, light silver leaves and pale rose-pink flowers with deeper pink tips.

Erica cinerea ○□

This is the familiar Bell Heather of the British moorlands. Plants have a rather lax habit, 15–75cm (1½–2½ft) tall. The leaves are in whorls of 3. The rosy-purple flowers occur in terminal racemes or umbels with numerous short leafy shoots developing beneath the inflorescence. Europe. May–September. 'Alba Minor'—abundant white flowers and pale apple-green leaves on a small, compact plant; 'Atroru-bens'—bright red flowers in long racemes; Coccinea'—a dwarf plant with green foliage and bright red flowers; 'C. D. Eason'—leaves deep green on a neat, free-growing plant, the flowers lilac-pink; 'Eden Valley'—a low spreading bush with light green leaves and abundant, lilac, white-based flowers; 'Golden Drop'—a foliage plant with golden to copper and red leaves, and rarely-produced pink flowers; 'Golden Hue'—golden leaves turning red in winter; 'P. S. Patrick'—erect and free-flowering with deep, glossy green leaves and rich purple flowers; 'Rosea'—bright pink flowers.

Erica vagans ○☆
The Cornish Heath is a native of SW Europe, including SW England. It is a neat, fast-growing, dwarf, spreading shrub with leaves in whorls of 4 or 5. Even small plants are very free-flowering and the dense inflorescence is composed of small flowers with protruding anthers which remain on the plant throughout the winter. May–August. This species is more tolerant of lime than most, but prefers a heavier, peaty soil. 'Lyonesse'—a tall, erect, floriferous plant with, fresh green leaves and white flowers with brown anthers; 'Mrs D. F. Maxwell'—a neat, bushy form with dark, glossy green leaves and cerise to dark red flowers; 'St Keverne'—produces fresh, vivid green leaves and abundant bright pink flowers.

Erica herbacea ○▯
A more familiar, though incorrect, name for this plant is *E. carnea*, and both names are listed in catalogues. One of the most popular small, winter-flowering shrubs in cultivation, forming a low, spreading, evergreen shrub, 15–25cm (6–10in) in height. It has whorls of 4 linear leaves and the rose-pink, urn-shaped flowers are borne in one-sided racemes. C and S Europe. December–April. One of the best species thriving equally well on acid or calcareous soils. 'Aurea'—bright gold leaves and flowers deep pink fading to white; 'Foxhollow'—a low, vigorous plant with pale yellow-green leaves deepening in winter to reddish-yellow, and white flowers deepening to pink; 'King George'—compact with dark, shining green leaves and deep pink flowers; 'Myretoun Ruby'—very dark green leaves and rich pink-red flowers; 'Springwood White'—vigorous trailing growth with bright green leaves and large white flowers with exerted brown anthers; 'Springwood Pink'—vigorous and spreading with mid-green leaves and white to pink flowers; 'Vivellii'—bronzed foliage and dark crimson-red flowers.

Erica × *darleyensis (E. herbacea* × *E. erigena)* ○
This is a floriferous, easily grown, vigorous hybrid in all its forms, attaining 30–36cm (12–15in), having typically bright rose-pink flowers. It rarely needs trimming and is the most easily suited of the heathers, surviving on the poorest of soils. 'Arthur Johnson'—pale green leaves, colourful juvenile growth and long racemes of bright mauve-pink flowers; 'George Rendall'—a good rich pink-flowered form; 'Jack H. Brummage'—leaves pale yellow or golden-green with a red tint, the juvenile growth yellow and pink and flowers deep pink (this form benefits from light trimming after flowering); 'Silberschmelze'—a neat plant with deep glossy green leaves and fragrant silver-white flowers with brown anthers.

ERIGERON (Compositae)
A genus of over 200 species of annual, biennial and perennial herbs, mostly native of North America. Although closely related to *Aster*, they are distinguishable from them by having slender ray-florets in several close whorls rather than a single ring. The disc-florets are nearly always yellow though the rays vary from pink through lilac to blue and purple. Most of those cultivated are indifferent to soil type and will thrive in any well-drained position, as long as maximum exposure to the sun is guaranteed. They are easily propagated from seed or by division of the parent plant.

Erigeron alpinus ○

The Alpine Fleabane is a native of N Europe with hairy lanceolate leaves arranged in a basal cluster. From these arise the slender stems, 15–20cm (6–8in) long, bearing attractive flower-heads of mauvish-pink and yellow, 20–30mm ($\frac{4}{5}$–1$\frac{1}{5}$in) across. June–August. A species of meadows and rocky habitats in the wild, from 1,500–3,500m (4,950–11,500ft) altitude.

Erigeron uniflorus ○☆

A fine plant with small clusters of spoon-shaped leaves and solitary flower-heads borne on stems 50–70mm (2–2$\frac{3}{4}$in) tall. The flower-heads are white, less commonly pink or mauve, the florets surrounded by a ring of purplish, woolly bracts. Mountains of Europe, N Asia and North America. July–August. A delicate little plant succeeding well on screes.

Erigeron aurantiacus ○

This species is native to W Asia, coming from Turkestan, where it forms clumps of bright green leaves, with equally leafy stems to 30cm (12in) tall. The relatively large flower-heads are a rich orange. June–August. Only really suitable for larger rock gardens because of its height, but the striking flowers make it most worthwhile.

Erigeron karvinskianus (*E. mucronatus* of gardens) ○◑☆

Another North American native which is widely naturalized in much of Europe and certainly worthy of cultivation. The flower-heads are numerous and are roughly the same size and shape as the common white daisy, often pink-tinged on the exterior. The stems are much-branched to form lax tufts 8–15cm (3–6in) tall. June–October. A delightful little plant ideal on a dry wall or in paving, but generally too invasive for the average rock garden.

ERINACEA (Leguminosae)

The genus takes its name from the Latin for hedgehog-like, in allusion to the spiny nature of the plant. It contains only one species, native to SW Europe and NW Africa.

Erinacea anthyllis (syn. *E. pungens*) ○☆

A spiny shrublet to about 30cm (12in) in height, forming dense tussocks. The branchlets are greyish-green, smooth and spine-tipped and the leaves are simple or trifoliate, deciduous. The blue-violet pea-like flowers, 16–18mm ($\frac{1}{2}$–$\frac{3}{4}$in) long, are borne in profusion in small clusters held just below the branch tips. May–June. A splendid rock plant preferring a sunny aspect and calcareous soils, although it is slow growing at first. Young plants often require some winter protection until they become properly established. Plants can be propagated from seed, when available.

ERINUS (Scrophulariaceae)

A genus of only 8 species, mostly native to South Africa, but with one indigenous to the mountainous regions of W Europe, where it occurs on rocky screes and stony grassland. All are perennials with alternate, divided leaves and flowers in short racemes. Readily propagated from seed.

Erinus alpinus ○▢☆

A very pretty, tufted plant only 50–70mm (2–2$\frac{3}{4}$in) high, with narrow-oblong, toothed leaves mostly held in basal rosettes. The racemes of rosy-purple, slightly

2-lipped, flowers are borne in profusion. W Europe. May–July. Several named colour forms exist including: var. *albus*—flowers white; 'Abbotswood Pink'; 'Mrs C. Boyle'—pure pink flowers; 'Dr Hanaele'—bright crimson flowers. Easily cultivated in a gritty soil, becoming naturalized from self-sown seed which are produced liberally.

ERIOPHYLLUM (Compositae)

A small genus of herbaceous perennials native to W North America which so far has only provided one species suitable for the rock garden. The stems and leaves are covered in a white mat of woolly hairs.

Eriophyllum lanatum ○☆
A sun-loving perennial with greyish-white hairy leaves, arranged alternately along the 5–20cm (2–8in) long stems. The small flower-heads are surrounded by dense woolly hairs and are about 20mm (⅘in) across, the florets a rich lemon-yellow, contrasting well with the grey foliage. NW North America where it is known as Oregon Sunshine. May–June.

ERODIUM (Geraniaceae)

A genus of about 90 species occurring in many parts of the temperate world, commonly referred to as Storksbills because of their long-beaked fruits. *Erodium* is closely related to *Geranium*, but differs from it by having pinnately divided, rather than palmately lobed, leaves and spirally twisted fruits. Many species are well suited to sunny places in troughs and in the rock garden and a few are widely available in the trade. Most are readily propagated by seed and may naturally increase in this way if left unattended.

Erodium chrysanthum ○☆
One of the most attractive species with basal clumps of finely divided silvery foliage from which the flower branches arise. The bright yellow flowers are one of the distinguishing features of this species, which is also unusual in having male and female flowers on separate plants. A native of S Greece where it occurs in open stony places on calcareous soils. May–June. Worth growing for its foliage alone.

Erodium reichardii (syn. *E. chamaedrioides*) ○☆
Another attractive species which has been cultivated since the eighteenth century, following its introduction from Mallorca. Plants form dense soft cushions of neat oval, toothed leaves. The flowers are borne very close to the foliage and vary in colour from white to rose-pink with purplish veins. Three cultivars are regularly offered: 'Album'—has white flowers; 'Roseum'—pale pink flowers; 'Merstham Pink'—deep rose coloured flowers. All June–July.

Erodium guttatum ○☆
A colourful and floriferous species forming a spreading plant up to 60cm (2ft) across, becoming rather woody at the base with age. The grey-green softly hairy leaves are heart-shaped and neatly toothed. The flowers are basically white, but with a prominent dark blotch on the upper two petals. SW Europe. June–September.

Erodium daucoides ○
Another European alpine species, occasionally offered for sale. It is well worth growing for its dense mats of rich green, finely divided foliage and delightful lilac

and white flowers which are delicately veined with deep purple and carried on short stalks, 5–10cm (2–4in) long. Spain. June–July.

ERYSIMUM (Cruciferae)

A large genus with some 100 species, including *Cheiranthus*, scattered across Europe and Asia, especially in temperate regions. They are annuals or short-lived perennials with slender, toothed or untoothed leaves and attractive racemes of yellow or purple flowers. They can be propagated from seed or cuttings. The named forms should be propagated only from cuttings as some produce variable offspring, seldom as good as the parent. Most require a sunny site and a well-drained soil. Most tend to become woody and straggly with age and need to be replaced regularly.

Erysimum cheiri (syn. *Cheiranthus cheiri*) ○☆
The Wallflower is well known and requires no description here. Most forms are unsuitable for the rock garden, being more generally used for spring bedding displays. 'Harpur Crewe'—only 30cm (12in) tall with double yellow, sweetly fragrant flowers.

Erysimum alpinum ○☆
A small wallflower only 15cm (6in) tall with narrow lanceolate, deep green leaves and condensed racemes of sulphur-yellow, fragrant flowers. Scandinavia. May–June. 'Moonlight'—a beautiful form with bright primrose-yellow flowers, taller than the type; 'Sunbright'—another good cultivar.

Erysimum helveticum (syn. *E. pumilum*) ○☆
A charming little tufted plant to 25cm (10in) tall, though often less. The leaves are grey-green and the 12–16mm ($\frac{1}{2}$–$\frac{5}{8}$in) flowers lemon-yellow. Pyrenees and Alps. April–July, but spasmodically almost throughout the year. The dwarfer forms (generally sold as *E. pumilum*), some only 60–80mm (2$\frac{1}{2}$–3in) tall, are worth seeking out. 'Aurantiacum'—orange-yellow flowers. *Erysimum rupestris* from Turkey is very similar, but taller.

Erysimum capitatum ○
A small, rather woody plant to 25cm (10in) tall with narrow deep green leaves and large condensed clusters of pale yellow flowers. W USA. May–July. A floriferous species.

Erysimum asperum ○
An unusual W USA species which is often biennial, though some cultivated forms are more reliably perennial. Plants grow to about 20cm (8in) tall, occasionally more, and bear yellow flowers suffused with copper. May–June.

Erysimum linifolium ○☆
A beautiful plant like a slender wallflower, to 30cm (12in) tall, sometimes more, with grey-green foliage and slender racemes of lilac flowers. Spain and Portugal. May–July, occasionally later. Easily raised from cuttings, but not completely hardy—requires a warm sheltered site. 'Bowles Mauve'—leaves suffused with grey-mauve and flowers deep mauve, fading with age; 'Variegata'—leaves variegated.

Erysimum mutabile ○
Similar to the previous, it hails from the cliffs of Crete up to an altitude of 1,000m (3,300ft). The flowers range from pale yellow to buff and mauve-purple, often all on the same raceme. May–July.

Various named cultivars are available from nurseries listed either under *Cheiranthus* or *Erysimum*. Their parentage is often unclear: 'Chequers'; 'Cream Beauty'; 'Dwarf Yellow'; 'Jubilee Gold'; 'Orange Flame'; 'Sprite'. All ○.

EUNOMIA (Cruciferae)

A charming little genus of 2 species which hail from the mountains of Turkey. They are related to *Aethionema* and should be treated in a similar manner.

Eunomia oppositifolia (syn. *Aethionema oppositifolia*) ○
A greyish prostrate perennial with numerous small, rather fleshy, paired oval leaves. The pink flowers are borne in condensed terminal racemes. The whole plant may reach 10–12cm (4–5in) tall in flower. June–July. Rather rare in cultivation and perhaps not hardy in colder districts. Worth a try when available.

EUPHORBIA (Euphorbiaceae)

A very large and diverse genus which contains the familiar spurges of our gardens. There are some 2,000 species scattered in many parts of the world. Many of those from the arid tropics are succulent, spiny and cactus-like. The herbaceous types have the familiar flower clusters surrounded by consipicuous green or yellowish bracts. Some of the larger hardy herbaceous ones are very statuesque, but alas too large for the average rock garden. All have milky juice. Propagation from seed or by mid-summer cuttings struck in a sand peat mixture.

Euphorbia mysinites ○☆
The finest species for the rock garden. Plants have rather sprawling stems decked with numerous bluish-grey fleshy leaves. The large flower-heads are bright yellowish-green. S Europe. Widespread in the mediterranean region. May–July. The stems die having flowered and fruited and should then be cut away to encourage plenty of new growths. Thrives best on a poor, well-drained soil, in full sun.

Euphorbia rigida ○
Similar, but larger and with erect stems to 40cm (16in) SE Europe. May–July. Less hardy than the previous species, requiring a sheltered site.

Euphorbia cyparissias ○◗
The so-called Cypress Spurge has erect leafy growths reminiscent of tiny fir trees. Plants form spreading tufts to 30cm (12in) tall, with numerous linear leaves and oblong heads of golden yellow flowers and bracts. Europe (including Britain). April–June. Can become invasive.

Where space permits other species should be considered such as *E. hyberna*, *E. polychroma* and *E. sikkimensis*.

EURYOPS (Compositae)

An interesting genus of about 70 species of evergreen shrubs or, less commonly, annual or perennial herbs, distributed from Arabia to southern Africa. They are characterized by having large yellow or orange daisy flower-heads. Most are too tender to survive long periods of frost and can only be successfully grown within the protection of an alpine house. However, one species is relatively hardy and makes an attractive and welcome addition to the rock garden.

Euryops acraeus (syn. *E. evansii*) ○☆
A shrubby perennial only fairly recently introduced from the Drakensberg mountains of Natal. Its well-branched stems are without leaves for much of their length and form low domes up to 30cm (12in). The leaves are crowded towards the tips of the stems and are greyish-green in colour, 3-toothed at the apex. The bright yellow flower-heads, 20–25mm ($\frac{4}{5}$–1in) across, are borne on 40mm ($1\frac{1}{2}$in) long stems from the upper leaf axils. May–June. Hardier than generally supposed. Old bushes tend to get rather straggly, but young plants are easily raised from summer cuttings or layerings. Requires full sunshine.

FIBIGIA (Cruciferae)

A small genus with 14 species from S and SE Europe and W Asia; related to *Alyssum*.

Fibigia clypeata (syn. *Farsetia clypeata*) ○
A tufted perennial herb, 30–70cm (12–28in) tall, with grey or grey-green woolly oblong leaves. The flowers, 9–12mm ($\frac{3}{8}$–$\frac{1}{2}$in) across, are bright yellow, borne in long racemes which lengthen when in fruit. The flattened fruits are elliptical, 14mm ($\frac{3}{5}$in) long or more. S and SE Europe. June–July. The dwarfer forms are worth seeking out. Requires a sunny, well-drained site on the rock garden.

FRANKENIA (Frankeniaceae)

A small genus of attractive subshrubs or perennials frequently referred to as the sea heaths, for they somewhat resemble heathers and generally inhabit coastal areas, although some favour inland salty regions. There are some 80 species in the genus, scattered in the northern hemisphere in temperate and subtropical regions. Propagation by division or summer cuttings.

Frankenia thymifolia ○☆
The finest species forming a low tufted mat to 80mm (3in) tall, with slender branched stems bearing numerous small, grey, triangular, hairy leaves; the stems become wiry with age. The tiny pink flowers are borne in small clusters. Spain and NW Africa. July–August.

Frankenia laevis ○
Another prostrate plant with wiry, reddish-brown stems. The linear leaves are slightly hairy and mostly borne on short lateral shoots. The pink flowers, 5mm ($\frac{1}{5}$in) across, are solitary. Europe to W Asia, including S Britain. July–August.

GALAX (Diapensiaceae)

There is only one species of *Galax*, which is native to North America. It is a tough perennial plant forming clumps of leathery, glossy, evergreen leaves, which in autumn become tinted with reddish-bronze. The inflorescences are spike-like with white flowers having 5 small oblong petals. The stamens are united into a tube which has 10 teeth, only 5 of which carry anthers. The fruit is a 3-celled capsule.

Galax urceolata (syn. *G. aphylla*) ○◑☐
The almost round or heart-shaped leaves are 5–10cm (2–4in) in diameter and are overtopped by slender 20–45cm (8–18in) stems, densely packed with small stemless white flowers, each less than 5mm (⅕in) across. E USA. June–August.

× GAULNETTYA (Ericaceae)

This genus is a result of several different crosses between *Gaultheria* and *Pernettya*. The cultivar 'Wisley Pearl' arose in cultivation and is often offered in catalogues as × *G. wisleyensis*, but this name has never been validated. The 2 genera are known to hybridize in the wild also. The correct, valid name for the genus, published in 1937, is × *Gaulnettya* × *Gaulthettya* is a synonym of × *Gaulnettya*.

× *Gaulnettya* 'Wisley Pearl' ◑☐
Plants form a neat, evergreen shrub 30cm (12in) or more in height, spreading by suckers, with 20–30mm (⅘–1⅕in) long leaves and long glandular racemes of white urn-shaped flowers. Fruits a fleshy, red-purple berry. May–June.

GAULTHERIA (Ericaceae)

A genus comprising 100–200 species of erect or prostrate, evergreen shrubs occurring naturally in Asia, Australasia and the New World. The leaves are alternate, usually more or less toothed. The flowers are solitary or in lax, axillary, racemes or panicles, the corolla urn- to bell-shaped; fruits often edible, berry-like. Very like *Vaccinium*, but easily distinguished by the relative positions of calyx and ovary. Gaultherias mostly require peaty acid soils and semi-shaded or woodland conditions. The smaller ones are useful peat-garden plants. Propagation by cuttings or layerings.

Gaultheria procumbens ◑☐☆
The North American Partridge or Checkerberry, also known as Canada Tea or Creeping Wintergreen, is the most familiar of the Gaultherias and the hardiest of the cultivated species. It is a creeping shrub which rarely exceeds 15cm (6in) in height, with crowded, glossy, aromatic leaves. The solitary nodding flowers are white flushed pink and are followed by comparatively large, bright red berries. July–August. Variegated plants are also known.

Gaultheria hookeri ◑☐
A popular, free-flowering species from Nepal, forming a dense tuft to 30cm (12in) in height and spreading by underground runners. Flowers white, succeeded by blue fruits. July–September.

Gaultheria miqueliana ◑☐
A plant 15–30cm (6–12in) in height, with a spread of up to 1m (3ft). It produces round, white flowers in early summer followed by edible, white, often pink-tinged, fruits. June–July. Very like *G. cuneata*, but with a hairless ovary.

Gaultheria cuneata ◑☐☆
A fully hardy, ground-covering species from China, which forms a creeping, compact shrub about 30cm (12in) high. Leaves leathery. Flowers white, in axillary, 10–30mm (⅖–1⅕in) long, racemes near the branch-tips. Fruit white, globose. June. It closely resembles *G. miqueliana*, but has a silky ovary.

Gaultheria trichophylla ◐☐
A densely tufted prostrate subshrub, a few centimetres in height, with crowded finely toothed leaves, solitary pink flowers and bright blue berries. Himalaya and W China. June–July. Unfortunately, fruits are not always freely produced in cultivation and sometimes not at all. *G. thymifolia* is very similar, but less common in gardens.

Gaultheria depressa ◐☐
A New Zealand species forming cushions woody at the base. The rounded leaves turn bronze late in the year. The pink and white flowers are succeeded by scarlet berries.

Gaultheria nummularioides ◐☐☆
A prostrate subshrub with many interlacing branches, covered in small oval leaves. The small pink flowers are succeeded by bluish-black berries. Himalaya and W China. June–July. Two particularly fine dwarf forms have been named 'Minor' and 'Minuta'.

Other small species sometimes listed by nurseries are *G. adenothrix* from Japan, *G. humifusa* from South America, *G. merilliana* from Taiwan, *G. pyrolifolia* from the E Himalaya and *G. sinensis* from S China and Burma.

GENISTA (Leguminosae)
Spiny or thornless shrublets with pale- to golden-yellow (rarely white) pea-like flowers, these usually borne in heads or racemes, or in small lateral clusters. The genus contains about 85 species native to Europe, the Canary Islands, North Africa and W Asia. Some of the species are evergreen, but many have deciduous leaves or are essentially leafless. Unlike its close relative, *Cytisus*, the genus has seeds without fleshy appendages. Species prefer well-drained soils and warm sunny positions in the garden. Plants can be propagated from cuttings or seed.

Genista tinctoria ○
Dyer's Greenweed was once valued for the deep yellow dye extracted from it. A very variable species forming an erect, thornless, deciduous shrublet, sometimes attaining 1m (3ft) or more in height. The leaves are simple, variable in shape and hairiness. The yellow pea-like flowers, each 8–15mm ($\frac{1}{3}$–$\frac{3}{5}$in) long, are borne in leafy terminal racemes, these sometimes aggregated together. May–August. Various dwarf, compact cultivars are available commercially although some of the names are rather obscure; 'Humifusa'—bright yellow flowers in terminal clusters; 'Florepleno'—a spreading shrub with double, deep-yellow flowers.

Genista januensis ○
A thornless species. Dwarf forms, rarely attaining 10cm (4in) in height, are generally grown in gardens. The stems and branchlets are usually 3-angled and the simple leaves hairless. The bright yellow flowers, each 10mm ($\frac{2}{5}$in) long, are borne in leafy racemes. June–July. Plants thrive best in a calcareous soil.

Genista lydia ○☆
A spreading green-stemmed thornless shrub with arching branches to about 60cm (24in) tall. The rather inconspicuous leaves are almost hairless and untoothed. The bright yellow flowers are 10–12mm ($\frac{2}{5}$–$\frac{1}{2}$in) long and borne in short racemes on

lateral branches. May–June. One of the loveliest and most popular shrubs for the rock garden. It looks at its best when allowed to hang over a large rock or wall.

Genista sericea ○☆
A dwarf thornless shrublet to 25cm (10in) in height with slender branchlets and simple silver-haired leaves. The golden-yellow flowers, 10–14mm ($\frac{2}{5}$–$\frac{3}{5}$in) long, are borne in terminal clusters of 2–5. SE Alps. May–June. In the wild this is a plant of rocky slopes to 1,300m (4,290ft) altitude. Deserves to be more widely grown in gardens.

Genista pulchella (syn. *G. villarsii*) ○
A spreading, thornless or weakly spiny shrublet, often forming compact mats little over 50mm (2in) in height. The young grooved branchlets and the simple leaves are grey with silky hairs. The golden-yellow flowers, 7–10mm ($\frac{1}{4}$–$\frac{2}{5}$in) long, are borne in leafy racemes. June.

Genista pilosa ○☆
A dwarf, thornless, creeping, prostrate shrublet to 15cm (6in) tall in cultivation (taller in the wild) and often with a spread of about 1m (3ft). The simple, dark green leaves are silkily hairy on the lower surface. The clear yellow flowers, *c*. 10mm ($\frac{2}{5}$in) long, are borne in great profusion, generally in short leafy racemes. A species tolerant of poor soils and rather adverse conditions. Europe. (April) May–July. 'Minor'—a prostrate form with a tangled mass of whip-like shoots.

Genista aspalathoides ○
An erect spiny shrub to about 10cm (4in) in height with grooved branchlets, hairy when young, but smooth and spine-tipped at maturity. The leaves are mostly trifoliate with narrow grey leaflets. The pale yellow flowers, 10–12mm ($\frac{2}{5}$–$\frac{1}{2}$in) long, are borne in lax leafy racemes. May–June.

Genista sylvestris (syn. *G. dalmatica*) ○
A dwarf shrub forming compact hummocks 15–30cm (6–12in) in height, weakly spined, and occasionally semi-prostrate and rock-hugging. The simple, dark green linear leaves are almost hairless and the bright golden-yellow flowers, 7–8mm ($\frac{1}{3}$in) long, are borne in long, lax terminal racemes. June–July.

Genista hispanica ○
The Spanish Broom is a densely branched shrublet to 30cm (12in) tall, but spreading more widely. The branches bear numerous, rather weak spines and simple leaves. The golden-yellow flowers, 6–8mm ($\frac{1}{4}$–$\frac{1}{3}$in) long, are borne in smaller clusters. E Pyrenees and N Spain. May–July. 'Compacta'—as the name suggests is a smaller more neatly rounded form. An easy and adaptable species.

Genista sagittalis (syn. *Chamaespartium sagittale*) ○◑☆
The Winged Greenweed is a dwarf, thornless, mat-forming subshrub with prostrate stems from which arise the ascending and herbaceous flowering branches. The rich green young branches are characteristically winged and flattened, and bear sparse simple leaves. The bright yellow flowers, 10–12mm ($\frac{2}{5}$–$\frac{1}{2}$in) long, are borne in dense terminal racemes. Mountains of C and S Europe. May–July. An easy and floriferous plant for the rock garden, spreading widely in time, and suitable for sunny or semi-shaded situations. In the wild a plant of mountain woodland and open rocky and grassy places, to 1,950m (6,400ft).

Genista delphinensis is sometimes recognized as a subspecies of *G. sagittalis* and is occasionally available commercially under its species name. It has a more prostrate habit and zig-zagged, winged stems with smaller flowers.

GENTIANA (Gentianaceae)

A large and beautiful genus much sought after by alpine gardeners. The genus has a world-wide distribution, but mainly restricted to mountain regions. Many are noted for their intense pure blue flowers and for the elegant trumpet shapes of many of the species. In most species the corolla tube has 5 lobes with additional lobe-like structures, known as plicae, alternating with the main lobes. All gentians have opposite, hairless, untoothed leaves and many die down to a resting bud in winter. Ease of cultivation varies very much, but all species thrive best if firmly planted in well-drained moisture-retentive soil, which should never be allowed to dry out. In general, European and New Zealand species enjoy full sun in any good well-drained soil, but Asiatic species usually prefer an acid peaty soil in light shade, although some do not mind full sun, provided plenty of moisture is available. Propagation in nearly all cases is easy from seed and by division. Cuttings taken in summer often provide a ready means of increase, as for example with *G. septemfida, G. sino-ornata* and related species and hybrids, and the Spring Gentian, *G. verna.*

Gentiana acaulis (syn. *G. kochiana*) ○☆

This is the well-known Trumpet Gentian of the European Mountains, the symbol of the Alpine Garden Society. Many people grow it, but not very many manage to bring it into full flower. This temperamental behaviour remains a mystery and a challenge. It forms flat, evergreen mats of rosettes of crowded, firm, elliptic leaves, from which rise short, upright stems with large solitary funnel-shaped flowers of an intense deep blue, speckled with brownish-green bands inside the tube. It requires very firm planting, best in well-drained heavy soil in full sun. If it fails to flower, try a range of different positions in the garden. Mountains of C and S Europe where it is a feature of rocky and grassy meadows to 3,000m (10,800ft). March–June. A must for every rock garden, despite not succeeding in all gardens.

G. alpina, G. angustifolia, G. clusii, G. dinarica and G. occidentalis are closely related, but less easily obtained.

Gentiana asclepiadea ◑

The Willow-leaved Gentian. A large but graceful species, with leafy erect or arching stems to 60cm (24in) tall. The 5–8cm (2–3in) long leaves are unstalked, oval and pointed. The flowers are borne 1–3 at a time in the leaf axils; the 30–50mm (1⅕–2in) long narrow trumpets are azure blue with darker striping outside and with reddish-purple spots within. C and S Europe and W Asia. July–September. Plants grow best in damp peaty soil in partial shade and are easy to cultivate. The corolla colour is variable, and a white form is known; however, one should select good forms.

Gentiana gracilipes (syn. *G. purdomii*) ◑▢

This pretty species forms a rosette of narrow, pointed, dark green leaves, to 15cm (6in) long. From this arise branching, decumbent, leafy stems bearing a single terminal long-stalked flower. The narrow bell-shaped corolla, 30–40mm (1¼–1½in) long, is greenish on the outside and deep purplish-blue within. W China. July–August. Fairly easy to cultivate and generally setting plenty of seed.

Gentiana kurroo ○□
This beautiful and graceful species is now very rare in cultivation. Plants sold as *Gentiana kurroo* are virtually always either *G. gracilipes* or *G. dahurica*. The true species forms a central rosette of 10–12cm (4–5in) long, rather narrow leaves. From this rise several unbranched stems, 10–30cm (4–12in) tall, with narrow linear leaves and a solitary terminal flower, sometimes 2 flowers together. The deep blue, narrow funnel-shaped corolla, 40–50mm ($1\frac{3}{5}$–2in) long, has 5 large spreading lobes and is spotted white and green within. W Himalaya. September–October. Plants require good drainage and will probably do best in scree or raised bed, but may not be completely hardy. This is a much sought after species, if one can find the real thing.

Gentiana lagodechiana see *G. septemfida* var. *lagodechiana*, p. 106

Gentiana lutea ○
The Great Yellow Gentian is a coarse plant, one of the tallest members of the genus. It is a stately species unsuitable for the smaller rock garden. The strongly ribbed elliptic leaves are up to 30cm (12in) long, and the erect, leafy, unbranched flowering stems may reach 100cm (40in) tall. The short-stalked yellow flowers are held in whorled clusters at the base of the upper leaves. Unlike most gentians, the corolla, 20–30mm ($\frac{4}{5}$–$1\frac{1}{5}$in) long, has a very short tube and long pointed lobes. Best grown in full sun in a rich, deep soil. Mountains of C and S Europe where it is a frequent plant of meadows. July–August. Plants may take up to 4 years, sometimes more, to come into flower.

Gentiana makinoi ○◑□
A bushy plant which sends up many 30–60mm (12–24in) long erect leafy stems. The lanceolate, pointed leaves are smallest at the base of the stem. The almost tubular slaty-blue flowers are heavily speckled and are borne in a dense cluster at the tip of the stems and at the upper leaf-axils; the corolla lobes are not spreading. Japan. July–September. Plants should be grown in a lime-free peaty soil in a sunny or partially shaded position.
  Gentiana scabra is very similar, but has later, bell-shaped flowers.

Gentiana prolata ◑□
A neat small species with spreading unbranched stems to 10–12cm (4–5in) which bear small elliptic leaves and erect terminal flowers. The narrow tubular corolla, 25–30mm (1–$1\frac{1}{5}$in) long, has slightly spreading lobes and is blue streaked with yellowish- or greenish-white. Himalaya. July–August. Plants grow well in a raised bed in peaty soil and require plenty of moisture.

Gentiana saxosa ○◑☆
A beautiful small species, well worth having in the garden. From a mat of rosettes of dark green, shiny, spatular-shaped, fleshy leaves arise prostrate leafy stems bearing a solitary or a small cluster of white, purply-brown-veined flowers; the open cup-shaped corolla, 18–20mm ($\frac{3}{4}$in) across, is divided almost to the base into blunt oblong lobes. New Zealand. July–September. This species does best in light sandy soil, or in scree or trough in full sun, but must be kept well watered.
  Gentiana bellidifolia is very similar, and differs mainly in its broader, spoon-shaped leaves. Both species are relatively short lived, and tend to be killed by a hard frost. Once established they will seed around, at least in some gardens.

Gentiana saxosa

Gentiana septemfida ○☆

An excellent, largely trouble-free, but very variable species. Plants send up several erect leafy, often spreading, stems, 15–30cm (6–12in) long. The leaves are stalkless and oval. The 5–8 flowers are borne in a tight head, terminally and from the topmost leaf-axils; the corolla, 30–40mm (1⅕–1⅗in) long, is narrow bell-shaped with spreading lobes and deeply cut plicae. It is very variable in colour, at its best deep blue with lighter spots inside the tube. W Asia and the Caucasus. July–August. One of the best species for the average garden, succeeding well in most soils, but best in full sun where it will remain more compact.

Var. *lagodechiana* from the E Caucasus is closely related, and differs by having prostrate stems, slightly stalked leaves, and generally only one terminal blue flower, which is very slender at the base. Many plants offered by the trade are forms of *G. septemfida* and not this variety. August–September.

Gentiana sino-ornata ○◑□☆

This marvellous species has been rated as one of the best plant introductions of this century and it is certainly one of the very finest alpines for gardens. From rosettes of narrow pointed leaves rise many prostrate stems, 15–20cm (6–8in) long, which root at the lower nodes and bear single upright terminal flowers. The corolla is funnel-shaped, up to 70mm (2¾in) long, with spreading lobes of a rich royal blue with 5 longitudinal bands of deeper blue alternating with greeny-yellow ones. SW China. September–October (–November). New plants develop round the rootstock and at the rooted nodes and provide a ready means of increase. This glorious species must have good deep lime-free soil, and plenty of moisture, if it is to succeed. In hot dry areas it does better in partial shade. At its best it forms a continuous green mat covered with flowers throughout the autumn, even into the November frosts. There is a white-flowered form, var. *alba*, and many cultivars, including 'Angels' Wings', 'Blue Heaven', 'Bryn form'. Related species such as *G. farreri* and *F. veitchiorum* are, alas, now rare in cultivation, but there are many splendid hybrids between these species.

Gentiana × inverleith (G. farreri × G. veitchiorum) ○◐□☆
Similar in general appearance to *G. sino-ornata*, but with a stronger rootstock and larger flowers of a deep Cambridge blue (intermediate between the bright Cambridge blue of *G. farreri* and the glowing deep purply blue of *G. veitchiorum*). The best cultivar is 'Susan Jane'.

Gentiana × caroli (G. farreri × G. lawrencei) ○◐□
A delicate and unmistakeable plant, with relatively small, narrow, funnel-shaped, pale blue, striped flowers, 40–50mm (1⅗–2in) long, borne on branched stems which rise from a rosette of narrow linear leaves.

Gentiana × macauleyi (G. sino-ornata × G. farreri) ○◐□☆
Similar in general appearance to *G. sino-ornata*, but with mid- to deep-blue flowers and long narrow leaves. There is a fine cultivar named 'Kingfisher'.

Gentiana × stevenagensis (G. sino-ornata × G. veitchiorum) ○◐□☆
Again, a plant similar in appearance to *G. sino-ornata*, but with branched stems, tighter habit and narrower flowers of a deeper blue which have a marked silky sheen. One of the best of the Chinese hybrid gentians. All these hybrids flower in September–October.

Gentiana ternifolia ○◐□
A recent introduction from SW China which has proved to be very amenable to cultivation and should shortly become widely available. It is a floriferous and very beautiful species similar to *G. sino-ornata* but with external green and white stripes. Cultivation as for *G. sino-ornata*.

Gentiana verna ○□
This lovely small plant, the Spring Gentian of the Alps, is not too easy in cultivation despite its wide distribution in the wild, but is worth every effort made to grow it. It forms a loosely tufted mat or mound of rosettes with elliptic, rather pointed leaves

Gentiana sino-ornata

Gentiana verna

to 20mm (⅜in) long. From the rosettes rise erect leafy stems to 8cm (3in), though often less, bearing a single deep azure-blue flower. The corolla consists of a narrow tube with wide spreading lobes and small plicae; the disc-like stigma appears as a contrasting central white 'eye'. Europe and W Asia. April–May. Plants grow well in scree, or in a trough or light soils, but greatly resent disturbance. Good forms can be increased by cuttings in early summer.

Var. *angulosa* (syn. *G. angulosa*) comes from the Caucasus and N Asia, and is somewhat larger and sturdier than the type. The corolla is of a paler blue and the calyx is more strongly winged. It is probably somewhat easier to maintain in gardens. May–June.

GERANIUM (Geraniaceae)

This genus, often referred to as the Cranesbills, has over 400 species throughout the world; it is particularly well known for its taller herbaceous species. It should not be confused with the 'Geraniums' grown as house or greenhouse specimens, which are largely South African members of the genus *Pelargonium*. *Geranium* is closely related to *Erodium* and differs by having palmately divided or lobed leaves and straight or slightly arced beaks on the fruit. Many species have scented foliage and a great variety of flower colours from the deepest blue to pale pink or white. Several are small enough to be grown in troughs and many are good subjects for the rock garden. Most can be propagated by division or from seed.

Geranium dalmaticum ○◑☆
This delicate species is native of S Yugoslavia and Albania where it occurs in rocky places often with little or no soil. As a result it thrives in virtually all conditions in cultivation and forms dense mats of glossy green leaves, which often colour well in autumn. The flowers are a rich pink and cover the plant in May and June. The white form 'album' is occasionally offered. One of the very best species for the rock garden.

Geranium cinereum ○☆
Another attractive species forming low tufts to 15cm (6in) tall. The grey-green leaves are deeply lobed and the flowers, often paired, are pale lilac-pink with deeper veins. Pyrenees. June–July. Perhaps better known and more commonly available is the hybrid between this species and *G. subcaulescens*, sold under the cultivar name 'Ballerina'. This combines the best attributes of both parents and forms neat clumps of silvery-green leaves from which arise numerous purple centred, lilac flowers.

Geranium subcaulescens ○☆
Like the previous, but flowers an intense magenta-red. SE Europe.

Geranium sanguineum ○◑☆
The Bloody Cranesbill is one of the few British native species commonly grown by alpine enthusiasts and with good reason, for it is an extremely attractive plant and very easy to grow. The leaves are finely divided into many narrow pointed lobes and remain close to the ground. The flowers may vary quite considerably in colour from a bright reddish-purple to pale pink and are carried on stems of 15–20cm (6–8in). Throughout much of Europe, inhabiting rocky places and open woods. June–September. The best-known selection of this species is 'Lancastriense' which has satin-pink flowers veined with wine red.

Geranium cinereum 'Ballerina'

Geranium sessiliflorum ○◑

A native of New Zealand forming a neat little plant with tiny white flowers. The leaves are small and in the cultivar 'Nigrescens' are chocolate coloured. May–July. A charming plant which needs to be viewed at close quarters to appreciate its full beauty.

Geranium farreri (syn. *G. napuligerum*) ○☆

This species is truly beautiful and forms close domes of olive green, kidney-shaped, lobed leaves up to 25cm (10in) across. From these arise pale pink flowers of great beauty with black anthers. SW China. June–July. The most beautiful of all alpine Geraniums. Seed is set sparingly and should be collected with care as plants are generally very difficult to divide. Plants resent wet soils and need adequate drainage.

GEUM (Rosaceae)

A genus of handsome perennials, often with yellow flowers, and pinnate leaves with a large end leaflet. The flowers are bowl-shaped, usually with 5–6 petals and a mass of stamens in the centre. The fruit clusters are often hooked, the barbs readily attaching themselves to clothing etc. Generally easy to cultivate and tolerant of a wide range of soil types. Many of the garden cultivars are too gross for the rock garden.

Geum montanum ○☆

The Alpine Avens is widespread in the mountains of C and S Europe, making tufts up to 12cm (5in) tall. The soft-green leaves have a very large end leaflet. The golden-yellow flowers are very handsome, 25–35mm (1–1⅜in) across. The fruits are not hooked. June–July. An easy and free-flowering plant deserving a place on any rock garden and not usually invasive.

Geum reptans ○▢▲

The Creeping Avens is essentially similar to the previous species, but is at once distinguished by its long reddish runners that root down at intervals forming new plants. European Alps. Unfortunately this desirable plant is fickle in cultivation and rarely succeeds for very long. It requires an acid soil, plenty of sunshine, but at the same time moisture below the soil surface. Plants rarely recover once they have been allowed to dry out. A natural hybrid between these two species, *G.* × *rhaeticum*, has intermediate characteristics, but lacks the runners of the latter whilst thankfully possessing the ease of cultivation of the former.

Geum rivale ◑

The common Water Avens, widespread in damp woods and pastures throughout Europe, with its delicate drooping cream or pale pink flowers, is not really worthy of cultivation. However, a cultivar, 'Leonard's Variety' with red flowers on stems to 30cm (12in) is well worth a semi-shaded corner.

Geum × borisii ○◑

A fine hybrid between *G. bulgaricum* and *G. reptans* noted for its glowing orange-yellow flowers on plants to 30cm (12in). It occurs naturally in the wild in Bulgaria and has long been established in cultivation. June–July, sometimes later.

GLOBULARIA (Globulariaceae)

The globularias are an aptly named group of perennials including both herbaceous and semi-woody species, all characterized by having small round heads of blue, or more rarely, white flowers. Although some are too large for growing in alpine troughs or pans, they do make good plants for the larger scree garden. Many are cushion-formers and eagerly sought after by enthusiasts who can offer the additional protection of an alpine house. The genus is quite small with just 15 species, most of which occur in S Europe. Many have persistent, glossy green leaves mostly arranged in basal rosettes. Propagation from cuttings or division, or from seed when available.

Globularia incanescens ○

A low-growing, cushion-forming plant with densely knit stems, 3–10cm (1–4in) tall, covered with oval, semi-deciduous, leaves. The foliage is bluish-grey throughout because of the accumulation of calcium deposits on the surface and this is one of the most distinguishing features of this species. The flower-heads are quite small, only 15–20mm ($\frac{3}{5}$–$\frac{4}{5}$in) across, and pale lavender blue. N Italy—native of the Apuan Alps and the N Apennines. May–July.

Globularia trichosantha ○

This is a larger plant than *G. incanescens* with stems reaching 20cm (8in). The leaves are toothed and grouped into basal rosettes. The stems are often stoloniferous and terminate in bright blue flower-heads up to 25mm (1in) across. This species has one of the eastern-most distributions, occurring in Bulgaria, Turkey and Russia. May–July.

Globularia punctata (syn. *G. aphyllanthes*, *G. willkommii*) ○◗☆

One of the most widespread species occurring throughout S Europe and extending into W Russia. A tufted evergreen perennial with erect leafy stems. The lower leaves are arranged in basal rosettes and the flower-stems reach 20–30cm (8–12in). One of the most distinctive features of this species is the collar of leafy bracts subtending the 10–15mm ($\frac{2}{5}$–$\frac{3}{5}$in) flower-heads. May–June. In the wild a plant of meadows, rocky places and open woods, generally on limestone and to 1,650m (5,450ft) altitude.

Globularia vulgaris ○◗

One of the larger members of the genus with flower-stems reaching 25–30cm (10–12in). The leaves remain close to the ground in basal rosettes and are distinct from other species with their long leaf-stalks which often exceed the leaf-blade in length. Europe. May–July. Two other species, closely related to *G. vulgaris*, which may be encountered, are *G. cambessedesii* (also known as *G. majorcensis*) and *G. valentina*.

Globularia cordifolia ○☆

This species is among the best known of the genus with its tight ground-hugging mats of woody stems from which the tiny dark green, leathery, notched leaves and small heads of rather deep blue flowers emerge. The flower-stalks rarely exceed 10cm (4in), often far less, and the flower-heads are usually between 10 and 20mm ($\frac{2}{5}$–$\frac{4}{5}$in) across. Mountains of C Europe and the E Pyrenees. May–June.

Globularia meridionalis (syn. **G. bellidifolia** or **G. cordifolia** subsp. **bellidifolia**) ○☆
Very similar to *G. cordifolia*, but differing in having un-notched leaves. It is also more robust, but none the less an equally attractive plant. Mountains of C and SE Europe. May–July. Both species are good choices if placed either near the edge of a wall or else close to a path where they can gracefully spill over, successfully hiding sharp corners. They will also succeed on a well-drained coarse scree.

Globularia repens ○☆
A third species in this group of shrubby globularias, but differing from the two previously mentioned by being much smaller. The plants formed by this species are very compact so it is rarely possible to see the tightly knit mats of woody stems which lie beneath the tiny leaves. The flowers are a deep lilac-blue and are held in heads no more than 10mm ($\frac{2}{5}$in) across, very close to the foliage mat. Pyrenees and SW Alps. May–July. Surely the finest alpine treasure in this attractive genus!

Globularia nudicaulis ○
This species is closer to *G. punctata* in size and overall appearance and probably has the largest flower-heads of all the species mentioned, 20–30mm ($\frac{3}{4}$–1$\frac{1}{4}$in) across, and a lovely rich blue colour. The specific name *nudicaulis* refers to the flower-stems which are leafless except for 2 or 3 tiny bracts; this makes it an easy plant to distinguish. Mountains of C and S Europe. May–July. The coarsest species, really unsuitable for the smaller rock garden.

GYPSOPHILA (Caryophyllaceae)

The name *Gypsophila* for many people conjures up thoughts of the large foamy sprays of small white flowers in florists' shops or herbaceous borders, provided by the species *G. paniculata*. There are about 125 other species in Europe and Asia, most of which are not in cultivation and barely worthy of garden space anyway, but a few of the dwarf ones are excellent hardy rock garden plants.

Gypsophilas have narrow, often greyish-green leaves and white or pink 5-petalled flowers like small *Dianthus* in overall form, but, unlike the latter, they have no epicalyx scales outside the true calyx.

Gypsophila aretioides ○
This very compact plant makes dense hard cushions of tiny green or greyish-green leaves. The flowers, which are not produced very freely in cultivation, are white and stemless, resting on the cushions. A form which makes particularly tight cushions is called var. *caucasica*. N Iran, Caucasus. June. Most often seen in the alpine house, but it will succeed outdoors given a well-drained rocky place in full sun.

Gypsophila repens (syn. **G. dubia**) ○☆
A species of prostrate habit with small hairless grey-green leaves and loose few- to many-flowered corymbs; the flowers are white or pink and 5–10mm ($\frac{1}{4}$–$\frac{1}{2}$in) across. A form sometimes found in catalogues as *G. repens* 'Dubia' or just *G.* 'Dubia' has bronze-coloured leaves; 'Letchworth Rose'—very floriferous with pink flowers; 'Dorothy Teacher'—a compact form with blue-grey leaves, producing rose-pink flowers over a long period in summer; 'Monstrosa'—a more robust form with white flowers; 'Fratensis'—has grey-green leaves and pink flowers; 'Rosea'—another good pink form; 'Rosea Plena'—has double pink flowers. The species is native to C, S and E Europe. June–August.

Gypsophila cerastioides ○
This species forms loose cushions of soft grey-green leaves, overtopped by sprays of flowers on stems to 10cm (4in) in height. The flowers are white streaked with purple and are 9–10mm ($\frac{2}{5}$in) across. Himalaya. May–July.

Gypsophila tenuifolia ○
A rather thrift-like plant with dense tufts of linear leaves. Stems 2–15cm ($\frac{3}{4}$–6in) long carry loosely branched sprays of white or pale pink flowers, 10–15mm ($\frac{2}{5}$–$\frac{3}{5}$in) across. Caucasus, E Turkey. June–August.

HABERLEA (Gesneriaceae)

A genus containing one or perhaps two species allied to *Ramonda*, but with trumpet-shaped, clearly lipped flowers borne in lax clusters on long stalks. Plants thrive in similar conditions to *Ramonda*, succeeding best in cracks in shaded walls or between blocks on the peat garden. Propagation by seed or division of the parent plant.

Haberlea rhodopensis ◑☆
Plants form deep rosettes of broad-elliptical, rather bright green, thick, toothed leaves. The flowers, 12–18mm ($\frac{1}{2}$–$\frac{3}{4}$in) long, are pale lilac with a whitish throat marked with pale yellow. The whole plant is about 15cm (6in) tall, the rosettes multiplying slowly over a number of years to form a large tuft. Balkans. April–June. 'Virginalis'—pure white flowers.

HACQUETIA (Umbelliferae)

A genus of just one species, native of central Europe and characterized by a slightly creeping stock and flowers which appear very early in the year, generally before the leaves. At first sight the golden yellow bracts look like petals and the plant could easily be mistaken for a species of *Ranunculus*.

Hacquetia epipactis ○◑☆
A leafy perennial 20–25cm (8–10in) high. Leaves glossy, 3-lobed, with long leaf-stalks. Flowers golden-yellow, appearing close to ground level at first and surrounded by petal-like, shiny green bracts. February–April. Normally grown as a woodland plant, but also at home in a shady or moist corner of the rock garden. A splendid species attractive from early spring and continuing well into summer. Plants form rounded mounds, often self-seeding once established.

HAPPLOPAPPUS (Compositae)

This large genus of 200 species of herbaceous and shrubby perennials is widely distributed throughout North and South America. It is characterized by having pure yellow daisy flower-heads and entire or slightly toothed, alternate leaves. Only one species is regularly grown as a rock garden plant.

Happlopappus coronopifolius ○
A low-growing shrubby perennial with erect and spreading stems forming semi-circular domes up to 15cm (6in) high. The leathery leaves are dark, glossy green and contrast well with the golden-yellow daisy flowers, 15–25mm ($\frac{3}{5}$–1in) across, held on reddish-brown stems up to 10cm (4in) long. June–August.

Hacquetia epipactis

HEBE (Scrophulariaceae)

The genus includes over 100 species of evergreen shrubs that are in the main confined to New Zealand. The genus is closely allied to *Veronica*, to which it once belonged, and from which it differs in various botanical minutiae. The flowers are arranged in simple or branched racemes or even spikes which can arise from the end of a shoot, as in the whip-cord species, or from a leaf axil, as is found in most other species. Some Hebes are tender and therefore best for a sheltered site in full sun. It is a very floriferous genus of easy cultivation in any well-drained soil. Most can be readily propagated from cuttings. Only a handful of the smaller species are included here.

Hebe rigidula ○

An erect, much-branched shrub to 30cm (12in) with slender branches covered by leathery, elliptical leaves which are green above and greyish beneath. The white flowers are borne in lateral racemes. New Zealand. June–July.

Hebe pinguifolia (syn. *Veronica* 'Pageana') ○☆

A small shrub, erect at first, but then becoming prostrate. Leaves oval, thickly textured, grey-green; flowers white, in crowded spikes up to 25mm (1in) long. New Zealand. May–August, occasionally earlier. The cultivar 'Pagei' is a much dwarfer selection up to 30cm (12in) tall, with plum-coloured stems and silvery-grey leaves. One of the finest and hardiest rock garden Hebes.

Hebe buchananii ○

A dwarf shrub to 30cm (12in) high, much-branched and of compact habit. The tiny leaves, which are closely set together, are rounded and leathery in texture. Flowers white, borne in a cluster of 3 or 4 spikes towards the shoot tips. New Zealand. June–July. A dwarf selection called 'Minor' has even smaller leaves.

Hebe pimeleoides ○☆
A loosely branched, spreading shrub to 30cm (12in) with dark-coloured branchlets. Its purplish blue flowers contrast extremely effectively with its greyish leaves, which are occasionally edged with red. New Zealand. July–August.

Hebe epacridea ○
A small prostrate shrub, to 40cm (16in) which is almost conifer-like having stems completely clothed with small, recurved, scale-like leaves. Its fragrant white flowers occur in dense terminal racemes up to 30mm (1⅛in) long. July.

Hebe 'Carl Teschner' ○☆
A popular plant said to be a hybrid between *H. elliptica* and *H. pimeleoides*. It forms a procumbent shrub, eventually reaching a height of 20cm (8in) and a width of 60cm (24in). Its dark, almost blackish stems carry dull green, elliptic leaves, about 10mm (⅜in) long. A free-flowering shrub with short racemes of violet flowers which have a white throat. June–July.

HELIANTHEMUM (Cistaceae)

The Rock Roses are a familiar group of plants, mainly represented in cultivation by a single species which has a myriad of cultivars much loved by gardeners. The genus contains about 100 species from North America, Europe, W Asia and N Africa. Some are evergreen subshrubs or herbaceous, whilst a few are annual. The flowers have 5 sepals and 5 petals, with a central boss of numerous stamens. All thrive in a well-drained soil in full sun where they will flower during the summer months. Plants can be raised from seed or midsummer cuttings. An easy and mostly reliable group of plants.

Helianthemum nummularium (syn. *H. chamaecistus*) ○☆
The Common Rock Rose is a widespread species from Europe (including the British Isles) which forms a spreading semi-evergreen shrub up to 30cm (12in) tall. Leaves green above, grey beneath; the flowers yellow, 14–22mm (½–⅞in) across, borne in many-flowered terminal racemes. June–August. The following are a selection of the most readily available cultivars: 'Ben Fhada'—bright yellow, orange centred; 'Ben Mohr'—burnt orange; 'Henfield Brilliant'—glistening brick red; 'Jubilee'—double, yellow; 'Mrs Earle'—double, red; 'The Bride'—white; 'Wisley Pink'—soft pink; 'Wisley Primrose'—soft yellow. Some forms with coloured foliage include 'Praecox'—grey foliage; 'Old Gold'—golden yellow leaves. The rock rose can be an imposing plant for the rock garden and needs to be heavily pruned after flowering.

HELICHRYSUM (Compositae)

A large genus of over 500 species native to the Old World, with the greatest concentration of species in southern Africa. Many inhabit areas where conditions are extremely arid and have become well adapted to periods of drought. They often have narrow hairy leaves and many produce papery 'everlasting' flower-heads. Only 3 species are commonly grown as rock garden plants, though many others have great merit and may become more widely available. The less hardy species are better grown in the alpine house.

Helichrysum orientale ○

A well-branched perennial arising from a woody stock reaching about 15–30cm (6–12in). The leaves and branches are covered with dense hairs, giving the plant a whitened appearance. A series of leaves, 20–50mm (⅜–2in) long, are crowded around the base of the stems, while those on the stems are a little shorter. The compound inflorescences may vary in size from 20–80mm (¾–3⅛in) across and contain tiny, bright, clear yellow flowers which have a glistening surface. This species is found on cliffs in mainland Greece and Crete. June–July.

Helichrysum bellidioides ○

Plants form low carpets of rooting, prostrate stems up to 60cm (24in) long; though often less; the branches are covered in white wool which has a cobwebby appearance. The oval leaves are very small, only 5–6mm (*c*. ¼in) long. Flower-heads creamy-white, 20–30mm (⅘–1⅛in) across. Native of New Zealand where it occurs in grassland. June–July. Can become invasive where suited, such as on a warm sunny bank or raised bed.

Helichrysum selago ○☆

Another New Zealand native, but with a very different habit. This species forms an erect branched shrub reaching about 15cm (6in). The hairy-margined leaves remain closely pressed to the stems, giving the plant a heath-like appearance. The solitary, pale yellow flowers are borne at the ends of the branches. June–July. This plant is probably best appreciated if grown in a trough or on a raised bed. Probably not hardy in colder, more northerly regions.

HELLEBORUS (Ranunculaceae)

The genus *Helleborus* contains a number of striking and extremely garden-worthy species, noted for their cupped flowers that are often shades of green and pink or purple. The large, deeply lobed, often shiny leaves are also an additional feature, persisting in some species throughout the year. Most of the species are far too gross for the rock garden, but two can often be found a corner, given a well-drained soil. Mature plants generally sulk when moved, but young plants are quick to establish and are generally readily raised from seed.

Helleborus niger ○◗

The lovely Christmas Rose needs no introduction. The leathery deep green leaves are persistent and the large white flowers, 40–90mm (1½–3½in) across, are borne on stout stalks from Christmas onwards. Each flower has a central cluster of bright yellow stamens. C and E Europe and W Asia. January–April. Unfortunately this superb plant is not always easy to please, succeeding in some gardens, failing in others. The shelter of a warm wall, away from cold winter winds will help protect the early flowers. A sheet of glass placed overhead will serve a similar purpose. The finest cultivar is 'Potter's Wheel' which bears extra large flowers held well above the foliage. Another good cultivar is 'Louis Cobbett'.

Helleborus orientalis ◗☆

The Lenten Rose is a native of Greece and Asia Minor. Plants form large tufts, up to 50cm (18in) tall with large, coarse, shiny green leaves. The flowers occur in clusters, ranging from white and pale green to deep purplish-pink. February–April. There are many fine modern cultivars, some with deep purplish-black flowers of great distinction. In recent times yellow as well as double-flowered forms have been produced.

HELONIOPSIS (Melanthaiaceae)

A small genus of Japanese and Formosan woodlanders, with small, lily-like, erect flowers, often foul-smelling. The species are more fascinating than beautiful. Propagation by division or from seed.

Heloniopsis japonica ◑☆
Plants to 20cm (8in) tall. The leaves are mostly basal, rather pale green, lanceolate. The spreading, drooping flowers are pale pink with darker stripes, borne in umbel-like clusters on long erect stems. Japan. April–May.

Heloniopsis breviscapa ◑☆
Plants have tufts of spatular-shaped leaves, and flowering scapes to 20cm (8in) tall, bearing a head of starry bluish-white flowers. Japan. May.

HEPATICA (Ranunculaceae)

A delightful genus closely related to the Anemones and generally distinguished by their 3 lobed leaves. The flowers, like those of *Anemone*, have petal-like sepals, often brightly coloured; each flower has a small ruff of 3, bract-like leaves immediately beneath. The species are mainly woodland plants in their native haunts, thriving best in a leafy moist soil in a semi-shaded position. They are resentful of disturbance, but can be increased by division of large old clumps. The species can often be found under *Anemone* in catalogues.

Hepatica nobilis (syn. *H. triloba*) ○◑☆
A widespread species found from Europe to Asia, as well as North America. The kidney-shaped deep green leaves have 3 triangular untoothed lobes. In some forms the leaves are pleasantly mottled. The flowers are 15–25mm ($\frac{3}{5}$–1in) across, with 6–9 deep blue, pink or white sepals. March–April. The deepest blue cultivar has been given the name 'Caerulea'. There are also double-flowered forms.

Hepatica transilvanica ◑☆
A more vigorous plant than the previous, with rather paler leaves, the lobes with a neat toothed margin. The flowers are generally a mauve-blue or pale pink. Romania. April–May. A hybrid between the above two species, *H* × *media*, is the finest of all Hepaticas, exceptionally vigorous, to 15cm (6in) tall. The best cultivar is 'Ballard's Var.' with numerous mauve blooms of great distinction.

Hepatica acutiloba ◑
Like *H. nobilis*, but with more pointed leaf-lobes. The flowers are smaller, ranging in colour from pale blue to pink and white. North America. Scarcely as good as the others.

HERACLEUM (Umbelliferae)

A genus of large leafy perennials, especially well known for its most notorious member, the handsome *H. mantegazzianum*, the Giant Hog-weed. Although there are only a few species, they show a great range in style and include in their ranks one small cousin that can claim a special place in the alpine, trough or scree garden.

Heracleum minimum ○

This delicate species is a biennial or short-lived rhizomatous perennial, rarely exceeding 15cm (6in) tall in cultivation. As a rather typical representative of the family it looks like a scaled-down version of a carrot, but with smooth divided leaves and umbels up to 60mm (2½in) across composed of tiny white or pale pink flowers. May–July. Sometimes seeds around, especially on screes.

HERNIARIA (Illecebraceae)

Rather insignificant plants of very little garden value which may be grown for their compact growth rather than for the flowers, which are minute. There are about 35 species in the Mediterranean region, W Asia and South Africa. Their stems are usually prostrate and much-branched in a mat-forming habit, bearing tiny opposite leaves and miniscule flowers in clusters at the leaf axils; each flower has 5 sepals and minute petals, or none at all. Unlike the related *Paronychia* there are no large papery bracts to provide a worthwhile display.

Herniaria glabra ○

A sprawling mat-forming perennial with many tiny yellowish-green, hairy, elliptical leaves only about 5mm (⅕in) long. The tiny green flowers, less than 2mm ($\frac{1}{10}$in) across, are produced in small dense clusters making almost spike-like inflorescences. Widespread in Europe. July–September.

HEUCHERA (Saxifragaceae)

There are between 35 and 50 species of *Heuchera* which are natives of North America. They have long-stalked basal leaves and the flowering stems carry the narrow panicles or racemes of flowers well above the foliage. They are probably most familiar as plants of the herbaceous border, but the following small species is suitable for the rock garden.

Heuchera racemosa (syn. *Elmera racemosa*) ○☆

A downy, tufted plant, the leaves with kidney-shaped blades. The flower-stems are 10–25cm (4–10in) tall and carry loose racemes of flowers which have a yellowish-green calyx and white petals, giving an overall creamy appearance; each petal is divided into 3–7 lobes. NW USA. June–August.

HIERACEUM (Compositae)

This large genus contains over 500 species, distributed throughout the world with the exception of Australasia. Most are rather weedy in habit and may be too invasive for cultivation, and certainly have no place in the rock garden. They resemble *Crepis* in having solitary golden yellow flower-heads, usually borne on long stems and arising from a basal rosette of leaves. A few of the alpine species are worthy of cultivation. They are readily raised from seed or by division.

Hieraceum waldsteinii ○☆

This beautiful species comes from the Balkans and is grown mainly for the effect of its lovely grey felted leaves, which are oval in shape and about 15cm (6in) long. The bright yellow flower-heads are borne on branched stems 20–25cm (8–10in) tall. The plant is herbaceous and dies down for the winter. July.

Hieraceum villosum ○☆
Another European species with downy, grey-silver leaves and stems; the basal leaves are oval and 40–80mm (1½–3⅕in) long and the stem-leaves decrease in size up the stem. The flower-heads are lemon-yellow, about 25mm (1in) across, and may be solitary or in small groups. June–July. Effective for its foliage alone. Plants become rather gross in time.

Hieraceum aurantiacum ○◐
The familiar Orange Hawkweed, or Fox and Cubs, which looks quite different in appearance from the two preceding species. Plants are strongly stoloniferous and as a result are inclined to spread rather rapidly if not checked. The green foliage is less hairy and the flowers rich orange to brick red, borne on branched stems 20–30cm (8–12in) tall. A native of the Alps, but widely naturalized elsewhere. June–July. Too invasive for all but the largest rock garden.

HIPPOCREPIS (Leguminosae)

The genus takes its name from the Greek for 'horse' and 'shoe', in allusion to the fruit segments. Most species are annual or perennial herbs or subshrubs with pinnate leaves. The genus contains 21 species, mainly in the Mediterranean, but extending to mainland Europe and W Asia. Propagation is by seed or division of the parent plant.

Hippocrepis comosa ○☆
The common Horseshoe Vetch is a prostrate, woody-based perennial herb. The yellow pea-flowers, 6–10mm (¼–⅖in) long, are clustered into small umbels, borne on long slender stalks. The fruit has a number of 1-seeded, horseshoe-shaped segments. Europe and W Asia. April–June. Plants prefer a calcareous soil and an open sunny position on the rock garden. 'E. R. James'—a more compact form with lemon-yellow flowers; the best form for gardens.

HORMINUM (Labiatae)

The genus contains a single species native to the Pyrenees and Southern Alps.

Horminum pyrenaicum
The Dragonmouth is a familiar plant of meadows and rocky places up to 2,500m (9,250ft), especially in the Pyrenees. The shiny, deep green leaves are mostly in a flat basal rosette, being oval or rounded, edged with blunt teeth. The flower spikes rise to 30cm (12in) though often less, and bear a succession of deep violet-blue flowers with protruding stamens. June–August. Forms large clumps once established. A white-flowered form is also known.

HOUSTONIA (Rubiaceae)

A North American genus of 50 species of hardy tufted perennials. Although several species are suited to the rock garden, only one of these is commonly grown in our gardens. Excellent for moist, shady sites, particularly between large stones, where it will often flower throughout the summer months.

Houstonia caerulea ◐☆
A native of North America where it is known as Bluets. A dainty, floriferous plant, forming loose mats of glossy leaves dotted with masses of tiny china-blue flowers, with pointed petals. Often represented in cultivation by 'Fred Millard', a sturdier

Horminum pyrenaicum

form with deeper-coloured flowers. Although perennial, its habit of flowering for much of the summer tends to make it short lived.

HUTCHINSIA (Cruciferae)

This familar genus of European mountains contains a single species. It is a small plant, quite hardy, but perhaps more easily appreciated in a trough or on a raised bed. However, it is equally at home on a fine scree, where it will seed around once established.

Hutchinsia alpina ○◐☆

The Chamois Cress is a low tufted perennial to 50mm (2in) tall, with shiny, deep green, pinnate, foliage. The small white flowers are borne in profusion in short fairly dense racemes. Like all crucifers there are 4 petals. Alps, Pyrenees and

Apennines. May–early July. The species inhabits limestone rocks and screes, to 3,400m (11,200ft) in the wild. Subsp. *brevicaulis* (syn. *H. brevicaulis)* is similar but more dwarf, often only 20–30mm ($\frac{4}{5}$–1$\frac{1}{5}$in) tall; the flowers have narrower petals. Subsp. *auerswaldii* (syn. *H. auerswaldii*) is taller than the type, to 15cm (6in), with flexuous stems. N Spain.

HYLOMECON (Papaveraceae)

An attractive genus of poppy-like plants relishing moist soils with plenty of peat and leaf-mould, being primarily woodlanders in their native habitat.

Hylomecon japonicum ◗☆

Forms mounds of bright green leaves, each with several pairs of sharply toothed leaflets. The golden-yellow poppy flowers, 40–50mm (1$\frac{1}{2}$–2in) across, have 4 petals and form a deep bowl, usually one to each stem. The pods, in contrast to true poppies, *Papaver*, are long and slender. Japan. April–May. A delightful plant despite the fact that it remains in flower for a relatively short time.

HYPERICUM (Hypericaceae)

This large genus contains about 400 species distributed throughout the temperate and mountainous tropical regions of the world. They all share the common floral characteristics of having 5 golden yellow petals surrounding a central boss of many radiating stamens. Plants of this genus vary greatly in size and habit, from large showy shrubs to ground-hugging herbs. Many are undoubtedly attractive and several make excellent plants for the rock garden or alpine trough. Most will flourish in any type of soil, in a sunny and open position. Propagation from seed or cuttings (of the shrubby types).

Hypericum balearicum ○

This is probably one of the most distinct species in the genus, forming a low hairless shrub to about 30cm (*c.* 12in) in cultivation. The opposite leaves are small, 8–10mm ($\frac{1}{3}$–$\frac{2}{5}$in) long, narrow and leathery with warty growths. The solitary, deep golden yellow flowers are 20–40mm ($\frac{4}{5}$–1$\frac{3}{5}$in) across. Balearic Islands. May–July. This species is hardy through all except the severest winters.

Hypericum aegypticum ○

Forms a low shrub, but is less erect in habit than the preceding species. In addition, the leaves are smaller, only 3–9mm ($\frac{1}{8}$–$\frac{3}{8}$in) long, greyish-green and crowded closely together. The yellow flowers are borne very close to the foliage and persist for some time. W Asia. May–June. A rather tender species that would probably do best given the protection of an alpine house.

Hypericum coris ○

A species related to *H. aegypticum*, but differing in flower and leaf arrangement. The leaves occur in whorls of 3 or 4 and the flowers are borne in pyramidal panicles. S Europe. June–July. A charming, small, rather heath-like plant that deserves to be more widely known.

Hypericum empetrifolium ○

A shrub with erect, closely packed, stems up to about 30cm (12in) with leaves in whorls of 3. The flowers are solitary or else borne in panicles like *H. coris* and are a rich golden-yellow. SE Europe and W Asia. June–August. One variety is widely grown, var. *prostratum*, which, as its name suggests, has low creeping branches.

Hypericum olympicum

Hypericum olympicum ○☆
This species differs from those described so far in that many parts of the plant are covered with black glands. Plants are really herbaceous, but sometimes become rather woody at the base. The stems are erect or slightly decumbent and bear oval to oblong, greyish-green leaves. The flowers vary in colour from a rich golden- to a pale lemon-yellow, 20–60mm ($\frac{4}{5}$–2$\frac{2}{5}$in) across. SE Europe and W Asia. May–July. One of the finest species for the rock garden, being hardy and floriferous. 'Citrinum'—pale yellow flowers.

Hypericum polyphyllum ○
This species is probably not distinct from the preceding species and is considered synonymous by some botanists. Plants offered for sale under this name are likely to be forms of *H. olympicum*.

Hypericum cerastioides (syn. *H. origanifolium, H. rhodopaeum*) ○
Closely related to *H. olympicum* and similarly a native of SE Europe. Plants are semi-prostrate subshrubs with oval leaves and flowers 20–40mm ($\frac{3}{4}$–1$\frac{1}{2}$in) across. May.

Hypericum trichocaulon ○
A slender evergreen, herbaceous species from Crete, with a low creeping habit, closely resembling *H. olympicum* in overall appearance. The leaves are rigid and the unopened flower-buds are quite distinct with their rich bronzy or reddish coloration. June. Still rather scarce in cultivation.

Hypericum reptans ○◑
This lovely Sikkimese member of the genus is the only species in this account to originate outside Europe. Like the preceding species, this also has bright red buds and a prostrate habit with stems of small oval leaves 10–15mm ($\frac{2}{5}$–$\frac{3}{5}$in) long. Flowers golden-yellow, 40–50mm (1$\frac{1}{2}$–2in) across. June–July. This species does best if placed above a rock or wall so that its stems may hang freely. Plants often colour well in the autumn.

HYPSELA (Campanulaceae)

A small genus of the southern hemisphere with species scattered in South America, Australia and New Zealand. They are creeping plants for cool peaty soils in shaded and semi-shaded positions. Only one species is in general cultivation. It may become invasive and is readily increased by division of the parent plant. The genus is often incorrectly spelt *Hypsella*.

Hypsela reniformis (syn. *H. longiflora*) ◑▢
A carpeting perennial forming bright green carpets of rounded or kidney-shaped leaves. The small solitary flowers are pale pink with crimson markings and have a neatly lobed lower lip. South America. Thrives best in a sheltered position.

IBERIS (Cruciferae)

This genus contains the common Candytuft, *Iberis amara*, grown as a summer annual. The alpine perennial species are attractive plants for the rock garden, thriving in sunny well-drained sites. Like other members of the cabbage family, *Cruciferae, Iberis* flowers have 4 petals; however in this genus 2 petals are long and 2 short, giving the flowers a lop-sided appearance.

Iberis gibraltarica
An evergreen subshrub to 30cm (12in) with dark green, rather leathery foliage; the leaves are wedge-shaped, sometimes toothed. The flat flower-heads are white to reddish-lilac. Gibraltar and Morocco, where it inhabits shady rock crevices. May–July.

Iberis semperflorens ○☆
The commonest candytuft in our gardens, it forms large spreading mats of deep green oblong leaves. Plants become quite woody with age, up to 1m (3ft) across, but only 30cm (12in) tall. The white flowers are borne in flattened heads. Sicily and W Italy, where it inhabits rock crevices and coastal cliffs. March–May. 'Pygmaea'—a dwarf form well worth seeking out.

Iberis sempervirens ○☆
Another evergreen subshrub with narrow spatular, untoothed, thick leaves. The white flowers are borne in racemes rather than flattened heads. Mediterranean Europe. April–June. 'Little Gem'—dark leaves and pure white flowers, only 12cm (4$\frac{3}{4}$in) tall; 'Snow-flake'—a similar cultivar.

Iberis saxatilis ○
A spreading evergreen subshrub, much branched, to 12cm (4$\frac{3}{4}$in) tall. Leaves cylindrical, linear and untoothed, rather yew-like. The flowers are white, being borne in flat heads. S Europe. April–June. The flowers occasionally have a mauve or pink tinge.

123

Iberis pruitii (syn. *I. jordanii*) ○

Another Mediterranean species. Plants form low cushions, perennial in the best forms, but sometimes annual. The fleshy leaves are spatula-shaped, sometimes toothed. The white, pink or lilac flowers are borne in flat heads. April–June. The dwarfer more compact forms are worth seeking out, although this species is not particularly common in cultivation.

INULA (Compositae)

This genus occurs in Europe, Africa and Asia and contains about 200 species. All are perennial herbs or low shrubs with simple leaves arranged alternately along the stems, which terminate in solitary golden-yellow flower-heads; both ray- and disc-florets being present. Only one species is small enough to be generally grown on the rock garden.

Inula ensifolia ○◑☆

An erect perennial 10–30cm (4–12in) tall with dark green lanceolate leaves finely hairy along the margins. The terminal, daisy flower-heads are 20–40mm ($\frac{4}{5}$–1$\frac{3}{5}$in) across. E and C southern Europe, as far west as Italy, where it is often found on the margins of woodland. July–August.

ISOPYRUM (Ranunculaceae)

A single species is in general cultivation.

Isopyrum thalictroides ◑

A charming and rather delicate plant forming lax tufts up to 15cm (6in) tall with grey-green leaves similar to a meadow-rue (*Thalictrum*). The small white flowers are like a miniature anemone, 10–20mm ($\frac{2}{5}$–$\frac{3}{5}$in) across, borne in lax clusters. Mountains of Europe. March–May. In its native haunts, it is a species of damp woodland soils, to 1,200m (3,900ft). In cultivation plants require similar shaded and moist conditions.

JANKAEA (Gesneriaceae)

The genus *Jankaea* contains a single species known only from the cliffs of Mount Olympus in Greece. The genus is closely related to *Ramonda*, but the flowers are more bell-shaped. It is one of the most beautiful and highly desirable of alpines, rather rare in cultivation, not very easy to grow and difficult to obtain, but well worth a try. Plants will thrive best wedged in a deep shady rock crevice, kept reasonably moist in summer, but dry in winter, as they greatly resent winter wet. Specimens are normally kept in the alpine house, but some skilled growers tend them quite successfully out-of-doors.

Jankaea heldreichii ○▲

Plants form a solitary or several close rosettes of thick, oval, silvery-grey felted leaves, rusted on the reverse. The flowers are pale violet, several borne on slender stalks to 70mm (2$\frac{3}{4}$in) long. April–May.

JASIONE (Campanulaceae)

An European genus of meadows and rocky mountain habitats, sometimes mistaken for species of *Scabiosa*. The species are herbaceous perennials thriving in well-drained sunny positions in the rock garden where the flowers are very attractive to butterflies. Propagation by division or seed.

Jasione montana ○☆
The so-called Mountain Sheepsbit is found throughout much of Europe including Britain and Ireland. Plants are erect, to 20cm (8in) tall with small wavy-edged leaves in the lower half. The flower-heads are blue, rarely pink or white, with protruding stamens. May–August. In the wild a plant of grassy, often rather dry, places on acid soils, to an altitude of some 1,700m (5,600ft).

Jasione crispa (syn. *J. humilis*) ○
Essentially like a short version of the previous species, rarely exceeding 12cm (9in) tall. The leaves, which are often toothed, are congested towards the base of the plant. Confined to the Pyrenees and Cevennes. July–August.

Jasione heldreichii (syn. *J. jankae*) ○☆
Like *J. montana*, but leaves clearly stalked. The flower-heads are a striking clear blue. Balkans. June–August. Perhaps the finest species for the rock garden.

Jasione laevis (syn. *J. perennis*) ○
The common Sheepsbit Scabious is widespread in a variety of grassy habitats and heaths in Europe. It is like *J. montana*, but of more robust habit and spreading by long runners, the old dead leaves persisting at the base of the stem. The flowers are bright blue. June–August. Generally less suitable on the average rock garden, being more invasive and less neat in habit.

JOVIBARBA (Crassulaceae)

A small genus of succulent perennials closely related to the houseleeks, *Sempervivum*, which they closely resemble. The main difference is seen in the flowers which are more bell-shaped (not starry) and with 6 toothed, rather than 10 or more untoothed, petals. Like *Sempervivum*, they have rosettes of fleshy leaves which produce offsets on short runners. The flowers are borne in erect inflorescences, branched towards the top; the flowering rosettes die after flowering, leaving the offsets to continue for future years. There are about 8 species native to the mountains of C and S Europe and W Asia. Like *Sempervivum* they thrive best in poor gritty or stony places—screes, rock crevices and troughs are ideal. Plants are extremely drought-resistant.

Jovibarba sobolifera (syn. *Sempervivum soboliferum*) ○☆
The Hen-and-Chickens Houseleek is an attractive little plant to 15cm (6in) tall in flower. The greyish-green globose leaf-rosettes are relatively small, with neatly incurving red-tipped leaves. The yellow flowers are 15–17mm ($\frac{3}{5}$–$\frac{3}{4}$in) long. C and E Alps. June–September. The offsets are attached by thread-like stalks to the parent plant and are easily detached, offering a simple means of propagation. A plant of dry, sandy and grassy habitats, often on acid soils, to 1,500m (4,950ft) altitude.

Jovibarba allionii (syn. *Sempervivum allionii*) ○
Similar to the preceding, but leaf-rosettes pale yellowish-green and hairy. The flowers are greenish-white. S and SW Alps. Rarer in cultivation than the previous species.

Jovibarba arenaria (syn. *Sempervivum arenarium*) ○
Another attractive little plant like *J. sobolifera*, but the leaf-rosettes bright green and more open. The flowers are pale greenish-yellow and upright, rarely produced

in cultivation. E Alps. July–September. The mature rosettes are only 18–20mm (¾in) across.

Jovibarba hirta (syn. *Sempervivum hirtum*) ○

Another species similar to *J. sobolifera*, but distinguished by its dark green, rather open hairy, leaf-rosettes; the leaves are not tipped with red. E and SE Alps. June–August.

Jovibarba heuffelii (syn. *Sempervivum heuffelii*) ○

A more distinctive species forming rather flat green rosettes, the leaves sometimes tipped with red. Plants rarely produce offsets, instead the parent-rosette divides into two equal daughter-rosettes. The cream or pale yellow flowers are borne on erect leafy stems to 15cm (6in) tall. SE Europe. July–September.

KALMIA (Ericaceae)

Evergreen, or occasionally deciduous, New World shrubs. The genus contains about 8 species in all, but only 2 or 3 are cultivated. The leaves are alternate, opposite, or in whorls; the flowers 5-parted borne usually in terminal and/or lateral, showy, umbel-like clusters; the corollas are cup-shaped, angular, with pouched 'shoulders' in which the 10 awn-less anthers nestle. A beautiful genus often referred to as calico bushes. They are plants for moist, acid, cool peaty soils.

Kalmia polifolia ○□☆

A dwarf, wiry shrub with glossy, dark green, leaves, whitish beneath. The large terminal clusters of purplish-pink flowers are each 10–20mm (⅖–⅘in) across. E North America. April. The best form is var. *microphylla* which grows up to 15cm (6in) tall.

Kalmia angustifolia ○□

Lamb Kill or Sheep Laurel is a native of E North America, but it is found naturalized in Germany and NW England. It is an evergreen, thicket-forming shrub to 1m (3ft) in height, with reddish-pink flowers 7–12mm (⅓–½in) in diameter. June. Forma *rubra* is similar, but the flowers are a deeper rose- or ruby-red.

LAMIUM (Labiatae)

The Deadnettles are familiar wild flowers throughout most of Europe. Most are vigorous carpeters easily grown on average garden soils, but generally too vigorous for the average rock garden; however, the following are worthy of consideration. Like most Labiates, plants have square stems and pairs of opposite leaves, with whorls of 2-lipped flowers. Propagation by division in the autumn.

Lamium maculatum ○◗

The Spotted Deadnettle is a strongly aromatic perennial with stems to 15cm (6in) tall, sometimes taller. The leaves are similar to the White Deadnettle, *Lamium album*, but are often marked with a silvery or white patch in the centre. The flowers are pinkish-purple. Widespread in Europe, W Asia and N Africa. April–October. 'Aureum'—leaves variegated with pale yellow; 'Roseum'—flowers pink.

Lamium garganicum ○

A S European mountain species with plain, brighter green leaves than the preceding. The flowers are pink to purple and stand erect. The common form is a tall plant, to 50cm (18in) but subsp. *pictum* is not more than 10cm (4in) and is a highly desirable, but little-grown, plant. The subspecies is restricted to the mountains of C and S Greece. June–July.

Lamium orvala ○◗☆
The Balm-leaved Archangel is a coarse but fascinating plant, a large deadnettle with triangular, heart-shaped leaves, irregularly toothed along the margin. The large flowers, 30–45mm (1⅕–1⅘in) long, are pink to dark purple, with a densely hairy upper lip. S and SE Alps, Hungary and W Yugoslavia. May–July. Perhaps too large for small rock gardens, but not an invasive species like the preceding.

LATHYRUS (Leguminosae)
This well-known genus contains amongst others the Sweet Pea, *Lathyrus odoratus*. Most are annual or perennial herbs with climbing stems and tendrils. The leaves are pinnate, although generally with few leaflets. The genus contains about 150 species mainly in Europe, Asia and North America, but extending to temperate South America and tropical E Africa.

Lathyrus vernus ○◗☆
The Spring Vetchling is a perennial forming tufts 30–50cm (12–20in) tall with angled stems. The leaves have 2–4 pairs of leaflets, but no tendril, and the blue-violet to reddish-purple, occasionally pink, pea-flowers are 13–20mm (½–⅘in) long, and borne in few-flowered racemes shorter than the leaves. Europe. May–June. An attractive, easy and floriferous plant, tolerant of a wide range of soils in sun and partial shade. In its native habitat a plant of wooded places to 1,900m (6,270ft) altitude.

Lathyrus cyaneus from the Caucasus is similar, but coarser and with striking bright blue flowers.

LAVANDULA (Labiatae)
The lavenders are a popular group of plants in gardens, widely used as a low hedge to edge paths or lawns. They are shrubby species becoming markedly woody with age. The majority of species are native to the Mediterranean region. The common lavender cultivated for ornament and perfumery is *L. angustifolia*.

Lavandula stoechas ○☆
The most charming of all Lavenders, but not always easy to please in gardens. Plants require as much sun as they can get, a well-drained soil and a sheltered site. Plants grow to 60cm (24in) tall, sometimes more, with numerous soft, grey-green linear leaves which are strongly aromatic when crushed. The deep purple, 4-angled flower spikes are topped by a curious, but attractive, cluster of deep purple-blue bracts which give the species its appeal. Mediterranean region and S Spain. July–August. The normal form has very short-stalked flower spikes, whereas subsp. *pedunculata* has far longer stalks, placing the flowers well above the foliage. The more dwarf forms of *L. stoechas* are well worth seeking out.

LEDUM (Ericaceae)
A small genus of aromatic, evergreen shrubs with 1–3 species. They have alternate, untoothed leaves and white or pink, 5-parted flowers with separate petals, borne in terminal umbel-like racemes. They require acid, cool soils; a semi-shaded position is preferable. Propagation by cuttings.

Ledum palustre ◐▢

The Labrador Tea is a circumpolar species of marshes, heather and coniferous woodland. It forms a low shrub up to 1m (3ft 4in), sometimes dwarf and prostrate at higher altitudes. The leaves are rusty-hairy beneath and with underrolled margins. The flowers, 10mm (⅜in) across, are white, sometimes pink, fragrant, and borne in terminal, umbel-like clusters; they produce copious nectar. April–May.

Subsp. *groenlandicum* (syn. *Ledum groenlandicum*) ◐▢

Is native to North America and W Greenland and is naturalized in a few places in Britain and W Germany. Preferable to *L. palustre* as a garden plant, being of denser growth, to 90cm (3ft) in height, with wider leaves, fewer stamens and a slightly longer flowering period, April to June. A compact form, 'Compactum', to 30cm (12in) tall, with woolly stems, short, broader leaves and small inflorescences, is also sometimes available.

LEIOPHYLLUM (Ericaceae)

A genus of 1–3 species, occurring naturally in E North America. The species have alternate or opposite, untoothed leaves and terminal clusters of pink or white, 5-parted flowers with separate petals. An attractive plant, distinguished from *Ledum*, to which it is closely related, by the longitudinally dehiscing anthers (*Ledum* releases pollen through apical pores) and the capsule, which splits from the top downwards, whereas *Ledum* capsules split from the base upwards. Like *Ledum* they require a lime-free, moist, leafy or peaty soil.

Leiophyllum buxifolium ◐▢

A tidy, erect, but low, evergreen shrub approximately 60cm (2ft) across, sometimes more, usually dense and twiggy, with reddish young wood and usually alternate, glossy green 'box'-like leaves. The flowers are rosy-pink in bud, with white petal-tips, paling to white when mature and carried on slender stalks in dense terminal clusters 20mm (⅜in) across. May and June. Var. *prostratum* is offered by nurserymen—a delightful low form.

LEONTOPODIUM (Compositae)

The genus contains the familiar Edelweiss, *L. alpinum*, as well as species scattered across Europe and Asia. They are perennial herbs with alternate entire leaves. Flower-heads are small and clustered, surrounded by a ruff of woolly, leaf-like bracts.

Leontopodium alpinum ○☆

This is the well-known Edelweiss which forms characteristic tufts of light greyish-green, hairy leaves, 15–40mm (⅗–1⅗in) long. The flower-stems vary from 5 to 20cm (2–8in) tall and terminate in almost round-headed groups of flower-heads, surrounded by leafy bracts, up to 50mm (2in) across. Individual florets are a yellowish-white. This species occurs throughout the mountains of S Europe, from the Pyrenees to the Rhodope Massif in SW Bulgaria. May–June. A selected form with a neater habit is the cultivar 'Mignon'. A superior form still is *L. nivale* from the Apennines, but this is scarce in cultivation.

Leontopodium haplophylloides ○

Like *L. alpinum*, but more slender, strongly scented of Lemon Verbena. W China. June–July. Rare in cultivation.

Leontopodium alpinum

LEPTARRHENA (Saxifragaceae)

A genus with only one species which comes from North America and Kamchatka. Like many of the genera in this family, it likes a cool, damp, shady position and will not tolerate full sun.

Leptarrhena pyrolifolia (syn. *L. amplexifolia*) ☽

Plants have glossy green, leathery leaves which are elliptic with blunt-toothed margins. The small white flowers are carried in compact, branched terminal clusters; the 5 petals are 1–2mm ($\frac{1}{25}$–$\frac{1}{8}$in) long, shorter than the 10 stamens. Canada and USA.

LEPTOSPERMUM (Myrtaceae)

A group of some 30 species of evergreen shrubs or small trees, mainly natives of Australia and Tasmania, but with a few species found in New Zealand, New Caledonia, the Malay Peninsula and Burma. The leaves are alternate, small and entire, and the flowers are solitary or in pairs or threes, each with 5 spreading petals which are normally white or occasionally pinkish; stamens numerous. The fruit is a hard woody capsule. Those cultivated are delightful and floriferous plants. They require a well-drained lime-free soil. Propagation from cuttings. They should be protected from severe frost.

Leptospermum humifusum ○□

A low spreading shrub up to 23cm (9in) high, with reddish stems. The thick, glandular, narrowly elliptic leaves, are 3–9mm ($\frac{1}{8}$–$\frac{2}{5}$in) long, glabrous and rounded at the apex. The small white flowers, 10mm ($\frac{2}{5}$in) in diameter, are borne singly in the leaf axils, smothering the branches. Tasmania. May–June. Very hardy and easy to grow in any good soil, but probably best in a light sandy loam. Excellent for draping a dry wall or rocks. Certainly the hardiest species in cultivation.

Leptospermum scoparium 'Nanum' Group ○◫
A variable group of small dense dwarf shrubs with linear-oblong to linear-lanceolate or ovate leaves that are a dark bronze-green in colour, reddish when young, sharply pointed, fragrant when bruised. The flowers are produced singly from the leaf axils, and range in colour from white through the various shades of pink to red. The species comes from New Zealand. May–June. Only hardy in S England. 'Red Falls', 'Redstart', 'Robin' and 'Wairere' are 4 recent introductions, but as yet are not readily available. 'Nicholsii'—a fine prostrate form with pale pink or rose-pink flowers.

LEUCANTHEMUM (Compositae)

The leucanthemums are a small group of about 20 species which at one time belonged in the genus *Chrysanthemum* and contain the common Ox-eye Daisy, *L. vulgare*. Most are European, though some come from N Asia, and are commonly known as marguerites, moon daisies or ox-eye daisies. They have large daisy flower-heads with large white ray-florets surrounding a central yellow disc. The foliage is usually divided into unequal lobes and is often rather fragrant. The species included here can be raised from seed or propagated by summer cuttings.

Leucanthemum hosmariense (syn. ***Chrysanthemum hosmariense***) ○☆
A sun-loving perennial from the Atlas mountains of Morocco with light greyish-green or silvery divided foliage and large daisy-like flower-heads to 40mm (1$\frac{3}{5}$in) across, borne on stems of 50–80mm (2–3in), eventually lengthening to 20–25cm (8–10in). May–June, occasionally earlier. One of the best rock garden daisies.

Leucanthemum niponicum ○
An interesting and pretty plant from Japan with rich green foliage and white or pinkish ray florets surrounding a yellow disc, the heads 30–40mm (1$\frac{1}{5}$–1$\frac{3}{5}$in) across. This species closely resembles the Ox-eye Daisy, but differs in having a shrubby rootstock and being generally shorter. June–July, occasionally later.

LEUCOPOGON (Epacridaceae)

A small genus of 150 species native to SW Asia and Australasia. They require a lime-free and semi-shaded position and the species included here is hardy in all but the coldest districts.

Leucopogon fraseri ○◫
A creeping subshrub, densely growing with erect leafy shoots to 80mm (3in) tall. The numerous leaves are small and heath-like, deep green but becoming bronzed or reddish-brown in the autumn and winter. The white flowers, 8–10mm ($\frac{1}{8}$–$\frac{2}{5}$in) across are 5-lobed. The fruit is a small berry, apricot-coloured when ripe. New Zealand. June–July.

LEWISIA (Portulacaceae)

Lewisias are among the showiest of all rock plants, especially the various forms and hybrids of *L. cotyledon*, and *L. tweedyi*. The genus contains about 18 species, mostly from mountainous rocky habitats.

The majority of species have a well-formed rosette of basal leaves which may be either evergreen or deciduous; the latter die down after flowering in spring; the leaves are fleshy to a varying degree and may be flat to almost cylindrical, often smooth at the margin, but sometimes toothed or undulate. The flowers are solitary on short stems in some species, but in most they are carried in loosely branched panicles, each branch and pedicel subtended by glandular-margined bracts. Each flower has between 2 and 4 sepals (or several in *L. rediviva*) often glandular-toothed, and between 4 and 18 petals which are mostly in the colour range white-pink-carmine to purple, often with darker veins or stripes; some selections of *L. cotyledon* and *L. tweedyi* are yellowish. The small capsules are circumscissile at the base, that is, breaking off like a cap to release the black, or dark brown, shiny seeds.

Lewisias require a sunny aspect and a very well-drained, lime-free, gritty soil, though not all demand an acid soil. The necks of the plants are often susceptible to rotting in winter, so that a collar of rocks or grit will help to keep them dry. Most species are best grown in pans in the alpine house, but a number will thrive in raised beds or troughs, or placed in a suitable crack in a retaining wall. On the flat, a sheet of glass or a cloche overhead will protect them from the worst of the winter wet. Propagation is generally from seed; the Cotyledon hybrids are especially easy from seed.

Lewisia cotyledon ○☆

This species from California and Oregon is the most widely cultivated, and indeed perhaps the easiest to grow. It has symmetrical evergreen rosettes of obovate or oblanceolate fleshy leaves, and panicles of very showy flowers, each 20–40mm ($\frac{4}{5}$–1$\frac{3}{5}$in) across. The most common colour is rose or salmon, often striped, but there are selections with soft yellow flowers (eg. 'Caroll Watson') and various strains with variable bright colours. 'Alba' and 'Siskyou White' have white flowers; 'Sunset Strain'—a variable group in pink, crimson, deep salmon, orange, apricot and yellowish colours. 'Birch Hybrids' are also a mixed group, some strikingly striped. Var. *cotyledon* has the leaves flat or slightly undulate and smooth at the margin. Var. *howellii* has the leaf margins conspicuously undulate-crisped and toothed. Var. *heckneri* has flat leaves with coarse fleshy teeth on the margins. All May–June.

Lewisia columbiana ○☆

This species also has neat rosettes of fleshy leaves, but they are much narrower, 3–8mm ($\frac{1}{8}$–$\frac{1}{3}$in) and always smooth-margined. The flowers are carried in loose panicles on slender stalks and are only 10–15mm ($\frac{2}{5}$–$\frac{3}{5}$in) across. Subsp. *columbiana* usually has magenta flowers and large leaf rosettes; subsp. *rupicola* (syn. *'Rosea'*) has smaller neater rosettes and rich rosy-magenta flowers; subsp. *wallowensis* usually has whitish flowers pencilled with purple veins. The species is native to N Oregon, Washington, W Idaho and S British Columbia. May–June.

'Edithae' is a garden form which is very like subsp. *rupicola*; it produces small stalked rosettes which can be detached and rooted as cuttings.

Lewisia leeana ○

Like *L. columbiana* in its general habit and flowers, but the leaves are more or less cylindrical, not flat. Oregon and California. May–June.

Lewisia congdonii ○

Like *L. columbiana* in its flowers, but the leaves are not evergreen and form loose erect tufts rather than symmetrical rosettes; they are flat and soft rather than stiffly fleshy, and are about 10–20mm ($\frac{2}{5}$–$\frac{4}{5}$in) wide. It is a much less attractive plant and far less often seen in cultivation. California. May–June.

Lewisia cantelovii ○☐

This has flattish neat evergreen rosettes of spatular leaves with very regularly toothed margins reminiscent of a saxifrage. The flowers are only 10–15mm ($\frac{2}{5}$–$\frac{3}{5}$in) across, whitish or pale pink, veined darker pink, and are produced in loose panicles on slender graceful stems. N California. May–June.

Lewisia tweedyi ○◑☐

A very beautiful species, popular for the alpine house. It has rosettes of large fleshy oval leaves which are narrowed to a stalk and are up to 50mm (2in) wide. The leaves are just overtopped by the large, usually soft apricot-pink or pale-yellow, flowers which are 50mm (2in) or more across. Selections have been made over the years, including 'Rosea' (pink) and 'Alba' (white). Washington State. April–May. This delightful species deserves every attention, though not particularly easy to grow; it will succeed outdoors in a wall crevice in some gardens.

Lewisia oppositifolia ○

A small plant with a few narrow basal leaves, not in an obvious rosette, and dying away in summer. The 10–20cm (4–8in) high stems also carry a few narrow leaves, the lower ones opposite. The flowers, 1–4 in number, are white or pinkish, 15–20mm ($\frac{3}{5}$–$\frac{4}{5}$in) across. Oregon and California. April–May.

Lewisia brachycalyx ○☐▲

An attractive dwarf species less than 10cm (4in) when flowering, dying down in summer. The flat fleshy leaves are dull greyish-green and spreading to form a rosette around the large short-stemmed white (occasionally pink) flowers, which are 30–50mm (1$\frac{1}{5}$–2in) in diameter. The 2 bracts are produced immediately below the 2 sepals, the flower thus appearing to have 4 sepals. California and Arizona. April–May. Generally rather difficult to cultivate successfully.

Lewisia nevadensis ○☐

A dwarf species with numerous linear basal leaves, becoming dormant in the summer. The usually single-flowered stems are shorter than the leaves and have a pair of bracts below their mid point; the stems often become curved and pressed onto the ground in the fruiting stage. The white flowers are about 15–20mm ($\frac{3}{5}$–$\frac{4}{5}$in) across and have entire sepals. Widespread in W USA. April–May.

Lewisia pygmaea ○

Like *L. nevadensis*, but having one or more white to deep pink flowers, 10–20mm ($\frac{2}{5}$–$\frac{4}{5}$in) across, with glandular-toothed sepals. The flowering stems are often prostrate. Widespread in the W USA. April–June.

Lewisia sierrae ○▲

Like *L. pygmaea*, but smaller, with pink flowers less than 10mm ($\frac{2}{5}$in) across and leaves up to 35mm (1$\frac{2}{5}$in) long. California. April–June. Rather rare in cultivation.

Lewisia longipetala ○▲

Like *L. pygmaea* in general appearance, but more robust with larger flowers, 25–35mm (1–1$\frac{2}{5}$in) across, the sepals with very conspicuous dark red glandular teeth. California. May–June. Rare in cultivation.

Lewisia rediviva ○□▲

A dwarf, large-flowered, highly decorative species, but requiring alpine house cultivation. Leaves linear, nearly cylindrical, fleshy, up to 50mm (2in) long, dying away at or before flowering time. Stems less than 50 mm (2in) long each, carrying a solitary rosy pink or white flower 50–60mm (2–2½in) across; they have 12–18 petals and 6–9 white or pinkish sepals. Widespread in W North America. June–July. Together with *L. tweedyi* the most desirable of *Lewisia* species.

Cultivars

Apart from the selections within the species mentioned above, there are various hybrids, many of them spontaneous ones with no recorded parentage, although it is usually possible to deduce what the most likely parents were. A selection of the best known is given here.

'George Henley'—a showy cultivar with the general appearance of *L. columbiana*, but with shorter and more compact inflorescences and rich rosy-purple flowers; 'Phyllellia' (*L. brachycalyx* × *L. cotyledon*)—has strong pink flowers produced throughout late spring and summer; 'Pinkie'—a dwarf hybrid with the habit of *L. longipetala*, but large pink flowers; 'Rose Splendour'—this may not be a hybrid, but a *L. cotyledon* selection with large clear pink unstriped flowers; 'Trevosia'—the general habit of *L. columbiana*, but the flowers are of a warm salmon-pink tone. All May–early July. ○

LIMNANTHES (Limnanthaceae)

This small genus of hardy annuals comes from California, where plants are normally found in damp ground. Indeed its name comes from the Greek, *limne-* meaning a marsh and *anthos-* a flower, referring directly to its preference for moist conditions. None the less, this genus performs equally well in drier conditions and can be a welcome addition to the larger rock garden, especially where a position in full sun can be guaranteed. Only one species is generally cultivated.

Limnanthes douglasii ○◑☆

A plant that is often referred to by its common name, Butter and Eggs. An overwintering or spring annual with brittle, divided, ferny leaves, to 25cm (10in) tall. The flowers have 5, toothed petals which are shining lemon yellow at the centre and pure glistening white at the edges. Pure yellow forms are sometimes seen. May–July. An easy and floriferous plant, but too invasive in confined areas.

LIMONIUM (Plumbaginaceae)

Also known as statice or sea lavender, this lovely genus produces small papery 'everlasting' flowers. Several of the 300 species are small enough for the rock garden and some are so small that they are best appreciated in a trough or pan. In most species the leaves are leathery, spatula- or spoon-shaped and arranged in basal rosettes; from these rise the slender wiry stems which carry the long-lasting membranous flowers. These vary in colour from white through pink and lilac to quite deep shades of purple and rose. Most occur in salt marshes or in steppe country in the wild.

Limonium bellidifolium ○☆

Plants remain quite compact in cultivation (5–15cm, 2–6in tall), but in the wild it may reach 30cm (12in). The leaves are spatula-shaped, each with 3–5 veins, and some frequently die off when the plant begins to flower. The tiny lilac-pink flowers are borne on slender stems. May–June. This species is probably best suited to a sunny corner in a trough rather than being placed in a rock garden situation where its beauty would be lost or overlooked.

Limonium minutum ○
Another very small species with flowering stems 3–15cm (1–6in) tall. The leaves only 8–10mm (*c.* ⅜in) long, have incurved margins and a single midvein. Native of SE France where calcareous cliffs are its usual habitat. May–June.

Limonium paradoxum ○☆
Another small tufted species 5–15cm (2–6in) tall with oval leaves up to 15mm (⅜in) long. The flowers are tiny, but a rich violet-blue colour. Ireland and Wales. May–June.

Limonium latifolium ○
Although considerably larger than the 3 preceding species this European native is a very attractive plant with flower-stems up to 50cm (20in) tall. In cultivation the elliptical leaves are 25–35cm (10–14in) long, but in the wild they often grow larger. The crowning glory of this plant is the branched inflorescence covered in large pale violet flowers. June–July. Generally too large for the small rock garden.

LINARIA (Scrophulariaceae)
The toadflaxes are a larger group of some 150 species of either annuals or herbaceous perennials. They have a wide distribution throughout the temperate western hemisphere. All enjoy a well-drained soil in full sun. Their narrow leaves occur in whorls in the lower part of the stem, becoming alternate in the upper part in most species. The 2-lipped flowers are borne in either terminal racemes or spikes and are characterized by having a conical spur protruding from the lower part of the flower and a hairy throat on the lower lip. Most are readily propagated from seed.

Linaria alpina ○☆
The Alpine Toadflax is one of the loveliest of alpine plants. It is a short-lived perennial, native to the mountains of C and S Europe, where it grows on rocky slopes and steep screes. The trailing stems have whorls of blue-grey leaves and dense racemes of violet and orange flowers. May–September. Several forms are grown including var. *alba*—flowers white; var. *rosea*—flowers of a delicate flesh-pink.

Linaria supina (syn. *L. pyrenaica*) ○
A perennial 8–15cm (3–6in) high with fine narrow, grey-green leaves carried on ascending branches. The flowers of this very variable species are usually yellow, sometimes tinged with violet. SW Europe. June–August.

Linaria tristis ○
This variable toadflax is native to Spain and Portugal where it grows amongst limestone rocks. Flowers yellow, variably tinged with purplish-brown. July–August.

Linaria maroccana ○☆
A bushy annual, 15–20cm (6–8in) high, with linear, light green leaves. Flowers normally bright violet-purple. NW Africa. June–August. Various colour forms exist including the following selections: 'Diadem'—flowers bright violet with a

white eye; 'Fairy Bouquet'—flowers white; 'Fairy Bridesmaid'—flowers citron-yellow.

LINNAEA (Caprifoliaceae)

A monospecific genus named in honour of Linnaeus (1707–78), the celebrated Swedish botanist. It is widely distributed in the colder part of the northern hemisphere including N Britain. Propagation by cuttings or rooted pieces of stem.

Linnaea borealis ○□☆

The Two-flowered Linnaea or Twin-flower is an old favourite with many gardeners. It forms prostrate tangled mats of slightly woody stems carrying oval to orbicular leaves. The delicate flesh-pink, fragrant, pendant, bell-shaped flowers, 5–9mm ($\frac{1}{5}$–$\frac{2}{5}$in) long, are borne in pairs on stems well above the foliage. May–July. A lover of shady places and moist peaty soils, greatly disliking drought. The American form, var. *americana*, is a larger version of the above with deeper pink flowers; this plant is generally said to be easier to establish in cultivation. *L. borealis* is one of the most delightful of creeping alpines easy to control should it become too invasive.

LINUM (Linaceae)

The flax genus contains about 230 species native to Europe and Asia, a few from the southern hemisphere. The perennial species are mostly attractive tufted plants with slender stems, small, often pointed leaves, and 5-petalled flowers in various shades of blue, pink and yellow, occasionally red. They are generally easy to grow in a sunny site on a well-drained soil. Propagation is easy from seed or by mid-summer cuttings. Most are hardy, but may succumb to winter wet. Slugs often take a liking to the young fleshy shoots.

Linum perenne ○☆

A hairless perennial to 40cm (16in), sometimes taller, with slender stems bearing numerous narrow-lanceolate grey-green leaves. The flowers, 18–25mm ($\frac{3}{4}$–1in) across, are a bright or pale blue, opening in succession along the stem tips. Europe, where it inhabits dry grassy places. June–August. Generally too tall, except on a large rock garden. However var. *alpinum (Linum alpinum)* is altogether finer, only 15–20cm (6–8in) tall with delightful, deep sky-blue, silky flowers, larger than the type.

Linum narbonense ○

Another tall-growing species, to 40cm (16in), bearing numerous bright blue flowers larger than the foregoing. C and S Europe. June–August.

Linum monogynum ○

Like a white version of *L. perenne*. The stems form dense tufts bearing numerous flowers. New Zealand. June–August. Not as hardy as the other species.

Linum suffruticosum ○☆

A tufted greyish perennial with short leafy non-flowering stems and long flowering shoots. The leaves are linear, alternate. The flowers are white-centred and veined with pink or violet. SW Europe. June–July. Subsp. *salsaloides* is the finest form for the rock garden, almost prostrate, the lower stems becoming woody with age. The flowers are 20–30mm ($\frac{4}{5}$–1$\frac{1}{5}$in) across, occasionally pure white. The whole plant rarely exceeds 15cm (6in) tall. In the wild this subspecies inhabits grassy and rocky habitats, to 1,750m (5,770ft), being frequent in parts of the Pyrenees and the

135

Cevennes. The form sold as var. *nanum* is even more compact and worth seeking out.

Linum flavum ○
A variable plant, to 30cm (12in) tall with spreading to erect stems bearing deep green lanceolate leaves. The flowers are bright yellow, 25–30mm (1–1⅛in), unfurling in sunshine like those of most other flaxes. C and S Europe, W and C Asia. May–July. The dwarfer more compact forms are worth finding, but not all are reliably hardy in the garden.

Linum arboreum ○
A Mediterranean species forming a small shrub to 20cm (8in) tall. The grey-green elliptical leaves are blunt and the flowers large, bright golden yellow. Crete, S Greece and SW Turkey. June–August.

Linum 'Gemmel's Hybrid' ○☆
A particularly fine and floriferous hybrid, more compact than *L. arboreum*, up to 18cm (7⅛in) tall, but often less, bearing a mass of bright yellow flowers. The best of the yellow flaxes for the rock garden.

LITHODORA (Boraginaceae)
A shrubby genus of 7 species, many of which, until recently, were included in *Lithospermum*. In the wild they are mainly confined to S Europe. The funnel-shaped flowers have 5 spreading lobes and are borne in leafy terminal racemes; their colour is usually purple-blue, but some species have white flowers. All parts of the plant are covered with pale, bristle-like hairs. In cultivation they thrive in a well-drained soil in an open, sunny sheltered position.

Lithodora diffusa (syn. *Lithospermum diffusum*) ○☐☆
A low evergreen shrub 20–30cm (8–12in) tall and forming a spreading mass up to 60cm (24in) wide. Leaves dark green, slender, 15cm (6in) long, clothed with pale hairs. Flowers stalkless, borne in the leaf axils in a terminal, leafy raceme, gentian-blue, faintly striped with reddish-violet. S Europe. May–June. 'Heavenly Blue'—has larger flowers that are of a paler blue; 'Grace Ward'—even larger flowers, the plant with a less spreading habit. The species and its cultivars thrive best in an acid or neutral soil.

Lithodora oleifolia (syn. *Lithospermum oleifolium*) ○
A laxly branched subshrub to 20cm (8in) tall, occasionally more, with dull green oblong leaves that are whitish beneath. Flowers sky-blue, pinkish in bud, borne in small clusters. E Pyrenees. June–July. Thrives on a limy soil.

LITHOPHRAGMA (Saxifragaceae)
There are 9 species in this genus, but only one is generally cultivated. The flowers have divided petals, 10 stamens and 3 stigmas.

Lithophragma parviflorum ◖
The Prairie Star has hairy, soft green leaves which are mostly basal or borne on the lower part of the stem; they are roundish and divided into 3 or 5 segments, which in turn are less deeply lobed. The heads of starry white or pink flowers are carried on stems about 15cm (6in) tall; each flower is 15–25mm (⅗–1in) across and each petal

has 3 or sometimes more narrow lobes. North America. April–May. A dainty plant with delicate stems which succeeds best in a moist peaty or leafy soil in partial shade.

LOBELIA (Campanulaceae)

A large genus with species scattered in both the old and new worlds. They range in form and size from prostrate carpeters to small annual species, *L. erimus*, much used as a summer bedding plant, to the giant monocarpic species with huge leaf-rosettes and spines of flowers endemic to the mountains of E Africa. Although several are cultivated by alpine gardeners, only one is widely grown and obtainable.

Lobelia syphilitica ○◑☆
A dwarf perennial species to 18cm (7in) tall, forming neat tufts, bearing fairly large pale blue flowers, lipped like those of other lobelias. E USA. September–October. Especially valuable for its late flowering habit. Readily grown in most average soils. 'Alba'—a white-flowered form.

LOISELEURIA (Ericaceae)

A genus containing one circumpolar species, growing in exposed situations on granite, and occurring naturally in the Highlands of Scotland.

Loiseleuria procumbens (syn. *Azalea procumbens*) ○☐
The Creeping Azalea forms a dwarf, prostrate, evergreen shrub with small, crowded, opposite, narrow leathery leaves, the margins underrolled to conceal the lower surface. The small, pink flowers, 5–6mm (⅕in), are 5-parted, solitary or in small terminal clusters; each is bell-shaped. The fruit is a many-seeded, 2–3-valved capsule. June–August. Although this plant is readily available commercially, it cannot be depended upon to produce flowers freely, especially in drier areas. It requires a well-drained leafy-loam without lime.

LOTUS (Leguminosae)

Annual or perennial herbs or small shrublets with about 100 species in northern temperate regions, but with a few scattered in Africa, Australia and the temperate regions of tropical South America.

Lotus corniculatus ○
This well known Bird's-foot Trefoil or the Bacon and Eggs Plant is a very variable and widespread species, a prostrate or ascending perennial herb reaching 60cm (24in) in lush conditions, but usually shorter. The pinnate leaves have 5 leaflets and the yellow pea-flowers, 10–16mm (⅖–⅝in) long, are often tinged with deep red. Widespread in Europe and Asia. May–September. Generally too invasive for the rock garden, but 'Flore-pleno' has showy double flowers and is rather less vigorous.

Lotus alpinus is like *L. corniculatus*, but smaller and with fewer flowers. Unfortunately, although occasionally seen in gardens, it is unavailable commercially.

LUETKEA (Rosaceae)

The genus contains a solitary species native to North America.

Luetkea pectinata ◑
A subshrub forming a dense mat of 3-lobed leaves. The flowers are white or pale yellow rather like those of *Spiraea*, borne in long spikes above the foliage.

June–August. Surprisingly little seen in cultivation and well worth seeking out. Plants thrive best in a rock crevice with a cool leafy moist root-run. In the wild *Luetkea* inhabits rocky places, gravels and screes close to, or above, the tree-line.

LUPINUS (Leguminosae)

A genus well known to gardeners by its showy Russell hybrids, but the small alpine species are much less robust and are worth considering. The genus contains about 200 species of annual or perennial herbs, mainly native to the Andes, Rockies and Mediterranean Europe, but with a few in the highlands of E Africa and E South America. The leaves are commonly palmate, often with 4–8 leaflets, and the pea-like flowers are borne in racemes. The four species listed below are native to North America.

Lupinus confertus ○
A woody-based perennial herb with erect or ascending leafy stems, 20–40cm (8–16in) in height, the whole plant invested with silky, golden hairs. The long racemes are many-flowered, blue, the standard petal with a central white blotch. June–August.

Lupinus ornatus ○
Another woody-based perennial herb, 30–40cm (12–16in) tall with silkily hairy leaves. Similar to *L. confertus*, but the flowers laxer and in longer racemes. May–June.

Lupinus lyallii ○☆
A mat-forming perennial herb to 10cm (4in) in height, with numerous silvery or greyish leaves. The blue flowers, 7–9mm ($\frac{1}{3}$–$\frac{3}{8}$in) long, are borne in compact racemes held well above the foliage on long stalks. W North America. June–August. Perhaps the loveliest species for the rock garden, thriving in a well-drained gritty soil, although like most lupins it is not particularly long lived and needs to be raised regularly from seed.

Lupinus littoralis ○
The Seashore Lupin or Chinook Licorice is a perennial, prostrate, mat-forming herb with ascending flowering branches reaching 50cm (20in) in height. The leaves are silvery- or golden-hairy beneath. The lax racemes of flowers are blue or purplish, sometimes with a lavender or white standard petal. May–July.

Other species to look out for, but only occasionally available, are *L. alopecuroides* and *L. lepidus*.

LYCHNIS (Caryophyllaceae)

A fairly small genus of about 12 species, the taller of which have large showy flowers, making excellent herbaceous border plants. They are all perennials with opposite leaves carried on the stems, sometimes all clustered together in basal tufts. The flowers have 5 petals, which are often notched or deeply bilobed. *Lychnis* is related to *Silene* from which it differs mainly in the number of tooth-like lobes at the apex of the capsule when it splits open; in *Lychnis* there are 5 such teeth, whereas in *Silene* there are 6, 8 or 10. There are no epicalyx scales surrounding the calyx as there are in the related *Dianthus*.

Lychnis alpina (syn. *Viscaria alpina*) ○☆
A charming, hairless, tufted plant with dark green, linear-lanceolate basal leaves. The flower stems are 5–15cm (2–6in) in height and carry 2–3 well-spaced pairs of leaves and a dense terminal head, 10–20mm ($\frac{2}{5}$–$\frac{4}{5}$in) across, of pinkish-purple flowers. Widespread in N Europe, including Britain, and in the Alps and Pyrenees. May–July. 'Rosea'—a slightly pinker selection.

Lychnis viscaria ○
The Sticky Catchfly is a widespread European and W Asian plant forming compact tufts of glabrous or slightly hairy, linear-lanceolate, basal leaves. These are overtopped by the flower-stems which have a few pairs of narrow leaves and sticky patches below the nodes; the height may be only 15cm (6in), but is usually much more. The flowers are produced in spike-like heads, pinkish-purple to dark purple, with entire or slightly notched petals. May–June. Very easy to grow, but short lived.

Lychnis flos-jovis ○
Although generally rather tall for the average rock garden, some forms may be as short as 20cm (8in) and therefore not entirely out of place. It has oval to spoon-shaped basal leaves which are covered in a dense silvery-white wool. Erect flower stems carry pairs of lance-shaped leaves and a terminal head of up to 10 flowers with broad bilobed petals, usually purplish-red, but sometimes pink or white. European Alps. June–July. 'Nana' is a slightly more compact version.

Lychnis × *haageana* ○
An attractive hybrid of robust upright habit, but only 20–30cm (8–12in) in height, with hairy, bronzed, lanceolate leaves and heads of very showy orange or scarlet flowers, each about 50mm (2in) across; the petals are bilobed and have a conspicuous tooth on each side. June–July.

Lychnis × *arkwrightii* ○☆
An excellent hybrid between *L* × *haageana* and the tall herbaceous *L. chalcedonica*. It is 20–35cm (8–14in) in height with erect stems bearing purplish-brown ovate-lanceolate leaves and loose heads of large intensely scarlet flowers some 40–50mm (1$\frac{1}{2}$–2in) in diameter, with bilobed petals. June–August. The young shoots are prone to attacks from ravenous slugs and can be protected by an encircling handful of sharp coarse grit or by a suitable slug bait. Readily raised from seed.

LYSIMACHIA (Primulaceae)

A large genus of about 200 species with a worldwide distribution. Most are herbaceous perennials too gross for rock gardens. The yellow, white or red flowers are borne singly at the leaf axils, or as racemes or spikes. The corollas are star- or bell-shaped with 5–7 petals. Most are easy to cultivate, relishing deep soils. They can be increased easily by division of the parent plant.

Lysimachia nummularia ○◗
The Creeping Jenny forms a mat of long prostrate leafy stems with opposite round leaves. The solitary, axillary, bright yellow flowers are cup-shaped, 8–16mm ($\frac{1}{3}$–$\frac{2}{3}$in) across. An attractive, if invasive, species, which should be cut back after flowering. Very easy in any situation except very dry ones. Europe. May–September.

Lychnis × arkwrightii

MAIANTHEMUM (Convallariaceae)

The genus contains a solitary species, the May Lily, a woodlander for moist shady places which is readily propagated by division of the parent plant.

Maianthemum bifolium ◐

A rhizomatous, carpeting perennial only 8–14cm (3–5½in) tall. The erect stems bear 2 pale green, glossy, heart-shaped leaves and a small cluster of fluffy white flowers. These are succeeded by small red berries. N temperate hemisphere. May–June.

MARGYRICARPUS (Rosaceae)

A small genus of Andean subshrubs well deserving a place on every rock garden. Only one species is commonly grown.

Margyricarpus setosus ◐☐

An evergreen subshrub to 20cm (8in) tall at maturity, with spreading branches. Leaves pinnate and spine-tipped. The flowers are rather dull, small and green, but are followed by showy snow-white berries which persist long on the plant. June.

MATTHIOLA (Cruciferae)

This genus includes the garden stocks, sweet-smelling spring and summer bedding plants derived from *Matthiola incana*. The genus contains some 50 species, primarily distributed in Europe and W Asia. Plants tend to be short lived and require a sunny sheltered site to be at their best but are often not hardy during severe winters. Propagation from seed. Many have strongly scented flowers.

Matthiola fruticulosa (syn. *M. tristis*) ○
A white or grey hairy perennial to 40cm (16in) becoming woody at the base. The linear to oblong leaves may be lobed or unlobed. The flowers vary from yellowish-brown to purplish-red and are borne in long racemes. S Europe. May–July. Subsp. *valesiaca* (syn. *M. valesiaca*) is a finer plant, more compact in habit and with dull mauve flowers (at least in the cultivated form). This subspecies is native to the mountains of C and S Europe.

MAZUS (Scrophulariaceae)
A group of small creeping perennials which are closely related to *Mimulus* and native of Asia, New Zealand and Australia. Flowers range from pale bluish to white and are borne singly or in one-sided racemes; each flower, which is large in comparison with the rest of the plant, has 2 lips, the upper being erect and the lower spreading and much larger. All are easily cultivated in a well-drained soil in full sun.

Mazus pumilio ○
Creeping underground stems bear short leafy branches of spatulate leaves, 20–70mm ($\frac{4}{5}$–2$\frac{4}{5}$in) long. The flowers are borne on 50mm (2in) long stems, white or bluish-white, with a yellow centre. Australia and New Zealand. July–August.

Mazus radicans ○
Forms prostrate mats with bronzed leaves and 15mm ($\frac{3}{5}$in) wide flowers, 1–3 to a stem, pure white and blotched with yellow in the centre. New Zealand. June–July.

Mazus reptans ○□
A mat-forming perennial with tufts of toothed, dark green leaves from which arise the relatively large purplish-blue flowers blotched white and yellow. Himalaya. June–August. A very good plant for a pan in the alpine house as well as on a scree outside. Probably the finest species in cultivation.

MECONOPSIS (Papaveraceae)
Perhaps the most popular of all the genera in the poppy family and noted primarily for the exquisite blue-flowered *M. betonicifolia* and *M. grandis* and their hybrids. *Meconopsis* is a relatively large genus with more than 40 species; however, few are suitable for the average alpine garden, being generally too gross. Besides the blue-flowered species, there are those with purple, red, yellow or white flowers. Some are truly perennial, whereas others form a handsome rosette for several years before flowering and dying. Apart from the Welsh Poppy, *M. cambrica*, they require cool leafy parts of the garden in which to succeed, mostly preferring acid rather than alkaline soils.

Meconopsis cambrica ◑☆
The Welsh Poppy is a native of Wales and the Pyrenees, but is widely established and naturalized in some areas. It is by far the easiest species to grow, often seeding around once established and it can prove bothersome on a scree garden. Plants form erect tufts to 30–40cm (12–16in) tall, with deeply lobed, often rather pale green foliage. The clear-yellow, crinkled poppy flowers are 40–70mm (1$\frac{3}{5}$–2$\frac{4}{5}$in) across and 4-petalled. June–August, sometimes later. There is a form with orange flowers, var.

aurantiaca, as well as those, in both colours, with semi-double flowers, 'Flore-plena'.

Meconopsis horridula ○◑□

This charming high alpine denizen of the Himalaya gets its name from the sharp straw-coloured spines that invest the leaves and stems. The lance-shaped leaves form a basal rosette from which eventually (generally 2–4 years) rises a column of blue or purple-blue, almost transparent flowers of great beauty, beset with a cluster of pale yellow stamens. Plants die after flowering and seed should be collected with care for future generations. June–July.

Meconopsis quintuplinervia ◑□

This is Reginald Farrer's Harebell Poppy, a charming perennial species for a cool peaty position. Plants form low tufts of lance-shaped, untoothed leaves and spread by short stolons to form extensive patches if the conditions suit them. The solitary pendant, half-open poppies are a pastel mauvish-blue, 25–30mm (1–1⅕in) long, borne on graceful spindly stalks up to 30cm (12in) long. W China.

The greatest alpine gem in the genus is undoubtedly *M. bella* from the C and E Himalaya, but it is frustratingly difficult in cultivation and has tempted many over the years, though few can boast to having succeeded with it for long. It can be likened to a blue alpine poppy—*Papaver alpinum*.

MENTHA (Labiatae)

The genus includes the mints which are mostly vigorous and invasive perennials to be kept away from the rock garden. One tiny species is, however, worth including.

Mentha requienii (syn. *M. conica*) ○◑

A prostrate green creeping perennial with thread-like stems and small elliptical or oval leaves, not more than 6mm (¼in) long. The tiny flowers are pale lilac and are borne in rounded clusters. The whole plant is strongly aromatic. Endemic to the islands of Corsica, Sardinia and Montecristo. June–July. Ideal for growing in cracks in paving and along the edges of paths. Spreads quickly, but dislikes a dry soil.

MENZIESIA (Ericaceae)

A genus of less than a dozen species native to North America and NE Asia, one of which, *M. ciliicalyx*, is more commonly grown than the rest, although several may be found listed in catalogues. The branches are frequently in tiers, and the leaves often clustered at the ends of the twigs. The flowers are terminal, borne in clusters at the end of previous year's growth; the corollas are bell- or urn-shaped.

Menziesia ciliicalyx ◑□

An attractive, slow-growing, deciduous shrub up to 1m (3ft) in height, somewhat resembling *Enkianthus* in the way the numerous, lantern-like flowers hang down beneath the branches. The twigs are smooth and slender, carrying the leaves in pseudowhorls at the branch ends; the leaves are bright green, 20–80mm (¾–3in) long. The flowers develop with the leaves and are borne in clusters; they are whitish-green at the base, pink to deep red at the lobes, 18–20mm (¾in) long. Japan. May–June. Var. *purpurea* has crimson to wine-coloured flowers covered with a dense blue-white bloom.

MERTENSIA (Boraginaceae)

A genus of 40 perennial herbs from Europe, including the British Isles and parts of North America and Asia. The alternate leaves are often bluish-green and bear small transparent dots. Flowers funnel- or bell-shaped with 5 lobes, mainly blue or purple, borne in terminal racemes. Most of the cultivated species eventually make low spreading plants, suitable for the more shady areas of the rock garden where they will flower in the spring or summer. Some have a reputation for being short-lived, but they are readily raised from seed sown the moment it is ripe, or by division in the early autumn.

Mertensia maritima (syn. *Pulmonaria maritima*) ○▲
This native of the shore of Britain and other parts of N Europe is sometimes known as the Oyster Plant, a very pretty flower in the wild. Plants form prostrate mats of slightly fleshy blue-grey leaves and bear flowers of turquoise which open from soft pink buds. July. Like many shoreline plants, it can be difficult to grow, but best results have been achieved by growing it in almost pure sand, or in an average sandy loam.

Mertensia virginica ◑☆
A native of North America where it is called the Virginian Cowslip, a splendid plant 30–40cm (12–16in) tall. Typically its foliage is of an amethyst-green from which grow drooping terminal heads of pink and mauve buds which open into luminous comfrey-like, sky-blue, flowers. April–May. A highly recommended spring-flowering plant for a shady position in the garden, preferring a light soil. A beautiful and striking plant when grown well.

MICROMERIA (Labiatae)

Small thyme-like aromatic herbs or subshrubs from warm dry regions requiring well-drained soils and plenty of sunshine. Most are not entirely hardy in Britain, but several are available from nurserymen. They can be propagated from seed or midsummer cuttings. They are especially valuable for mid- and late-summer flowering.

Micromeria microhpylla ○
Perhaps the finest, forming a twiggy shrublet to 30cm (12in) high eventually. The small grey-green, paired leaves are triangular-oval. The purple flowers are 5–6mm (¼in) long. A native of Corsica, Italy and Sicily. August–September.

Micromeria marginata (syn. *M. puperella, Thymus marginata*) ○
Another delightful aromatic shrub, to 20cm (8in), with broad-oval, untoothed leaves. The flowers are purple to violet, 12–16mm (½–⅔in) long. Endemic to the Maritime Alps of SE France and NW Italy. August–October.

MIMULUS (Scrophulariaceae)

The monkey flowers or musks are a large group of showy plants which are cosmopolitan in their distribution and include several suitable for the rock garden. They mostly have lush green leaves with serrated margins, occurring in opposite pairs. The snapdragon-like, open-mouthed flowers have 2 lips. Interestingly the stigma consists of 2 plates which, on being touched, close together. Flower colours range from pure yellow through orange to red. Most are short-lived perennials which flower during the summer months and require a moisture-retentive soil.

Mimulus 'Andean nymph'

Mimulus luteus ○◑

A North American plant similar to *M. cupreus*. The flowers are yellow with two dark marks near the mouth. The dwarf variety *alpinus* is more suitable for the rock garden: a perennial with 1–4-flowered stems of bright yellow flowers which arise from densely matted stolons. June–September.

Mimulus cupreus ○◑☆

A Chilean species closely related to *M. luteus*, but differing in its more tufted habit. Flowers yellow at first, then becoming copper-coloured, throat yellow, spotted brown. June–August. Its many forms are more widely cultivated than the wild type and include: 'Bee's Dazzler'—bright crimson-red; 'Brilliant'—deep purple-crimson; 'Red Emperor'—bright crimson scarlet; 'Whitecroft Scarlet'—vermilion, 20–30mm (8–12in) tall, the best-known cultivar. *M.* × *burnetii*, a hybrid between *M. cupreus* and *M. luteus*, with coppery-yellow, spotted flowers.

Mimulus primuloides ◑☆

A tufted downy perennial of North American origin forming neat flat mats of oval hairy leaves. Its solitary yellow flowers are borne on 8–10cm (3–4in) high, leafless stems. W USA. A choice plant requiring a gritty soil in a cool moist position. Plants spread by radiating runners.

Mimulus moschatus ○◑

The Common Musk is generally too coarse for the average rock garden, but worthy of a place where space allows. The old-fashioned musk-scented forms of this plant appear to be very rare in cultivation today.

Mimulus 'Andean Nymph' ○◑☆

This fine plant, now widely available, hails from the Andes, and represents an as yet undescribed species. It is most notable for its attractive pale cream blooms flushed with pink and delightfully spotted in the throat. May–July.

MINUARTIA (Caryophyllaceae)

The sandworts constitute a large genus of some 120 species distributed widely, but mainly, in northern temperate regions. They are mostly not showy enough to be worth cultivating, but two of the cushion-forming species may be found in gardens.

Minuartias are annuals or perennials with narrow, often spiky, paired leaves and mostly white flowers carried in loose clusters, sometimes solitary. There are 5 petals which are entire, not notched at the apex as in many *Caryophyllaceae*, and each flower has 10 stamens and 3 styles. The capsules, when they split open, have 3 teeth at the apex whereas the related *Arenaria* has capsules with twice as many teeth as styles, usually 6.

Minuartia stellata ○
A cushion-forming perennial with densely packed rosettes of lanceolate leaves, each up to 10mm (⅜in) long, overtopped by short stems carrying solitary (rarely 2) flowers. These are white and about 10mm (⅜in) across. Greece and Albania. May–June.

Minuartia verna (syn. *Alsine verna*) ○
The Vernal Sandwort is a loose cushion-forming perennial with very narrowly linear-lanceolate sharply pointed leaves up to 20mm (¾in) long. The loosely branched inflorescences carry one to several flowers, 6–8mm (¼–⅓in) in diameter, white with contrasting purple anthers. S, W and C Europe. May–July.

Subsp. *gerardii* is sometimes seen in catalogues, but is now considered to be only a slight variant of subsp. *verna* and not worthy of separate recognition.

MITCHELLA (Rubiaceae)

There are only 2 species in this genus, one indigenous to North America and the other to Japan; both grow in peaty soil in woodland shade, and are trailing evergreen perennials with woody stems, rooting at the nodes. The leaves are borne in opposite pairs, glossy and heart-shaped. Flowers pink, fragrant. Only one species is commonly grown.

Mitchella repens ◑☆
A native of North America, where it is known as the Partridge Berry. Prostrate, soft-wooded shrublet only 20mm (⅜in) tall. Its square stems support small cordate leaves, which are glossy-green with white veins. Flowers stalkless, pink, flushed with red, tubular with 4 lobes, daphne-like and fragrant. The scarlet berries are an additional feature. June–July.

MITELLA (Saxifragaceae)

A genus of 12 species from E Asia and North America—only American species are presently in cultivation. They all like cool, dampish conditions and are useful for a shady spot in the rock garden. A feature of Mitellas is the 5 divided or fringed petals. The plants are covered in short glandular hairs and have long-stalked leaves which are mostly basal. Propagation by division of the parent plant, although once established, plants often seed around rather freely.

Mitella diphylla ◑☆
A tufted plant with glossy, stalked, maple-shaped leaves with 3 or 5 lobes; the 15–25cm (6–10in) tall, slender stems bear a pair of leaves (hence the epithet *diphylla*). The small white flowers are about 4mm (⅛in) across, borne in spikes; the

petals are fringed. North America. April–May. A useful woodlander for semi-shaded places.

Mitella breweri ☽☆
Plants form mats of lobed, kidney-shaped leaves. The stems, up to 25cm (10in) tall, carry many greenish flowers. The fringed petals alternate with the stamens. North America. May.

Mitella nuda ☽
Another mat-forming species producing slender stolons, which help it to spread. The leaves are kidney-shaped or rounded, with blunt-toothed margins. The stems are 3–15cm (1–6in) tall, bearing spikes of greenish or brownish flowers. The petals have long spreading segments and 10 stamens (the other species have only 5 stamens). North America. May.

Mitella pentandra ☽
Plants have roundish, bluntly toothed leaves on long stalks. Leafless stems, 25–30cm (10–12in) tall, carry lax racemes of greenish-yellow flowers; each flower is about 6mm (¼in) wide and has fringed petals which are opposite the stamens. North America. May–June.

Mitella caulescens ☽
A low-tufted plant with hairy heart-shaped leaves which are usually 5-lobed and irregularly toothed. Drooping racemes are carried on stems 10–15cm (4–6in) tall. The flowers, which open from the top of the raceme downwards, are pale yellow and the petals alternate with the stamens. North America. May.

MOLTKIA (Boraginaceae)

A small genus of 8 species native to Europe and Asia and closely related to *Lithospermum*, with which it is sometimes confused in cultivation. They can be herbaceous perennials or subshrubs, with roughly hairy, alternate leaves. The flowers are tubular or funnel-shaped, ranging in colour from purple and blue to yellow. All are summer flowering and require a hot sunny position in a very well-drained, limy soil. Plants are most readily raised from cuttings taken during the summer.

Moltkia petraea (syn. *Lithospermum petraeum*) ○☆
A small semi-evergreen shrub 15–30cm (6–12in) tall, with stems and leaves covered in grey hairs. Flowers produced in small dense clusters at the end of the shoots; these are pinkish-blue in bud, but open to a deep violet-blue, about 8mm (⅓in) long, with long-protruding stamens. June.

Moltkia × *intermedia* (syn. *Lithospermum* × *intermedium*) ○
An attractive hybrid between *M. petraea* and another species, *M. suffruticosa*, 20–25cm (8–10in) tall with brilliant blue flowers produced in spreading heads. June.

MONARDELLA (Labiatae)

This American genus contains several delightful little species of small bergamot-like plants, mostly with red, blue, purple, or white flowers. They require a sunny sheltered position on the rock garden and a good gritty well-drained soil.

Monardella macrantha ○
The most readily available species, but by no means common in cultivation. Plants form small tufts to 20cm (8in) tall, though often less, with a creeping rootstock. The leaves are oval and toothed and like the stems they are often flushed with purple or red. The scarlet, tubular flowers are borne in tight heads surrounded by purplish bracts. California. July–August.

MONTIA (Portulacaceae)

A genus of about 50 species, mostly rather uninteresting from a horticultural stand-point. Some Montias are weedy and in general they are the poor relations of the Lewisias which are much more showy. They have somewhat fleshy foliage and smallish, white to pinkish-purple flowers, borne in racemes. They are mostly North American, but there are a few in Europe, Asia and Australasia; only one species is generally listed in catalogues—described here.

Montia australasica (syn. *Claytonia australasica*) ○◗
This is a neat species with creeping stems forming mats of growth with many upright, linear leaves, amid which arise umbels of small white flowers, each less than 10mm (⅜in) across. The whole plant is usually not more than 50mm (2in) in height. Australia and New Zealand. June–August.

MORISIA (Cruciferae)

This charming little genus contains only a solitary species native to sandy habitats on the islands of Corsica and Sardinia. A plant for poor well-drained soils, succeeding well on screes or in troughs or pans. Plants can be propagated from seed, or alternatively by root cuttings.

Morisia monanthos (syn. *M. hypogaea*) ○
A hairy little perennial to 50mm (2in) tall with pinnately lobed leaves borne in neat rosettes, dark shiny green. The flowers are golden-yellow, solitary, erect, but curving down to the soil surface in fruit. April–June, sometimes later.

MYOSOTIS (Boraginaceae)

The forget-me-nots, or scorpion grasses, are a very familiar group of about 40 annual or perennial herbs, native to temperate regions of the world, but most commonly found in Europe. The familiar flowers occur in terminal spiralled racemes, each flower tube being short with 5 spreading lobes. Some species are white or even yellow, but most are blue, these sometimes changing to a reddish-pink with age. A moist soil suits most, but few are cultivated on rock gardens as many are either short lived or are weedy and not suited to such specialized treatment. Most are readily raised from seed.

Myosotis alpestris ○
A tufted perennial up to 20cm (8in) tall covered with azure-blue flowers 6–9mm (¼–⅜in) across with a yellowish eye. A native of European mountains, where it inhabits damp woods and meadows above 1,500m (4,950ft). June–July. Several named clones are grown, including 'Ruth Fischer' with larger leaves which are curled and crimped and larger flowers borne on shorter stems; 'Aurea'—has attractive yellow leaves.

Myosotis australis ○◗

A hairy forget-me-not from New Zealand, 20cm (8in) in height, erect and branching from the base. The narrow leaves are up to 50mm (2in) long and the flowers white, or more commonly yellow, 8–10mm (*c.* ⅜in) across. June–July. A charming species.

Two further New Zealand species, *M. explanata* and *M. saxosa*, are also occasionally seen in cultivation. Like so many New Zealand alpines, both have white flowers. The latter is a small plant to 80mm (3⅛in) tall with rosettes of leaves, the former taller and stouter, to 15cm (6in).

MYRTEOLA (Myrtaceae)

An offsplit from the much larger genus *Myrtus, Myrteola* comprises some 12 species of dwarf shrubs native to South America. They have opposite leaves, covered in gland dots and pleasantly fragrant when crushed. The white flowers are axillary and solitary, each with 4 sepals and 4 petals. The berry-like, edible fruit has a persistent calyx.

Myrteola nummularia (syn. *Myrtus nummularia*) ◗☐

The plant forms a tangled mass of prostrate foliage and reddish woody stems. The tiny leathery, oval leaves, 4–10mm (⅕–⅖in) long, are hairless, with decurved margins. The small flowers, 3–5mm (⅛in) across, are produced from the upper leaf-axils, on very short stalks. The pink berry is edible. A plant for the sheltered peat garden, but it is quite hardy in more temperate areas. Well suited for carpeting moist areas and large rocks. Straits of Magellan and Falkland Islands. May. Propagation by cuttings or self-rooted pieces. Plants can be clipped back lightly in late spring to keep them in check and tidy.

NIEREMBERGIA (Solanaceae)

A small Mexican and South American genus of great charm belonging to the potato family, which has few other members suitable for the alpine garden; there are about 35 species in the genus. They are fairly easy to grow, preferring a sheltered, sunny though moist site, disliking long droughts in particular. Propagation by division or from seed.

Nierembergia caerulea (syn. *N. hippomanica*) ○☆

A dense, bushy little plant to about 15cm (6in) tall with bright green lanceolate leaves. The numerous flowers are upturned, bell-shaped and deep mauve and, at a distance, similar in appearance to some bellflowers (*Campanula*). Argentina. June–September. Especially valuable for its long-flowering season, though only half-hardy in less mild districts.

Nierembergia repens (syn. *N. rivularis*) ○☆

Another pretty species, but quite distinct from the previous; a mat-forming plant, creeping and rooting about, not more than 50mm (2in) tall. The deep green leaves are lanceolate and the widely opening, bell-shaped flowers pure white, large for the size of the plant. Argentina, Chile and Uruguay. July–August. Well worth growing—hardier than *N. caerulea*.

OENOTHERA (Onagraceae)

The evening primroses are mostly far too gross and invasive for inclusion here, but there are several more dwarf species worthy of consideration. The genus contains some 80 species, primarily native to the Americas. The flowers are usually large and showy with 4 overlapping petals which open in the evening in the majority of species. Most are short lived, but are readily propagated from seed or by root cuttings.

Oenothera acaulis (syn. *O. taraxicifolia*) ○
One of the finest, a prostrate leafy plant with grey-green elliptical, somewhat toothed and lobed leaves. The large flowers, 50–80mm (2–3⅛in) across are white, flushing pink as they age. Chile. July–September. A lovely plant, not always easy to please, but deserving every bit of attention.

Oenothera missouriensis (syn. *O. macrocarpa*) ○☆
More vigorous than the previous species with trailing stems and green lanceolate, toothed leaves. The huge yellow flowers, up to 15cm (6in) across, are very beautiful, but often seem disproportionately large, almost vulgar in the rock garden setting. S USA. July–September.

Oenothera caespitosa ○
A small, practically stemless species, to 12cm (4¾in) tall, with a lax rosette of grey-green spatular-shaped, somewhat lobed leaves. The white flowers, to 90mm (3½in) across, flush with pink as they age, the petals deeply notched. W North America. July–August. Var. *crinita* is even more desirable with its grey-hoary foliage.

Oenothera pumila (syn. *Kneiffia perennis*)
A slighter species to 15cm (6in) tall with a basal tuft of narrow-lanceolate leaves. The erect leaf spikes carry a series of small yellow flowers, about 25mm (1in) across. E North America. July–September.

Oenothera fruticosa ○
Like the previous, but a taller, more leafy plant to 30cm (12in) with large yellow flowers. E North America. A variable species—some forms are too tall for the rock garden.

Oenothera speciosa ○
A small tufted species to 20cm (8in) tall. The leaves are oblong, toothed or somewhat lobed. The flowers are rose-pink, about 25–35mm (1–1⅜in) across and borne in succession. North America. July–August. Often sold under the incorrect name of *O. mexicana* var. *rosea*, a quite distinct species. The usual form of *O. speciosa* sold by nurseries is var. *childsii*.

OMPHALODES (Boraginaceae)

A delightful genus of annual and perennial plants, most of them easily cultivated. The forget-me-not-like flowers are carried in loose, spiralled racemes and their colour is predominantly blue, although white forms do occur. The 30 species within the genus are widely distributed throughout Europe and Asia, where they are found in a variety of habitats, ranging from exposed rocks to damp shady woodlands, to open maritime sands. Only 3 are commonly cultivated and these flower in spring and early summer, occasionally later.

Oenothera missouriensis

Omphalodes cappadocica ◐☆

A rhizomatous perennial with slender erect stems forming tufts up to 15cm (6in) tall. The pale green, heart-shaped, leaves arise mainly from the base of the plant on long stalks. The intense azure-blue flowers are only 5mm ($\frac{1}{5}$in) wide and form graceful loose racemes. Caucasus. March–May. The clone 'Anthea Bloom' is sometimes grown and has grey-green leaves and paler blue flowers.

Omphalodes verna ○◗

This S European species, commonly known as 'Blue-eyed Mary', is a trailing perennial 15cm (6in) tall. Its long-stalked leaves are 90mm (8in) long and heart-shaped. Flowers solitary or two to each raceme, blue with a white throat. February–May. Can prove invasive and not always very floriferous if too vigorous. 'Alba'—pure white flowers.

Omphalodes luciliae○▲

An immensely attractive plant which inhabits rock crevices in the mountains of Greece and W Asia. Plants form loose tufts up to about 15cm (6in) tall with striking blue-grey leaves. The few-flowered racemes are rose-coloured at first, but soon change to a beautiful sky-blue. June–July. 'Alba'—a white-flowered form. The normal blue-flowered form is one of the most desirable and much sought after alpines. It demands a gritty, well-drained, compost with a rich loam and added mortar rubble, but is not the easiest of plants to accommodate. Some people succeed with it outdoors on a scree, or raised bed in a sunny sheltered site, although it is safest to confine it to a pan in the alpine house.

ONONIS (Leguminosae)

The rest-harrows are annual or perennial herbs or dwarf shrubs with about 75 species, mainly in the Mediterranean but with a few species found further north in Europe, in the Canary Islands, and West Asia. Plants are often sticky with glandular hairs. The clover-like leaves have toothed leaflets. The pea-flowers may be yellow, pink, purple or white and are borne in spikes, racemes or panicles. Easily raised from seed, or the shrubby ones can be propagated from cuttings.

Ononis rotundifolia ○

A dwarf, erect, deciduous subshrub, 35–50cm (14–20in) in height forming a rounded bush. The stems are hairy and glandular and the trifoliate leaves are covered with short hairs. The rose-pink or whitish flowers, 16–20mm ($\frac{3}{5}$–$\frac{4}{5}$in) long, are borne in axillary racemes, the standard-petal striped with deep pink. Mountains of C and S Europe.May–August. A delightful plant, seldom long lived, but easily raised from seed. Plants prefer a calcareous soil.

Ononis fruticosa ○

The Shrubby Rest-harrow is a compact dwarf shrublet, 30–60cm (12–24in) in height. The flowers are rose-pink, 10–20mm ($\frac{2}{5}$–$\frac{4}{5}$in) long, the standard-petal with a central blotch, the wing-petals generally paler. Pyrenees and SW Alps. June–August. In the wild a plant of dry rocky places, to 1,600m (5,280ft).

Ononis cristata (syn. *O. cenisia*)

A mat-forming, rhizomatous perennial attaining a height of about 20cm (8in) and a spread of 25–30cm (10–12in). The solitary pink flowers, 10–14mm ($\frac{2}{5}$–$\frac{3}{5}$in) long, are borne on slender stalks. Mountains of C and S Europe and North Africa. June–September. Prefers calcareous soils.

Ononis natrix ○☆

A much-branched dwarf subshrub, 20–60cm (8–24in) in height and densely glandular-hairy. The flowers are borne in lax leafy panicles, 14–16mm ($\frac{3}{5}$in) long, and deep yellow with the standard-petal often striped with blood-red or violet veins on the reverse. C and S Europe. May–August. A very variable species which makes a magnificent plant for a sunny position on the rock garden or scree, preferring a calcareous soil. Plants can be pruned hard back in the spring to encourage a nice even mound of growth. Often seeds around once established, but surprisingly uncommon in cultivation.

ORIGANUM (Labiatae)

The marjorams are an interesting genus of aromatic herbs native mainly to the Mediterranean region and W Asia. The Common Marjoram, *O. vulgare*, is a familiar European species, widely cultivated, but too gross for the rock garden. There are, however, several other exciting species, well deserving a place in any collection. They are mostly subshrubs with wiry stems and opposite pairs on untoothed leaves. The flowers are partly concealed by large conspicuous bracts which give the plants their great appeal. The flowers are highly attractive to bees, sometimes butterflies. Propagation by seed, cuttings or division.

Origanum dictamnus ○▲
The Dittany is a native of the hot rocky slopes of Crete. It is a charming plant, but by no means hardy in most gardens and is best tried within the confines of an alpine house—its chief enemy being winter wet. This super little plant forms domed tufts to 20cm (8in) tall, the rounded leaves covered in a dense layer of soft hairs. The drooping flower-heads have pink flowers and green leaf-like bracts which are generally tinged with pink. June–September.

Origanum laevigatum ○
A Turkish species fairly recently introduced to cultivation, but hardy in the garden, forming spreading tufts to 15cm (6in) tall. The dark green oval leaves are not felted as in the previous species. During the later summer the thin stems produce branched sprays of small reddish-purple flowers. August–October. Well worth growing.

Origanum hybridum ○
Another Turkish species which has proved amenable to cultivation. Plants have larger and rounder leaves than the foregoing and the flower-heads are pink or purplish. July–September.

Origanum amanum ○☆
Perhaps the finest species for the alpine gardener, generally seen in the alpine house, but hardy enough on the rock garden wedged in rock crevices and shielded from winter wet. Plants form small tufts to 10cm (4in) tall, with spreading wiry stems. The leaves are oval or rounded and generally bright green. The long tubular, 2-lipped, flowers are a bright rose-pink, each up to 30mm ($1\frac{1}{8}$in) long. The bracts are rather less conspicuous than in the other species referred to. Turkey. July–August.

Origanum rotundifolium ○☆
Another fine Turkish species, hardier in the garden than once supposed. Plants form rounded tufts to 20cm (8in) tall, with rather rounded leaves. The flowers are small and pinkish, but the drooping heads are surrounded by large and conspicuous apple-green bracts of great charm. July–September. The attractive bracts remain fresh on the plant long after the flowers have faded.

OROSTACHYS (Crassulaceae)

A small genus of about 20 species from temperate Asia, with succulent leaf-rosettes, reminiscent of those of the houseleeks, *Sempervivum*. They are reliably hardy only

Origanum amanum

in the mildest districts and elsewhere require some form of winter protection. They make ideal pan plants, readily propagated from offsets.

Orostachys chanetii (syn. ***Sedum chanetii***) ○
The greyish-green leaf-rosettes are rather flat, sometimes with a pleasant pinkish tinge. The small pink flowers are borne in an erect pyramidal inflorescence, up to 20cm (8in) tall. C China. June–August.

Orostachys spinosum (syn. ***Cotyledon spinosa, Umbilicus spinosus, Sedum spinosum***) ○
A handsome plant forming symmetrical rosettes of spine-tipped lanceolate leaves— the leaves are thick and fleshy and during the winter close into a tight ball with many upward projecting spine-tips. The yellow flowers are borne in a spike to 13cm (5in) tall. C Asia. June–August. Perhaps hardier than *O. chanetii*.

OTHONNOPSIS (Compositae)

A genus of about 8 glabrous shrubs, mainly from South Africa. They are related to *Senecio* and have similar, yellow, daisy flower-heads. In cultivation they require a dry, sunny, sheltered position.

Othonnopsis cheirifolia ○
A spreading, evergreen, grey-green shrub, to 30cm (12in) high, with lanceolate or elliptical, untoothed leaves, thick and rather fleshy. Flower-heads bright yellow, 30–35mm (1⅕–1⅖in) across, solitary or laxly clustered. N Africa. June–July. Requires some protection in colder districts.

OURISIA (Scrophulariaceae)

A genus of about 25 species native of New Zealand, Australia and temperate South America. Most are low herbaceous perennials, often forming mats of foliage which

Othonnopsis cheirifolia

arise from a creeping underground rhizome. The flowers can be white, pink or scarlet and are borne in whorled racemes. In the wild they are found in open sites close to streams where the soil is moist; however, in cultivation a little shade is necessary in order to provide shelter from drying winds; a peaty, lime-free soil is preferred.

Ourisia caespitosa ◑☐

The smallest species, forming a tight mat with tiny, silvery-green leaves which are slightly notched. Flowers white with a shade of yellow in the throat, 4–5 borne on slender 10cm (4in) tall stems. May–June. The variety *gracilis* is even smaller in the size of its leaf and flower. Both are ideally suited to the peat garden which provides both moisture and shade.

Ourisia coccinea ◑☐☆

A charming plant from the Chilean Andes, which has bright green, toothed leaves with well-defined venation. Its tubular, scarlet flowers, which are about 40mm (1⅝in) long, hang in loose racemes. May–September. A moist peaty soil in a shady position is best.

Ourisia macrocarpa ◑☐
A vigorous plant with coarse, fleshy foliage, light green in colour and up to 12cm (4¾in) in length. Although this species is sometimes shunned because of its large foliage it is worth growing for its panicles of pure white flowers, each 25mm (1in) wide and opening 4–8 in a whorl. New Zealand. June. A moist peaty soil is best.

Ourisia 'Loch Ewe' ◑☐☆
A beautiful hybrid betwen *O. coccinea* and *O. macrophylla*, which has recently been raised at Inverewe Gardens in Scotland. It forms mats of rich green foliage and loose panicles of delicate pink flowers. 30cm (12in). June–August.

OXALIS (Oxalidaceae)

This large genus is familiar to many gardeners not so much for its decorative members, but for some of the pernicious and invasive species which it contains. These aside, there are a number of beautiful subjects well deserving attention here. The genus contains about 800 species widely scattered in both hemispheres, especially in the tropics and subtropics. Many have trefoil-like leaves and bear clusters of rather Flax-like flowers which open in sunshine. Those listed here are reasonably easy to grow given a well-drained soil and sunny aspect, except where indicated. Propagation by seed or offsets.

Oxalis acetosella ◑
The familiar Wood Sorrel is a charming and well-known plant, with its pale green, trefoil leaves and dainty white flowers. Plants form spreading mats, creeping below ground by slender stems. Widespread in northern temperate regions. March–April. Requires a cool shaded position—dislikes drought. 'Rosea'—rose-red flowers.

Oxalis oregana ◑
From W North America, is like a small pink-flowered version of the previous species.

Oxalis adenophylla ○◑☆
One of the most select species which, when well grown, is a superb plant. Close to the soil surface, the fibrous bulb produces a tuft of silvery-grey leaves, not trefoil-like but with 10 or 12 folding leaflets like miniature umbrellas. The flowers are pink, paler in the centre, funnel-shaped. Chile. April–May. Plants die away completely in the autumn. An attractive pan subject.

Oxalis laciniata ○◑
Another bulbous species, but distinguished by its narrow trefoil leaves. The flowers are pink or mauve, occasionally nearly blue. Patagonia. May–June.

Oxalis enneaphylla ◑☆
A low rhizomatous perennial. The leaves mostly have 9 heart-shaped leaflets. The pearly white flowers are solitary, very similar to those of *O. acetosella*. Patagonia and the Falkland Islands. May–July, sometimes later. 'Rosea'—pink flowers, the best form.

Oxalis depressa (syn. *O. inops*) ○
A spreading, sometimes invasive species with green trefoil leaves and pretty, large, rose-pink flowers with a yellowish centre. The whole plant is about 7.5cm (3in) tall.

155

Oxalis articulata (syn. *O. floribunda* Hort.) ○❶
Another invasive species but attractive and worthy of a place where space permits. Plants grow to 25cm (10in) tall and have pale green trefoil leaves. The long stalks bear a lax cluster of showy bright pink, funnel-shaped flowers. June–September. Argentina. Several different plants are sold under this name and it is often difficult to be sure one has the right subject.

Oxalis deppei ○
Another species with a bulb-like rootstock. Plants form a tuft of leaves from which arise the clusters of brick-red flowers on slender stalks to 20cm (8in) tall. Mexico. May–June.

Oxalis chrysantha ○
A Brazilian species, low growing, to 15cm (6in) tall in flower, and spreading by runners. The leaves are green, trefoil-like, and the flowers bright yellow. June–September. Probably not hardy in less mild districts.

Oxalis obtusa ○
Another prostrate species with trefoil leaves. The flowers are rose-pink. South Africa.

Oxalis lobata ○
A tufted perennial with rather bright green trefoil leaves. The solitary bright yellow flowers are borne above the foliage, the whole plant about 8–10cm (3–4in) tall. South America. August–September. The leaves die away during the early summer, but a new crop appears with the flowers in the autumn.

Oxalis magellanica ○❶
A creeping perennial with small leaves and stemless white flowers close to the ground. South America.

Two further species sometimes seen in plant catalogues are *O. patagonica* and *O. speciosa*.

OXYTROPIS (Leguminosae)

The genus takes its name from the Greek for sharp keel with reference to the beaked keel-petals which distinguish this from its close generic relative, *Astragalus*. There are about 300 species distributed in Eurasia and North America. They are perennial herbs or subshrubs, sometimes stemless, the pinnate foliage forming a rosette at ground level. Propagation is generally from seed.

Oxytropis lambertii ○☆
A handsome silvery tufted perennial to 20cm (8in) tall. The carmine or purplish flowers are borne in long-stalked clusters, each flower with an inflated silvery calyx. North America. June–July. The most charming species in cultivation.

Oxytropis megalantha ○
An almost stemless, densely hairy, perennial herb to 25cm (10in) in height with bluish pea-flowers aggregated into long-stalked racemes which well exceed the leaves in stature. Japan. May–June.

Oxytropis shokanbetsuensis ○❶
Also from Japan, this little-known, almost stemless, perennial herb has purplish flowers, about 20mm (⅘in) in length, borne in racemes. June–July.

Oxytropis montana ○
A plant from the European Alps, rare in cultivation, but worth growing. More delicate than the preceding species, it is almost prostrate with deep green leaves and blue, purple or reddish-purple flowers. April–May.

PAEONIA (Ranunculaceae)

Most of the paeonies are far too gross for the average rock garden, but one, *P. cambessedesii*, is worthy of attention, being generally dwarfer than the other types.

Paeonia cambessedesii ○
A very beautiful species to 45cm (18in) tall with striking grey-green, almost metallic-looking, deeply lobed leaves, which are backed with reddish-purple. The solitary, deep rose blooms are 6–10cm (2½–4in) across, with a central boss of yellow stamens. Balearic Islands. June–July. Resents disturbance like most species of paeony.

PAPAVER (Papaveraceae)

This large genus is too well known and widely grown to warrant description other than to mention that few are really suitable for the alpine garden and certainly many of the coarse annual ones should be kept well away in case they invade screes and crevices with the copious seedlings.

'Papaver alpinum' ○☆
The Alpine Poppy is here stressed because most experts today recognize it as representing an aggregate of species native primarily to the higher regions of the Alps and Pyrenees. They are delightful and cheerful little plants, generally behaving as short-lived perennials. The one normally seen forms small tufts of finely cut grey-green foliage and white or golden-yellow flowers, 30–50mm (1⅕–2in) across, borne on slender erect stalks to 15cm (6in) tall. The white-flowered plant is correctly *P. burseri* or *P sendtneri*, which differ primarily in fine details of the leaves. The yellow-flowered plants are usually referable to *P. rhaeticum* (including *P. pyrenaicum*); however, all these are found in catalogues usually as *P. alpinum* and, to complicate matters, they all tend to hybridize. Despite this, they are well worth growing.

Papaver miyabeanum ○
A Japanese alpine poppy rather like the previous but generally a smaller plant with yellowish-green foliage and pale creamy yellow flowers. Not a difficult plant to grow, preferring scree to open soil, but not yet widely available.

Papaver rupifragum ○
From the mountains of Andalucia, with terracotta flowers, and the closely related *P. atlanticum* from Morocco, with orange flowers, are sometimes seen on rock gardens, but are generally too vigorous and invasive.

PARAHEBE (Scrophulariaceae)

A small genus of semi-woody shrubs which are closely allied to, and sometimes confused with, both *Hebe* and *Veronica*. The flowers closely resemble those of the speedwells and are borne in loose racemes, ranging in colour from white, pink through various shades of blue. All are summer flowering and prefer a sheltered position exposed to full sun. They are natives of New Zealand.

Papaver rhaeticum

Parahebe lyalli ○☆

A semi-prostrate subshrub to 20cm (8in) tall and frequently rooting from where the branches touch the ground. Leaves thick and leathery with a few coarse teeth, sometimes reddish when young. The flowers occur in slender racemes and are white, sometimes veined with rose. August–September.

Parahebe catarractae ○

An erect bush to 20cm (8in) in height, with purplish young shoots and leaves which are oval or narrow-oblong with saw-like teeth. The flowers are borne in the leaf axils on the upper part of the shoots and are white with rose-purple veining. August–October.

PARAQUILEGIA (Ranunculaceae)

Paraquilegia is one of those genera guaranteed to excite interest amongst growers of alpines. As is often the case, the attraction of these plants lies not only in their beauty, but also in their difficulty of cultivation which provides growers with an irresistible challenge.

Paraquilegia anemonoides ◖
A tufted perennial with delicate grey-green ferny foliage similar to that of a small meadow-rue (*Thalictrum*). The solitary flowers, 20–30mm ($\frac{4}{5}$–1$\frac{1}{5}$in), are a delicate shade of mauve-blue, occasionally white, half-nodding on slender stalks. Himalaya and W China. April–May. A plant of rock crevices in the wild, requiring alpine house conditions or a trough sheltered from the worst of the winter weather. Not difficult once well established, but it is not always easy to obtain plants. Seed is occasionally available.

Paraquilegia microphylla ◖
Similar to the previous species but with much more finely divided leaves and smaller, white, occasionally pale pink, flower. The plants are up to 12cm (5in) tall. W Himalaya. April–May. Rarer in cultivation.

PAROCHETUS (Leguminosae)

A genus of one species native to the high mountains of both Asia (to 4,000m (13,200ft) in the Himalaya) and East Africa, but the African form is eventually to be given a separate species name, as it differs in several characteristics. Easily propagated by division.

Parochetus communis ◖☆
The Shamrock Pea or Blue Oxalis is a creeping or trailing perennial herb rooting at the nodes and rarely attaining a height of more than 80mm (3in). The trifoliate, oxalis-like, leaves have heart-shaped leaflets with a basal brown crescent, the margin slightly toothed. The cobalt blue pea-flowers are solitary or paired, up to 20mm ($\frac{4}{5}$in) across, sometimes with pinkish wings. October–February. A half-hardy species that will survive outdoors in a sheltered site in all but the severest winters. The protection of a pane of glass or cloche will help to ensure survival.

PARONYCHIA (Illecebraceae)

A large, but little-known group, horticulturally speaking, and mostly of only slight ornamental interest. There are about 50 species widely distributed in the world. They are annuals or perennials, often prostrate, and much-branched with small opposite leaves with conspicuous papery stipules adjacent to them. The flowers are very small, usually borne in the leaf axils in rounded clusters surrounded by large and conspicuous silvery bracts; each flower consists of a 5-lobed calyx and minute petals, or no petals at all. It is the papery bracts which constitute the most attractive feature of these plants. They require a well-drained, gritty compost and plenty of sunshine.

Paronychia argentea ○
An attractive cushion or mat-forming plant with oval or lanceolate leaves 5–10mm ($\frac{1}{5}$–$\frac{2}{5}$in) long. The clusters of tiny flowers are surrounded and hidden by the silvery-white bracts, each whole cluster being some 10–15mm ($\frac{2}{5}$–$\frac{3}{5}$in) across. S Europe. May–June.

PARNASSIA (Parnassiaceae)

A north-temperate genus of 50 species. Most of the species grow in upland bogs. They are perennial herbs with simple leaves, most of which are basal. The flowers are solitary with 5 sepals and petals. Inside and opposite the petals are 5, usually fringed, staminodes (modified stamens) which have nectaries on the upper surface.

159

Parochetus communis

They grow best in a wettish place in the garden, though not necessarily a shady one; a peaty soil suits most of them. They flower from summer to early autumn. Plants can be propagated by division or from seed. The family Parnassiaceae is closely related to the Saxifragaceae, indeed sometimes it is included within it.

Parnassia palustris ○◐

The Grass of Parnassus grows throughout the temperate northern hemisphere, including parts of Britain. The flowers, 15–25mm ($\frac{3}{5}$–1in) across, are borne on stems 10–20cm (4–8in) tall which rise from tufts of heart-shaped leaves. The petals are white with 7–13 green veins, and smooth margins. The staminodes are fringed with narrow projections, each with a globular tip. July–September. A lovely plant which is well worth growing, though not always easy to please. In Britain and some parts of Europe it is a protected species.

Parnassia fimbriata ◐

A very handsome species which has larger flowers than *P. palustris*, and can grow to 30cm (12in) tall. The petals are fringed on the lower edges and the staminodes are fringed with rather stubby projections. W North America. July–August.

Parnassia parviflora ○◐

Similar to *P. palustris*, but the leaves are oval or oblong and the flowers, which are about 12mm ($\frac{1}{2}$in) across, have petals with green or pale purple veins. North America.

Parnassia nubicola ○◑
Rather like a daintier version of *P. palustris*. The heart-shaped leaves and branched stems carrying white, green-veined, flowers about 15–20mm (⅗–⅘in) across. The petal edges are often finely toothed and the staminodes 3-lobed. Himalaya. August–September.

Parnassia foliosa ○◑
A distinctive species which has the leaves in tiers up the stem. Plants grow to about 20cm (8in); the flowers have fringed petals, and the staminodes have 3 lobes with a spherical gland at the tip of each lobe. China, N India, Japan. July–September.

PENSTEMON (Scrophulariaceae)
A very beautiful genus of up to 150 species, natives of North America and Mexico, with one in NE Asia. They can be herbaceous, half-hardy perennials or semi-shrubby with a tendency of being short-lived. The flowers are 2-lipped, the upper lip 2-lobed and the lower 3-cleft; they are snapdragon-like and very showy, ranging in colour from red, pink and blue through to white, and are generally borne in many-flowered racemes. All those described here require a hot sunny position in a light, well-drained soil. Propagation from mid-summer cuttings or from seed.

Penstemon davidsonii (syn. *P. menziesii*) ○
A variable species that has in the past been much confused with *P. rupicola*. In its best form it is a creeping, mat-forming shrub with flower-stems 6–10cm (2½–4in) tall. The small leaves are oval or elliptical and the flowers, which are 25–40mm (1–1⅜in) long, are lavender to violet in colour, borne in a few-flowered raceme. California. June–July.

Penstemon newberryi ○☆
A mat-forming, evergreen subshrub only 10–15cm (4–6in) high in which the young stems are covered with a fine, spreading down. Leaves rather leathery, dull green and broadly elliptic in shape with an almost rounded apex. Flowers 2–8 in a rather crowded raceme, bright cerise-crimson, up to 30mm (1⅕in) long and funnel-shaped. W USA. July. A charming and very worthwhile plant.

Penstemon rupicola ○
Closely allied to *P. newberryi* and differing by its prostrate, creeping habit and thick grey-blue-green leaves. It also has fewer flowers to each raceme; these are rose-carmine. California and Oregon. May–June. Another fine species, though rather less brilliant than *P. newberryi*.

Penstemon roezlii ○
The status of this species is uncertain and plants distributed under this name are most likely to be *P. newberryi* or a form of it.

Penstemon pinifolius ○☆
A very distinct species with sharply pointed, needle-like leaves, about 25mm (1in) long, giving plants an overall feathery effect. It is a spreading subshrub up to 20cm (8in) high which supports narrow panicles 10cm (4in) long, of tubular, bright scarlet flowers. NW North America. August. A super plant only comparatively recently introduced into cultivation.

Penstemon scouleri ○☆

An erect subshrub to 30cm (12in) tall with lanceolate leaves 50mm (2in) long and only 6mm (¼in) wide. This floriferous plant has lavender or pale purple flowers that are arranged in opposing racemes. NW North America. May–June. 'Alba'—a good white-flowered cultivar which is sometimes seen in cultivation. Two fine hybrid cultivars also worth growing, both 20–30cm (8–12in) tall and with pink flowers, are 'Six Hills' and 'Pink Dragon'.

PERNETTYA (Ericaceae)

A small genus of about 24 species, distributed in Central and South America, with one species confined to New Zealand and Tasmania. The South American *P. mucronata* is one of the hardiest species, and, together with its many cultivars, is the most popular and the most commonly grown of its group. Several other species are almost as readily available from nurserymen, but they do not produce anything like the colour range of the berries of *P. mucronata*. Pernettyas are low evergreen shrubs grown for their fruits rather than for the small, typically Ericaceous flowers. The leaves are also small and variably toothed, while the flowers are 5-parted, urn-shaped, white. The characteristic fruit, a hairless, round, many-seeded berry, overwinters on the plant. For a plentiful crop of berries, it is wise to ensure that each collection includes at least one male plant as a pollinator. This is essential with *P. mucronata*, *P. leucocarpa* and *P. pumila*, and it is a good idea to plant these species in groups of 3 or more, including a male plant in each group. Pernettyas require a lime-free, leafy, moist but well-drained soil in an open or slightly shaded position.

Pernettya mucronata ○◑◐□☆

Plants spread rapidly by suckers, the stems reaching a height of 60cm (24in) or more in time. The leaves, 10–20mm (⅖–⅘in) long, are spine-tipped, shiny and hairless. The small white flowers are followed by berries 8–12mm (⅓–½in) in diameter, typically red, but ranging from white to purple in the many cultivated forms. May–June. The following cultivars are generally the easiest to obtain: 'Bell's Seedling'—large, bright, carmine-red berries, particularly long lasting; 'Alba'—white berries; 'Davis's Hybrids'—a selection of plants producing a variety of berry colours. A male form of *P. mucronata* is offered by many nurseries.

Pernettya tasmanica ◑□

This is another desirable and dwarf species, but it is comparatively rare in cultivation, possibly because it is not fully hardy. It is a prostrate plant forming cushioned mats with red, pink or yellowish berries which are produced in profusion. Tasmania. June. Generally grown within the shelter of an alpine house or frame, where it makes an attractive pan plant. 'Alba'—a white berried form.

Pernettya nana ◑□

A low subshrub to 12cm (5in) tall with slender wiry branches bearing tiny oval leaves and later, red berries. New Zealand. June.

PETROCALLIS (Cruciferae)

A small genus distributed in the mountains of C and S Europe. Plants can be propagated from seed or by late summer cuttings.

Petrocallis pyrenaica (syn. *Draba pyrenaica*) ○
A low, densely tufted, grey-hairy perennial to 40–50mm (1½–2in) tall at the most. The wedge-shaped leaves are lobed at the top and the small pale lilac or pink, very occasionally white, flowers are borne in short racemes. Pyrenees and Alps, where it inhabits limestone rocks and screes above 1,700m (5,600ft) altitude.

PETRORHAGIA (Caryophyllaceae)

A mainly European group of plants related to *Dianthus* and *Gypsophila*. Only one species is cultivated to any extent by rock gardeners since most of them are rather tall. There are about 20 species, mainly Mediterranean in origin.

  Petrorhagia species are mostly perennials with pairs of slender linear-lanceolate leaves and either loosely branched inflorescences or very dense heads of flowers; these have a tubular 5-toothed calyx and 5 petals, 10 stamens and 2 styles and, when the capsule opens, 4 teeth at the apex. The petals may be rounded, toothed or 2-lobed at the apex.

Petrorhagia saxifraga (syn. *Tunica saxifraga*) ○
The Tunic Flower is a loosely growing, hairless, perennial, 10–30cm (4–12in) in height when in flower. It has narrow, pointed, greyish-green leaves and solitary upright flowers, or sometimes a few flowers in a branched head. These are pale pink, about 5–10mm (⅕–⅖in) across, with petals that are notched at the apex. Well-grown plants may be very floriferous. C and S Europe. June–August. There is a double-flowered form in cultivation, 'Flore Plena', which is darker pink than the single form usually seen.

PHUOPSIS (Rubiaceae)

A genus from the Caucasus Mountains containing a single species which is very closely related to the genus *Crucianella*. A hardy perennial herb for an open sunny position. Readily increased by division of the parent plant.

Phuopsis stylosa ○☆
A spreading perennial with stems to 25cm (10in). Leaves slender and pointed, arranged in whorls of 6–8 on the stem. Flowers small, funnel-shaped, pink, borne in flat heads. May–June. The whole plant emits an unpleasant musky scent, which is especially evident after a rainfall. Generally too invasive for the smaller rock garden although plants can be trimmed back severely to keep them in check.

PHYLLODOCE (Ericaceae)

A small genus of dwarf, evergreen, prostrate shrubs, widely distributed over the northern hemisphere in Europe (including the British Isles), Asia and North America. The leaves are crowded, linear and with underrolled toothed margin. The 5-parted, urn-shaped flowers are nodding, borne in sub-terminal racemes. Beautiful little shrubs for humus-rich, lime-free soils, preferring semi-shaded positions. Propagation by cuttings or seed.

Phyllodoce caerulea (syn. *P. taxifolia*) ○▢
A native of northern regions of Asia, America and Europe, this species is also a rare native of N Britain, where it is commonly called the Mountain Heath. Plants grow to 15–35cm (6–14in) in height bearing prostrate and/or ascending branches. For the first few years one stem only is produced, but as the plant matures, this primary stem

Phuopsis stylosa

dies back and is replaced by new shoots arising from its base, which eventually form a dense cushion. The leaves are dark, glossy green and the nodding, urn-shaped, lilac-purple flowers are 7–11mm ($\frac{1}{4}$–$\frac{2}{5}$in) long, borne near the top of the stems. May–June. In the wild a plant of heaths and moors up to 2,600m (7,480ft) altitude.

Phyllodoce aleutica ○◐☐
This species is native to the Aleutian Islands and is also found in Alaska, Japan and Kamchatka. It is a dwarf, compact, carpeting species up to 23cm (9in) tall. The leaves are dense, dark green above, yellowish beneath, and the flowers pale yellow or creamy-white borne in clusters at tips of shoots. May–June.

Phyllodoce empetriformis (syn. *Menziesia empetriformis*) ○◐☐☆
Ths W North American alpine species, which occurs naturally above 2,300m (6,900ft) is considered to be the easiest of the genus to grow in cultivation and is certainly one of the best. It is a tufted shrub up to 25cm (10in) in height with erect stems, at least when young. The leaves are linear and toothed. The bright red-purple flowers are produced in clusters of up to 6 at the uppermost leaf-axils, each corolla 7–9mm ($\frac{1}{3}$in) long. April–May.

Other species frequently offered in catalogues are:

Phyllodoce glanduliflora ◐☐
A small, semi-erect shrub to 20cm (8in) tall, the leaves 4–14mm ($\frac{1}{5}$–$\frac{3}{5}$in) long, with a median white line beneath. The flowers are in clusters of 3–8, sulphur-yellow, hairy outside. Alaska and NE Asia. May–June.

Phyllodoce × *intermedia* ◐☐
A natural hybrid between *P. empetriformis* and *P. glanduliflora* found in British Columbia. It is much easier to grow than many Phyllodoces, producing vigorous, densely leafy mats of growth, and reaching 25cm (10in) in height. Flowers rose-pink or mauve. May.

Phyllodoce breweri ○☐
A lax, somewhat spreading subshrub, to 23–30cm (10–14in) in height. The leaves are 6–20mm (⅕–⅘in) long and the flowers comparatively large, rosy-purple, saucer-shaped with a deeply lobed corolla; stamens protruding. California—Sierra Nevada. May–June.

Phyllodoce nipponica ◐☐
This is a beautiful plant when well grown. It hails from Japan and is an erect, compact shrub, 15–23cm (6–10in) in height, with finely toothed leaves, white-felted beneath. The bellflowers are white, occasionally pink-tinged, and borne in clusters of 3–10, each 7–8mm (⅓in) long. May–June.

PHYTEUMA (Campanulaceae)

A widespread genus with species in Europe and W Asia. They are fairly close to *Campanula* but, with their heads or spikes of narrow, often curved, flowers, they tend to look very different. Each flower has 5 narrow petals which are joined together close to the base, but also at the tip with the 2-lobed stigma projecting through the fused petals. The higher alpine species are the finest for the rock garden, though they are not easy to please and are prone to attacks from slugs. For this reason they are most often seen in pans in the alpine house, in screes or raised beds.

Phyteuma globulariifolium ◐☐
A low perennial scarcely exceeding 50mm (2in) tall with tufts of oblong or spoon-shaped leaves and heads of pretty deep violet flowers, distinctly curved in bud. E Alps. July–September. A plant of acid rocks and screes in the wild from 2,000 to 3,000m (6,600–9,900ft) altitude.

Phyteuma humile ◐☐
Superficially like the previous species, but with narrower leaves and flower-heads with long, pointed bracts. Restricted to the SW Alps. July–August.

Phyteuma hedraianthifolium ○◐
Forms erect tufts to 15cm (8in) tall, though often less, with long grass-like toothed leaves. The dark, violet-blue flower-heads are subtended by several long leaf-like bracts of varying length. C Alps (excluding Austria). July–August. In the wild a plant of rocky and stony places between 1,800 and 3,100m (5,900–10,200ft) altitude.

Phyteuma hemisphaericum ○◐☐
Very like the previous species with dense tufts of grassy leaves—usually untoothed. The globular flower-heads are subtended by several oval, rather short, bracts. Mountains of C and S Europe. June–August. This species inhabits meadows, rocks or screes, generally growing in acid soils.

Phyteuma scheuchzeri ○◐
A taller species to 30cm (12in). The toothed leaves are a bluish-green, the lower lanceolate to heart-shaped, the upper longer and narrower. The flowers are deep

blue, strongly curved in bud and forming dense heads below which trail several long, slender, pointed bracts. S Alps. May–August.

There are several taller coarser species such as *P. betonicifolium, P. nigrum* and *P. spicatum*, which, though attractive garden plants, are generally too gross for all but the largest rock garden, though they look well enough on the margins of small streams.

Phyteuma comosum ○▲
The so-called Devil's Claw is one of those curious plants that every alpine grower simply has to have in his collection. Plants form low tufts of fleshy, kidney-shaped or oblong, coarsely toothed leaves. Sitting on the middle of the leaf-rosette appear dense heads of pinkish-lilac flowers tipped with blackish violet, each flower 16–20mm (⅗–⅘in) long. A native of the SE Alps, particularly the Dolomites, where it inhabits deep crevices in limestone and dolomitic formations to about 2,000m (6,600ft) altitude. A very distinctive and intriguing species which is not always easy to please. However, its chief requirements are a well-drained compost, particularly a rock crevice, or rocks wedged in around its neck. Plants do best in the alpine house, though fine ones can be found on raised beds or in troughs or screes outdoors, where they must be protected both from winter wet and the depredations of slugs and snails which can quickly demolish a healthy specimen. This should not deter enthusiasts from trying this gem.

PLANTAGO (Plantaginaceae)
A well-known genus with some 260 species widely distributed in the world. Many of the European ones are invasive weeds with little place in the alpine garden, but one or two are worth some attention. Propagation easy from seed.

Plantago nivalis ○
A charming little plant only 25–50mm (1–2in) tall with small leaf-rosettes, the leaves lanceolate, blunt, covered in a web of silvery hairs. The greyish-green flower spikes are small blobs on leafless stalks. Spain. May–July.

Plantago major ○
The common Broad-leaved Plantain has no place in the rock garden; however, two forms are worthy of consideration: 'Rosularis'—similar to the familiar wild plant, but the flower-spikes are converted into rose-like rosettes with numerous large, overlapping leafy bracts; 'Rubrifolia'—has leaves stained with purple or crimson. Can be invasive.

PLATYCODON (Campanulaceae)
A small genus from E Asia variously known as balloon flowers or Chinese bellflowers because of the broad, round, bell-shaped flowers which are inflated and balloon-like in bud. In general appearance they resemble lush large-flowered campanulas. They are generally easily grown in sunny well-drained soils and are best propagated from seed or division of the roots. However, they generally dislike disturbance.

Platycodon grandiflorum ○☆
An herbaceous perennial to 30cm (12in) tall, occasionally more, with erect stems bearing numerous bluish-green broad-oval leaves. The flowers are generally solit-

ary, large, open bells, blue or purplish-blue, paler on the outside, each up to 50mm (2in) across. N China, Korea and Japan. July–August. The typical plant is too gross for the average rock garden and is better placed at the front of an herbaceous border. There are, however, two fine dwarf forms which are excellent for the rock garden. Var. *mariesii* grows to 20cm (8in) tall with flowers of deep purplish-blue, or occasionally pink. 'Apoyama' (syn. *P. apoyama*)—a dwarf cultivar, 10–13cm (4–5in) tall, bearing even larger purplish-blue flowers.

POLYGALA (Polygalaceae)

The milkworts are a very large group of colourful plants with flowers resembling small pea-flowers. Although many are very attractive, few of them are cultivated to any extent. There are over 500 species, distributed worldwide, particularly in temperate and subtropical regions.

Polygalas may be annual or perennial, sometimes shrubby; they have alternate, often leathery, leaves. The flowers appear in the leaf axils or in terminal racemes; their structure is complicated, with 5 sepals, 2 of which are much larger and form conspicuous 'wings'. There are 5 petals, 2 of which are very small or lacking altogether; the lower petal forms a tube-like 'keel' which has a lobed or fringed apex.

Polygala calcarea ○☆

A low clump-forming species with loose rosettes of spoon-shaped, rounded, basal leaves and slender trailing stems 30–60mm ($1\frac{1}{5}$–$2\frac{1}{2}$in) long, bearing narrower lanceolate leaves. The tips of the stems turn upwards and bear dense terminal racemes of deep blue flowers, each about 5mm ($\frac{1}{5}$in) long, with a paler fringe at the apex of the lower 'lip'. Widespread in W Europe including Britain. May–June.

Polygala chamaebuxus ◑□☆

The Shrubby Milkwort is by far the finest species for the rock garden, requiring a moist lime-free soil. Plants form a low spreading shrub 5–15cm (2–6in) in height with tough, leathery, lanceolate leaves 15–30mm ($\frac{3}{5}$–$1\frac{1}{5}$in) long. The solitary flowers are borne at each of the upper leaf axils and are 10–15mm ($\frac{2}{5}$–$\frac{3}{5}$in) long; each has 2 large erect, white or yellow 'wing' sepals and a lip which is bright yellow and 2–6-lobed at the apex; in older flowers the lip becomes tinged with pink or orange-brown. Alps and Carpathians. April–June. In the wild a plant of woods, rocky pastures and slopes, to 2,500m (8,250ft). Var. *purpurea* has purple wings and a yellow lip—the finest form.

Polygala vayredae ◑□

Rather like *P. chamaebuxus*, but a wiry, more slender dwarf shrub with much narrower, linear to linear-lanceolate, leaves. The large 'wing' sepals, and the basal part of the keel petal are coloured purple, but the apex of the lip, and its crest of 5–9 narrow lobes, is bright yellow. E Spanish Pyrenees. April–May.

POLYGONUM (Polygonaceae)

A genus of about 150 species, widely scattered in temperate regions of the world. Many are weedy annuals and perennials with no place in the rock garden; several, however, deserve to be considered. *Polygonum* species have a characteristic sheath on the stem immediately above each leaf. The flowers, which are small and generally 5-parted, are aggregated into spikes or clusters. Most are easy to grow on average garden soils. Propagation by division of the parent plant.

Polygala chamaebuxus

Polygonum affine ○◑☆
The finest species is a mat-forming perennial to 22cm (9in) tall in flower. The deep green, rather leathery leaves are oblong and become bronzed during the autumn and winter. The flower-spikes are rose-red, almost carmine in the best forms. Himalaya. August–September. 'Donald Lowndes'—the finest form.

Polygonum vaccinifolium ○☆
Another prostrate perennial, but more slender than the previous, with stems to 22cm (9in) tall in flower. Leaves oval to elliptical, short-stalked, bright green, but sometimes flushed with red. Flowers bright rose-pink, borne in slender, tapered spikes, reminiscent of *Calluna* from a distance. Himalaya. September–October.

POTENTILLA (Rosaceae)
A large and complex genus with species scattered in many parts of the world, more especially in temperate regions. Many of the low growing yellow-flowered species are difficult to separate. They are generally easy to cultivate in open positions on well-drained soils.

Potentilla fruticosa ○☆
The Shrubby Cinquefoil is a familiar garden shrub to 1m (3ft) tall with much-branched twiggy growth. The small pinnate leaves, deep green above but greyish or whitish beneath, are shed in the late autumn. The typical 5-petalled potentilla flowers are bright yellow, 15–25mm (⅗–1in) across, borne in small clusters. Widespread in the temperate regions of the northern hemisphere. June–September. The large cultivars are generally too gross for the smaller rock garden, but there are a number of fine lower-growing cultivars that provide interest over a long season. 'Ben Bannoch'—40cm (16in) with deep golden flowers; 'Daydream'—40cm (16in), tangerine flowers; 'Elizabeth'—60cm (24in), bright yellow flowers; 'Kathleen Dykes'—80cm (32in), silvery leaves and yellow flowers; 'Tangerine'—60cm (24in), orange flowers.

Potentilla aurea ○
The Golden Cinquefoil, widespread in the mountains of C and S Europe, is a low-growing, mat-forming perennial, with neat 5-lobed leaves with silky margins.

The golden-yellow flowers often have an orange centre, 15–25mm ($\frac{5}{8}$–1in); the petals are slightly notched. June–September. There is a form with double flowers, 'Plena'.

Potentilla crantzii ○

The Alpine Cinquefoil is similar to the previous species, but with more erect flower-stems to 15cm (6in), the margins of the leaves not silky with hairs. Mountains of Europe, W Asia and North America.

Potentilla eriocarpa ◖☆

A Himalayan species becoming more widespread in cultivation and relatively easy to grow. Plants form a mass of woody, rather brittle, spreading stems. The deeply lobed grey-green leaves are a good foil to the clear yellow flowers, 20–25mm ($\frac{4}{5}$–1in) across. June–September. Good in rock crevices, on screes or in large troughs.

Polygonum affine

Potentilla brauniana (syn. *P. dubia*) ○
A charming little tufted plant, rarely exceeding 80mm (3in) and often less. The leaves are 3-lobed and the small yellow flowers 7–11mm (⅛–⅖in) across. Pyrenees and Alps. June–August. Occurs on limestone rocks in the wild, frequently by snow patches.

Potentilla alba ○
Essentially like a white-flowered *P. aurea*, the leaves with 3–7 lobes. C and S Europe. Occasionally seen in cultivation.

Potentilla nitida ○☆
A delightful low cushion- or mat-forming perennial with numerous 3-lobed silvery leaves. The rose-pink to rose-red flowers, 22–26mm (⅞–1in) across, are held slightly above the foliage and seem almost too large compared to the leaves. S Alps and N Apennines. June–July. A real gem, fairly readily available, preferring limy to acid soils, reasonably easy to cultivate, but not always flowering with great enthusiasm. However, the leaves make amends for any paucity in bloom.

Potentilla × *tonguei* ○
A striking hybrid with apricot flowers and a contrasting crimson centre. Stems spreading, to 18cm (7in) . June–September.

PRATIA (Campanulaceae)

A small genus of creeping perennials with often inconspicuous lobelia-like flowers which are often followed by attractively coloured berries. They thrive best in moist, but well-drained soils and can be propagated by division or fragments—the creeping stems generally root down as they go.

Pratia treadwellii ◗
A mat-former with slender pinkish stems and pale green practically round, alternate leaves. The stemless white, often purple-streaked flowers are followed by bright purple berries. April–May, sometimes early. This plant appears to be of garden origin and is possibly only a very good form of *P. angulata*; it sometimes appears in literature as *P. angulata* 'Treadwellii'.

Pratia angulata ◗
Very like the preceding, but generally inferior with smaller leaves and flowers. The berries are less bright. New Zealand. March–April.

Pratia repens ◗
Like the previous species, but generally recognizable on account of its kidney-shaped leaves. The small white flowers are flushed with purple. Falkland Islands. June–October.

Pratia pendunculata ◗☆
A spreading carpeter, often very invasive, forming mats of pale green, thread-like stems and oval, slightly toothed leaves. The solitary, pale mauvish-pink flowers are borne on long stalks, often as much as 30mm (1⅛in) in length. June–October. Perhaps the best species in cultivation, thriving on peat banks and in moist areas of the rock garden. Although invasive by nature this charming plant seldom swamps its taller neighbours.

Pratia pendunculata

PRIMULA (Primulaceae)

One of the most attractive and best loved of genera, it contains the common Primrose, Cowslip and Oxlip. The 300 or so species are to be found mostly in the temperate zones of the northern hemisphere and show a very wide range of forms and flower colour. They all possess a more or less branching rhizome which develops rosettes of basal leaves from which rise one or several inflorescences in the form of a leafless stalked (e.g. the Cowslip) or stalkless (e.g. the Primrose) umbel of one to several flowers. A few species develop two or more umbels in tiers one above the other (candelabra types). In general, primulas thrive best in regions of plentiful summer rainfall and humidity, and in a well-drained soil. The soil should never become waterlogged, especially in winter, as this encourages root rot. Most European and American species do well in full sun. Asiatic species, however, need light to medium shade, although some will also do well in a sunny position if the soil is kept really moist. Many species benefit from winter protection, and most respond well to alpine house treatment, but here there is a greater danger of winter rots.

Propagation of most species is best achieved from seed; good forms are selected on flowering, and the rest thrown away, but beware, the appearance of chance hybrids is to be expected. Division after flowering in summer is also applicable to all species, but this, though easy, is a slower method of increase. Some species, especially in the Auricula group, can be propagated from cuttings; the last two methods have to be used if the propagation of a good form is desired.

Primula allionii ◑

This delightful primula is a great favourite among enthusiasts and is one of the main features of early spring alpine flower shows. Plants form tight low mounds of small, rather flat, leaf-rosettes covered in stemless bright magenta-pink flowers with a white eye. W Europe, Maritime Alps. March–April. It is a very variable species, both in leaf form and flower size and colour, hence the existence of many named cultivars. Of these the most frequently available are the following: 'Crowsley Variety'—smaller flowers of a deep rich crimson-magenta and clear white eye; 'Avalanche'—large white flowers with overlapping petals; 'William Earle'—large lilac-pink flowers with overlapping petals. *Primula allionii* does best in an alpine house or cold frame in a moist open compost watered from below. Wetting the aerial parts must be avoided, especially in winter, and plants should be kept in a semi-shaded position in summer. Grows readily from cuttings.

Primula allionii

Primula alpicola ◗☆
Close to *P. sikkimensis*, but with a truncate leaf base. The 30–90cm (12–36in) stalk bears a cluster or two whorls of pendent flowers, broadly funnel-shaped, mostly yellow, but often white or violet, sometimes purple and beautifully scented. Tibet. May–June. 'Luna'—yellow; 'Violacea'—violet-purple. A good species for a moist soil in semi-shade.

Primula anisodora ◗
A striking if lanky species. From spreading rosettes of large, shiny, toothed leaves, which in spring smell of aniseed, rise candelabra flower stalks up to 70cm (28in). These bear 3–5 whorls of nodding, very deep purple flowers with a clear yellow eye. W China. May–June. A moisture-loving species, thriving near water; even moderately dry soil harms it.

Primula aurantiaca ○◗
Another species from W China and the smallest and most brilliantly coloured of the candelabra section. Plants bear rosettes of rather large, toothed leaves. The flower stems, which are somewhat drooping, rise to 30cm (12in) and carry 2–6 whorls of small, but rich reddish-orange flowers with a coppery sheen. June–July. Plants tend to form leafy growths in the umbels, which when removed can be treated as cuttings. The species requires a moist position.

Primula aureata ◗▲
This highly prized species comes from the mountains of C Nepal and is becoming more readily available due to tissue culture propagation. A petiolarid primula, it

produces a cluster of 3–10 creamy-yellow flowers with a deeper yellow central zone shading to orange; the petals are toothed. The leaf-rosettes are flat, composed of oval toothed, mealy, leaves up to 10cm (4in) long. March–April. This most beautiful species does best under alpine house conditions, but it is not all that easy to keep.

Primula auricula ○◐☆

The common Auricula is an easy but variable garden plant and, at its best, a very beautiful one. Plants form rosettes of large, oval, somewhat fleshy, leaves which may or may not be mealy. The stalks, 10–15cm (4–6in) long, bear umbels of many pale to deep yellow, funnel- to saucer-shaped, flowers, 15–25mm (⅜–1in) across, with a mealy eye, fragrant in some forms. Alps and Apennines. April–May. Many colour forms are offered in commerce: 'Alpina', 'Albo-cincta', 'Ciliata', and 'Old Yellow Dusty Miller' are close to the wild type, but there are many garden auriculas which are of hybrid origin, such as 'Blue Velvet' and 'Old Red Dusty Miller'. Always buy auriculas in flower, so that the best types can be selected. 'Blairside Yellow' is a delightful quite small form. All are easily grown in the open garden.

Primula 'Beatrice Wooster' (P. allionii × P. 'Linda Pope') ○◐

This is a lovely form, with leaves like *P. allionii* but larger, and umbels of large clear pink flowers held just above the leaves on mealy stalks. March–April. Better in the alpine house, or outdoors with the benefits of a pane of glass overhead during winter.

Primula beesiana ○◐☆

One of the coarser candelabra species and which hybridizes with some of the other related species so readily, that the true species is difficult to obtain. The large leaves grow to 40cm (16in) long after flowering. The flower stems, up to 60cm (24in) long, bear 2–8 superposed umbels of many nodding rosy-carmine flowers. W China. May–June. Plants require a cool moist soil.

Primula 'Belluensis'

This name is widely offered in the trade, but the plants are nearly always *P.* × *pubescens* 'Freedom'.

Primula ×berninae (P. latifolia × P. hirsuta) ○☆

In many of its forms, this hybrid is strikingly beautiful the form most frequently offered is the floriferous 'Windrush Variety' which has the small stature of *P. hirsuta*, with heads of reddish-purple flowers. March–April.

Primula × bilekii see P. × forsteri

Primula bracteosa ◐

This petiolarid species forms a flat rosette of whitish-mealy toothed leaves, up to 15cm (6in) long. A cluster of 10–20 pinkish-lilac flowers, with toothed petals and a yellow eye surrounded by a white halo, sits in the centre of the rosette. Does well outside in moist shady conditions, but is best in northern regions. April.

Primula bulleyana ◐☆

Another Chinese plant, a large, but attractive candelabra species, to 70cm (2ft 4in) tall. From large rosettes of ovate, toothed, leaves rise stiff stalks bearing 5–7 whorls of many spreading, deep orange-yellow flowers, each 18–20mm (⅘in) across.

Hybridizes readily, so that propagation, if one wants to maintain the species, is best by division. June–July.

Primula burmanica ◯◑
Similar to *P. beesiana*, but with more attractive corolla colours which are mostly reddish-purple with a yellow eye. June.

Primula capitata ◑
This quite handsome Himalayan species forms a flattish rosette of oblong, sharply toothed, leaves. The flower scapes rise 15–40cm (6–16in) bearing a very characteristic flattened white-mealy cluster in which most of the funnel-shaped flowers point sideways or downwards. The flower colour ranges from a rich violet-blue to deep purply-blue. July–August. Subsp. *mooreana* is a fine variant, larger in all its parts.

Primula chionantha ◑☆
A beautiful species related to *P. sinopurpurea*, fairly easy of culture and well worth having in any collection. The rosettes of large upright lanceolate, finely toothed leaves are powdered on the underside with pale yellow meal (farina). The flower stalks, 30–60cm (12–24in) tall bear up to 4 whorls of white, fragrant, nodding flowers, each about 30mm (1⅕in) across. W China. May.

Primula chungensis ◯◑
A large species in the Candelabra section, with coarse leaf-rosettes, each leaf up to 30cm (12in) long, oblong, toothed and spreading. The flower scapes, to 80cm (2ft 8in) long, bear 2–5 whorls of many pale orange, nodding flowers with reddish tubes, each flower 18–20mm (¾in) across. E Himalaya and W China. May–June.

Primula clarkei ◑
A very pretty small species, which is not now as floriferous in cultivation as it used to be, perhaps due to virus infection. The small round, finely toothed, long-stalked leaves develop after the flowers. These rise mostly singly on 30–50mm (1⅕–2in) long stalks, but can also appear in lax umbels of 2–6. The pleasing bright rose-pink flowers, 12–18mm (½–¾in) across, have a yellow throat and a wide white 'eye', Kashmir. March–April. This species needs a lot of moisture, and does well in peaty soil, both in the open and in the alpine house. A more vigorous hybrid with *P. rosea* is sometimes sold as *P. clarkei*.

Primula clusiana ◯
A rather beautiful species native to the N and NE Alps. It forms rosettes of stiff, elliptic, shiny dark green leaves, which can be up to 90mm (3½in) long. The umbels of up to 4 bright rose-magenta flowers have a prominent white eye, each flower 25–40mm (1–1½in) across. May–June. Often a shy flowerer in cultivation, so it is wise to seek out a good, more floriferous clone. 'Murray-Lyon'—one of the best clones.

Primula cockburniana ◑
The smallest species in the candelabra section. From rosettes of oblong finely toothed leaves up to 15cm (6in) long rise slender stalks bearing 2–3 whorls of many nodding orange-red flowers, each about 15mm (⅗in) across. The species is short-lived, but produces plenty of good seed. W China. May–June.

Primula cortusoides ◐

An attractive slender woodland plant. The lax rosettes are made up of downy, heart-shaped leaves, 60–90mm (2–3½in) long with a fairly long stalk. The flower stems rise 15–30cm (6–12in) and bear a fairly tight umbel of 2–15 rose to rose-violet or red flowers, 15–20mm (⅗–⅘in) across. Plants offered by nurserymen as *P. cortusoides* are often *P. polyneura* or *P. saxatilis*, and it is in fact doubtful that the true species is still in commerce.

Primula darialica

Most if not all the *P. darialica* offered in commerce are *P. frondosa*.

Primula denticulata ○◐☆

This is the extremely popular Drumstick Primula and deservedly so, for it is an easy and accommodating plant. The coarse rosettes of oblong or oval leaves enlarge greatly after flowering. The stout, mealy stems, 10–25cm (4–10in) long, bear large globular heads of very many funnel-shaped flowers varying in colour from mauve to purple. Sino-Himalaya. March–May. The natural variability of the species has been exploited to produce many splendid hybrid cultivars from pure white to deep purple, even to a glowing purple as in 'Pritchard's Ruby'.

Primula 'Dianne' ○

This charming hybrid is close to *P. × forsteri* which is the seed parent. The pollen parent is unknown, but is probably a *P. × pubescens*. The rosettes of dark green, broadly spatular-shaped, toothed leaves are 20mm (⅘in) long. Short-stalked umbels bear 1–3 deep magenta to crimson flowers. April–May. Easy to grow in the open garden.

Primula edgeworthii (syn. *P. winteri*) ○☆

A lovely petiolarid which has been in cultivation for a long time. From a rosette of white-mealy, spatular-shaped leaves rises a low umbel of many pale mauve to deep blue-mauve flowers with an ochre yellow eye surrounded by a white halo; the petals are toothed. C Himalaya. January–April. Fairly easy to please; it can be grown outside in partial shade in moist leafy soil, if given winter protection. 'Alba'—a pleasant white form.

Primula elatior ◐☆

The Oxlip is a well-known and much-loved species, distinguished from the Cowslip (*P. veris*) by its closely fitting cylindrical calyx and by its primrose-yellow, shallow funnel- to open saucer-shaped flowers which are usually held in a one-sided umbel. Europe to W Asia in both lowland and mountain habitats. March –May.

    Primula amoena (syn. *P. elatior* subsp. *meyeri*) is identical, except for the bright magenta colour of its flowers. This Caucasian species is sometimes offered in commerce.

Primula ellisiae ○☆

An attractive and elegant species which forms rosettes of fairly large leaves, lanceolate and finely toothed, up to 15cm (6in) long. From these rise scapes, to 20cm (8in) long, bearing open umbels of 4–8 flowers. The corolla colour varies from rose-magenta to rose-violet, occasionally shading towards blue, and is darker round the yellow eye; each flower is shallow funnel-shaped, 20–30mm (⅘–1⅕in) across. USA–New Mexico. May–June. This species does well in the alpine house, and also in the open in scree or in a well-drained but moist soil.

Primula farinosa

Primula 'Ethel Barker' (*P. allionii* × *P. hirsuta*) ○◑

A beautiful and floriferous hybrid half-way in appearance between the parent species. The bright carmine flowers are borne 3–5 in an umbel on quite short stalks. April. Easy in the alpine house, but plants may suffer from winter wet in the open garden unless covered with a pane of glass.

Primula farinosa ○◑

The Bird's-eye Primrose is a delightful small plant familiar in many parts of Europe and N Asia, especially in the mountains. The rosettes of small elliptic or blunt leaves are white-mealy on the undersurface. The flower-scapes rise to 5–15cm (2–6in), and bear tight umbels of 10–25 lilac-pink flowers with a yellow eye, each shallowly saucer-shaped, 10–15mm ($\frac{2}{5}$–$\frac{3}{5}$in) across. March–April. Does well in a sunny position with plenty of moisture at the roots, though it tends to be short lived in cultivation.

Primula florindae ○◑

A large version of *P. sikkimensis* with roundish leaves which hails from Tibet. The stout scapes, up to 100cm (3ft 4in) tall, bear an umbel of 30–80 pendent, funnel-shaped, sulphur-yellow, scented flowers. June–July. Easily grown, although best in wet ground by a stream or pond in semi-shaded places. Too gross for smaller rock gardens.

Primula × forsteri (*P. minima* × *P. hirsuta*) ○

This horticultural form is a lovely plant, close to *P. minima* in general appearance, but with large, brighter, deep pink, white-eyed flowers, 23–25mm (1in) across, held close to the leaves, 1–3 in an umbel. April–May. There is another similar horticultural variety with slightly smaller, but deeper pink flowers, forma *bilekii* (syn. *P.* × *bilekii*). *Forma steinii* (syn. *P. steinii*) is a vigorous and attractive clone close in appearance to *P. hirsuta* with spoon-shaped, toothed, leaves and 20mm ($\frac{4}{5}$in) crimson flowers with a white eye.

Primula frondosa ○◑☆
An easy and vigorous species which is similar to *P. farinosa*, but with larger leaves and much laxer flower-heads. It forms rosettes of rough spatular-shaped leaves, up to 10cm (4in) long, with crinkled margins, densely white-mealy on the undersurface. The lax umbel, 10–18cm (4–7in) tall, bears 5–12 or more lilac to reddish-purple flowers, 10–15mm ($\frac{2}{5}$–$\frac{3}{5}$in) across, each with a small yellow eye. Europe. March–April.

Primula glaucescens ○
Similar to *P. clusiana*, but with smaller leaves. It is usually shy flowering, but there are a couple of good clones in commerce. Grows well in the open garden in full sun. Europe. May–June.

Primula gracilipes ◑☆
One of the easier species in the Petiolaris section. A dome of bright magenta-pink to purple-pink flowers, each 25–30mm (1–1$\frac{1}{5}$in) across, with an orange-yellow eye surrounded by a white halo, sit on a flat rosette of toothed, spatular-shaped leaves up to 15cm (6in) long. C and E Himalaya. April–May. This pretty species does well in the open garden, especially in N Britain, preferring a moist leafy soil in partial shade with some form of winter protection. It also responds well to alpine house treatment.

Primula halleri (syn. ***P. longiflora***) ○◑☆
An easily grown species close to *P. farinosa*, but distinguished by its very long flower-tube. It forms rosettes of 40–80mm (1$\frac{1}{2}$–3in) long leaves, which are creamy-mealy on the undersurface. The flower-scapes, 8–18cm (3–7in) long, bear tight and often one-sided umbels of 2–12 lilac-mauve to violet flowers, 15–20mm ($\frac{3}{5}$–$\frac{4}{5}$in) across, with a yellow eye; the flower-tube is 20–30mm ($\frac{4}{5}$–1$\frac{1}{5}$in) long. Europe. April. Plants thrive best in a sunny position in scree, but will tolerate light shade.

Primula helodoxa ○◑☆
A large bog-loving species in the candelabra section known in cultivation as the 'Glory of the Marsh'. The coarse leaf-rosettes of broad, oblong, spreading leaves are up to 35cm (14in) long. The flower-scapes rise to 50–120cm (1$\frac{3}{4}$–4ft), bearing 4–6 whorls of many rich golden-yellow, fragrant, spreading flowers, each 22–25mm (1in) across. W China and N Burma. June–July.

Primula hirsuta (syn. ***P. rubra***) ○◑☆
A lovely, free-flowering and quite variable species which forms rosettes of slightly sticky, roundish to elliptical, coarsely to finely toothed leaves. The bright magenta-pink to mauve flowers, 15–25mm ($\frac{3}{5}$–1in) across, have a clear white eye and are held several to an umbel on short stalks just above the leaves. Europe. April–May. Occasionally suffers from winter rot, so winter cover may be beneficial in some areas. A very distinct form, var. *exscapa*, has very tight, almost unstalked, umbels. 'Nivea'—a fine white form. Plant names 'Stuart Bootham' or 'Bootham's Var.' are offered as *P. hirsuta*, but they are almost certainly of hybrid origin.

Primula integrifolia ○◑

One of the smallest European species often prolific in moist swards in the Alps and Pyrenees. A very pretty carpeter, but often shy-flowering in cultivation; free-flowering clones should be sought. The long, branching, prostrate stems bear many rosettes of small elliptic, untoothed leaves. The flowers, 15–25mm (⅗–1in) across, are rose to magenta and do not have a white eye; they are solitary or borne 2–3 together on a common stalk. April–May. As a way to encourage flowering, some people advocate growing this species in close association with other plants, such as *Campanula cochleariifolia* or *Gentiana verna*, or even in short grass.

Primula involucrata ◑

This delicately attractive species has rosettes of oval or oblong long-stalked leaves. The flower-scapes, 10–30mm (⅖–1⅕in) long, bear a fairly lax umbel of 2–6 fragrant, nodding flowers, usually white, sometimes white tinged with brownish-purple or purple; each flower is 15–20mm (⅗–⅘in) across, has a yellow eye and is of a lovely crystalline texture. Himalaya. May–June. In gardens this species requires moist rich soil and shady conditions.

Primula ioessa ◑

This attractive species is in the *P. sikkimensis* section. It has narrow, oblong, toothed leaves in a lax rosette. The flower-scapes, 20–25cm (8–10in) tall, bear an umbel of 2–8 broadly funnel- to cup-shaped flowers, white or pale madder-pink to violet, semi-pendent and fragrant, mealy white within; the calyx is almost black. Tibet. May–June.

Primula japonica ○◑☆

Perhaps the most extensive and popular of all candelabra primulas, long established in cultivation. From the rosettes of broad-oblong, finely toothed leaves, arise the flower-scapes to 45cm (18in), bearing 1–6 superposed whorls of many purplish to deep red flowers, each 18–22mm (¾in) across. Japan. May–July. This fine species usually comes true from seed, and is very easily grown in a moist rich loamy soil; the parent plant needs to be divided regularly. There are many named varieties differing in the nature of the red colour of the corolla; one of the finest is 'Miller's Crimson'. 'Postford White'—white with a yellow eye.

Primula juliae ○◑☆

A delightful and floriferous small species related to the Primrose which comes from the Caucasus. From mats of heart-shaped and toothed, long-stalked leaves rise several bright deep purplish-magenta, yellow-eyed flowers, 20–30mm (⅘–1⅕in) across. March–April. The key parent of the wonderful hybrid *P.* × *pruhoniciana* (syn. *P* × *juliana*).

Primula latifolia (syn. *P. viscosa*) ○◑☆

One of the larger European species which is very distinct and attractive, with mostly upright, broadly elliptic leaves and a tall stalk, up to 20cm (8in), bearing a one-sided umbel of long-tubed, funnel-shaped, scented flowers of a rich reddish-violet, sometimes an intense purple. May. A variable species; it pays to select good forms.

Primula 'Linda Pope' ○

The most widely grown of the *P. marginata* hybrids, whose pollen (male) parent is not known. It bears umbels of 4–6 large rounded flowers of an attractive mauve-blue with a white-mealy eye on an erect 15cm (6in) stalk. The large, toothed leaves are powdered with whitish meal. April–May. A strong grower which is seen at its best in a pan in the alpine house, although it can be grown outdoors.

Primula macrophylla ○◑▲
An attractive and variable species which, like many of its close cousins, is not particularly easy to grow. The rosettes of upright, lanceolate, finely blunt-toothed leaves, are mealy-white on the undersurface. The flower-scapes rise to 10–25cm (4–10in) and bear umbels of many bluish-violet to purple, fragrant flowers, each 20–30mm (⅘–1in) across, and with a darker eye. May. Outdoors it requires overhead protection during the winter.

Primula 'Marven' (*P. marginata* × *P. venusta*) ○◑
A gorgeous and widely grown hybrid. The rosettes of mealy-edged leaves give rise to stout 20cm (8in) scapes bearing tight umbels of up to 15 rounded, intensely violet-blue flowers, with overlapping petals and a dark eye ringed with white meal. April–May. Does best in a pan in the alpine house, although it can be grown in the open.

Primula marginata ○☆
One of the loveliest of European primulas, this beautiful and very popular species should be in every collection. It forms aerial branching stems which can lead to leggy plants, or to fairly tight domes of leaf rosettes, depending on the clone. The coarsely toothed leaves are very attractive, as they always have dense farina along the margins. The flower-scapes, 2–12cm (¾–5in) tall, bear open umbels of 2–20 long-tubed flowers varying from lilac-lavender to blue-lavender, sometimes to violet, rarely pinkish, and all with a white mealy eye. April–May. Var. *alba* of commerce is rarely pure white; 'Beatrice Lascaris'—clear blue flowers; 'Caerulea'—has farinose leaves and blue flowers; 'Holden's Var.' or 'Holden Clough'—has farinose leaves and smallish blue flowers; 'Kesselring's Form'—deep lavender flowers; 'Pritchard's Var.'—a larger form with lilac-purple flowers. Other generally inferior forms often masquerade under the last two names.

Primula melanops ○◑
From rosettes of large elliptical, finely toothed leaves covered below with white meal, rise 25–35cm (10–14in) stalks bearing umbels of nodding, deep violet to purple fragrant flowers, 18–20mm (⅘in) across, with an almost black eye. W China. May–June. In commerce *P. melanops* not infrequently turns out to be *P. sinopurpurea*, which does not have a black eye.

Primula minima ○
A charming, quite small, mat-forming species of very distinct appearance. Its very small, dark shiny-green leaves are wedge-shaped with a deeply toothed truncate apex. The flowers are mostly solitary and very short stemmed. The corolla is bright magenta-pink with a white eye, and the remarkable Y-shaped petal-lobes form a wide funnel-shaped limb. Europe. April–May. The true species is, unfortunately, nearly always very shy flowering in cultivation. There is also a pure white form.

Primula modesta ○◑☆
A small, graceful, but variable Japanese species fairly close to *P. farinosa*. Plants form open rosettes of mealy, spatular-shaped leaves with undulate, blunt-toothed margins, with dense yellow meal on the undersurface. The flower-scapes, 10–12cm

(4–5in) tall, bear open umbels of 2–15 pinkish-purple flowers, each 10–15mm ($\frac{2}{5}$–$\frac{3}{5}$in) across. April–May. There are many named varieties.

Primula parryi ◑
This vigorous and attractive species does well in cultivation, but is often shy flowering and sometimes dies suddenly for no apparent reason. It forms rosettes of very large, leathery, erect, finely toothed leaves, up to 30cm (12in) long. The stout, 10–40cm (4–16in) long scapes bear a one-sided umbel of 3–20 strongly scented, bright magenta to reddish-purple flowers, each 20–30mm ($\frac{4}{5}$–1$\frac{1}{5}$in) across, flat to shallow saucer-shaped, with a yellow eye surrounded by a dark halo. North America. May–June.

***Primula* 'Peter Klein'** ○◑☆
Another fine and vigorous plant, possibly a hybrid between *P. rosea* and *P. clarkei*. It has small rounded leaves like *P. clarkei* and bright pink flowers with a white eye borne 3–8 in an umbel on 80mm (3in) long stalks. March–April. Easy to cultivate in the open garden in a moist peaty soil.

Primula petiolaris ◑
A delightful species which forms a tight flattish, crisped, rosette of toothed leaves, small at flowering time. From the centre of the rosette rises a tight stalkless cluster of many magenta-pink to magenta-purple flowers to about 20mm ($\frac{4}{5}$in) across, with a yellow eye surrounded by a thin white border. The flowers form a lovely dome of bloom. Nepal. March–April. Does well in moist leafy soil in half-shade given winter protection; a good alpine house plant.

Primula poissonii ○◑☆
A candelabra species with rosettes of narrow oblong, finely toothed, spreading leaves. The scapes, up to 45cm (18in), bear 2–6 whorls of many deep reddish-purple, spreading flowers, each 20–30mm ($\frac{4}{5}$–1$\frac{1}{5}$in) across. W China. June–July. An easy species for moist soils.

Primula polyneura (syn. ***P. veitchii, P. lichiangensis***) ○◑
A variable species both in size and flower colour. It forms lax, soft downy rosettes of 7–11-lobed, large, rounded leaves, heart-shaped at the base and long-stalked. The flower-scapes, 10–50cm (4–20in) tall, bear 1–3 whorls of 2–12 flowers which are pale rose to purple with a yellow eye, each 15–25mm ($\frac{3}{5}$–1in) across. W China. May.

Primula* × *pruhoniciana (syn. ***P.* × *juliana***) ○◑☆
A large aggregate of very successful horticultural hybrids originating from crosses between *P. juliae* and coloured cultivars of the common Primrose, *P. vulgaris*. These are easy in moist rich soil, with plenty of organic matter present. March–May. 'Kinlough Beauty'—has the Polyanthus habit and salmon-pink flowers with a cream stripe down each petal; 'Lady Greer'—has pale yellow flowers and the Polyanthus habit; 'Wanda'—has the primrose habit and intense purple-red flowers—one of the most popular primulas.

Primula* × *pubescens ○◑☆
This aggregate contains very many extremely successful and easily grown plants, all of which form stout branching rhizomes bearing medium-sized leaf rosettes and stems with many-flowered umbels of well-shaped blooms in various shades of pink, red, mauve and white. They all derive originally from various crosses between *P. auricula* and *P. hirsuta*, which, over many decades, have been interbred and

selected into stable cultivars. The following is a selection of the most widely grown—all April–May: 'Bewerley White'—creamy-white flowers; 'Boothman's Variety'—neat habit, bright crimson flowers with a clear white eye; 'Christine'— deep rose flowers with a white eye; 'Crimson Velvet'—a compact plant with deep crimson flowers; 'Faldonside'—dusky reddish-pink, white-eyed flowers; 'The General'—few-flowered umbels of rich velvety-red flowers with yellow eyes; 'Freedom'—deep lilac flowers; 'Harlow Car'—large creamy-white flowers; 'Mrs J. H. Wilson'—fragrant purple, white-eyed blooms—an old and very popular variety; 'Rufus'—a large variety with large red (tending to brick-red) flowers with a golden eye.

Primula pulverulenta ◑☆

A handsome and popular candelabra species in gardens. The rosettes of oval, toothed leaves are up to 30cm (12in) long. The mealy flower-scapes rise up to 100cm (3ft 4in) and bear several whorls of many purple to deep red flowers with a darker eye. W China. June–July. Several excellent varieties are available, the best known being the pink 'Bartley Strain'.

Primula reidii ◑

A most delightful, fragrant gem from the Himalaya. The rosettes of soft, woolly, elliptic, lobed leaves give rise to 10–15cm (4–6in) long flower-scapes bearing a very tight umbel of 3–5 white, nodding, bowl-shaped flowers, each 18–20mm ($\frac{4}{5}$in) across. May. The species itself is difficult to obtain, but var. *williamsii* is available commercially. It is somewhat larger than the type, with flowers of a most beautiful pale blue, or white, or pale blue shading to white. It needs plenty of moisture in the growing season, but should be kept dry in winter to prevent rotting.

Primula rosea ◑☆

Another striking Himalayan species. The 15–20cm (6–8in) long lanceolate leaves are finely toothed, but are only slightly developed at flowering time. The flower-scapes are 4–15cm (1½–6in) long at flowering and lengthen greatly in fruit. The umbels of 4–12 glowing carmine-rose flowers are 15–20mm ($\frac{3}{5}$–$\frac{4}{5}$in) across, with a pleasing yellow eye. April–May. There are two cultivars: 'Grandiflora'—larger flowers than the type; 'Micia Visser de Geer'—flowers of a deeper colour. Often seeds around once established.

Primula × *scapeosa (P. scapigera* × *P. bracteosa)* ◑

A vigorous petiolarid hybrid which forms a lovely mound of rosy-mauve flowers, 22–25mm (1in) across, with toothed petals and a yellow starry eye surrounded by a white halo. The rather large leaves are coarsely and irregularly toothed. February– March.

Primula scotica ○◑

Everyone should grow this delightful little fragrant jewel which is endemic to N Scotland. The flattish rosettes of elliptical 30–50mm (1¼–2in) long leaves are densely farinose on the lower surface. The flower-scapes are usually short and bear a tight umbel of 1–6 flowers; the flower tube is yellow and mealy, and the 5–8mm ($\frac{1}{5}$–$\frac{1}{3}$in) limb is flat and a strikingly dark purple with a yellow eye. April–May. Best grown in a pot, but will do well in a raised bed in moist well-drained soil in sun or light shade.

Primula secundiflora ◗☆

This sturdy and attractive species is related to *P. sikkimensis*. The rosettes of oblong, relatively narrow, short-stalked leaves bear scapes mostly 30–50cm (15–20in) tall, bearing an often one-sided umbel of 5–20 nodding funnel-shaped flowers ranging in colour from reddish or violet-purple to deep rose-red; each flower is 15–25mm (⅗–1in) across. SW China (including SE Tibet). June.

Primula sinopurpurea ◗

This species comes close to *P. chionantha*, but it is not as easy to grow. The rosettes of long upright, elliptical, finely toothed leaves have much yellow meal (farina) on the lower surface. The flower-scapes, 30–70cm (12–28in) tall, bear an umbel, or 2–3 whorls of many nodding purplish-violet flowers with a whitish eye, each 25–35mm (1–1½in) across. W China. May–June. Requires protection in winter.

Primula sonchifolia ◗☆

One of the most spectacular of the petiolarid Primulas. The large bulb-like winter-resting buds begin to open in the late winter and produce a large rounded cluster of up to 20 good-sized flowers on stout, though short, mealy stalks. The flower is of various shades of delicate blue to bright, even indigo, blue, all with an ochre yellow eye surrounded by a pentagonal white halo. The leaves continue to develop after flowering to form a quite large rosette. W China, SE Tibet and N Burma. February–March.

Primula steinii see *P.* × *forsteri*

Primula sieboldii ◗☆

This species has long been in cultivation, and there are now many cultivars in gardens. The downy, long-stalked, heart-shaped leaves die down soon after flowering. The thin flower-scapes, 10–30cm (4–12in) tall, bear one or two loose whorls of 6–10 flat-faced flowers, 20–35mm (⅘–1⅖in) across, which can vary from rosy- to lilac-purple, even to deep crimson, generally with a white eye; pure white forms are also known. NE Asia and Japan. May–June. Plants generally need some protection from hard frosts.

Primula sikkimensis ◗☆

A deservedly popular and attractive species native to the high meadows of the Sino-Himalaya. Plants have rather large, elliptic, long-stalked leaves and from these rise 30–60cm (12–24in) long scapes bearing one, sometimes two, whorls of numerous pendent, funnel-shaped, yellow, fragrant flowers. May–June. This charming plant, like other bog-loving primulas, looks at its best planted close to water, around a pool or lake or along a stream bank.

Primula veris ○

The Cowslip is a well-known British native, but it is a widespread species in Europe, W and N Asia. It is characterized by an umbel of 5–15 semi-pendent flowers with a baggy calyx and a rather small (10–15mm, ⅖–⅗in) bowl-shaped, deep golden-yellow corolla with internal orange markings. April–May. Of the several subspecies, the most readily available is subsp. *macrocalyx* (syn. var. *uralensis*) with a wide conical calyx and rather larger flowers.

Primula vialii (syn. *P. littoniana*) ◗☆

One of the most distinctive of all Primulas, often mistaken at a distance for a marsh orchid. The rosettes of erect lanceolate hairy leaves, 20–30cm (8–12in) long, bear

1   *Anagallis monelli*

2   *Anagallis tenella* 'Studland'

3   *Androsace sarmentosa*

4   *Campanula cochlearifolia*

5 *Campanula raineri*

7 *Clematis alpina*

6 *Campanula zoysii*

8   *Cyclamen graecum*

9   *Dionysia tapetodes*

10 *Draba polytricha*

11 *Erinus alpinus*

13   *Gentiana saxosa*

14   *Geum montanum*

15   *Globularia meridionalis*

16   *Linaria alpina*

17 *Lithospermum diffusum*

18 *Omphalodes luciliae*

19 *Oxalis enneaphylla*

20   *Primula edgewirthii*

21   *Pterocephalus perennis*

22 *Pulsatilla halleri*

23 *Rhododendron forresti* var. *repens*

24   *Salix reticulata*

25   *Saponaria ocymoides*

26   *Saxifraga longifolia*

27   *Saxifraga sempervivum*

28 *Soldanella alpina*

29 *Thlaspi rotundifolium*

30 *Tropaeolum polyphyllum*

31   *Viola calcarata*

32   *Vitalliana primuliflora*

erect flower-scapes, 30–60cm (12–24in) tall, with dense spikes of numerous semi-pendent bluish-violet flowers. The unopened buds are bright crimson so that the immature spike presents a striking appearance. W China. June–July. This exciting species does best in a rich moist compost in a shaded position, preferably near water.

Primula × *vochinensis* (syn. *P. minima* × *P. wulfeniana*) ○

A pretty hybrid which usually flowers well. The forms offered generally have the habit of *P. minima*, but with large flowers of an attractive magenta-pink, with a purply sheen contributed by *P. wulfeniana*. The flowers are held just above the leaves. April–May.

Primula vulgaris ◐☆

The Common Primrose is a well-loved species, thriving in some gardens, but often struggling in others for no apparent reason. It forms a rosette of large blunt rather rough leaves. At flowering time the foliage is partially hidden by a dome of soft yellow flowers, each 20–30mm ($\frac{4}{5}$–1$\frac{1}{5}$in) across, borne on long pedicels; there is no scape. Europe, Turkey and W Asia. March–April. Subsp. *sibthorpii* has pale to bright pink flowers with a yellow eye, but various forms are offered by nurserymen, some rather poorly coloured. The subspecies comes from NE Greece, Turkey and the Caucasus.

Primula waltoni ◐▲

This beatiful species is said by some to have disappeared from cultivation, but at least 4 well-known nurseries are offering plants under that name. The true species, which comes from Tibet and Bhutan, is difficult in cultivation. It is like a *P. sikkimensis*, but with pink or dark-lilac to deep wine-purple flowers. The corolla is mealy within, but has a clear band like a pink eye round the throat. The mealy calyx is often stained with purple. May. Unlike other species in the *P. sikkimensis* section, this species does not like wet ground, doing best in rich, moist, leafy soil near shrub roots.

Primula 'Wanda' see *P.* × *pruhoniciana*

Primula warschenewskiana ◐

This is a much diminished relative of *P. rosea*, also flowering before the leaves are fully developed. The mature oblong leaves are finely toothed, up to 70mm (3in) long. The tight umbel of 1–8 flowers is held on a very short, almost absent, scape. The rose corolla, 7–12mm ($\frac{1}{3}$–$\frac{1}{2}$in) across, has a yellow eye surrounded by a white 5-lobed ring. Turkestan and NW Pakistan.

Primula whitei ◐☆

A gorgeous and not too difficult petiolarid species. From a compact, crisped rosette of sharply toothed leaves arises a tight umbel of 5–20 delicate pale to dark blue flowers with a white or greenish-white eye, forming a posy sitting on the leaves. E Himalaya. March–April.

Primula yargongensis ○◐

This lovely plant is very similar to *P. involucrata*. The rosettes of long-stalked ovate leaves bear long scapes with a rather open umbel of 3–8 pale mauve to pink or purple, flat-faced, fragrant flowers with a yellow eye surrounded by a white ring. SW China and SE Tibet. May–June.

PRUNELLA (Labiatae)

The genus contains the common Self-heal, *P. vulgaris*, widespread in Britain and Europe. Several species are well worth cultivating, but strangely only one is generally seen in gardens. They are easy and amenable plants for a sunny or semi-shaded site and because of their drooping habit are readily increased by division of the parent plant.

Prunella grandiflora ○◑☆

The Large Self-heal is a European native, though not a British species. Plants form spreading tufts to 16cm (6in) tall, with deep green oval or diamond-shaped leaves, which generally have a few blunt teeth. The dense oblong flower-heads are deep purple, or violet-blue, each flower 20–25mm (⅘–1in) long. June–September. Various colour forms are available including 'Pink Loveliness' and 'White Loveliness'.

PRUNUS (Rosaceae)

A large genus containing many large shrubs and trees—the plums and cherries belong here. Few are small enough to be considered suitable subjects for the rock garden.

Prunus prostrata ○

A twiggy deciduous shrub to 30cm (12in), occasionally more. Leaves small, oval and toothed. Flowers small and clear pink, like a tiny almond. The small, red, cherry-like fruits are rarely seen on cultivated specimens. W Asia. March–April. Plants require a well-drained sunny position and are most often seen in a trough or in a pan in the alpine house.

Prunus tenella (syn. *Amygdalus tenella, A. nana*) ○

The Russian Almond is an erect deciduous shrub with slender stems carrying numerous small bright pink flowers along their length, before the leaves appear; leaves are bright green, elliptical. Russia and SE Europe. March–April. A delightful shrub, but with a nasty habit of producing copious suckers which can be very annoying. The normal forms grow to 1m (3ft) tall, sometimes more, but the dwarfer ones, some only 30cm (12in) tall, are worth seeking out.

PTERIDOPHYLLUM (Papaveraceae)

A choice and much sought-after plant for shady woodland soils. The only species commonly cultivated is *P. racemosum*, a native of Japan. The rosettes of leaves are remarkably fern-like, but the branched spikes of small white flowers tell otherwise. Each flower is 4-petalled like a small poppy and the spikes reach up to 15cm (6in) in well-grown specimens. May–early June. ◑

PTEROCEPHALUS (Dipsacaceae)

A small genus of scabious-like plants, with 25 species in the Mediterranean region and Asia. Only one species is in general cultivation, thriving in sunny places on screes or rocks, and disliking too rich and moist soils. Propagation by division or seed.

Pterocephalus perennis (syn. *P. parnassii, Scabiosa pterocephalus*) ○☆

Plants form spreading mats of soft, velvety, grey leaves, which are oblong, toothed, short-stalked. The pink or mauvish scabious flower-heads, 24–28mm (1–1⅛in) across are borne amidst the foliage on short stalks. The whole plant scarcely exceeds

80mm (3⅛in), often lower. Greece. June–August. A charming plant, ideal for the front of a rock garden or scree.

PTILOTRICHUM (Cruciferae)

A small genus with about 15 species distributed primarily in SW Europe and related to *Alyssum*. They thrive best in a sunny well-drained site; a scree or trough suits them admirably. Propagation from seed or cuttings.

Ptilotrichum spinosum (syn. *Alyssum spinosum*) ○
A small much-branched subshrub with spiny branched twigs. The small oval leaves are hoary with hairs, those on the flowering stems narrower than the others. The flowers are white in the typical form, borne in short racemes. The whole plant is about 20cm (9in) tall, occasionally more. E and S Spain and S France. June–July. 'Roseum'—flowers pale to deep pink.

PULSATILLA (Ranunculaceae)

The pasque flowers were formerly included in *Anemone*, but can be readily distinguished by the feathery appendages to the fruit clusters. Most of the species are highly desirable in cultivation and are easy to propagate from seed. Young plants should be set out in the open in the spring and established plants will generally not tolerate disturbance. As in *Anemone*, the flowers have a whorl of 3 leaves closely below them.

Pulsatilla vernalis ○☆
The Spring Pasque Flower is the earliest to come into bloom. The whole plant is only 10cm (4in) tall (taller in fruit), with small pinnately lobed leaves with broad segments. The superb flowers are woolly on the outside and flushed with pink, violet or purplish-blue, but open to reveal a white interior with a central boss of golden stamens. Mountains W and C Europe. April–May. One of the most beautiful of all European alpine plants.

Pulsatilla vulgaris ○☆
The Common Pasque Flower is a larger plant, to 25cm (10in) tall, taller in fruit, with finely cut, rather ferny foliage. The flowers are half nodding at first, but open to a wide erect star-shape, 50–80mm (2–3¼in) across. The common colour forms are a rich purple, but many different shades exist in cultivation, including mauve, pink and white. Europe, including Britain. April–May. Widely cultivated in gardens. In the wild a plant of meadows over limestone.

Pulsatilla rubrum ○☆
Very similar to *P. vulgaris* but with rich reddish-brown to deep red blooms. C and S France. May–June. Hybrids between the two species (*P. vulgaris* and *P. rubrum*) exist in gardens.

Pulsatilla halleri ○
Like *P. vulgaris*, but plants more densely woolly with large rich purple blooms. Mountains of E Europe, including the E Alps. 'Budapest' is the finest cultivar, but the true plant is very rare in cultivation.

Pulsatilla alpina ○☆
A familiar and widespread species in the mountains of W and C Europe. More vigorous than the previous species, forming large tufts to 30cm (12in) tall, often

more. The deep green leaves are rather carrot-like and fringed with hairs. The glistening white, cup-shaped flowers, 40–60mm (1½–2¼in) across, are often flushed with bluish-purple on the outside, with a boss of bright yellow stamens inside. The flowers are followed by striking feathery fruits borne on elongating stems. May–June. The yellow form, subsp. *apiifolia* (syn. *P. sulphurea*), is equally delightful. It has a similar distribution in the wild, though preferring acid, rather than calcareous, soils. *P. alpina* is not difficult to cultivate, but it is often a shy flowerer in gardens, though not in all. The decorative fruits often attract attention.

Pulsatilla caucasica ○
Plants, to 15cm (6in) tall, have finely cut deep green leaves with small bell-shaped flowers ranging in colour from greenish-yellow to pink or purplish. W and C Asia. May. Scarcely as good as a garden plant as the preceding species. The same applies to the North American *P. occidentalis* which bears small flowers similar in shape to *P. alpina*, white or pinkish in colour.

PYROLA (Pyrolaceae)

A delightful group of low-growing, creeping, evergreen woodland plants which are unfortunately not easy to grow, although by no means impossible. There are about 20 species in the northern temperate regions. In cultivation they require cool, moist, leafy soils and partial shade; they greatly resent disturbance. Pyrolas have rather long-stalked leaves, often rounded, and produced near ground level. The leafless flower stems grow above the leaves and usually carry a raceme of smallish white, pink or purplish flowers, but sometimes the flowers may be solitary. Their 5 petals usually curve inwards in the shape of a cup, with 10 stamens inside.

Pyrola rotundifolia ◑
The Round-leaved Wintergreen is one of the best for garden value, reaching 15–25cm (6–10in) tall in flower and with rounded to oval, almost entire, leaves. Long racemes carry 10–20 scented white flowers, each about 10mm (⅖in) across, with a strongly bent S-shaped style which protrudes conspicuously from the corolla. Europe, including Britain, and North America. May–July.

Pyrola media ◑
Similar to *P. rotundifolia*, but with smaller flowers and a straight style, although fairly long and protruding beyond the pale pinkish corolla. Europe, including Britain. June–July.

Pyrola minor ◑
The Common Wintergreen is smaller than either of the preceding species with slightly toothed leaves and short racemes some 10–15cm (4–6in) high. The small white or pale pink flowers have a straight style which is short, not protruding from the corolla. Europe, Britain and North America. June–August.

Pyrola secunda (syn. *Orthilia secunda*) ◑
Wavering Bells is a less showy plant, only 5–10cm (2–4in) in height, with ovate toothed leaves and small bell-shaped greenish-white flowers in a one-sided spike. Europe, Britain, Asia and North America.

Pyrola uniflora (syn. *Moneses uniflora*) ◑▲
A lovely plant, but difficult to cultivate. It has wiry stems 8–15cm (3–6in) in height with the leaves carried on the lower part of the stem and overtopped by a solitary

Pyrola rotundifolia

nodding, scented, white flower, flattish, 10–15mm ($\frac{2}{5}$–$\frac{3}{5}$in) across, and with a wax-like texture. Europe, including Britain, Japan and North America. June.

RAMONDA (Gesneriaceae)

A popular group amongst alpine enthusiasts. The genus contains 3 species, all native to S Europe where they inhabit shaded cliff crevices. They form basal flat rosettes from the centre of which arise the flat flowers on leafless stalks; they are reminiscent of African Violets, *Saintpaulia*, to which the genus is distantly related. They thrive in a moist leafy compost and are at their best placed in a shaded rock crevice or north-facing wall. Plants are long lived and remarkably drought resistant once established; however, an occasional soaking during dry spells will help to keep them healthy. They also make excellent plants for the peat garden, or in a pan in the alpine house. Propagation from seed is slow, but with care the tiny seedlings can be nursed on for a year or two until large enough to plant out.

Ramonda myconi (syn. *R. pyrenaica*) ◑☆
Plants form large deep green, rough-leaved rosettes up to 25cm (10in) across, rusty-golden beneath. The flowers are mauve to bluish-violet, 20–30mm ($\frac{3}{4}$–1$\frac{1}{4}$in) across, 5-petalled. The yellow stamens form a cone in the centre of the flower. Pyrenees. April–May. The commonest forms in cultivation are: 'Alba'—white flowers; 'Coerulea'—blue flowers; 'Rosea'—clear pink flowers.

Ramonda nathaliae ◑
Similar, but a neater plant, with paler, more shiny and less rough leaves. The flowers are usually 4-petalled, deep mauve-blue in the best forms, with a cone of yellow anthers. S Yugoslavia and Bulgaria. April–May. 'Alba'—a particularly fine white form.

Ramonda serbica ◗▲
Like the previous in its leaf rosettes, but the flowers are more cupped, with distinctive purple stamens. Balkans. April–May. Rarer and less easy in cultivation than the other species.

RANUNCULUS (Ranunculaceae)

The buttercups are familiar plants of meadows and waysides. The genus, however, contains many species distributed throughout the world, except for the tropics. Apart from the coarser meadow species, there are many delightful mountain species. Some are easy to cultivate, others more demanding. On the whole, a well-drained gritty compost will suit most of the commoner ones available. Seed is best sown as soon as it is ripe.

Ranunculus gramineus ○☆
One of the most distinctive with its narrow grass-like leaves, unlobed, and the usual bright yellow buttercup flowers. Plants grow to 30cm (12in) tall, but the best forms are more dwarf. Late June–August, sometimes later. SW Europe.

Ranunculus pyrenaeus ○
Rather like the previous species, but the leaves greyish-green and the flowers more delicate, 10–20mm ($\frac{2}{5}$–$\frac{4}{5}$in), white with a central boss of golden stamens. Plants grow to 18cm (7in) tall, though often less. April–May. Alps and Pyrenees. A plant of mountain meadows over limestone, often growing close to snow patches. Not common in cultivation.

Ranunculus × *arendsii* ○☆
A charming hybrid between the previous two species, producing sulphurous yellow flowers throughout the late spring and summer. Well worth acquiring.

Ranunculus parnassifolius ○
One of the gems amongst the alpine buttercups. Plants are small, 7–10cm (3–4in) tall, usually with a basal rosette of dark green heart-shaped leaves. The flowers, 20–25mm ($\frac{4}{5}$–1in) across, are white, but turn pink or reddish as they age. The stamens are bright yellow. Alps and Pyrenees. April–May. A plant for a sunny scree, but like the previous species it should not be allowed to dry out, especially during the summer months. In the wild *R. parnassifolius* is a plant of rocks, screes and moraines at altitudes between 1,900 and 2,900m (6,270–9,570ft).

Ranunculus amplexicaulis ○
A Pyrenean meadow species to 20cm (8in) tall, with rather large oval basal leaves. The erect stems bear several small stalkless leaves and white buttercup flowers, 16–20mm ($\frac{5}{8}$–$\frac{4}{5}$in) across. May–June.

Ranunculus calandriniodes ○
Another gem, this delightful species comes from the High Atlas of Morocco. The attractive greyish leaves are oval with a distinctive wavy margin. The large flowers, 30–50mm (1$\frac{1}{5}$–2in) across, are poppy-like, white flushed with pink, with a large boss of golden stamens. Plants grow to 15cm (6in) tall, occasionally more. December–February. A hardy species that will succeed outdoors, but because of its time of flowering it is generally grown in a large pot in the alpine house. The leaves appear above ground during the autumn.

Ranunculus pyrenaeus

Ranunculus ficaria ○
The familiar Lesser Celandine is a species which many would wish they could eradicate from their gardens, for it often becomes an invasive weed. However, there are a number of forms worth cultivating. The species has basal tufts of heart-shaped, sometimes dark-marked, leaves. The starry, glistening yellow, flowers have 10 or more narrow petals. Widespread in Europe and W Asia. 'Albus'—a white-flowered form; 'Aurantiaca'—flowers of coppery gold; 'Cupreus'—copper flowers; 'Flore-pleno'—an attractive form with rich yellow double blooms; 'Major'—a larger plant to 30cm (12in) and large golden flowers; 'Primrose'—flowers pale creamy-yellow.

Ranunculus glacialis ○□▲
Another gem, but by no means one of the easiest to cultivate. The basal leaves are thick and rather fleshy, rounded in outline, but deeply lobed. The stems rise to 10cm (4in), though often less, and generally carry several white flowers, 25–40mm (1–1⅗in), which become delicately flushed with pink. Mountains of Europe, Iceland and Greenland. April–July. It inhabits high alpine moraines and screes, often close to snow patches.

Ranunculus seguieri ○
Rather like the previous, but smaller and more delicate with more finely divided leaves and pure white flowers, the petals slightly notched. Alps and Apennines. May–July. A denizen of high damp meadows and screes, growing, unlike *R. glacialis*, on calcareous soils.

Ranunculus hybridus (syn. *R. × phthora*) ○
A small plant to 80mm (3in) tall with 2 large basal leaves, kidney-shaped, but coarsely toothed at the top. The delicate stems have a few small bract-like leaves and carry one or often several buttercup-flowers, each 12–25mm (½–1in) across. E and SE Alps. March–June. A plant of high limestone screes and moraines.

Ranunculus crenatus ○

Another little curiosity, not unlike the previous species, but smaller and often with only a single leaf that enfolds the flowers in bud. The bright yellow flowers give the plant a Winter Aconite appearance. Mainland Greece and Hungary. May–June. Another dweller amongst high alpine screes and moraines.

Ranunculus asiaticus ○

Perhaps the most remarkable of all the buttercups, this Mediterranean species has long been cultivated in gardens, where there exist both single and double-flowered forms. The wild forms with their gorgeous poppy-like blooms are, however, the most delightful. Plants persist by means of an underground tuber like a bunch of stiff claws and can be purchased as such. The lobed basal leaves are generally deep green. The wiry stems to 40cm (16in) tall carry several large flowers 40–60mm ($1\frac{3}{8}$–$2\frac{2}{3}$in) across, bright red, bright yellow or satiny white, contrasting with a central cluster of black stamens. June–July. Hardy in warmer areas, but unfortunately this plant seldom persists for long in the garden. Grown in a pot in the alpine house some have been known to survive year after year, given a summer baking, and little or no water once the foliage begins to die down. All who see this plant for the first time will want to cultivate it.

RAOULIA (Compositae)

The plants in this curious genus of about 25 species of Australasian herbs are sometimes called 'vegetable sheep', a name referring to their dense, tufted, greyish foliage. The tiny rosettes of leaves are only a few millimetres high and form dense cushions or hummocks, sometimes very hard, often spreading up to 1m (3ft) across in the wild, although in cultivation this is rarely the case. The flowers are rather insignificant and are either white or pale yellow, resembling the helichrysums. They are generally difficult to raise from seed, but rooted tufts or cuttings afford the best means of increase. A sheet of glass placed overhead will protect these plants outdoors from the worst of the winter weather.

Raoulia australis ○

A species from New Zealand with tiny leaves up to 2mm ($\frac{1}{12}$in) long that are finely covered with silver hairs. The flowers occur throughout the summer and are a delicate, pale sulphur yellow, 4–5mm ($\frac{3}{16}$in) across.

Raoulia hookeri ○

Slightly larger than the preceding species with prostrate stems rooting at the nodes, bearing pale green leaves, 3–5mm ($\frac{1}{8}$–$\frac{1}{5}$in) long. The flowers are a paler yellow and 5–7mm (to $\frac{1}{4}$in) across. July–August.

Raoulia haastii ○☆

This species is similar in habit and size to the two preceding ones, forming hard mounds of rich green foliage, which turns brownish in winter. The stemless flowers are white and papery, up to 5mm ($\frac{1}{5}$in) across. New Zealand. July–August. A useful scree or alpine plant species.

Raoulia tenuicaulis ○☆

Closely related to the previous species having leaves 5mm ($\frac{1}{5}$in) long covered in a dense whitish wool. The flower-heads are slightly larger, up to 6mm ($\frac{1}{4}$in) in diameter and creamish-white. New Zealand. July–August. This is probably the easiest of the group to cultivate.

Other species available are *R. glabra, R. grandiflora* and *R. lutescens*, all of which come from New Zealand. The former two have small white flower-heads, the latter lemon-yellow. All will succeed on a fine scree or raised bed, given perfect drainage.

RHODIOLA (Crassulaceae)

This genus contains the well-known Roseroot, *Rhodiola rosea*. The species, about 50 in number, were formerly included in the stonecrops, *Sedum*. They are widely distributed in the northern temperate hemisphere. They require a well-drained, gritty compost and are reasonably easy to cultivate, though infrequently seen in gardens.

Rhodila rosea (syn. *Sedum roseum*) ○◑☆
A grey-green tufted, fleshy, perennial to 20cm (8in), though often lower, the stems often flushed with purple. The leaves are oval, thick and toothed. The small, dull yellow flowers, are borne in dense, rather flat, clusters at the stem tips. May–July. Widespread in the northern hemisphere. In the wild, a species of rocky meadows, rocks and screes to 3,000m (9,900ft); plants may occur on acid or calcareous soils. Flowers are either male or female and are borne on separate plants.

RHODODENDRON (Ericaceae)

Rhododendron is one of the largest genera in the plant kingdom, comprising approximately 800 species of which vast numbers are in cultivation. Some of these have been used to produce innumerable hybrids and cultivars and it would be impossible in the space allotted here to give a comprehensive list, but growers are many, and catalogues readily available, and the reader is referred to them. Some of the more commonly grown, easily obtainable members of this genus are listed below.

Rhododendrons form dwarf to large, evergreen or deciduous, trees or shrubs with alternate leaves frequently clustered beneath the inflorescences in pseudowhorls. The usually showy flowers are borne in spring in clusters; the corolla shape varies from salver to funnel or trumpet shape. Most species require a moist leafy or peaty lime-free soil. The smaller ones make excellent pan plants; the pans can be sunk in the garden or in a shaded frame during the summer. All heartily dislike drought. A selection of the smaller and most useful species is included below.

Rhododendron anthopogon ◑☐
A dwarf shrub to 1m (3ft) high with rounded heads of small white to deep pink flowers. Flowers are often more sparse in young plants. Himalaya and Tibet. May–June.

Rhododendron campylogynum ◑☐
A spreading shrub to 1.3m (4½ft) in height, but creeping in habit with long shiny deep green leaves. The long-stalked, bell-shaped flowers are cream, pink, or shades of plum-purple, borne in clusters of 1–3, usually with a blue-white bloom. SW China, Burma and Tibet. May. Some forms are variably hardy, but all are worth cultivating.

Rhododendron camtschaticum ◑☐
A very beautiful deciduous shrub up to 20cm (8in) tall, with oval bright green leaves

and pink salver-shaped flowers borne clear of the foliage. NE Asia and NW North America. May–early June.

Rhododendron fastigiatum ◐☐
Usually less than 1m (3ft) in height, a dense, mound-forming shrub with small, glaucous leaves. The flowers are numerous, mauve to purple. SW China. April–May. Rather like a more erect *R. impeditum*.

Rhododendron ferrugineum ◐☐☆
The Alpenrose, is a hardy, late-flowering, European species which can reach 1.5m (5ft) in height, but is usually more compact. The attractive leaves are rust-coloured beneath. The small trumpet flowers are closely clustered, frequently pink, but the colour varies from white to crimson. June–July. A familiar plant of mountain slopes, open woods and scrubland to 3,200m (7,600ft) in the mountains of C and SW Europe.

Rhododendron flavidum ◐☐
A shrub eventually up to 2.5m (9ft) tall, but more usually only 1m (3ft) in height. The leaves are glossy and the flowers pale yellow. Subject to die-back if not completely happy.

Rhododendron forrestii ◐☐▲
A fairly robust creeping shrub with oval leaves which are often purple beneath. The comparatively large, waxy bell-shaped flowers are scarlet to blood-red, borne singly or in pairs. SW China and Tibet. April–May. Plants are subject to damage from spring frosts. A beautiful plant when well grown, but not one of the easiest. Var. *repens* (syn. *R. repens*) is the normal form offered by nurseries—the leaves are green beneath.

Rhododendron hanceanum 'Nanum' ◐☐
A very dwarf form of *R. hanceanum*, slow growing and free flowering, with clear yellow flowers. May–June.

Rhododendron hippophaeoides ◐☐
A small-leaved plant to 1.25m (4ft) high with racemes of blue, mauve, pink or white flowers. E Himalaya and SW China. April–May.

Rhododendron impeditum ◐☐☆
A dense low evergreen shrub up to 40cm (16in) tall, but often less. The small leaves are deep green, but are very variable in different forms. The flowers vary from mauve to purplish-blue, borne in profusion. SW China. May–early June. One of the best—the more dwarf forms are worth seeking out.

Rhododendron lepidostylum ◐☐
An aromatic small shrub, worth growing for the blue bloom of the young foliage. The yellow flowers are borne in clusters of 1–3. May.

Rhododendron leucaspis ◐☐
Plants to 1m (3ft) tall with blue-green leaves. The white, sometimes pink-tinged, saucer-shaped flowers, 50mm (2in) across, have chocolate-brown stamens. China and Tibet. February–April. Unfortunately, not hardy except in milder areas of Britain, but well worth trying in a container as it is one of the loveliest of all small rhododendrons.

Rhododendron pemakoense ◑▢
Forms a dense shrub up to 60cm (2ft) in height with a suckering habit. A very floriferous plant, with comparatively large, pink-mauve trumpet-shaped flowers. China and Tibet. April. The flowers are sometimes caught by a late frost, so a protected position is advisable.

Rhododendron prostratum ◑▢
As the name implies, this species is completely prostrate, forming a dense mat of oval leaves with rather flat pinkish-purple flowers. W China. April.

Rhododendron racemosum ◑▢
A normally compact shrub, 15–40cm (6–16in) in height, which occasionally produces lax growth. The stems are usually red and the flowers pale pink, crowded and many in short or longer racemes. E Himalaya and SW China. April–May.

Rhododendron russatum ○▢
A variable twiggy shrub to 1.8m (6ft) tall, but often less, with oval dark green leaves, 20–30mm ($\frac{3}{4}$–1$\frac{1}{8}$in) long. The flowers are blue to purple, frequently with small white eye, wide trumpets with protruding stamens. SW China. April–May. The small-leaved forms tend to be more compact.

Rhododendron saluenense ◑▢
An erect shrub, becoming leggy as it ages. The flowers are comparatively large, open-faced, magenta to plum-purple, generally crimson-spotted, borne on a plant up to 1.2m (4ft) in height. SW China. April–May. Var. *chamenum* is a more compact form.

Recommended cultivars are: *Rhododendron* × 'Blue Diamond' ('Intrifast' × *R. augustinii*)—scaly aromatic foliage and bright or violet-blue flowers; 'Carmen' (*R. sanguineum* subsp. *didymum* × *R. forrestii* 'Repens')—a compact dwarf shrub with comparatively large, dark red, waxy, bell-shaped flowers; 'Chikor' (*R. rupicola* var. *chryseum* × *R. ludlowii*)—compact dwarf, yellow-flowered, shrub; 'Cilpinense' (*R. ciliatum* × *R. moupinense*)—a compact, early and free-flowering dwarf shrub with neat, glossy, ciliate foliage, bronzed when young, and large pink, funnel-shaped flowers; 'Elizabeth' (*R. griersonianum* × *R. forrestii* 'Repens')—low-growing and free-flowering with red flowers; 'Pink Drift' (*R. calostrotum* × *R. polycladum*)—compact dwarf shrub with pink to pinkish-mauve flowers, borne in profusion; 'Praecox' (*R. dauricum* × *R. ciliatum*)—a showy plant which can attain 2m (6ft) or more in height with pinkish-lilac flowers in profusion. All ◑▢☆.

RHODOHYPOXIS (Hypoxidaceae)

A small genus of charming and much sought-after plants from South Africa. Only one species is widely grown. It is reasonably hardy in milder districts, but elsewhere is safest in a pan in the alpine house. Propagation by division of the rootstock or seed, if available.

Rhodohypoxis baurii ○☆
A small tufted plant to 80mm (3in) tall, though often less. The basal leaves are spreading, lanceolate and silky with hairs. The solitary flowers come in a wide range

193

of colours from pale pink to deep rose, carmine, purple, as well as pure white; each flower is rather flat with 2 sets of 3 overlapping petals, looking like a miniature flattened iris. A long flowering season from April onwards. Plants thrive best in a sunny well-drained soil, that should not be allowed to dry out during hot weather. A number of named forms are available.

RICOTIA (Cruciferae)

A small genus with about 10 species. Only one is included here, which, though not common in cultivation, is worth seeking out. Plants are reputed to be short lived, but can be propagated from seed. Useful in a pan or trough.

Ricotia davisiana ○
An attractive little plant to 80mm (3¼in) tall with greyish 3-lobed leaves which are almost succulent. The flowers are pink. Turkey. April–May.

ROMANZOFFIA (Hydrophyllaceae)

A small genus of only 4 species from E North America and the neighbouring parts of NE Asia. Only two species are generally available, requiring semi-shaded places and moist leafy soil. Generally easily grown and propagated by seed or division.

Romanzoffia californica (syn. *R. sitchensis*) ◐
A small tufted plant with erect stems up to 15cm (6in) though often less, somewhat resembling the Meadow Saxifrage, *Saxifraga granulata*. The leaves are kidney-shaped, with blunt lobes, and flowers are borne in branched sprays; the anthers are golden. NW North America. April.

Romanzoffia unalaschkensis ◐
Similar to the preceding, but only 50mm (2in) tall with glossy leaves and white or pale purple flowers. E Siberia, W Canada and Alaska. April.

ROSA (Rosaceae)

A large and familiar genus, widespread in temperate regions of the northern hemisphere; however, only one is really suitable here.

Rosa pendulina (syn. *R. alpina*) ○☆
The Alpine Rose is a characteristic plant of woods and open mountain slopes to 2,600m (8,500ft) in the mountains of C and S Europe. It is essentially a briar rose with thornless stems to 1m (3ft), though much dwarfer in the best forms. The flowers are deep purplish-pink, 25–40mm (1–1⅜in), strongly cupped and with cream stamens. These are followed by the usual red, flask-shaped hips. May–July. Plants sucker around freely and this habit should be borne in mind when choosing a suitable site. 'Elliot's Var.'—a good reliable dwarf form.

ROSCOEA (Zingiberaceae)

An Asian genus with some 15 species, members of the ginger family. They are rhizomatous perennials with grassy leaves enfolding one another at the base. The large, but rather delicate, flowers are hooded, with a prominent, often lobed lip and only one large stamen. Attractive plants, but the flowers are rather fleeting, though often borne in succession. They prefer a deep humus-rich soil; most are reasonably hardy, but a sheltered site is advisable.

Roscoea alpina ◗
The smallest species in general cultivation, only 10–16cm (4–7in) tall with few leaves and solitary pinkish-purple flowers set low down amongst the foliage. Himalaya and SW China. June–July.

Roscoea humeana ◗
A more robust plant, to 30cm (12in), with broad, lanceolate leaves which are only partly developed at flowering time. The large violet-purple flowers are borne in close succession, each with a broad hood and a cleft lip. SW China. June–July.

Roscoea purpurea ◗☆
Another robust species, to 30cm (12in) tall, sometimes more, with deep green, maize-like leaves and up to 4 purple flowers with a narrow wedge-shaped hood and a cleft lip. Himalaya. June–August. A very handsome plant. Var. *procera* (syn. *R. procera*) is very similar, but larger, with broad leaf-sheaths and substantially larger flowers.

Roscoea cautleoides ○◗☆
A more slender species, to 20cm (8in) tall, occasionally more. The leaves are rather narrow and the elegant flowers a soft primrose yellow. There is also a purple-flowered form. SW China. June–July. Perhaps the finest and easiest species for the average garden.

ROSMARINUS (Labiatae)

The rosemarys are familiar aromatic shrubs of our gardens noted for their bright flowers and as a herb for flavouring food. Most are too gross for the rock garden, but a prostrate form of the Common Rosemary is worth consideration.

Rosmarinus officinialis var. ***prostratus*** (syn. ***R. lavandulaceus***) ○
A dwarf prostrate shrub eventually reaching 1m (3ft) or more across. The dark glossy-green slender leathery leaves are familiar, as are the pale violet 2-lipped flowers. Mediterranean region and W Asia. Rosemarys demand a well-drained soil and sunny sheltered site. Cuttings overwintered in a frame will ensure a supply of plants should those outdoors succumb to a severe winter.

ROSULARIA (Crassulaceae)

Succulent plants, resembling houseleeks, and with rosettes of thick leaves and bell-shaped flowers borne in lateral inflorescences. The genus contains about 25 species although only a few are in general cultivation; they come from the E Mediterranean, W and C Asia. The two included here are only hardy in the mildest districts, elsewhere requiring the protection of an alpine house. Plants need a very well-drained compost and sunny sheltered aspect. Propagation by offsets or from seed.

Rosularia pallida (syn. ***R. chrysantha, Cotyledon chrysantha, Umbilicus chrysantha***) ○
Plants grow to 16cm (6½in) tall in flower. The leaf-rosettes are green, the individual leaves rather small, oval and hairy along the margins. The creamy-white flowers are borne in an erect, spike-like raceme. W Asia—primarily Turkey. July–August.

Rosularia platyphylla (syn. ***Cotyledon platyphylla***) ○
Similar to the preceding. The flowers are white. Altai. July.

Another species occasionally encountered is *R. persica*, but it is a scarce plant in cultivation with little merit over those already referred to.

RUBUS (Rosaceae)

This extensive genus is widespread in many parts of the world and includes the brambles, as well as the Raspberry and Loganberry. Needless to say most are wholly unsuitable for the rock garden. A few are worthy of some attention; all those mentioned die down in the winter and all can prove invasive.

Rubus arcticus ○◑
The Arctic Bramble is a short, creeping perennial, not prickly, with 3-lobed, toothed leaves. The solitary bright red flowers, 15–25mm ($\frac{3}{5}$–1in) across, arise on erect stalks clear of the foliage. The fruits are dark red. Arctic and sub-Arctic regions. June–July.

Rubus chamaemorus ○◑
The Cloudberry will be familiar to those who have trampled the moors and bogs of Britain and N Europe. Plants are creeping and downy, rarely more than 15cm (6in) tall with lobed leaves reminiscent of an *Alchemilla*. The pure white flowers, 15–20mm ($\frac{3}{5}$–$\frac{4}{5}$in) across, are followed by edible berries which are a glowing orange when ripe. June–July.

Rubus illecebrosus (syn. ***R. sorbifolius***) ○◑
The Strawberry Raspberry hails from Japan; dwarf, like the previous species, but certainly sturdier, to 30cm (12in) tall. Leaves pinnate, with pointed, toothed leaflets. Flowers solitary or few, white 25–30mm (1–1$\frac{1}{5}$in) across. The large mulberry-red fruits are an attractive bonus in the late summer and autumn. July. The fruits are edible, but rather insipid.

RUPICAPNOS (Papaveraceae)

Rupicapnos africana ◑
A small tufted fumitory-like plant to 15cm (6in) tall. Leaves rather ferny and somewhat white, often tinted with pink, 8–10mm ($\frac{1}{3}$–$\frac{3}{8}$in) long, borne in delicate racemes just clear of the foliage. NW Africa. June–August. Generally hardy, but short lived and disliking excessive winter wet. Seed is generally set, but needs to be collected before the fruits burst.

SAGINA (Caryophyllaceae)

The pearlworts are mainly weedy plants which the alpine gardener tries to rid himself of rather than encourage; several can be a menace in pots, frames and along pathways. However, a few are of value and are non-invasive. There are some 20–30 species, widely distributed in the world, particularly in the northern temperate regions. The leaves of saginas are, in most species, short and needle-shaped but soft, forming prostrate mats or, in some cases, cushions. In spring and summer the insignificant flowers are produced, consisting of 4 or 5 green sepals and very small green or white petals which are sometimes absent altogether.

Sagina boydii ◑
This is one of the most desirable members of the group, forming tight hummocks of glossy deep green leaves; it is for these cushions that it is cultivated, since the flowers

are of no ornamental value. It is thought to have been found in Scotland, but has not been rediscovered in the wild. June–August.

Sagina glabra ◑

A carpeting plant forming mats of short needle-like leaves. The cultivar with golden foliage, 'Aurea', is the only form which is planted to any extent. The white flowers are small and starry and carried on short stems. Europe. July–September.

SALIX (Salicaceae)

The willows are a familiar group of plants. The genus contains about 500 species scattered in many temperate and Arctic regions of the world. They range from large trees to bushes and tiny undershrubs. A number are very suitable for the rock garden grown for their attractive leaves and catkins or their shape or coloured stems. Catkins are either male or female and are borne on separate plants. All the species are deciduous. Male forms make attractive plants for the garden. Most require a moist, humus-rich soil and dislike drought. Propagation from cuttings; seed is short-lived and difficult to germinate.

Low-growing species

Salix reticulata ◑

A small prostrate species eventually becoming much branched and woody. The attractive shiny oval leaves are covered in a fine mesh of veins, silvery-white with hairs beneath. The catkins are long-stalked, held above the foliage. Europe (including Britain). June–July. Slow-growing and not always easy to please, but perhaps the finest species for the rock garden or trough. Prefers a cool aspect. A plant of damp rocks and screes in the wild, to 2,500m (8,250ft).

Salix retusa ◑☆

Another mat-former with creeping stems, more invasive than the previous. The small oblong leaves, often notched at the apex, are shiny above. The small catkins are yellow. Mountains of C and S Europe. June–July. Like *S. reticulata*, it hugs the ground and rocks with which it comes into contact.

Salix serpyllifolia ◑

Like the previous, but even more compact and ground-hugging, the leaves only about 6mm (¼in) long. The stems become very congested in time. European Alps. May–June.

Salix herbacea ○◑

The Least Willow is another charming ground-hugger, forming an intricate web of interlacing branches in time. The small leaves are rounded, slightly toothed, and glossy on both surfaces. The small catkins are bright yellow. Europe (including Britain) and W Asia.

Salix hylomatica ◑☆

A creeping and trailing undershrub with slender stems rooting down readily into the soil. The numerous, bright, shiny green leaves are oval or elliptical and slighty toothed. The catkins are not very conspicuous, but the plant is pleasing none the less. Himalaya. June–July.

197

Taller growing species

Only a small selection is given here; there are many others worth considering for the large rock garden.

Salix lanata ○☆
The Woolly Willow forms a low spreading shrub to 1m (3ft) tall eventually, with thickly felted twigs. The broad, oval leaves are yellowish-hairy at first, but later the hairs become silky-grey. The yellow catkins are borne before the leaves expand. N Britain and Scandinavia. April–May. A very fine plant.

Salix lapponum ○
Grows more upright and taller with narrower leaves crowded at the stem tips. W and NW Europe. April–May.

Salix helvetica ○
A shrub to 2m (6ft) tall, but often far less, with thin greyish-brown stems. The oval leaves are shiny and greenish above, but white-felted beneath. The large yellow catkins have short stalks and are borne with the young leaves. Alps. May–June.

Salix arbuscula ○
In the wild, the Mountain Willow usually forms a low gnarled bush to 2m (6ft), but the form in cultivation will only reach 80cm (32in) in time. The leaves are elliptical, pointed and toothed, shiny green above but grey beneath. The narrow catkins are greyish, becoming yellow in the male plant. C and N Europe. A plant of damp mountain meadows and moraines. The dwarfer, high-mountain form is the finest—generally the form supplied by nurseries.

Salix × boydii ○☆
This rare plant was only once found in the wild in the Scottish Highlands and all those in cultivation are descended from it. Plants are very slow growing, forming a gnarled bush with thick stems and small rounded grey leaves at the branch tips. Will reach 60cm (24in) high after many years. May–June.

Other species worth considering if space permits are *S. fargesii, S. gillotii, S. × grahamii, S. mooreanus* and *S. wehrhahnii*.

SANGUINARIA (Papaveraceae)

The genus contains a single species native to woodland in North America, where it is widely known as Bloodroot, and is much sought after in gardens, especially the double-flowered forms. They require semi-shaded spots in a peaty lime-free soil.

Sanguinaria canadensis ◐□☆
A tufted perennial with coarse fleshy rhizomes which exude a red-sap when damaged, hence Bloodroot. The grey-green leaves unfurl with the flowers and are rounded in outline and with blunt uneven lobes around the margin. The anemone-like white flowers are solitary, about 35–40mm ($1\frac{2}{5}$–$1\frac{3}{5}$in) across with a central boss of yellow stamens. The whole plant is rarely more than 15cm (6in) tall, often less. April–May. The double-flowered form 'Flore Pleno' has longer-lived, more substantial blooms and is generally the better garden plant.

SAPONARIA (Caryophyllaceae)

The soapworts, so called because the leaves of *S. officinalis* produce a lather if rubbed in water, are a large and colourful group of plants, mostly easily cultivated. Some are compact enough to be of value to the rock gardener. There are about 30 species in Europe and Asia, but they are mainly Mediterranean in distribution.

Saponaria species may be annual or perennial, often with linear leaves, or sometimes ovate, lanceolate or spatula shaped; they are usually hairy to some extent on leaves, stems and calyx, the hairs frequently stickily glandular. The flowers have 5 petals and 5 sepals, the former joined into a tube, and in most species reddish-purple, although there are some yellow-flowered ones. They resemble *Silenes*, but have a calyx with 5, not 10, veins and usually 2 styles (not 3 or 5). The fruit-capsule opens at the apex into 4 or rarely 6 teeth (in *Silene* 6 or 10 teeth).

Saponaria ocymoides ○☆
The Rock Soapwort is a colourful loosely matted hairy perennial less than 15cm (6in) high, with dark green oval leaves. The small sprays of bright reddish pink flowers, each about 10mm ($\frac{2}{5}$in) in diameter, with blunt, not notched, petals, are borne in masses, often completely covering the plant. S Europe. April–August. There is a white form, 'Alba', and a more compact-growing selection known as 'Rubra Compacta'.

Saponaria pumilio (syn. ***Silene pumilio***) ○◫
The Dwarf Soapwort is one of the most desirable species, forming compact tufts, almost hairless, with fairly long, linear, pointed leaves. The large solitary pinkish-purple flowers, 15–20mm ($\frac{3}{5}$–$\frac{4}{5}$in) across, are carried on very short stems over the cushions; the petals are distinctly notched. Austria, Italy. August–September. In the wild, a species of rock meadows on acid soil between 900 and 2,600 (2,900–8,500ft).

Saponaria caespitosa ○
The Tufted Soapwort is another perennial species forming dense, nearly hairless, cushions, to 15cm (6in) tall, with pointed linear-lanceolate leaves. These are overtopped by small tight clusters of pinkish purple flowers, each about 10–15mm ($\frac{2}{5}$–$\frac{3}{5}$in) across, the petals rounded, not notched. Pyrenees, growing in rocks and screes. June–August.

Saponaria × *olivana* is a hybrid forming tight green cushions with larger near-stemless pink flowers. A very good rock garden plant. ○☆

Saponaria pulvinaris ○
A very compact species making hard dense hairless cushions of small linear leaves. The stems, 20–60mm ($\frac{4}{5}$–2$\frac{2}{5}$in) high, bear several smallish bright pink-red flowers, 7–10mm ($\frac{1}{3}$in) across, with notched petals. Generally not very free-flowering in cultivation. Turkey, Lebanon. June–July.

SARCOCAPNOS (Papaveraceae)

Very similar to *Rupicapnos* and requiring similar conditions in cultivation. Out of doors plants require a well-drained position and some form of winter protection—a sheet of glass is normally sufficient. Plants, however, produce seed readily and this acts as a useful insurance against fatalities.

Sarcocapnos enneaphylla ○◖

A low cushion-forming perennial to 12cm (4¾in) with delicate, rather fragile stems and pretty, grey-green, ferny foliage. The fumitory-like flowers are white with yellow and purple markings, each 8–10mm (⅓–⅖in) with a short spur. Spain and N Africa. Late May–July.

SATUREJA (Labiatae)

A moderately sized genus with some dozen species in Europe alone. Most are too coarse for the rock garden. They have the typical 2-lipped labiate flowers and opposite leaves.

Satureja montana ○

A very variable species from C and S Europe, with several subspecies recognized. The normal form, subsp. *montana*, forms tufts up to 30cm (12in) tall, with finely hairy stems and lanceolate or oval leaves which are hairy only on the edge. The flowers are deep mauve, 6–12mm (¼–½in) long, borne in dense crowded whorls. From S Spain, E to NW Yugoslavia. June–July. The plant is highly aromatic when crushed. The form generally found in cultivation is 'Pygmaea', which scarcely reaches 15cm (6in) tall, a charming plant well worth growing in a sunny, well-drained position.

SAXIFRAGA (Saxifragaceae)

The genus *Saxifraga* contributes many of the most popular plants to the rock garden. There are over 350 species, most of which are mountain plants and they occur throughout the northern hemisphere; a few species are native to the Andes. Most are perennial and very variable in their leaf characters; some have the ability to deposit calcium on their leaves by evaporation of hard water from special pores. Some species produce runners or bulbils which can effect propagation. The flowers are borne singly or in small clusters or large panicles; they have 5 sepals, 5 petals and 10 stamens, and flowers occur in every colour except blue.

Saxifrages are mercifully free from most pests and diseases—blackbirds probably do most of the damage by pulling at the plants while looking for grubs or other food, but other birds can equally well destroy a plant. Occasionally, the cushion species are attacked by a fungus when conditions are too wet.

In such a large genus, botanists have found it convenient to group the species into sections, and these have been used in the following account, thus species with certain features in common will be found near one another.

Propagation is by cuttings or from seed. Some of the mat-forming types can be readily increased by simply dividing the parent plant. A few species can be propagated by the bulbils or runners which they produce.

Section Hirculus

This section contains over 170 species, though only a very few are in cultivation. They have undivided leaves which do not form rosettes as in many saxifrages, but which are borne on the flower-stems as well as at the base of the plant. The flowers are yellow or pale orange.

Saxifraga hirculus ○◖

The Marsh Saxifrage is a tufted species to 15cm (6in) tall, though often less, with lanceolate untoothed leaves. The flowers are bright yellow, 20–30mm (⅘–1⅕in)

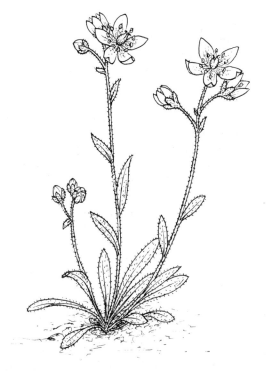

Saxifraga hirculus

across, one or several borne on the erect stems. In the best forms the petals are delicately spotted with red. May–July. Widespread in the mountains of Europe and Asia where it inhabits wet places.

Saxifraga flagellaris ◑
This species has 3 or 4 bright yellow flowers with petals 7–9mm ($\frac{1}{3}$–$\frac{3}{8}$in) long, carried on a stem which grows from a mat of leaves. The plants produce conspicuous red runners from the base of the stem when the flowers have finished, and each runner ends in a bud which eventually produces a new plant. Arctic Europe and Asia, Himalaya, Canada, extending down the Rockies as far as Arizona. July–August. For most people alpine house culture is probably best, as *S. flagellaris* likes some dampness in the summer, but cannot stand wet in winter.

Saxifraga brunoniana ◑
Rather like *S. flagellaris*, but with flowers of a paler yellow. The runners are even more shiny red. Himalaya and W China. July–August. Easier to grow out-of-doors than *S. flagellaris*.

Saxifraga diversifolia ◑
A laxly tufted species. The basal leaves are heart-shaped with long stalks. Golden-yellow or dull yellow flowers are borne on stems 15–20cm (6–8in) tall which have smaller, short-stalked leaves. W China and the Himalaya. June–August. In the wild a plant of meadows and open woodlands. In cultivation it thrives best in a moist shady place.

Section Robertsoniana

Plants evergreen, producing overground runners. The flower-stems are usually leafless, and the rosette leaves are more or less spoon-shaped, leathery, with unevenly toothed margins. The petals are white or pink, often finely spotted; the sepals are often downturned. Perhaps the easiest group of Saxifrages to cultivate.

Saxifraga umbrosa ◑

Plants form dense mats made up of almost flat leaf-rosettes; the leaf-stalks are densely hairy, and the blades are usually oval with a scalloped margin. The numerous flowers are carried in a lax panicle; the petals are white with red spots. W and C Pyrenees, but it has occasionally become naturalized in Britain. June–early August. Easily grown, but mostly superseded by the following hybrid.

Saxifraga × *urbium* ◑☆

This is the well-known and popular London Pride and is often incorrectly called *S. umbrosa* in gardens. It is a hybrid of garden origin, between the true *S. umbrosa* and *S. spathularis*. Plants can grow to 30cm (12in) tall and produce starry white flowers, the petals spotted with red. In all features it is intermediate between its parents. May–June. An easy and useful plant for semi-shaded places. Good as a path edger. 'Avreopunctata'—yellow-variegated leaves and prefers a sunny position; 'Clarence Elliott'—a smaller version, only to 15cm (6in) tall, and with rose-pink flowers ('Walter Ingwersen' is probably the same); 'Primuloides'—small leaves and bright pink flowers.

Saxifraga spathularis ◑

Rather rare in gardens, this species produces mat-forming rosettes. The spoon-shaped leaves have 4–7 coarse teeth on each side. The flower-stems are 10–40cm (4–16in) tall and the white petals have 1–3 yellow spots at the base as well as tiny scattered red dots. N Portugal, NW Spain and Ireland. June–July.

Saxifraga cuneifolia ◑☐☆

A carpeting species which has been in cultivation for almost two centuries. The leaves are spoon-shaped, the margins only slightly toothed. The flowering stems grow 8–25cm (3–10in) tall and the starry white flowers are rather small, 5–8mm ($\frac{1}{5}$–$\frac{1}{3}$in) across. Mountains of C and S Europe. May–July. This species does not like lime; it grows happily in semi-shade; in the wild it inhabits wooded places and shaded rocks, to 2,300m (7,500ft).

Saxifraga × *geum* ◑

A hybrid between the true *S. umbrosa* and *S. hirsuta*, being intermediate between its parents. The flower-stem is relatively sparsely branched, 18–30cm (7–12in) tall, and carries flowers with white petals, spotted with red and yellow. Pyrenees, where the parent species grow in close proximity. June–July. In gardens it thrives best in cool, semi-shaded places.

Section Cymbalaria

A group of annual species with rather ivy-shaped leaves. The flowers are usually yellow, sometimes white, with oval, clawed petals.

Saxifraga cymbalaria ◑☆

A slender plant with weak stems up to 20cm (8in) long. The leaves are usually kidney-shaped with 7–9 teeth. The bright yellow flowers have petals 3–5mm ($\frac{1}{8}$–$\frac{1}{5}$in) long, each with an orange blotch at the base. Romania and N Africa to the Middle East. March–September. This and the following two species do best in shady, rather damp places and are useful for making cheerful yellow splashes. They self-seed abundantly, but, thankfully, they are easily weeded out from places where they are not wanted.

Saxifraga hederacea ◑

A shorter plant than *S. cymbalaria* reaching only about 10cm (4in). The leaves have 3–7 blunt or pointed lobes and the white or pale yellow petals are only 2–3mm ($\frac{1}{12}$–$\frac{1}{8}$in) long. Sicily, Yugoslavia and Greece, east to Syria. March–June.

Saxifraga sibthorpii ◑

This species differs from *S. cymbalaria* in having larger petals, 5–7mm ($\frac{1}{5}$–$\frac{1}{3}$in) long, and sepals which reflex after flowering. Greece and Turkey. March–June.

Section Nephrophyllum

Plants usually with soft kidney-shaped leaves, and often with bulbils in the axils and at the base of the plant. The flowers are generally white.

Saxifraga latepetiolata ○

A glandular-hairy biennial which, in its first year, produces a rosette of recurved, kidney-shaped leaves with long stalks. In the second year it flowers, producing a leafy branched panicle 15–30cm (6–12in) tall, with numerous white flowers; the petals are 8–9mm ($\frac{1}{3}$–$\frac{3}{8}$in) long. E Spain. May–June. In the wild a plant of limestone rocks. In cultivation it requires some protection from frost and prolonged wet conditions.

Saxifraga irrigua ◑

A tufted plant with loose rosettes composed of pale green hairy leaves which are divided into 3 and then again divided into 9–25 segments. The flower-stems grow 10–30cm (4–12in) tall and are branched in the upper half, bearing many white flowers with petals 10–14mm ($\frac{2}{5}$–$\frac{3}{5}$in) long. USSR (Crimea). June. Despite being perennial, the plants often die after flowering, but are easily raised from seed. They grow best in shady conditions, either outdoors or in the alpine house.

Saxifraga biternata ○◑

This species forms a loose cushion with procumbent stems which bear bulbils in the lower leaf-axils; after flowering these grow into young plants which eventually become detached from the parent plant. The leaves are rather fern-like and covered with glandular hairs. The flower-stems, 15–25cm (6–10in) tall, carry numerous white flowers; petals 15–20mm ($\frac{3}{5}$–$\frac{4}{5}$in) long. In the wild it is found only at El Torcal de Antequera in S Spain, where it grows on limestone cliffs. May–June.

Saxifraga granulata ○◑

The Common Meadow Saxifrage is an extremely variable species with a wide distribution through Europe and the USSR to North America. It has mostly basal leaves, borne in loose rosettes, with a kidney-shaped, blunt-toothed blade. Bulbils are produced on the lower, underground part of the stem and these enable the plant to propagate itself. The glandular-hairy stems are 25–50cm (10–20in) tall, branched in the upper half to form a loose panicle of white flowers, each 10–18mm ($\frac{2}{5}$–$\frac{3}{4}$in) across. May–June. It will grow in most soils, except those with excessive calcium, but with a preference for soil which is not too dry. It is often naturalized in grassy areas in the garden, but is also suitable for growing in clumps in the rock garden. There is a double variant, *S. granulata* 'Plena'.

Saxifraga corsica ◖

Similar to *S. granulata*, but with 3-lobed leaves which are deeply scalloped, and flower-stems which are branched almost from the base. Corsica, Sardinia, the Balearic Islands and E Spain. The Spanish form is distinguished as subsp. *cossoniana*, a more robust plant with more deeply lobed leaves; it does well in the alpine house. This species needs a shady position in the garden.

Saxifraga sibirica ◖

A delicate, hairless or slightly hairy plant, 7–20cm (2¾–8in) tall, with white flowers 8–15mm (⅓–⅝in) long. The leaves are kidney-shaped, scalloped or 5–9-lobed, and with long stalks. There are underground bulbils in the axils of the basal leaves. A variable species which occurs from SE Europe through Turkey and the Caucasus into C and N Asia. May–July. In the wild it inhabits shady moist rocks and should be given these conditions in the garden where it deserves to be more widely grown.

Section Dactyloides

The Mossy Saxifrages. They have dense cushions or mats of rosettes made up of leaves which are variously forked or notched, and covered with hairs or glands; the rosettes do not die after flowering. The flowers are white, pink, red or yellow. This section contains numerous and often confusing species and the reader can be forgiven if they do not always seem easy to tell apart.

Saxifraga pentadactylis ◖☐

A species which forms loose cushions. The leaves have 3–5 narrow segments and are sticky, but hairless. The flower-stems are 6–20cm (2–8in) tall and each carries 3–30 star-shaped white flowers, tinged with cream. E Pyrenees and the mountains of N and C Spain where it is confined to acid rocks between 1,800 and 2,900m (5,940–9,950ft) altitude. May–June. Not long-lived in gardens and really does better with the protection of an alpine house.

Saxifraga corbariensis ◖

Rather similar to *S. pentadactylis*, but the leaves are scarcely sticky and are 3-lobed, each lobe being further divided to give 5–11 segments. E and NE Spain, SE France (Corbières). May–June. It always grows on limestone rocks and soils, generally in semi-shaded places. Best grown in a frame or alpine house.

Saxifraga camposii ○

A cushion-forming species with sticky leaves divided into 5–11 segments. The white petals are 8–11mm (⅓–½in) long, longer than the 4mm (5⁄16in) petals of *S. pentadactylis*. Limestone rocks, SE Spain. May.

Saxifraga trifurcata ○

A mat-forming plant whose sticky, dark green leaves are divided into many, pointed segments. The flower-stems grow 15–20cm (6–8in) tall and carry panicles of small white flowers. N Spain. May–June. In the wild a species of sunny limestone rocks.

Saxifraga geranioides ○☐
Superficially similar to *S. corbariensis*, but the sticky-hairy leaves are even more divided, having 9–27 segments. The 6–9 white flowers are in a compact inflorescence on a stem to 20cm (8in) tall; they are slightly fragrant, 22–24mm ($\frac{6}{7}$–1in) across. E Pyrenees and NE Spain. May–June. A plant of acid rocks and screes in the wild; in cultivation a cool, moist shady position suits it best.

Saxifraga vayredana ◑
A floriferous species forming rounded bright green cushions. The leaves have 3–7 segments and are covered in short glandular hairs which give off an aromatic smell. The flower-stems grow to 10cm (4in) tall, reddish in the upper part, and bear white flowers. NE Spain, where it inhabits shady places. Not completely hardy and best grown in an alpine house.

Saxifraga pedemontana ◑
A cushion-forming species with a wide range of habitats from the Cevennes eastwards to the Balkans and Carpathians. The slightly hairy, broad-stalked leaves are cut into 5–11 segments and the white flowers are borne in a close cluster, each flower 18–26mm ($\frac{3}{4}$–1in) across. May. In the wild a plant of shaded siliceous rocks.

Saxifraga androsacea ◑☐
A slightly hairy, cushion-forming species. The leaves are all basal and can be unlobed or with 3 short teeth. The 1–3 creamy-white flowers, 10–12mm ($\frac{2}{5}$–$\frac{1}{2}$in) across, are carried on slender stems up to 80mm (3in) tall. Mountains of Europe (Pyrenees and Alps) extending to the E Altai and E Siberia. May–June. It likes somewhat acid conditions in a moist, semi-shady position; in the wild, plants grow on damp screes and by snow patches.

Saxifraga muscoides ○◑
A dwarf species which forms soft cushions. The unlobed, lanceolate leaves persist on the plant when dead, and turn a conspicuous silvery colour. The flowers may be white or pale lemon-yellow, 1–3 being borne on a flowering stem 50mm (2in) or less tall. C and E Alps. June-August. The mats have a tendency to die from the centre outwards and it is a good idea to divide the clumps when this happens, before the whole plant is thus affected.

Saxifraga moschata ○◑☆
A species which forms moderately dense to very dense cushions or mats. The pale green leaves are divided into 3 blunt lobes, and the upper surface does not have channels. The flower-stems can reach 10cm (4in) tall and carry 1–7 small flowers 5–8mm ($\frac{1}{5}$–$\frac{1}{3}$in) across which are cream or yellowish, sometimes tinged with red. Mountains of C and S Europe, the Caucasus and Altai Mountains; usually found on calcareous rocks and screes. May–June. An accommodating species which will succeed happily out-of-doors in a sunny position. 'Cloth of Gold'—a form with golden leaves; the colour is retained all the year round, but it does best in shade.

Saxifraga exarata ○◑
Very similar to *S. moschata*, but the leaves have a channel down the middle of each segment. S Europe, Turkey and the Caucasus. May–June. Perhaps happiest within the confines of a frame or alpine house.

Saxifraga cebennensis ◑
Like *S. exarata*, but a larger plant with tighter, very sticky cushions of a pale

grey-green colour. The leaves have longer glandular hairs than those of *S. exarata*. The white flowers are 12–14mm ($\frac{1}{2}$–$\frac{5}{8}$in) across, with broad rounded petals. S France (Cevennes) where it inhabits shady limestone rocks. May.

Saxifraga pubescens ○

This species usually forms large dark green cushions and has leaves normally divided into 5 lobes and densely covered with long glandular hairs. There are two subspecies recognized in the wild and the one most commonly grown is subsp. *iratiana* which is compact with flowering stems 2–6cm ($\frac{3}{4}$–$2\frac{2}{3}$in) tall. The flowers, 8–12mm ($\frac{1}{3}$–$\frac{1}{2}$in) across, have white petals with reddish veins and anthers. C and E Pyrenees. May–June.

Saxifraga rosacea (syn. *S. decipiens*) ◑☆

A variable species which can produce tight cushions or loose mats. The hairy leaves usually have 5 lobes. The flower-stems, to 25cm (10in) tall, bear 2–5 white or pale pink flowers. NE and C Europe. May–July. A parent of a large number of 'Mossy Hybrids'. The species will thrive in both shaded or semi-shaded places, preferring a moist soil.

Saxifraga hypnoides ○◑

This species produces leafy shoots bearing widely spaced leaves which can be unlobed or 3-lobed; at the end of each shoot is a rosette of leaves which are 3–9-lobed. The flower-stems usually reach about 20cm (8in) and carry 3–7 large white flowers which open from nodding buds. Sub-Arctic regions southwards through NW Europe south-eastwards to the Vosges. May–June. 'Kingii'—very dwarf, turning red in the autumn; 'Whitlavei'—much more free-flowering than the type with more flowers on a stem, but less compact in habit.

Saxifraga tenella ◑

The plants form mats of creeping stems, with resting buds in the leaf-axils. The linear, leaves are about 10mm ($\frac{3}{8}$in) long, and hairy on the edges, especially near the base. The hairless flower-stems, 5–10cm (2–4in) tall, carry 2–8 creamy flowers. SE Alps. June. A useful plant for a moist shady part of the garden. In the wild this species inhabits shady rock and screes, generally on limestone, to 2,400m (7,900ft) altitude.

Saxifraga demnatensis ○

Forms a mat of pale green aromatic leaves covered in sticky hairs. The flower-stem usually grows 50–80mm (2–3in) and bears about 10 white flowers with green veins. Atlas Mountains of NW Africa. May–June. Best grown with the protection of an alpine house or frame.

The Mossy Saxifrages include a large range of hybrids, many of which are of unknown parentage. Normally spring-flowering, they provide useful hummocks of colour on the rock garden, whilst the compact dwarf ones are ideal subjects for troughs. The following selection is grouped according to flower colour:

RED: 'Ballawley Guardsman'—clear red, 50–90mm (2–3$\frac{3}{8}$in); 'Carnival' and 'Sanguinea Superba'—sun-proof; 'Dubarry'—20–25cm (8–9$\frac{3}{4}$in) with large flowers; 'Elf'—50–80mm (2–3in), late flowering; 'Peter Pan' and 'Triumph'—compact cushions.

PINK: 'Blutenteppich' (also called 'Flower Carpet')—free-flowering, likes a dampish position; 'Dartington Double'—slow-growing with double flowers; 'Gaiety'—neat cushions, early-flowering; 'Pixie'—compact, to 50mm (2in); 'Winston Churchill'—vigorous, 10–15cm (4–6in).

WHITE: 'James Bremner'—20–25cm (8–10in), vigorous, with very big flowers; 'Pearly King'—8–10cm (3–4in), floriferous.

YELLOW: 'Flowers of Sulphur'—somewhat spreading with pale lemon flowers, to 10cm (4in).

Section Trachyphyllum

Mostly small species which form mats and have unlobed linear-lanceolate leaves. The flower-stems have rather few branches and carry whitish or yellowish flowers.

Saxifraga bryoides ◖

Plants produce large, pale green mats from which arise 2–8cm ($\frac{4}{5}$–3in) stems bearing a solitary cream-coloured flower. The non-flowering shoots are densely leafy and buds develop in the axils of the incurved leaves. Mountains of Europe from the Pyrenees to the Balkans. April–May. Often called the Mossy Saxifrage despite belonging to a different section to the other 'mossy' species.

Section Xanthizoon

The plants produce loose mats of stems which have narrow leaves; the leaves are unlobed and have notched or bristly margins. The flowers are yellow, orange, purplish or red and are carried singly or in loose umbels. Only one species is cultivated.

Saxifraga aizoides ◯◖

This species forms mats of prostrate and upright branched stems, with rather fleshy, linear leaves. The flowers are produced 2–10 together at the ends of the flower-stems which vary from 5–30cm (2–12in) tall; the petals are usually yellow or pale orange, but in var. *atrorubens* they are deep red. The species has a wide distribution in the northern hemisphere, occurring in the northern parts of all continents and on mountains further south. June–July. In the wild it grows in wet, but not stagnant, conditions, on damp scree, stream banks or even in the beds of shallow streams and these conditions are not easy to reproduce in most gardens. It can survive in drier places, but must be given a lot of water to look its best. *S. aizoides* has hybridized with *S. × urbium* 'Primuloides' (in section *Robertsoniana*) to produce *S. × primulaize*. This fine hybrid looks like a small 'London Pride' and is very easy to grow, particularly on dampish soil in semi-shade. Mats of evergreen rosettes give rise to branched stems 50–80mm (2–3in) tall which carry deep pink or salmon-pink flowers.

Section Euaizoonia

These are the Encrusted or Silver Saxifrages. The rosettes are made up of stiff leaves which are encrusted with deposits of lime, often giving them a grey or silvery effect; lime-excreting pores can be seen at the tips or round the margins of the leaves. The flowers are produced in spikes, panicles or umbels and are usually white, the petals often with red spots. After flowering, the rosettes die, but usually new rosettes are produced on slender overground runners. In the wild most of the species grow on limy soils, generally amongst rocks or on cliffs.

Saxifraga paniculata (syn. *S. aizoon*) ○☆

A clump-forming plant with rosettes 10–60mm (⅜–2¼in) across, composed of toothed, elliptical- to spoon-shaped leaves which are somewhat incurved at the tips. The amount of lime-encrustation on the leaves is very variable. The flower-stems are 2–45cm (⅘–18in) tall and unbranched for most of their length. The small white, cream or occasionally pink flowers are 8–11mm (⅓–½in) across; the petals may be spotted with red. May–July. An extremely variable species with a wide distribution from S and C Europe to the Arctic, Turkey and the Caucasus and NE America. Nursery catalogues offer a bewildering array of names, the following being the most frequently encountered (inclusion here does not imply that they should be regarded as accepted botanical entities): 'Balcana'—white flowers with red spots; 'Baldensis' (syn. *S. aizoon* var. *baldensis*)—very small rosettes and reddish flower-stems; subsp. *cartilaginea*—leaves with sharp, pointed tips and white, freely produced flowers; var. *carinthiaca*—rosettes with fewer leaves which are densely lime-encrusted, and hairless flower-stems; 'Correvoniana'—produces flower-stems up to 10cm (4in) tall; 'Koprvnik'—the leaves are slightly hairy; 'Labradorica'—flower-stems only about 80mm (3⅛in) tall borne on silver-grey cushions; 'Lagraveana'—petals with rounded teeth; 'Lutea'—pale yellow flowers; 'Minor' (syn. *S. paniculata* subsp. *brevifolia*)—leaves only about 10mm (⅜in) long which form silvery rosettes; var. *minutifolia*—even smaller leaves than the previous, only 4–6mm (1/16–¼in) long and brownish flower-stems; 'Orientialis'—creamy flowers with red spots; 'Portae'—particularly tiny leaf-rosettes; 'Rex'—creamy unspotted flowers carried on brownish red stems; 'Rosea'—leaf-rosettes of a yellowish green colour and pale pink flowers; var. *sturmiana*—small rosettes, and brown stems carrying white flowers. (All ○☆)

Saxifraga kolenatiana (syn. *S. cartilaginea* var. *kolenatiana*, *S. paniculata* subsp. *kolenatiana*) ○

Very similar to *S. paniculata*, but with narrower leaves which taper gradually towards the tip, and pinkish purple flowers. Turkey, Caucasus. May–July.

Saxifraga callosa (syn. *S. lingulata*) ○

The leaf-rosettes are rather irregular, dying after flowering, but the plant produces short lateral stolons which bear new rosettes. The leaves are 5–8cm (2–3in) long, narrow, blue-green and lime-encrusted. The flower-stem rises up to 35cm (14in), arching and carrying numerous white flowers; the petals are 6–9mm (¼–⅜in) long, often with red spots at the base. S France and Italy. June–July. In cultivation it will thrive in a sunny position and likes a limy soil; a plant of limestone rocks and screes in the wild. A variable species: names have been given to a number of varieties which are in fact impossible to distinguish in the wild. Subsp. *catalaunica*—broader leaves than the type and a glandular-hairy flower-stem; var. *bellardii*—pure white flowers carried on a hairless stem; var. *lantoscana*—the variety seen most often in gardens which has short, blunt, lime-encrusted leaves; var. *lantoscana* 'Superba'—has taller flower-stems; 'Albertii'—larger rosettes than the type and a spreading inflorescence 25–30cm (10–12in) tall (it may possibly be a hybrid).

Saxifraga cotyledon ◑☐

The large rosettes measure up to 15cm (6in) across, and have strap-shaped, toothed leaves, somewhat broader towards the tip, and scarcely, if at all, lime-encrusted. The flower-stem is 15–90cm (6–36in) tall, and branched from the base to form a pyramidal panicle of numerous flowers; the white petals are 6–10mm ($\frac{1}{4}$–$\frac{2}{5}$in) long, sometimes spotted with red. Mountains of Europe and North America. June–August. A very handsome plant, which in cultivation dislikes lime and grows best in shade or semi-shade. A very variable species; gardeners have selected and named some of the more attractive variants: 'Caterhamensis'—flowers densely spotted with red; 'Norwegica'—leaves tapering to a short point, and white flowers; 'Pyramidalis'—bears a splendid inflorescence which is almost as broad as long.

Saxifraga cochlearis ○

Similar to *S. callosa*, but a smaller plant. The rosettes are crowded together to form a mound and the leaves are spoon-shaped and heavily encrusted with lime, 5–40mm ($\frac{1}{5}$–1$\frac{3}{5}$in) long. The flower-stems are 15–20cm (6–8in) tall, branched in the upper half, hairless or with only sparse glandular hairs. SW Alps. May–June. 'Major'—larger rosettes than the type and is thought possibly to be a hybrid with *S. callosa*; 'Minor'—a dwarf form suitable for a crevice in the rock garden. In the wild *S. cochlearis* inhabits limestone rocks to 1,900m (6,200ft) altitude.

Saxifraga crustata ○◗

An attractive lime-encrusted species which forms a mat with leaf-rosettes 20–80mm ($\frac{4}{5}$–3in) across; the leaves are 20–60mm ($\frac{3}{4}$–2$\frac{1}{4}$in) long, linear. The flower-stems, 12–35cm (4$\frac{4}{5}$–14in) tall, are glandular-hairy and branched in the upper half. The white or cream flowers, 8–11mm ($\frac{1}{3}$–$\frac{2}{5}$in) across, sometimes have red dots on the petals. Alps, south to C Yugoslavia. June–July. This species prefers a poor soil and semi-shade although it will put up with full sun; it is another limestone dweller in the wild.

Saxifraga hostii (syn. *S. altissima*) ○◗

This species differs from *S. paniculata* by its leaves which curve outwards at the tips, and in being larger in all its parts: leaves up to 10cm (4in), flower-stem to 60cm (24in), and petals 5–8mm ($\frac{1}{5}$–$\frac{1}{3}$in). E and SE Alps. May–June. In cultivation it is a vigorous plant and can be grown in full sun, although it prefers a little shade. In autumn the leaves take on a reddish hue. There are two subspecies, subsp. *hostii* and subsp. *rhaetica*—the former is the one most commonly cultivated and is often sold as *S. hostii* var. *altissima*. The leaves of the former subspecies have obtuse tips, whereas those of subsp. *rhaetica* have pointed tips.

Saxifraga longifolia ○☆

One of the most spectacular of all Saxifrages. A long-lived plant with a beautiful solitary leaf-rosette up to 15cm (6in) across which dies after flowering. The leaves are arranged very irregularly and are linear, wider towards the tip, 3–10cm (1$\frac{1}{5}$–4in) long and lime-encrusted. The flower-stem is glandular-hairy, 30–70cm (12–28in) tall, branched for its entire length and forming a pyramidal panicle with up to 1,000 white flowers! Pyrenees and E Spain. June. One of the grandest sights of the High Pyrenees in the summer are limestone cliffs decorated with white plumes of *S. longifolia* in full flower, the panicle swaying in the mountain breezes. A beautiful species which usually flowers from seed in 4–6 years; no offsets are produced so propagation has to be from seed which is usually abundant. 'Francis Cade'—a form with fine silvery leaf-rosettes. *S. longifolia* hybridizes freely with *S. paniculata*; the offspring are very reliable, but perennial, forming clumps of rosettes. The finest of these has been called 'Tumbling Waters' though it is not always possible to get the genuine article.

Saxifraga florulenta ○□▲

Often called the Ancient King, this species is unmistakeable. The solitary leaf-rosette is flat, 10–15cm (4–6in) in diameter, and composed of dark green, pointed leaves 50–75mm (2–3in) long; they are not lime-encrusted. The leaves tend to remain on the plant, so old specimens bear a green rosette on top of a cylinder of dry brown leaves. The flower-stem is about 45cm (18in) tall and carries a panicle of dirty pinkish white, bell-shaped flowers 5–7mm ($\frac{1}{5}$–$\frac{3}{10}$in) long. C Maritime Alps of France and Italy—in the wild it is so rare that it is legally protected. June–July. *S. florulenta* is not an easy plant, disliking lime in any form and hating a moist position or over-watering. For this reason it is normally grown in a pan in the alpine house. In the wild it is a species of granite cliffs between 1,900 and 3,250m (6,200–10,750ft). Specimens must not on any account be removed from their habitat. Like *S. longifolia*, plants die after flowering, so seed offers the only means of increase.

Saxifraga mutata ◑

The large rosettes are 4–13cm (1$\frac{3}{5}$–5in) across and form loose clumps; the leaves are shiny dark green, not lime-encrusted, more or less strap-shaped and often upcurved, with a distinct whitish border. The flower-stems are rather stout, 30–50cm (12–20in) tall and glandular-hairy, the petals dark yellow or orange, narrow, 5–8mm ($\frac{1}{5}$–$\frac{1}{3}$in) long. Alps and S Carpathian mountains. May–July. In the wild this species inhabits damp limestone rocks. In the garden it can grow without lime, and prefers a semi-shady situation where it will usually live for two or three years and die after flowering. Unfortunately in cultivation it often seems reluctant to produce offsets; however, it is readily raised from seed. *Saxifraga mutata* has produced a natural nybrid with *S. aizoides* (in section *Xanthizoon*) called *S.* × *hausmanii*. This hybrid is found in the Alps and looks more like *S. mutata* than its other parent; the flowers are coppery-orange and carried on stems 7–10cm (2$\frac{3}{4}$–8in) tall. May–June. In cultivation it tends to be short lived.

Saxifraga valdensis ○

A cushion-forming species with narrow spatula-shaped leaves, 40–60mm (1$\frac{3}{5}$–2$\frac{2}{5}$in) long, lime-encrusted and reflexed. The flower-stems grow 5–15cm (2–6in) tall and are covered with reddish glandular hairs; they carry 5–10 white flowers. SW Alps of France and Italy where it grows tightly wedged into crevices in limestone rocks. May–June. A slow-growing plant which enjoys full sun and does best in the alpine house. Often confused with *S. cochlearis* 'Minor', but has a more clustered inflorescence and narrower leaves.

Section Porophyllum

This section used to be known to gardeners as *Kabschia* and at one time the subsection *Engleria* was also included here, but recently it has been put into section *Tetrameridium*. *Porophyllum* Saxifrages produce firm, tight evergreen cushions made up of numerous small rosettes which do not die after they have produced flowers. The leaves are small, stiff and narrow, often sharp, and with few or many lime pores. The white, pink or yellow flowers are carried on short stems, singly or several together. The plants flower in the spring, some of them very early.

Saxifraga marginata ○

A cushion-forming species which has been known to produce plants eventually to over 50cm (20in) across. The narrow leaves are bluish green, lime-encrusted,

3–13mm ($\frac{1}{8}$–$\frac{1}{2}$in) long. The flower-stems are 30–90mm (1$\frac{1}{5}$–3$\frac{3}{5}$in) tall and cary a cluster of 3–8 white, or sometimes pale pink, flowers. Mountains of S Europe. March–April. In the wild it is a plant of limestone rocks. The following are to be found in nurserymen's catalogues, but the plants offered rarely correspond to the described varieties: var. *coriophylla*, var. *karadzicensis* and var. *rocheliana*.

Saxifraga scardica ◑▲

Like *S. marginata*, but with pointed grey-green leaves 4–17mm ($\frac{1}{6}$–$\frac{3}{4}$in) long and with more numerous (4–13) white flowers on each reddish stem. Balkan Peninsula. March–April. A species which is easier to grow under glass than out-of-doors as it appears to dislike both a lot of wet in winter and a lot of sun in summer. Forma *erythrina* (sometimes known as var. *rosea*) has pink flowers; it was orginally described as having flowers of deep purple, but this is now thought to be an error. Var. *obtusa* has green leaves and flowering stems, and the petals tend to separate and twist outwards with age giving a rather untidy appearance. In gardens it will put up with more sun than *S. scardic* itself. Recent studies suggest that it may not belong to *S. scardica* but be a species in its own right; further work is needed before a final judgement can be made.

Saxifraga spruneri ○▲

This is the only European *Porophyllum* Saxifrage with hairy leaves. The cushions are domed, the individual leaf-rosettes 5–13mm ($\frac{1}{4}$–$\frac{1}{2}$in) across. The 6–12 white or yellowish green flowers are borne on a stem 40–80mm (1$\frac{3}{5}$–3in) tall; the petals are 3–6mm ($\frac{1}{8}$–$\frac{1}{4}$in) long. Albania, Yugoslavia, S Bulgaria and N Greece. April–May. Another inhabitant of limestone rocks in the wild. Not very easy to grow, requiring lots of sun.

Saxifraga diapensioides ○◑▲

A very slow-growing species which forms hard, tight cushions made up of rosettes 5–10mm ($\frac{1}{4}$–$\frac{1}{2}$in) in diameter. The leaves are 4–6mm ($\frac{1}{8}$–$\frac{1}{4}$in) long, usually encrusted with lime. The flower-stem is glandular-hairy and varies in height from 20 to 80mm ($\frac{4}{5}$–3$\frac{1}{5}$in) and bears 2–6 white flowers, occasionally more. France, Switzerland and Italy—primarily the SW Alps. April–May. Not easy in cultivation and only flowers well when it is absolutely happy. Too much wet in winter will kill it, so it is best given the protection of an alpine house or frame.

Saxifraga tombeanensis ○

This species, which is confined to limestone rocks in the mountains of N Italy, is very similar to *S. diapensioides*, but has shorter leaves, 2–4mm ($\frac{1}{12}$–$\frac{1}{6}$in) and larger petals, 8–14mm ($\frac{1}{3}$–$\frac{3}{5}$in). April–May. In the wild the cushions can grow to 30cm (12in) across. In cultivation, it responds best to being grown on tufa.

Saxifraga vandellii ○

The rosettes of this plant grow tightly together to form hard, compact cushions up to 75mm (3in) in diameter. The green, glossy leaves are 6–10mm ($\frac{1}{4}$–$\frac{3}{8}$in) long and the glandular-hairy flower-stems 30–80mm (1$\frac{1}{5}$–3in) tall. There are 3–8 white flowers to a stem. N Italian Alps, where it inhabits limestone rocks. April–May. Some of the plants being sold in Britain as *S. vandellii* have been found to be hybrids with *S. marginata*.

Saxifraga burseriana ◑☆

A beautiful species which forms mats or low cushions up to 15cm (6in) across. The narrow, pointed leaves are grey-green, 5–12mm ($\frac{1}{5}$–$\frac{1}{2}$in) long and have 5–7 lime

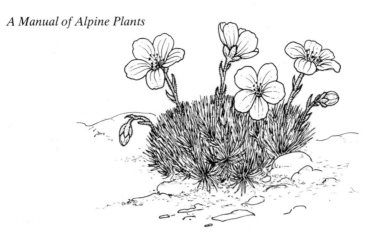

Saxifraga burseriana

pores. The reddish-brown flower-stems bear a solitary flower (occasionally 2); they are relatively large, 16–24mm ($\frac{1}{2}$–1in) across, white, sometimes with reddish veins. E Alps and Karawankan—another limestone dweller. February–April. Botanists do not generally consider the varieties of *S. burseriana* to be worthy of recognition; however, they will be found in nursery catalogues. Var. *burseriana* (syn. var. *minor*)—rosettes 6–8mm ($\frac{1}{4}$–$\frac{1}{3}$in) across, 1-flowered stems and petals 5–9mm ($\frac{1}{5}$–$\frac{3}{8}$in). Var. *major* (syn. var. *tridentina* var. *tridentata*)—a larger plant with rosettes 8–16mm ($\frac{1}{3}$–$\frac{2}{3}$in) across, flower-stems with 1 or 2 flowers, the petals 8–11mm ($\frac{1}{3}$–$\frac{2}{5}$in). *Saxifraga burseriana* is particularly useful because of its early-flowering habit, though preferring not to be grown in full sun. The following cultivars are available: 'Brookside'—large flowers with petals 10–12mm ($\frac{3}{8}$–$\frac{1}{2}$in); 'Crenata'—notched, weather-resistant petals; 'Gloria'—particularly early-flowering, the petals are 11–17mm ($\frac{2}{5}$–$\frac{2}{3}$in).

Saxifraga juniperifolia ◑☆
This species forms dark green low cushions or mats of spiky rosettes; the leaves are 10–14mm ($\frac{2}{5}$–$\frac{3}{5}$in) long, lanceolate with tiny marginal teeth in the lower half, pointed, not encrusted with lime. The hairy flower-stems bear a cluster of 6–11 bright yellow flowers with protruding stamens. Mountains of Bulgaria, Turkey and the Caucasus. May–June. Like *S. burseriana* it is best grown in a semi-shady place.

Saxifraga sancta (syn. *S. juniperifolia* subsp. *sancta*) ◑
Very similar and closely related to *S. juniperifolia*, indeed some botanists consider it to be a subspecies. It differs in having the tiny marginal teeth almost to the leaf-tip, and non-hairy flower-stems bearing fewer (3–7) flowers. Greece and NW Turkey. March–April. Not very free-flowering in cultivation and old plants have a tendency to turn brown and die off in the middle; if this happens it is best to divide the plant and grow the resulting pieces as new plants. Var. *macedonica* (syn. *S. juniperifolia* var. *macedonica*) carries its flowers on stems 70–80mm ($2\frac{4}{5}$–3in) tall, and flowers a little later.

Saxifraga caucasica ◑
A species native to the central Caucasus and represented in cultivation by var. *desoulavyi*. Plants form tight cushions made up of small leaf-rosettes. The bright yellow flowers are borne on hairless stems, 3–7 together in a compact head. March.

212

This species needs good drainage and if happy, will prove free-flowering in cultivation.

Saxifraga kotschyi ◑

This species forms cushions up to 45cm (18in) across in old specimens. The leaves are grey-green and encrusted with lime, the old dead leaves are retained on the shoots. The yellow flowers are borne in clusters of 4–13, the petals are 3–6mm ($\frac{1}{8}$–$\frac{1}{4}$in) long, shorter than the stamens. Turkey, N Iran. March. Not as common in cultivation as *S. juniperifolia* and not too easy to obtain, as many of the plants sold as *S. kotschyi* are misidentified.

Saxifraga ferdinandi-coburgi ◯◑

This plant produces a dense, hard, bluish-green cushion; the leaves are 5–8mm ($\frac{1}{4}$–$\frac{1}{3}$in) long, narrowly oblong with an incurved pointed tip. A cluster of 7–13 bright yellow flowers is carried on a 25–70mm (2–2$\frac{4}{5}$in) stem, the petals 5–7mm ($\frac{1}{5}$–$\frac{2}{7}$in) long. Mountains of Bulgaria and N Greece. March–April. A free-flowering species in cultivation. Nurseries offer var. *radoslavoffii* which is said to be more vigorous with larger flowers and leaves. The name is commonly mis-spelt and often appears in catalogues as *radislavii*, *radowslawoffii* or even *prawislavii*!

Saxifraga aretioides ◑

A native to limestone rocks in the Pyrenees. Similar to *S. ferdinandi-coburgi*, it differs in having slightly wider, greener leaves with almost blunt tips, and fewer (3–5) flowers with slightly larger petals. April–May. Rather rare in cultivation, but seems to thrive best in a position away from direct sunlight.

Saxifraga luteoviridis ◑

The flattish rosettes of this species are 15–35mm ($\frac{3}{5}$–1$\frac{2}{5}$in) across and form mats or low cushions. The bluish green leaves are 13–20mm ($\frac{1}{2}$–$\frac{4}{5}$in) long, often purple beneath and have obvious lime pores. Up to 15 greenish yellow flowers are borne on a stem; they have a densely glandular-hairy calyx. Romania and Bulgaria, extending eastwards into Turkey, where it inhabits limestone mountains. April. A slow-growing plant which needs some shade in summer, and protection from frost in winter.

Saxifraga sempervivum (syn. *S. porophyllum* var. *thessalica*, *S. porophyllum* var. *sibthorpiana*, *S. sempervivum* forma *alpina*) ◯

Plants form dense cushions; the pointed leaves are narrow-oblong, 8–18mm ($\frac{1}{3}$–$\frac{3}{4}$in) long and lime-encrusted. The flower-stems are 3–18cm (1$\frac{1}{5}$–7in) tall, glandular-hairy, and carry 10–18 almost stalkless flowers in a spike which is enveloped in a crimson-purple felt of hairs. The flowers range from deep red to purple, the petals 4–5mm ($\frac{1}{6}$–$\frac{1}{5}$in) long, more or less equal in length to the sepals. Balkans and NW Turkey. March–May. 'Waterperry'—purplish flowers, fits within the natural variation. In the wild *S. sempervivum* inhabits limestone rocks and screes. This striking species is particularly attractive as the inflorescences unfurl, perhaps less so when they are in full bloom.

Saxifraga grisebachii ◯

A very beautiful plant which forms loose clumps of rosettes. The rosettes are relatively large, 20–75mm ($\frac{4}{5}$–3in) across; the leaves spoon-shaped, heavily lime-encrusted and silvery-grey. The flower-stems rise to 10–18cm (5–7in) tall, with reddish, green-tipped, recurved stem-leaves, covered with silky glandular hairs.

The reddish purple flowers are borne in a somewhat nodding cluster, the petals only 1–2mm ($\frac{1}{25}$–$\frac{2}{25}$in) long. Balkan Mountains. March–April. A fine pan plant for the alpine house or frame, also succeeding on a good scree or raised bed—does best in a limy soil. 'Wisley' is especially vigorous with beautiful colouring.

Saxifraga porophylla ○
Related to *S. grisebachii* but differing in having shorter leaves (6–15mm long) and fewer flowers on a stem only 50–75mm (2–3in) tall. S and C Italy. March–May.

Saxifraga stribrnyi ○
Differs from *S. grisebachii* in having a branched inflorescence, and flowers with petals to 4mm ($\frac{1}{6}$in) long. More restricted in distribution, being found only in Bulgaria and N Greece. March–May. Plants do particularly well in an alpine house.

Saxifraga media ○
Plants form silvery-grey cushions up to 15cm (6in) across; the leaves are spoon-shaped, 7–20mm ($\frac{2}{5}$–$\frac{4}{5}$in) long, with a sharply pointed tip. The flower-stem is densely glandular-hairy, bearing a raceme of pink or purplish flowers, which often appears to be one-sided. Pyrenees. April–May. In the wild a plant of limestone rocks or shale to 2,150m (7,090ft). *S. media* crosses in the wild with *S. aretioides* to produce a range of variable hybrids which have been given the name *S. × luteopurpurea*. Of these, *S. × luteopurpurea* var. *aurantiaca* is the one most often seen in cultivation; the flowers are yellowish orange.

Saxifraga lilacina ◑
A species which forms mats of small rosettes. The greyish green leaves are up to 5mm ($\frac{1}{4}$in) long and the solitary flowers are deep violet with darker veins, and have rather recurved petals, 8–11mm ($\frac{1}{3}$–$\frac{1}{2}$in) long. W Himalaya. March–April. In the wild a plant of damp rocks. In cultivation *S. lilacina* is a lime-hater and grows best in a semi-shady position which is not too dry; it requires plenty of water when actively growing, but it must also have good drainage.

Saxifraga hypostoma ○◑▲
The tight cushions of this species can reach a diameter of 8–10cm (3–4in) in favourable conditions. The leaves are 4–6mm ($\frac{1}{6}$–$\frac{1}{4}$in) long with rounded tips and with small marginal hairs in the upper half. The solitary white flowers appear to be stalkless, but in fact have short stalks about 3mm ($\frac{1}{8}$in) long. The sepals are glandular-hairy and the white petals somewhat wavy, 4–5mm ($\frac{1}{6}$–$\frac{1}{5}$in) long. C Nepal where it grows at altitudes above 4,500m (14,800ft) on rocks and open stony slopes. March–April. In cultivation it flowers well and is happiest with the protection of an alpine house. Still rather rare in cultivation, but a beautiful sight in full flower.

Saxifraga stolitzkae ◑
An especially pretty Himalayan saxifrage, found in Nepal, Bhutan and N India. Plants may eventually produce cushions up to 15cm (6in) across. The leaves are rather fleshy, heavily lime-encrusted and 6–9mm ($\frac{1}{4}$–$\frac{3}{8}$in) long. The flower-stems are 15–50mm ($\frac{3}{5}$–2in) long, covered with pink, glandular hairs and bearing 4–7 white, rarely pink, flowers which are faintly scented. March–April. This species likes a well-drained gritty soil, but one which does not dry out, especially during the summer. A useful scree or trough plant out-of-doors, but also looks fine in a pan in the alpine house.

Saxifraga andersonii ○▲
Like *S. stolitzkae*, but differs in that the leaves bear only traces of lime and the flowers are smaller with the petals 3–6mm (⅛–¼in) long, pink, or white, ageing to pink. Nepal, China (Tibet) and Bhutan. May–June. Rather shy flowering in cultivation; it needs plenty of water and can stand more sun than *S. stolitzkae*

Saxifraga wendelboi ○
Plants form a hard, compact cushion, the individual leaf-rosettes 5–10mm (⅕–⅖in) across. The glandular-hairy flower-stems are 30–60mm (1–2½in) tall and carry 3 or 4 white flowers each with a purplish calyx; petals 7–10mm (⅓–⅜in) long. Iran. March–April. A fairly recent introduction which is still rare in cultivation, but, like the previous few species, well worth obtaining and adding to a collection. As it flowers so early, plants are best given some protection from frost as the flower-buds may easily be damaged.

The species of section *Porophyllum* have been extensively hybridized. The following hybrids and their cultivars are available commercially. They are listed alphabetically. Many are listed in catalogues under more than one name so they need selecting with care—synonyms are put in wherever they are known.

S. × anglica (S. lilacina × S. × luteopurpurea) ◑☆
This fine hybrid has flat or domed cushions; the leaves normally green and linear. The flower-stems are usually 1–3-flowered with pink to purplish flowers. March–May. Almost 30 cultivars are available and of these the most commonly seen are: 'Arthur'—deep purplish flowers; 'Beatrix Stanley' (syn. 'Lady Beatrix Stanley')—a beautiful free-flowering plant with rich red flowers on stems 30–50mm (1⅕–2in) tall; 'Christine' ('Cerise Gem'; 'Cerise Queen')—silvery leaves and stems with 1–3 flowers which are red to salmon-pink; 'Clare'—solitary lilac-pink flowers; 'Cranbourne'—a reliable and popular plant with large pinkish red to lilac flowers which fade with age; 'Grace Farwell'—flowers of wine or carmine red, 2 or more on each stem; 'Myra'—silvery-grey cushions and flowers of a deeper colour than 'Cranbourne', but a less vigorous plant; 'Winifred'—small grey-green cushions and deep pink flowers with darker centres, borne on 30mm (1⅕in) stems.

S. × apiculata (S. lilacina × S. marginata) ○◑☆
A hybrid which is very easy to grow and quickly forms green mats or cushions up to 40cm (16in) across, which look especially good growing on a wall or scree. The flowers are usually yellow. March–April. 'Alba'—white flowers, but in other respects is similar to 'Gregor Mendel', which produces clusters of up to 15 pale yellow flowers; 'Primrose Bee'—slightly larger yellow flowers.

S. × arco-valleyi (S. lilacina × S. marginata) ○◑
This hybrid has dense cushions and is slow-growing. The solitary flowers are normally pale lilac-pink. March. 'Arco'—pale lilac-pink flowers on 30mm (1⅕in) stems; 'Dainty Dame'—pale salmon-pink flowers on slightly longer stems; 'Hocker Edge'—can have 2 or 3 pinkish lilac flowers per stem; 'Ophelia' ('Alba')—white flowers.

S. × biasolettii (S. grisebachii × S. sempervivum) ○
Usually found in cultivation as the cultivar 'Crystalie', a vigorous plant which grows quickly and is intermediate in appearance between its parents. Plants produce lots of side-rosettes and the crimson flowers are borne on stems 15–18cm (6–7in) tall.

S. × bilekii (S. ferdinandi-coburgi × S. tombeanensis) ◑
Cultivated as 'Castor' which has grey-green cushions up to 12cm (4⅘in) across, and produces 3–6 pale yellow flowers on stems 5–8cm (2–3in) long. April.

S. × boeckeleri (S. ferdinandi-coburgi × S. stribrnyi) ○
Intermediate between its parents and available commercially as 'Armida'. Tight greyish cushions produce dull orange-yellow flowers which droop at first, on stems 6–7.5cm (2⅖–3in) tall. March–April.

S. × borisii (S. ferdinandi-coburgi × S. marginata) ○
Over 20 cultivars of this hybrid have been named, but only 2 are commonly available: 'Sofia'—bluish green leaves and 6–7.5cm (2⅖–3in) long, glandular-hairy, stems which carry 7–12 yellow flowers; 'Vincent van Gogh'—flowers of a deeper yellow. Both March–April.

S. × boydii (S. aretioides × S. burseriana) ○◑☆
A hybrid with tight, spiny cushions and large, usually yellow flowers similar in size and shape to those of *S. burseriana*. Almost 20 cultivars are available—the following are the most often grown; 'Aretiastrum' (syn. 'Valerie Finnis')—a beautiful plant that produces lots of pale yellow solitary flowers, and is very strong and reliable—it is often sold under the name *S. burseriana lutea*; 'Cherrytrees'—1–3 lemon-yellow flowers on 20–30mm (⅘–1⅕in) stems; 'Faldonside'—1 or 2 flowers of a variable yellow, on stems 20–30mm (⅘–1⅕in) tall; 'Hindhead Seedling'—40–70cm (16–28in) stems carrying 2 or 3 pale yellow flowers; 'Luteola' (syn. *S. burseriana* 'Major Lutea') and 'Sulphurea' (syn. *S, burseriana sulphurea* and *S.* 'Moonlight')—both have solitary pale yellow flowers.

S. × bursiculata (S. burseriana × [S. marginata × S. sancta]) ○
Usually grown in gardens under the name 'King Lear'. Plants have tight grey-green cushions and 40–90mm (1⅗–3⅗in) flower-stems bearing 3–5 rounded white flowers. February–March.

S. × edithae (S. marginata × S. stribrnyi) ○◑
This hybrid has rather small flowers and silvery or greyish, tight cushions. 'Bridget'—7–20 flowers of pale mauve-pink on stems 8–12cm (3–5in) tall. 'Edith'—flower-stems 5–10cm (2–4in) tall, each with 4–15 pale pink flowers. Both March–April.

S. × elizabethae (S. burseriana × S. sancta) ○☆
A hybrid which has about 20 named cultivars, most with yellow flowers. They are vigorous, fast-growing plants which will tolerate full sun. 'Boston Spa'—grey-green cushions and 3–6 light yellow flowers on 30–45mm (1⅕–1⅘in) stems; 'L. G. Godseff' (syn. *S. × godseffii*)—2–4 flowers of a brighter yellow on 20–40mm (¾–1½in) stems; 'Ochroleuca'—an easily grown cultivar with 20–30mm (¾–1¼in) flower-stems which carry 2–4 pale yellow flowers. March–April.

S. × eudoxiana (S. ferdinandi-coburgi × S. sancta) ○◑
A fast-growing hybrid which quickly forms mats. The flowers are yellow and borne in compact heads. 'Eudoxia'—flower-stems 50–70mm (2–2⅘in) tall, each with 3–10 pale yellow flowers; 'Gold Dust'—50–90mm (2–3⅗in) flower-stems with up to 15 bright yellow flowers; 'Haagii'—a less compact plant than the other cultivars with rather narrow-petalled golden-yellow flowers.

S.* × *geuderi ([S. aretioides* × *S. burseriana]* × *S. ferdinandi-coburgi) ○
In cultivation as 'Eulenspiegel'. Plants have solitary bright yellow flowers on 30mm ($1\frac{1}{4}$in) stems. March.

S.* × *gloriana (S. lilacina* × *S. obtusa) ◑
The cultivar most often grown is sold under the name 'Amitie', but this is an incorrect name for the cultivar 'Godiva'. To make matters more confusing, 'Godiva' also masquerades under the names 'Felicity' and 'Gloriana'. Whatever its name this is a delightful plant with large lilac-pink flowers borne singly on 20–40mm ($\frac{4}{5}$–$1\frac{3}{5}$in) stems; the flowers become paler as they age. March–April.

S.* × *gusmusii (S. luteoviridis* × *S. sempervivum) ○
The leaf-rosettes, 10–30mm ($\frac{3}{8}$–$1\frac{1}{4}$in) across, produce glandular-hairy flower-stems 6–12cm ($2\frac{3}{8}$–$4\frac{3}{4}$in) tall bearing 3–10 orange-red, rather bell-shaped flowers. March.

S.* × *hardingii ([S. aretioides* × *S. burseriana]* × *S. media) ◑
Usually grown as the cultivar 'Iris Pritchard', which can flower as early as January in a sheltered place. The silvery cushions are covered with 50–60mm (2–$2\frac{2}{5}$in) long flower-stems, usually bearing 3 flowers which can vary from apricot to pale pink.

S.* × *heinrichii (S. aretioides* × *S. stribrnyi) ○◑
Cultivated as the cultivar 'Ernst Heinrich'. Plants form slow-growing cushions and produce flower-stems 40–70mm ($1\frac{3}{5}$–$2\frac{3}{4}$in) tall, covered with purple glandular hairs, and bearing 10–12 flowers which have contrasting purplish red sepals and pale yellow petals.

S.* × *hofmannii (S. burseriana* × *S. sempervivum) ◑
A hybrid forming rather loose cushions bearing small flowers in short racemes. 'Bodensee'—flower-stems 7–16cm ($2\frac{4}{5}$–$6\frac{2}{5}$in) tall with up to 25 dingy pink or yellowish flowers. April–May.

S.* × *hornibrookii (S. lilacina* × *S. stribrnyi) ○◑☆
Some of the 9 cultivars of this hybrid have been named; 2 are fairly readily available: 'Delia'—heavily lime-encrusted rosettes and stems 20–50mm ($\frac{4}{5}$–2in) tall, carrying 1–3 purple to violet-pink flowers which become paler as they age; 'Riverslea'—slightly taller stems with 2–5 purplish red flowers. Both are beautiful additions to the rock garden.

S.* × *irvingii (S. burseriana* × *S. lilacina) ○◑☆
A slow-growing hybrid forming tight cushions. The flowers are normally solitary and are similar to those of *S. burseriana*, but in various shades of pink. March–April. There are many named cultivars of which the following is only a selection: 'Gem'—flowers pale lilac-pink to whitish; 'His Majesty'—white flowers flushed with pink in the centre (sometimes 2 to a stem); 'Jenkinsiae'—pale pink flowers with darker veins—a fine and reliable cultivar; 'Rubella'—pale pink to whitish flowers on short stems; 'Timmy Foster'—deep lilac-pink flowers which are often larger than those of the other cultivars—the petals are usually twisted and waved; 'Walter Irving'—a very reliable flowerer with pale pink or lilac flowers which fade with age.

S.* × *kellereri (S. burseriana* × *S. stribrnyi) ○◑
A vigorous easily-grown hybrid, of which several cultivars can be obtained. 'Johann Kellerer'—early-flowering, with silvery rosettes and 1 or 2 lilac-pink or peachy flowers; 'Kewensis' (syn. *S. kewensis* 'Big Ben')—very glandular-hairy stems

4–7.7cm ($1\frac{3}{5}$–3in) tall, bearing 1–3 pale pink flowers which often fail to open completely; 'Suendermannii'—bright red flower-stems topped by 1–4 long-lasting pink flowers; 'Suendermannii Major'—differs from 'Suendermannii' in having smaller, but more numerous, almost white flowers, faintly flushed with pink.

***S.* × *landaueri* ([*S. burseriana* × *S. stribrnyi*] × *S. marginata*)** ◑
Similar to *S.* × *kelleri*, but generally smaller. 'Schleicheri'—somewhat hairy flower-stems 30–90mm ($1\frac{1}{5}$–$3\frac{3}{5}$in) tall, with 3–6 pink flowers.

***S.* × *mariae-theresiae* (*S. burseriana* × *S. grisebachii*)** ◑☆
A slow-growing hybrid with tight clusters of rosettes forming cushions up to 10cm (4in) across. The flower-stems are bright purplish red, 40–80mm ($1\frac{1}{5}$–$3\frac{1}{5}$in) tall and carry 6–10 small lilac-pink flowers. March. A striking plant which attracts attention.

S.* × *megaseaeflora ◑
A complex hybrid which involves 4 species (*S. aretioides, S. burseriana, S. lilacina* and *S. media*) in its parentage. March–April. Several cultivars have been named of which probably the most attractive is 'Robin Hood'—1-flowered stems 3–7.5cm ($1\frac{1}{5}$–3in) tall and flowers a deep rose-pink with clawed, wavy petals—it should be grown in a sheltered position or under glass; 'Mrs Gertie Prichard'—flowers in which the pale pink petals overlap.

***S.* × *paulinae* (*S. burseriana* × *S. ferdinandi-coburgi*)** ◑
The cushions are tight and domed, the flowers large and yellow. 'Franzii'—hooked tips to the leaves and deep yellow flowers, 3–7 to a stem; 'Kolbiana'—1–4 pale yellow flowers and leaves with pointed, but not hooked, tips—it flowers very early, from November to January; 'Paula'—leaves with slightly incurved tips and stems with usually 1–3 pale yellow flowers, larger than those of 'Kolbiana'—a prolific flowerer.

***S.* × *petraschii* (*S. burseriana* × *S. tombeanensis*)** ○◑
Thirteen cultivars exist of this hybrid which has tight cushions, white flowers and leaves usually with hooked tips; the flowers are 15–25mm ($\frac{3}{5}$–1in) across. The following cultivars are most often seen; 'Affinis'—a dwarf plant with 40–60mm ($1\frac{1}{2}$–$2\frac{3}{8}$in) flower-stems bearing 1 or 2 flowers; 'Kaspar Maria Sternberg'—greyish cushions and 30–70mm ($1\frac{1}{5}$–$2\frac{4}{5}$in) stems carrying 1–3 beautiful white flowers which open from reddish buds and have wavy petals.

***S.* × *prossenii* (*S. sancta* × *S. stribrnyi*)** ○
'Regina' is the cultivar usually grown of this hybrid. Plants have deep green cushions, up to 15cm (6in) across, from which arise stems 3–7.5cm ($1\frac{1}{5}$–3in) tall with 6–30 flowers with deep red sepals and orange-yellow to brownish yellow petals. March–May. An unusual colour combination liked by some growers.

***S.* × *pseudo-kotschyi* (*S. kotschyi* × *S. marginata*)** ◑
This hybrid is found in cultivation under the name 'Denisa'; it differs from *S. kotschyi* in having pale green rosettes and flower-stems 30–40mm ($1\frac{1}{5}$–$1\frac{3}{5}$in) tall with fewer (3–7) starry yellow flowers.

***S.* × *salmonica* (*S. burseriana* × *S. marginata*)** ○◑
A pretty, white-flowered hybrid with many easily-grown cultivars. The following are recommended: 'Kestoniensis' (syn. *S. burseriana* forma *kestoniensis*—rosettes 5–15mm ($\frac{1}{5}$–$\frac{3}{5}$in) across and flower-stems 20–70mm ($\frac{4}{5}$–$2\frac{4}{5}$in) tall with 1–3 crinkly

petalled flowers; 'Maria Luisa ('Marie Louise')—larger rosettes 9–20mm ($\frac{3}{8}$–$\frac{3}{4}$in) across, and 2–5 flowers; 'Obristii' (syn. *S.* × obristii)—flower-stems 4–12mm tall carrying 3–7 large flowers; '*Salomonii*')—small leaf-rosettes and flower-stems 20–50mm ($\frac{4}{5}$–2in) tall usually bearing 2 or 3 small flowers.

S. × *semmleri ([S. ferdinandi-coburgi* × *S. sancta]* × *S. pseudolaevis)* ○
Grown as 'Martha', an undemanding plant with rather soft cushions. The flower-stems reach only 20–30mm ($\frac{4}{5}$–1$\frac{1}{5}$in) and carry 4–8 small deep yellow flowers.

S. × *stuartii (S. aretioides* × *S. media* × *S. stribrnyi)* ○◑
A vigorous hybrid forming loose cushions which produce many lateral rosettes. April–May. 'Lutea'—flowers with reddish sepals and yellow petals, on stems 6–7.5cm (2$\frac{2}{5}$–3in) tall; 'Rosea'—purplish-brown flowers.

Porophyllum cultivars of unknown parentage
These cultivars are included below because they are worth growing and available in the trade. All flower March–April unless otherwise stated.

'Appleblossom'—densely glandular-hairy stems 30–60mm (1$\frac{1}{5}$–2$\frac{2}{5}$in) tall; 'Camyra'—1–4 pale yellow flowers on stems 20–45mm ($\frac{3}{4}$–1$\frac{3}{4}$in) tall; 'C. M. Prichard'—stems with 2 or 3 large creamy-white flowers with reddish brown veins; 'Coningsby Queen'—deep red flowers on rather domed cushions; 'Goeblii'—5–18 pink flowers which are deeper-coloured in the centre, borne on 40–70mm (1$\frac{3}{5}$–2$\frac{4}{5}$in), glandular-hairy stems; 'Rosemarie'—tight cushions with 10–30mm ($\frac{2}{5}$–1$\frac{1}{5}$in) tall stems carrying 1–4 large rose-pink flowers. February–April.

Section Porphyrion
The species of this section form low evergreen mats of creeping shoots which usually root down where they touch the soil. The small, opposite leaves are dark green and leathery and the almost stemless flowers range from pink to purple, or occasionally white.

Saxifraga oppositifolia ◑☆
The Purple Saxifrage is one of the most familiar Saxifrages on the mountains of Europe, including the British Isles, but it also encircles the North Pole and is found on mountains further south in North America and N and C Asia eastwards to W Xizang (Tibet) and Kashmir. It has no particular preference for limestone or acid rock and is usually found on rocks, scree, river gravels or alpine grassland. Plants form flat mats and the creeping stems bear stiff leaves in 4 rows. The flower-stems are almost absent to 25mm (1in) tall, and carry only one flower which varies in colour from deep red to purplish pink, turning more violet with age. May–June. In gardens, this species grows best on an east- or west-facing slope; it should not be exposed to mid-day sun. Plants can also be grown in a north-facing position, but will not thrive in deep shade. The soil should not be allowed to dry out, nor should it be water-logged. A very variable species in the wild and a number of subspecies can be recognized. Added to these are the variations and cultivars which have been selected in cultivation. Subsp. *latina*—very short stems with deep rose-purple flowers, a reliable flowerer; var. *alba*—white flowers, and although less vigorous, flowers well when it is growing well; 'Ruth Draper'—large satiny, bright rose flowers on 20mm ($\frac{4}{5}$in) stems; 'Splendens'—stemless purplish pink flowers; 'W. A. Clark'—crimson-red flowers.

Saxifraga oppositifolia

Saxifraga retusa ◗

Similar to *S. oppositifolia*, but the flower-stems carry up to 5, usually smaller flowers, 8–9mm (⅓–⅜in) across which have sepals without a fringe of hairs. Pyrenees and Alps eastwards to Bulgaria. April–May. Plants should be grown in a well-drained soil, though not one which dries out; perhaps seen at its best as a pan plant in the alpine house, although disliking too much bright sunshine.

Section Diptera

Species of this section have rounded, stalked leaves which appear rather leathery. The flowers usually have petals unequal in size giving them an elegant air; they are pure white or may have coloured spots.

Saxifraga fortunei ◗☆

A useful and pretty plant for a shady corner of the garden; the flower-stems reach 40cm (16in) so it is suitable only for a larger rock garden. The glossy, brownish green leaves are 7-lobed and red beneath, with long stalks. The flowers are white, with 5 narrow petals; the lower 1 or 2 are often toothed and are 3–4 times longer than the upper ones. Japan. September–October. Sometimes regarded by botanists as a variety of *S. cortusifolia*. 'Rubrifolia'—red flower-stems and attractive red-brown leaves; 'Wada's Form'—purplish leaves, very handsome.

Saxifraga stolonifera (syn. *S. sarmentosa*) ◗●

A well-known house plant which is often called 'Mother of Thousands' because it sends out numerous slender reddish runners which develop plantlets at their tips; these can be detached and grown into new plants. The species is not really frost-hardy, but its cultivar 'Cuscutiformis' is compeletely hardy and can be grown in the rock garden. The rounded leaves have 7–10 lobes and are brownish green, veined with pale grey, hairy above, hairless and reddish beneath. The flower-stems are 20–40cm (8–16in) tall and carry elegant white flowers. China and Japan. July–August. Often offered by nurseries under the erroneous name *S. cuscutiformis* (see below). It does best in a shady place in soil with plenty of humus.

Saxifraga cuscutiformis ◗

Related to *S. stolonifera* but smaller. The leaves are bronzy and have a network of white veins. The flower-stems grow to only 10cm (4in) tall and carry pure white flowers. Plants will not stand frost and should be grown outside only in mild areas.

Saxifraga veitchiana ◑
Similar to *S. stolonifera* but a smaller plant. The leaves do not have whitish veining, but are plain dark green and hairy beneath. The flowers have white petals with pink dots towards the tips and a yellow flush below—they are carried on 10cm (4in) stems. W China. August–September. It is not particularly free-flowering and is usually grown for its rosettes which produce red runners.

SCABIOSA (Dipsacaceae)

A genus of some 100 species native primarily to Europe and Asia, but also represented in the mountains of E and S Africa. Several are familiar garden plants, and include both annual and perennial scabiouses. Most are too vigorous for the rock garden, but there are several small ones that are well suited, being both easy to grow and floriferous. Propagation by division or from seed. They prefer sunny sites and well-drained limy soils.

Scabiosa graminifolia ○☆
The finest species for the rock garden forming tufts to 20cm (8in) tall. The numerous slender leaves are silvery grey and contrast perfectly with the pinkish-lavender flower-heads. S Europe. July–September. Although reasonably hardy, plants can be killed back to ground level during severe winter weather.

Scabiosa columbaria ○☆
A familiar European (including Britain) plant typical of chalk downs. The usual form reaches 50–60cm (20–24in) tall, bearing its bluish-purple flower-heads throughout the summer. There are dwarfer mountain forms, some only 12–15cm (5–6in) tall, that are much better suited to the rock garden—they are often called *S. alpina*, 'Nana' or *S. columbaria* 'Nana'. July–October.

Other small species that would make useful subjects for the rock garden are *S. lucida* and *S. vestina*, both native to the European Alps.

SCHIVERECKIA (Cruciferae)

A genus of only 5 species closely related to *Draba* and *Alyssum*. Propagation best by seed, although short cuttings can be taken in midsummer.

Schivereckia podolica (syn. *Alyssum podolicum*) ○
A prostrate, grey or silvery rosetted alyssum-like plant. The leaves are oblong and toothed, the flowers small and white, borne in short racemes, to 14cm (5½in) tall. W Ukraine to NE Rumania. April–May.

Schivereckia doerfleri (syn. *Draba doerfleri*) ○
A more laxly tufted species; like the previous but the stem leaves not clasping the stem and often untoothed. SW Yugoslavia, April–May. Rather rare in cultivation.

SCLERANTHUS (Illecebraceae)

A small, horticulturally unimportant, genus of some 10 species distributed in Europe, Asia, Africa, Australia and New Zealand. They can be annual or perennial, generally with a loose sprawling habit, but two of the southern hemisphere species are nicely compact making useful cushion plants. They have tiny flowers which lack petals, consisting of 5 sepals and 10 stamens.

Scleranthus biflorus ○
A dense, domed, cushion plant with needle-like pale green leaves and minute green flowers, usually in pairs, carried on 10mm (⅜in) stalks, protruding above the cushion. Australia, New Zealand. July–September.

Scleranthus uniflorus ○
Similar to *S. biflorus*, but an even more densely leafy plant; the tiny green flowers are solitary, not held well above the cushions, but carried on very short stalks at the tip of each shoot. New Zealand. Summer.

SCUTELLARIA (Labiatae)
The skullcaps are so-called because of the rounded erect flange on the upper lip of the calyx which resembles a skullcap. The genus contains several fine species with colourful, tubular, 2-lipped flowers. Those normally seen in gardens are easy and adaptable plants for an open well-drained position.

Scutellaria alpina ○☆
The Alpine Skullcap is widespread in the Pyrenees, the W and S Alps and the Apennines, where it inhabits limestone rocks and screes, as well as grassy places, up to an altitude of some 2,500m (8,250ft). Plants form spreading tufts to 20cm (8in) with oval, toothed leaves. The hooded, rather erect flowers are deep purple with a whitish lower lip; they are borne in small clusters, each flower 20–25mm (⅘–1in) long. July–August. Good deep-coloured forms are worth seeking out, as some of those in cultivation are poorly coloured.

Scutellaria orientalis ○☆
An equally attractive species widespread in rocky mountain habitats in SE Europe and W Asia. Plants form small subshrubs to 30cm (12in), becoming rather woody at the base. The oval deep green or grey-green leaves are deeply toothed or even lobed. The flowers are generally bright yellow, the lower lip often marked with reddish-brown; each flower is 20–30mm (⅘–1⅕in) long. July–August.

Scutellaria scordifolia ○
A fine species which hails from Korea, where it forms bushy tufts up to 15cm (6in) high bearing brilliant deep blue flowers from July–September. Not widely available, but well worth seeking out.

Scutellaria indica var. *japonica* ○☆
A widely cultivated species which comes, as the varietal name suggests, from Japan. Plants form bushy tufts to 15cm (6in) tall, with small, greyish-green, oval slightly toothed leaves. The skullcap flowers are a rich purplish blue and borne in profusion from July until September. Perhaps the best skullcap for the rock garden.

SEDUM (Crassulaceae)
The stonecrops are one of the most popular groups of alpine plants. They are a diverse group of succulent plants, ranging from tiny annuals to vigorous perennials. There are about 600 species widely distributed in the world, but particularly in the mountains of the northern hemisphere. They are characterized by flattened or rather cylindrical, fleshy leaves and branched clusters of star-shaped flowers, with 5–8 narrow petals. Many species are cultivated, but only relatively few are distinguished enough for the rock garden. Most are easy and prolific growers requiring little attention, though thriving best on a well-drained, gritty or rocky

Scutellaria alpina

ground, though a few require cooler shadier conditions. Propagation is easy from cuttings, although many seed around or self-propagate from detached pieces.

The species included here can be divided conveniently into the 3 main groups or series: *Genuina* which includes all the familiar stonecrops, *Telephium* and *Aizoon*. The numerous tender Mexican species are not included.

Genuina Series

The majority of species belong here. They are mostly perennials with fibrous roots and fleshy untoothed leaves, which are often rounded or oval in cross-section.

Sedum acre ○☆

The Wallpepper is a familiar stonecrop of walls and rooftops in W Europe. Plants form spreading tufts to 50mm (2in) tall, the slender stems clothed with alternate egg-shaped, bright green leaves. The flowers are bright yellow, 8–10mm ($\frac{1}{3}$in), borne in small clusters; very floriferous. Europe, W Asia and NW Africa. June–July. A plant of rocky and sandy habitats in the wild. 'Aureum'—an attractive form with mats of golden leaves.

Sedum sexangulare ○

Similar to the preceding, but even dwarfer with narrower leaves set in 5–6 close rows. N and C Europe. June–July.

Sedum altissimum (syn. *S. nicaense*) ○

A tufted species with linear-lanceolate leaves with a slender pointed tip, grey-green. The flowers are borne on long stems 30–40cm (12–16in) tall, and are whitish-green. S Europe and the Mediterranean region. June–July.

223

Sedum reflexum ○

The Rock Stonecrop is another familiar species. More vigorous than the previous, it forms spreading mats with flowering stems up to 20cm (8in) tall. The stems are clothed with many slender, cylindrical, pointed leaves. The flower clusters characteristically droop in bud, but open erect, yellow and each 12–14mm ($\frac{1}{2}$in) across. Mountains of Europe. June–July. Rather too invasive for the small rock garden. Various forms are sold by nurserymen including 'Cristatum'.

Sedum ochroleucum (syn. *S. anopetalum*) ○☆

Essentially like *S. reflexum*, but a finer plant with attractive mats of grey-green leaves and cream to pale yellow flowers, the clusters erect in bud. Mountains of C and S Europe. June–July.

Sedum rupestre ○

A low, tangled mat-forming species to 40mm (1$\frac{1}{2}$in) tall. The crowded linear leaves are pointed, oval in section and a rather dull grey-green, but becoming reddish in the autumn. The flowers are golden-yellow, borne in small compact inflorescences. W Europe. June–July.

Sedum album ○

The White Stonecrop forms spreading tufts up to 12cm (5in) tall. The shiny, bright green, shortly cylindrical, leaves are often tinged with red; they are alternate. The starry white flowers, 4–8mm ($\frac{3}{16}$–$\frac{5}{16}$in) across are borne in lax flat clusters on reddish stalks. Europe to Asia and N Africa. June–August. Another very easy and prolific grower, generally too invasive for the average rock garden. 'Chloroticum'—has deep green leaves; 'Micranthum'—stems forming flat carpets bearing very small leaves; 'Murale'—leaves mahogany-red and flowers pink; 'Murale Coral Carpet'—leaves and flowers pink.

Sedum anglicum ○

Lower growing than the previous, forming rather flat tufts, greyish or reddish. The leaves are egg-shaped, generally tinged with red and the flowers white or pale pink 6–9mm ($\frac{1}{4}$–$\frac{3}{8}$in) W and SW Europe. June–September.

Sedum dasyphyllum ○◗

Similar in size to *S. anglicum*, but leaves mostly opposite, not alternate, and sticky with down. The flowers are pure white or very pale pink, 5–6mm ($\frac{1}{4}$in). Mountains of C and S Europe. June–August. A plant of acid rocks, walls and banks in the wild, to an altitude of 2,500m (8,250ft). 'Glanduliferum'—an especially hairy form.

Sedum brevifolium ○

Like a smaller *S. dasyphyllum*, scarcely 30mm (1$\frac{1}{8}$in) tall in flower. The whole plant is mealy, suffused with pink. The leaves are borne in 4 rows along the stem. SW Europe and NW Africa. The usual form sold is 'Quinquefolium'. Many plants sold under the name *S. brevifolium* turn out to be *S. dasyphyllum*, so buy plants with care.

Sedum hispanicum ○

A low plant forming spreading greyish-blue hummocks, rarely more than 40mm (1$\frac{3}{8}$in) tall. The stems are very leafy, the leaves narrow and pointed, pressed close to the stem. The flowers are small and white, quite pleasing. S Europe and W Asia. June–July. The plants become leafless in the autumn and die back to a few parched twigs. A charming curiosity. 'Minus'—even dwarfer.

Sedum dasyphyllum

Sedum lydium ○
Another dwarf, densely tufted carpeter to 70mm (2⅘in) tall. The narrow cylindrical leaves are heavily flushed with red. The small flowers are white. W Turkey. June–July.

Sedum tatarinowii ○
A curious plant with a perennial stock from which arise erect annual stems to 15cm (6in) tall. The semi-cylindrical leaves are alternate and up to 25mm (1in) long. The pinkish-white flowers are borne in dense terminal heads. N China. July–August. Useful for a scree.

Sedum humifusum ◐
A rather rare species in cultivation. It is an attractive plant which comes from Morocco, forming tangled mats of creeping shoots to 50mm (2in) tall covered with tiny green leaves, which become flushed with pink or red as they age. The flowers are (unusually) solitary and bright yellow. April–June. Unfortunately, this species is not reliably hardy, succumbing to frost and winter wet. However, when available, it makes an excellent subject for a pan or trough, given some form of winter protection and shady conditions.

Sedum spathulifolium ○☆
One of the most popular succulent plants for the rock garden. Plants form brittle tufts with numerous flattish rosettes of spoon-shaped leaves which are grey-green or whitish, sometimes tinged with pink. The flowering stems rise to about 80mm (3in) although often rather sprawling, and carry a flat head of yellow flowers up to 8cm (3in) across. W North America. July–August. 'Capa Blanca' has attractive white-powdered leaves which contrast with the clear yellow flowers. The foliage may be damaged by inclement winter weather. 'Purpureum'—a handsome form with purple-flushed leaves. A number of other forms are listed by nurseries, but are scarcely as good as the former.

Sedum oreganum (syn. *S. obtusatum*) ○
Another species which hails from W North America. Similar to the previous, but the leaves handsomely flushed with crimson. A rather dwarfer plant. July–August.

Sedum populifolium ○
A stout tufted perennial species to 40cm (16in) tall, though often less. The erect stems bear fleshy holly-shaped leaves. The white flowers have a pleasant hawthorn

225

scent and occur in much-branched lax clusters. Siberia. July–August. Only properly hardy in the mildest districts, otherwise it is best confined to the alpine house.

Sedum spurium ○☆

A widely cultivated species which forms spreading tangled mats. The oval, slightly toothed leaves are borne in opposite pairs. The flowers range in colour from white to pale or deep pink. July–August. Caucasus and N Iran. Best on acid soils in semi-shaded places. 'Album'—a good white-flowered form; 'Coccineum'—deep pink; 'Roseum'—rose-pink; 'Schorbuser Blut' one of the finest with deep red flowers. Various other cultivars are also offered.

Sedum stoloniferum ○

Similar to *S. spurium*, but a more erect and daintier species. The slender creeping and rooting stems are bright red and the leaves smaller and pale green. The flowers are pink. Turkey and the Caucasus. June–July.

Sedum divergens ○

A dense creeping perennial to 50mm (2in) tall. The slender prostrate stems are much-branched, with short shoots clothed in closely set pairs of egg-shaped, deep glossy-green leaves. The flowers are relatively large, bright yellow and borne in forking clusters which form a flattish head. W North America. June–July.

Sedum ternatum ○◖

Another species from W North America distinguished by having its oblong, blunt leaves in groups of 3. Plants are low-spreading, up to 12cm (5in) tall, the stems creeping and rooting down in places. The leaves are pale green and the flowers white, with only 4 petals. June. A plant for a sheltered moist site.

Sedum nevii ○◖

Related to *S. ternatum*, but lower growing (to 50mm; 2in), the leaves alternate below, but condensed into pseudorosettes near the stem tips and pale green, often purplish at the apex. The flowers are white with purple anthers and have 5 petals. E USA. June–July. Rather rare in cultivation, requiring, like *S. ternatum*, a moist sheltered site.

Sedum moranense ○

A dense dwarf plant, rarely more than 80mm (3in) tall. The slender stems are red and clothed with numerous triangular yellowish-green leaves, giving the plants a feathery look. The flowers are white, flushed with pink or red on the reverse, borne in a small inflorescence. Mexico. July. One of few Mexican species reliably hardy in temperate gardens.

Sedum palmeri ○

Another Mexican species. Plants form branched tufts to 24cm (9½in) tall, each branch terminating in a rosette of broad pale grey-green leaves, bluntly-pointed. The inflorescences are lateral with several drooping branches bearing numerous attractive double rows of orange-yellow flowers. May–June, also sometimes a second crop in August. Only hardy in the mildest districts, otherwise requiring winter protection.

Sedum pruinatum ○

An interesting and distinctive species with tufts of wiry red stems, bare except for the tips, which bear a cluster of slender pinkish-grey leaves. The stems root down late in the year. The flowers are straw-coloured, but are only produced occasionally. Portugal. June–July. Plants grow to 30cm (12in) high.

Sedum pulchellum ○☆
One of the most beautiful of the North American species. It forms close tufts branched low down, the stems erect and reddish, to 90mm (3½in) tall. The leaves are crowded, linear-lanceolate, half-clasping the stem, pale green. The flowers are an attractive rosy-purple, 4-petalled, borne in a 3–5-forked inflorescence, the branches recurved. C USA. July–August.

Sedum rubroglaucum (syn. *S. jipsonii*) ○
A Californian species forming low tufts to 80mm (3in) tall. The club-shaped leaves are often slightly notched at the apex, flattish and clasping the stem at their bases; they are borne in opposite pairs. The flowers are relatively large and bright yellow, on curving branches. September. A useful, non-invasive species for the rock garden, adding colour at the end of the summer.

Sedum sarmentosum ○◐
A prostrate perennial with rapidly extending stems which are slender and reddish and eventually rooting at the tips. The leaves are borne in threes and are broad-lanceolate, pointed and flat, pale green, clasping the stem at their base. The flowers are bright yellow, borne in flat-topped clusters. N China and Japan. June–July. A hardy plant, but often dying back to the rooting tips—some of these can be removed and over wintered under glass to ensure material for the following year.

Sedum lineare ◐
Similar to the previous species but with more numerous, denser trailing stems and the leaves linear-lanceolate with recurved tips. N China and Japan. Requires similar winter treatment to *S. sarmentosum*. 'Variegatum'—white-margined leaves.

Telephium Series

Members of this series have thick fleshy roots forming a crown from which annual shoots arise. The leaves are characteristically flat. This series contains the popular and widely grown *Sedum spectabile*, used in herbaceous borders, but too gross for the rock garden.

Sedum telephium ◐
The Orpine is a variable species, to 50cm (20in) tall, though often less. The stems are erect and carry flattened oval or rounded, toothed, fleshy, alternate leaves. The flowers range in colour from white to yellowish-green or purplish-red, borne in dense, rather flat terminal heads. Europe and Asia, including Britain, being a plant of woods, rocks and shady habitats to 1,800m (5,900ft) altitude. July–September. 'Autumn Joy'—the best form with heads of salmon and bronze flowers.

Sedum anacampseros ○◐
Rather like the previous species, but the stems more sprawling, often trailing and bearing elliptical, bluish-green, untoothed, alternate leaves. The flowers are deep red inside, but bluish-lilac on the reverse, borne in dense rounded clusters. Mountains of SW and C Europe. Late June–August. Grows on acid rocks in the wild, above 1,400m (4,600ft) altitude.

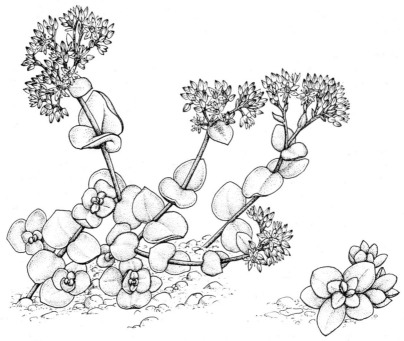

Sedum ewersii

Sedum ewersii ○◐☆

Another sprawling and spreading species with trailing stems with pairs of rounded, greyish-blue fleshy leaves. The flowers are pink or red, borne in slightly rounded heads up to 40mm (1½in) across. Himalaya to Mongolia. August–October. Can prove invasive; the cultivar 'Homophyllum' is a miniature version better suited to the smaller rock garden, with pink flowers.

Sedum sieboldii ○◐

This species is perhaps best known as a house plant or as a subject for a hanging basket. Plants are tufted with slender unbranched, spreading or trailing stems. The leaves occur in threes and are grey-green, rounded in outline and slightly toothed. The flowers are pink. Japan. September–October. Grown primarily for its foliage. The plants die down in the winter. Will survive most mild winters outdoors, though it cannot be relied upon to be completely hardy. 'Variegatum'—handsome leaves variegated with cream.

Sedum cyaneum (syn. *S. pluricaule*) ○◐

A beautiful species somewhat resembling *S. ewersii*. The tufts produce arching grey branches which creep and root down, becoming woody at the base. The leaves are alternate and opposite, oblong, but broadest above the middle, a charming lilac-grey colour. The rosy-purple flowers are borne in broad, rather flat clusters. The whole plant is only 50–80mm (2–3in) tall. Siberia. July–August.

Sedum cauticola ○◐

Not unlike the previous species, but the leaves in pairs and the flowers deep crimson. Japan. September–October. Hardy and particularly useful as a late flowering plant for a raised bed on a dry wall.

Sedum pilosum ○

A choice species, but rare in cultivation. Plants form soft, hairy, rounded rosettes which eventually flower; the flower clusters are rose-pink and often smother the rosette completely. The whole plant is scarcely 80mm (3in) tall. W Asia to Iran and the Caucasus. May–June. A fine pan subject for the alpine house. Plants die after flowering (monocarpic), but may take several years to do so; they are readily raised from seed.

Aizoon Series

Members of this series have a thickened woody rootstock. New stems arise at the base of the current year's stems in the autumn and bear alternate, flat leaves. The large inflorescence is leafy and branched, persisting brown and dry long after the flowers have faded.

Sedum kamtschaticum ○◐☆

A vigorous species forming twiggy tufts to 15cm (6in) tall. The leaves are fleshy, glossy, deep green, spatular-shaped, blunt-toothed in the upper half. The golden-yellow flowers are borne in lax flat terminal clusters. E Siberia to N China. July–September. Good in semi-shaded positions; an easy and tolerant species. 'Variegatum'—leaves margined with white; the usual form offered by nurseries which is less vigorous than the type.

Sedum middendorffianum ◐

Similar to the previous, but distinguished by its dull, rather than glossy green, narrow leaves, which are sharply toothed. The yellow flowers are smaller and borne in a denser head. Siberia and Korea. July–August.

Sedum ellacombianum ○◐

This species, which hails from Japan, is related to *S. kamtschaticum*, indeed it is sometimes treated as a variety of it. However, it has a distinctive look with its fleshier, arching stems and broad, pale, yellowish-green leaves. The flowers are yellowish-green, being borne in a broad leafy cluster. The plant is generally 14–16cm (5½–6½in) tall. July–August.

Sedum floriferum ◐

Another species of the *S. kamtschaticum* persuasion. The stems spread sideways and branch freely. The flowers are greenish-yellow, the sepals are linear rather than broad—a useful character if other methods of distinguishing this plant fail. NE China. August. 'Weihenstephener Gold'—the finest form.

Sedum selskianum ◐

A rare plant in cultivation, forming erect tufts as much as 30cm (12in) tall. The stems and leaves are hairy which makes it an easy plant to distinguish from the preceding species. The flowers are yellow. Korea. July–August.

Rhodiola Series

Generally treated as a distinct genus, *Rhodiola*, under which name the species will be found. The genus contains the well-known Roseroot, *Rhodiola rosea*.

SEMIAQUILEGIA (Ranunculaceae)

The species of *Semiaquilegia* were for a long time included amongst the columbines, *Aquilegia*; however, they can be easily distinguished by their spurless flowers. Only one species is generally cultivated.

Semiaquilegia ecalcarata ○◑☆

A delicate plant to 30cm (12in), with ferny, columbine-type foliage, often stained with red or purple. The small nodding flowers, dusky-purple or brownish-purple, are borne in profusion in airy sprays on slender stalks, each flower 12–18mm ($\frac{1}{2}$–$\frac{3}{4}$in) long. W China. June–July. An excellent scree plant, often seeding itself around once established. However, it crosses readily with other allies, especially *Aquilegia vulgaris*, *A. alpina* etc.

SEMPERVIVELLA (Crassulaceae)

A small genus with 4 species native to the W Himalaya. The species look rather like *Sempervivum* in their leaf-rosettes but the inflorescences are borne laterally rather than terminally. Readily propagated from offsets or seed. Plants require a well-drained gritty compost. Only one species is in general cultivation.

Sempervivella alba ○◑

Plants form low mats to 50mm (2in) tall. The small green, succulent, velvety rosettes are often flushed with red or purplish-red. The cream-coloured flowers are borne in rather lax arching racemes, smothering the plant; they are relatively large and star-shaped, generally 6–7-petalled. Himalaya. August–early October.

SEMPERVIVUM (Crassulaceae)

This familiar genus contains the houseleeks. The most commonly cultivated is *S. tectorum*, often seen naturalized on old walls or tiled rooftops. There are about 25 species scattered in the mountains of S Europe and W Asia. Most are easily cultivated, thriving best on poor dry, exposed places—screes, raised beds, pans and troughs are ideal. Indeed they make fine pan plants and a collection of different types filling a stone trough can look most effective. The species have fleshy leaf-rosettes, generally producing offsets on short lateral runners which afford a ready means of propagation. The flowers are borne in a rather flat, branched, head on a stout leafy stem; each flower generally has 10 or more narrow pointed petals which open widely into a star-shape. Leaf-rosettes die having flowered. Most are perfectly hardy, though some dislike too much winter wet. Although there are relatively few species, there are innumerable named cultivars; only a selection is presented here; not all are free-flowering.

Sempervivum tectorum ○☆

The Common Houseleek has large open, flattish leaf-rosettes, to 90mm (3½in) across; the succulent leaves are a bluish-green tipped with purple and bristle-edged. The flowers are deep pink, 18–20mm (¾in) borne on stout stems to 30cm (12in) tall. Mountains of C and S Europe. July–September. A widespread and variable species. 'Calcareum' (syn. var. *calcareum*)—has particularly well-coloured leaf-rosettes, the leaves tipped with brownish-purple; 'Triste'—leaves tipped with reddish-brown, the stem leaves reddish-brown all over. Other cultivars include 'Alpinum', 'Royanum', 'Sunset' and 'Violaceum'.

Sempervivum × *calcaratum* ○☆
A stout hybrid with *S. tectorum* in its parentage. Plants to 30cm (12in) tall with rosettes up to 15cm (6in) across; leaves blue-green, tipped crimson sometimes. The flowers are reddish-purple. A fine plant.

Sempervivum schlehanii (syn. *S. marmoreum*) ○☆
Very like *S. tectorum*, and best known for several good cultivars. Var. *rubrifolium* (syn. *S. rubicundum*) has crimson, green-tipped leaves. 'Ornatum'—bright crimson-red leaves tipped with green and whitish flowers, each petal striped with red—one of the finest cultivars.

Sempervivum calcareum ○
Rather like the previous species, but the leaf-rosettes are more globose, blue-green, the leaves tipped with purplish-brown or reddish-purple. The flowers are pale pink, 14–16mm (⅝in) SW Alps. July–September.

Sempervivum atlanticum ○
Closely allied to *S. tectorum*, this vigorous species forms clusters of rosettes, each up to 20mm (2¾in) across, the leaves broad, green, but sometimes tipped with red, finely hairy. The flowers are 12-parted, about 30mm (1⅛in) across, the petals white with a median band of reddish-purple. Morocco. June–July.

Sempervivum caucasicum ○
Another ally of *S. tectorum*. The rosettes are similar, but the leaves hairy only along the margin. The flowers, 22–25mm (⅞–1in) across, are a rose-red, deeper along the centre of each narrow petal. Caucasus. July. Rather rare in cultivation.

Sempervivum montanum ○☆
The Mountain Houseleek is another widespread species in the mountains of C and S Europe where it inhabits acid rocks and screes above 1,500m (4,950ft). Plants have clusters of small, dark green, resin-scented, hairy rosettes, each up to 40mm (1⅜in) across. The flowers are reddish-purple, 24–30mm (1–1⅛in) across. The whole plant can reach 12cm (4¾in) tall. June–September. A prolific grower which hybridizes readily with other species, *S. arachnoideum*, *S. tectorum* and *S. wulfenii* in particular. Such crosses may occur in the wild as well as in cultivation. Var. *burnatii* (syn. '*Burnatii*') has larger rosettes to 80mm (3⅛in); SW Alps. Var. *stiriacum* (syn. '*Styriacum*') has small rosettes, to 45mm (1⅜in) the leaves tipped with red; E Alps.

Sempervivum dolomiticum ○
Rather like the previous species, but with more globular, less hairy rosettes, bright green, the leaves tipped with brown. The flowers are deep pink. Dolomites. July–September. Hybridizes with *S. montanum*.

Sempervivum cantabricum ○
Similar to *S. dolomiticum* but with larger darker green rosettes, the leaves tipped with red. The flowers are reddish purple. N Spain, Picos de Europa. July–August.

Sempervivum kosaninii ○
A species from SE Europe with large, rather flat rosettes to 90mm (3½in) across, the leaves purple-tipped. The flowers are red or reddish-purple. The plant grows to 20cm (8in) tall; a handsome species with stout runners, producing numerous offsets. S Yugoslavia and Greece. July–September.

Sempervivum kindingeri, S. leucanthum, and *S. ruthenicum* are similar to *S. kosaninii*, but have yellow flowers. They are all offered by some nurserymen. ○

Sempervivum arachnoideum ○☆
The well-known Cobweb Houseleek is an extremely variable species. The rounded rosettes can measure up to 15mm ($\frac{5}{8}$in) across, but often less and are covered in a characteristic web of whitish hairs. The rosettes are crammed together to form a flattish mat. The flowers are reddish-pink, 14–18mm ($\frac{2}{5}$–$\frac{3}{4}$in) across, borne on leafy stalks up to 12cm (4$\frac{3}{4}$in) tall. Alps and Apennines. June–September. A plant of acid rock and screes up to 3,100m (10,200ft) in the wild. Subsp. *tomentosum* has larger rosettes, to 25mm (1in) across. In the best forms the rosettes are tight balls completely enveloped in cobwebbed hairs. 'Minor'—a fine small cultivar. Hybrids with *S. grandiflorum, S. montanum, S. nevadense, S. pittonii* and *S. wulfenii* are offered in the trade.

Sempervivum grandiflorum (syn. ***S. gaudinii***) ○
Plants grow to 18cm (7in) tall and bear fairly large flat hairy rosettes 25mm (1in) across; they are resin-scented, dark green with brown leaf-tips. The flowers are yellow, 20–36mm ($\frac{4}{5}$–1$\frac{2}{5}$in) each petal with a purple spot at the base. 'Fastigiatum'—one of the best cultivars. Hybrids with *S. montanum* and *S. tectorum* are often offered by nurseries.

Sempervivum pittonii ○
Similar to the previous species, but rosettes smaller and grey-green, not resin-scented. The flowers are greenish-yellow. E Alps.

Sempervivum wulfenii ○
One of the most handsome species with its large bluish-green leaf-rosettes, 40–50mm (1$\frac{3}{5}$–2in) across; the leaves have a bristly margin, but are otherwise hairless. The lemon-yellow flowers are 20–22mm ($\frac{4}{5}$–$\frac{7}{8}$in) across, each petal with a purple spot at the base. C and E Alps. July–August. Rather rare in cultivation. The central rosette leaves form a distinctive cone as the young leaves emerge.

Sempervivum pumilum ○
Plants with small open rosettes to 18mm ($\frac{3}{4}$in) across, the leaves plain green and hairy; offsets produced on delicate, thread-like stems. Flowers rose-purple, 20mm ($\frac{4}{5}$in) across. Caucasus. July–August.

Sempervivum ciliosum (syn. ***S. ciliatum***) ○
Another species with relatively small rosettes, 20–45mm ($\frac{4}{5}$–1$\frac{4}{5}$in) across. The leaves are very hairy and pale green, forming a rather closed, globose rosette. The flowers are greenish-yellow borne in a compact cluster on a stiff stem with closely overlapping leaves. Bulgaria. July–August. *S. borisii* is sometimes considered a distinct subspecies or variety, but is of rather dubious status.

Sempervivum erythraeum ○
Plants produce rather open flat rosettes to 50mm (2in) across, greenish-purple or grey-green, minutely hairy. The flowers, 18–20mm (*c.* $\frac{3}{4}$in) across are reddish-purple, borne on a stiff purplish scape. Bulgaria. July.

Sempervivum macedonicum ○
Similar to *S. erythraeum*, but forming a loose mat because the offsets are long- not short-stalked. The rosette leaves are pale green, often tipped or flushed with red and the flowers are rather smaller. Macedonia. June–July.

Catalogues and lists include a number of other species and a confusing array of cultivars and supposed hybrids, and it is best to consult a good selection of these. However, potential buyers should be rather careful as the same plant may sometimes be found under various names in different catalogues.

Of the hybrids the following 5 are particularly fine: *S. × barbulatum* (*S. arachnoideum × S. montanum*); *S. × fimbriatum* (same parentage as the previous); *S. × funkii* (a triple hybrid; *S. arachnoideum × S. montanum* hybrid crossed with *S. tectorum*); *S. × hookeri* (*S. arachnoideum × S. montanum*)—a particularly small and neat form of this hybrid; *S. × thomsonii* (*S. arachnoideum × S. tectorum*).

SENECIO (Compositae)

Despite containing several pernicious weeds (groundsels and ragworts), this genus also boasts many attractive members among its over 2,000 species. Most have yellow or orange daisy flower-heads, although some are without ray-florets. Many have leafy stems as well as basal clusters of leaves. Despite their huge numbers only one is regularly offered for the rock garden.

Senecio incanus ○▯

This species forms small rosettes of deeply lobed hairy grey leaves. The flower-heads are button-like and borne on stems 5–10cm (2–4in) tall; they are a lovely rich golden-yellow, but their small size renders them somewhat insignificant. The variety *carniolicus* is often grown instead since it has slightly larger flower-heads. Alps and Apennines, where it inhabits pastures and rocky places on acid soils, 1,700–3,500m (5,600–11,500ft) altitude. July–August.

SERRATULA (Compositae)

Like many other genera in the daisy family, *Serratula* is better known for its large herbaceous members. It is reminiscent of the hardheads and thistles, with its constricted flower-heads of similarly shaped and coloured flowers. The leaves are often divided and usually occur along the stems as well as in basal clusters.

Serratula 'Shawii' ○

This cultivar has been grown in gardens for several decades and is possibly just a dwarf form of the Sawwort, *S. tinctoria*, a native throughout much of Europe. The short stems bear several heads of mauve flowers, the total height of the plant rarely exceeding 20–25cm (8–10in). July–September.

SHORTIA (Diapensiaceae)

A small genus of low, almost shrubby, plants, perhaps among the most beautiful of all alpines and requiring cool lime-free growing conditions in a moist humus-rich soil. There are about 7 species distributed in Taiwan, Japan, China and E North America.

Shortias have rather leathery, shiny, evergreen leaves which become attractively coloured in autumn and winter. The pink or white flowers are bell-shaped with 5 toothed or frilled lobes, reminiscent of a large *Soldanella*.

Shortia uniflora ○▯

A clump-forming plant increasing slowly by wiry stolons. The leathery leaves are carried mostly at the ends of the shoots, rounded in outline and undulate-toothed, 25–70mm (1–3in) in length. The leafless flower-stems rise to 10–15cm (4–6in) and bear solitary, widely bell-shaped or flattish, pale pink, scented flowers, horizontal

Shortia soldanelloides

or slightly drooping, and 25–30mm (1–1⅕in) across. Japan. March–April. Var. *grandiflora* has fragrant pink flowers up to 50mm (2in) across; a deeper pink form of this has been named 'Rosea'.

Shortia soldanelloides (syn. **Schizocodon soldanelloides**) ◗☐☆
Similar in general appearance to *S. uniflora*, but with very smooth shiny leaves about 30–60mm (1⅕–2⅖in) long, conspicuously toothed at the margins and colouring to a rich reddish brown in the autumn. The deep rose-pink flowers are seldom solitary, usually 3–10 in a one-sided raceme 10–20cm (4–8in) in height; they are more narrowly funnel-shaped than those of *S. uniflora* and pendant with promi-nently fringed lobes. Japan. April–May. A delightful species that deserves to be in any collection and well suited to the peat garden. Forma *alpina* is a dwarf alpine version with very small, almost untoothed leaves, only 10–20mm (⅖–⅘in) long and with usually only one flower per stem. Var. *magna* (syn. *Shortia magna*) has larger leaves, 8–12cm (3–5in) long, and as much across, with many rather small teeth along the margins. Var. *ilicifolia* (syn. *Schizocodon ilicifolius*) has small leaves with sharply triangular teeth along the margin. 'Alba'—a good white-flowered form. Var. *intercedens* has white flowers, and the leaves are whitish on the underside with up to 15 coarse teeth on each side.

Shortia galacifolia ◑▢
In this species the shiny green leaves are carried on long stalks, the blade wavy-edged, nearly orbicular and about 50mm (2in) in diameter, becoming bronze-tinted during the autumn. The solitary white flowers are widely bell-shaped, about 25mm (1in) across and facing out horizontally on stems 10–12cm (4–5in) tall. E USA—N Carolina. April–May. A pale pink form is also known.

SILENE (Caryophyllaceae)

A very large group of plants which includes the campions and catchflies, the latter so called because the stems and leaves are furnished with sticky glands to which small insects become stuck. There are many attractive species well worth cultivating, but often they are too tall for the rock garden and are better used in a border or a semi-wild situation. There are some 500 species distributed throughout the northern hemisphere. They are generally easy to cultivate, often seeding around once established.

Silenes may be annual, biennial or perennial, sometimes even shrubby, with opposite leaves varying widely in shape and size. The flowers have a tubular calyx with 5 teeth and many (10–20) veins along its length, the particular number being a distinguishing character between different groups of species. There are 5 petals with an expanded showy blade narrowed to a claw at the base and often either notched or more deeply bilobed at the apex. There are 10 stamens and usually 3 (rarely 5) styles. The fruit capsule, on splitting open, normally has 6 teeth at its apex.

Silene acaulis ○☆
The Moss Campion is among the best known and most beautiful of European alpine plants, with its mossy, bright green cushions of small, hairless, linear leaves. The solitary, rose-pink flowers are carried on very short stalks so that they appear almost stemless on the cushions and are about 5–10mm ($\frac{1}{5}$–$\frac{2}{5}$in) across, rounded in outline but with notched petals. Widespread in Arctic regions and on the higher mountains of Europe including Britain and Ireland. June–August. A good plant for a sunny scree. 'Alba'—a white-flowered form. Var. *pedunculata* has long-stalked flowers.

Silene alpestris (syn. *Heliosperma alpestre*) ○
A loosely tufted perennial with lanceolate leaves, which are wider towards the tips, and branching sprays, 10–30cm (4–12in) in height, of rounded white flowers 8–10mm ($\frac{2}{5}$in) across, with 4–6 teeth at the apex of each petal. E Alps of Europe. June–August. 'Flore-pleno'—a form with tightly double flowers.

Silene elizabethae ○
This perennial species forms tufts of loose rosettes of lanceolate leaves. The 10–20cm (4–8in) tall flower stems carry one or more upright, very large, deep reddish-purple flowers, 30–45mm (1$\frac{1}{5}$–1$\frac{4}{5}$in) across, which have a stickily-hairy calyx about 2cm ($\frac{4}{5}$in) long; the petals are bilobed at the apex. Italian Alps. June–August. Deserves to be more widely grown in gardens.

Silene keiskei ○◑
A sprawling perennial with upright flower stems 5–20cm (2–8in) in height, bearing well-spaced, glabrous or sparsely hairy, lanceolate leaves. The pink flowers are carried in few-branched heads and are 15–30mm ($\frac{3}{5}$–1$\frac{1}{5}$in) across, with deeply bilobed petals and a glabrous or hairy calyx about 10–15mm ($\frac{2}{5}$–$\frac{3}{5}$in) long. Japan. July–August. This is a variable plant and several different forms have been

introduced into cultivation. Those with compact growth and large flowers are the most desirable for the rock garden. 'Minor'—a dwarfer form is occasionally offered in catalogues.

Silene saxifraga ○
The Tufted Catchfly is a much-branched tufted perennial with an almost woody base, forming soft hummocks of narrowly linear, pointed, slightly hairy, leaves up to 15mm ($\frac{3}{5}$in) long. The many flower-stems, 5–20cm (2–8in) in height, carry 1 or 2 white flowers, 10–15mm ($\frac{2}{5}$–$\frac{3}{5}$in) across, with bilobed petals and a club-shaped calyx; the petals are often suffused green or reddish on the outside. Mountains of S Europe. June–July.

Silene italica ○
A rather tall plant, 20cm (8in) or more when in flower, and suitable only for the larger rock garden. It forms tufts of elliptical leaves, the basal leaves being broadest above the middle. The loose panicles of creamy-white flowers are borne on sticky stems, each flower 15–20mm ($\frac{3}{5}$–$\frac{4}{5}$in) across, with deeply bilobed petals which are often suffused green or red on the outside. Widespread in C and S Europe. June–July.

Silene maritima (syn. ***S. vulgaris*** subsp. ***maritima***) ○◑
The Sea Campion is a widespread British native which forms a more or less prostrate hairless plant with grey-green, narrowly lanceolate leaves. The erect or spreading flower-stems, 5–25cm (2–10in) in height, carry solitary (sometimes up to 4) white flowers which are 15–20mm ($\frac{3}{5}$–$\frac{4}{5}$in) across. These have a very inflated waxy-looking calyx with a netted pattern of veins, often suffused with green or purple. Coastal areas of W Europe. May–August. 'Flore Pleno'—has large double flowers which are often too heavy for the stems so that the whole plant, including flowers, is prostrate.

Silene schafta ○☆
A prostrate or clump-forming plant with mats of slightly hairy elliptical, pointed leaves, 10–30mm ($\frac{2}{5}$–1$\frac{1}{5}$in) long, and spreading flower-stems 2–15cm (1–6in) tall. These carry solitary or sometimes several deep pink, magenta or rarely white flowers, 15–25mm ($\frac{3}{5}$–1in) across, with deeply notched petals; the slender 10-veined calyx is usually suffused with purple. N Iran, Caucasus. June–August. A very variable plant usually with single-flowered stems in the wild, but more branched in cultivation. 'Abbotswood'—a good and floriferous cultivar.

SISYRINCHIUM (Iridaceae)

A genus of about 100 species of charming tufted perennials from America, the West Indies, the Falkland Islands and several other places. Only the smaller ones are suitable rock garden subjects. Most form tufts of small fans of iris-like leaves. The petalled flowers are short-lived, but borne in succession, close to the tip of a scape. Propagation by division or from seed; some species seed around freely and may become a nuisance on a scree.

Sisyrinchium bermudianum ○☆
The Blue-eyed Grass forms tufts to 20cm (8in) tall bearing small, but brilliant, violet-blue flowers, often in profusion. Bermuda and Ireland. June–September. One of the hardiest.

Silene schafta

Sisyrinchium angustifolium ○
Similar to the previous species, but more slender and with purer, bluer flowers. North America. July–September. Also often called Blue-eyed Grass.

Sisyrinchium bellum ○☆
Like *S. angustifolium*, but with shorter spathe-valves and the flowers held well clear of the bracts, blue-violet with a yellow throat. North America. June–August. 'Album'—a fine dwarfer form with pure white flowers.

Sisyrinchium brachypus ○
A shorter sturdier plant than the previous species to 10cm (4in) tall, with broader fans of leaves and golden flowers. North America. June–August.

Sisyrinchium californicum ○
Like the previous, but taller and with bright yellow flowers. W USA. July–August.

Sisyrinchium douglasii (syn. *S. grandiflorum*) ○☆
Tufts of narrow leaves to 20cm (8in) tall and paired, drooping bell-shaped flowers of satiny purple. North America. Late June–August. Plants die down completely after flowering ceases, so care should be taken not to dig them up by mistake. 'Album'—a fine white version.

Sisyrinchium filifolium ○◑
Rather like the previous but a slender, often shorter plant. The broad bellflowers are satiny white with pale purplish veins. Falkland Islands. May–June.

SOLDANELLA (Primulaceae)

This lovely genus of less than 10 species derives its name from the round leaves, which resemble a coin (Latin = soldus, Italian = soldo). They are further characterized by small umbels of bell-shaped flowers, delightfully fringed along the edge. In the wild, *S. carpatica, S. hungarica,* and *S. villosa* are essentially woodlanders, whilst *S. alpina* and *S. minima* are alpine meadow species.

In cultivation they thrive best in a cool, moist position, especially in peaty soil, but preferably not under trees. They will also succeed in a sunny position provided there is plenty of moisture at the roots. Most will benefit from overhead protection in winter, but will survive without, although they may not flower so freely. Slugs and snails may eat flower buds in late winter, so protection with slug pellets is advisable. For pot culture an acid open compost with plenty of peat or leaf mould seems to be the best.

Soldanella alpina ○▢
The Alpine Snowbell forms a mat of thickish dark green rounded leaves, up to 35mm (1⅜in) in diameter. The scapes rise to 10cm (4in) each bearing 2–4 pendent, flared, violet or blue-violet bells, 9–12mm (to ½in) long. The corolla is deeply cut giving it a very frilly appearance. Mountains of C and S Europe. April–May. It is usually shy flowering in cultivation, and some clones tend to lack vigour. Sometimes other species, especially *S. hungarica*, are sold under the name *S. alpina*. In the wild this delightful species occurs on wet pastures and stony places to 3,000m (9,900ft), being especially prominent by snow patches.

Soldanella carpatica ○◑▢
Very similar to *S. alpina*, differing mainly in the violet undersurface of the leaves (in *S. alpina* it is green). W Carpathians. April–May. It is probably somewhat more vigorous in cultivation and tends to flower more freely. A very nice white form is also seen in gardens.

Soldanella hungarica (syn. *S. montana* subsp. *hungarica*) ○◑▢
Very much like a larger *S. alpina*, but with rather smaller flowers. The umbel of 3–10 flowers is borne on a scape 10–20cm (4–8in) long. The main difference from *S. alpina* can be seen in the short hairy leaf-stalks, the larger leaf-blades with slightly toothed or uneven margins, often violet below. Carpathians and the Balkans. A vigorous species which is happy in the open garden.

Soldanella minima ○
The Least Snowbell is a delightful small carpeting species which responds well to cultivation. The rounded dark green leaves are 5–10mm (⅕–⅖in) in diameter. The pendent flowers are usually solitary, white to pale violet, narrow bells, 12–15mm (½–⅗in) long, fringed close along the rim (much less deeply so than *S. alpina*). E Alps and Carpathians. March–May. In the wild a plant of damp soils and turf over limestone, to 2,500m (8,250ft).

Soldanella villosa (syn. *S. montana* subsp. *villosa*) ○◑▢☆
This is a large and vigorous species which differs from *S. hungarica* only by its shaggily hairy leaf-stalks and generally longer scapes which rise from 10 to 30cm

(4–12in). W Pyrenees. May–June. Does well in the open garden, particularly on raised peat borders. Perhaps the easiest and most accommodating species in cultivation.

SOLIDAGO (Compositae)

The genus contains the goldenrods, a group of about 100 species all native to North America except for one which is European. The plants are all perennials with leafy stems and congested heads of small daisy-like flowers, with disc- and ray-florets. Alpine forms of the European species are fairly compact and have been grown in rock gardens for many years.

Solidago virgaurea ○◑

The Common Goldenrod is surprisingly attractive. It bears many heads of golden-yellow flowers which are held in pyramidal racemes on stems 20–25cm (8–10in). July–September, The dwarfer forms are sold under several varietal names such as var. *minuta* and var. *alpestris*. *Senecio brachystachys* is very similar.

SORBUS (Rosaceae)

Only one species is suitable for rock gardens, a pigmy mountain ash.

Sorbus reducta ○☆

A dwarf bush to 40cm (16in) after many years. Leaves pinnate, deep green, red-tinted in autumn. Flowers creamy white, borne in dense clusters to 15mm ($\frac{5}{8}$in) across. These are followed by crimson or pink berries in the autumn. W and SW China, N Burma. July. Well worth growing.

SPIRAEA (Rosaceae)

A large genus of shrubs much grown in gardens. Several of the smaller ones can find a useful niche on the rock garden. They are easy to cultivate, preferring sunny or semi-shaded aspects.

Spiraea × bullata ○

A dense bush with numerous rusty-brown stems to 30cm (12in). Leaves dark green, oval toothed. Flowers deep rose-pink, borne in small, flat clusters. July–September. Useful for its late summer flowers, often borne until the first frosts of autumn.

Spiraea × brumalda ○☆

Similar to the previous species. The leaves are paler green and more pointed, and the flowers bright rose-red. June–July. The best cultivars are 'Nana'—a prostrate form not more than 15cm (6in)tall; 'Nyewoods'—rich rose-red flowers, stems to 40cm (6in).

Spiraea hendersonii ○

A subshrub forming low hummocks of deep green, elliptical leaves. Flowers cream, borne in long, dense spikes above the foliage, the whole plant not more than 15cm (6in) tall. North America—Rocky Mountains. June–July.

STACHYS (Labiatae)

The common *Stachys* of gardens, *S. lanata* or Lamb's-ears, is well known, though far too coarse and invasive for the rock garden. The genus contains the betonys and Woundworts with many species scattered across the northern hemisphere, but most, like *S. lanata*, are too coarse to be included here. Two are worthy of mention, succeeding in a sunny position on any well-drained soil.

Stachys corsica ○

A southern European species occupying damp rocky habitats in the wild. Plants form spreading mats with creeping and rooting stems rising to only 50–60mm (2–2½in), and numerous bluntly toothed, rather rounded shiny green leaves. The flowers are white to purple, the darker-flowered forms being the more desirable in gardens; each flower is 12–18mm (½–¾in) long, 2-lipped. July–September.

Stachys lavandulifolia ○

An E Turkish species, taller than the previous one, often reaching 30cm (12in) high. The elliptical, toothed, felted grey-green leaves are rather handsome and contrast nicely with the whorled spikes of reddish-purple flowers. July–August.

SYMPHYANDRA (Campanulaceae)

A beautiful genus of *Campanula*-like plants, with large bellflowers, which well deserve to be more widely grown. They look well on the higher part of the rock garden or in a raised bed where their beauty can be all the more readily appreciated. They thrive in well-drained, gritty loams and are especially valuable for their late summer flowering habit.

Symphyandra hoffmannii ○◗☆

A biennial species forming a rosette of rather pale green, rough, elliptical leaves and a narrow pyramid of numerous pendent creamy-white bells, each 20–30mm (⅘–1⅕in) long. The whole plant is about 20cm (8in) tall, sometimes more. W Yugoslavia. July–September. Seeds need to be saved regularly as this is a biennial species; however, it will seed itself about in some gardens.

Symphyandra wanneri (syn. *Campanula wanneri*) ◗

A more splendid plant than the previous. It is a perennial to 15cm (6in) tall, with sharply toothed lanceolate leaves. The bellflowers, 20–35mm (⅘–1⅖in), are a translucent purple-blue of great charm. Bulgaria, Romania and E Yugoslavia. July–September. In the wild a plant of shady mountain rocks and cliffs.

TALINUM (Portulacaceae)

A genus of 30–40 species with fleshy stems and leaves, related to *Lewisia*. They are distributed in North America, Asia and Africa and are seldom cultivated, but two attractive species from the USA are grown by specialist rock gardeners, mainly as alpine house subjects.

Talinum okanoganense ○

This is a very dwarf plant with branching fleshy stems forming loose cushions. The grey-green leaves are also fleshy and are nearly cylindrical, about 5–10mm (⅕–⅖in) long, deciduous and leaving the basal part of the midribs as persistent, but rather soft projections. The flowers are few, 10–15mm (⅖–⅗in) across, white, short-stemmed and carried just above the leaves. USA—Washington State and British Columbia. May–June.

Talinum spinescens ○

This also has tufts of fleshy green leaves, but they are longer than those of *T. okanoganense* and the midribs persist as hard spines on the older parts of the stems which become trunk-like as the plants mature. The flower-stems are taller, up to 15cm (6in), carrying more numerous pink to magenta flowers, 15–20mm ($\frac{3}{5}$–$\frac{4}{5}$in) across. USA—Washington State. May–June. A double-flowered form is also known.

In addition to these two species there is an intermediate hybrid between them which is also in cultivation.

TANACETUM (Compositae)

An interesting genus of about 50 species of herbaceous plants including the Common Tansy, long known for its use as a medicinal herb. Several members of the genus are grown for their attractive flowers and foliage. The flower-heads are compound, containing either disc- and ray-florets or just disc-florets; they vary in colour from yellow to white, including shades of lemon.

Tanacetum bipinnatum ○

An attractive species 5–30cm (2–12in) tall which is native to the arctic regions of the world, occurring in Scandinavia, Russia and Canada. It forms basal clumps of silky, hairy, finely divided leaves up to 25cm (10in) long. The solitary flower-stems are sometimes branched in the upper half, the yellow flower-heads up to 25mm (1in) across. July–August.

Tanacetum densum ○☆

An interesting, spreading species from Turkey, grown largely for its delicate filigree foliage which is silvery-grey. The flowers are rather insignificant. It is surprisingly hardy, but needs to be planted either in or on a wall, scree, or a raised bed where good drainage is guaranteed. A sunny sheltered aspect is essential. The subspecies *amani* (syn. 'Amanum') is usually offered for sale. Formerly sold under the name of *Chrysanthemum haradjanii*.

TANAKEA (Saxifragaceae)

There is only one species of *Tanakea* and it looks not unlike a small *Astilbe*. In cultivation it needs a lime-free soil and does best in a shady place. Propagation is by division of the rhizome in the spring, or from seed.

Tanakea radicans ◗□

A tufted species, 10–20cm (4–8in) tall, producing short running stems which bear long-stalked evergreen, rounded or heart-shaped, somewhat leathery, leaves with toothed margins. The flower-stem is leafless, and carries flowers which, instead of petals, have a greenish white calyx and 10 stamens. China, Japan. Late Spring. A charming little woodlander.

TELESONIX (Saxifragaceae)

A genus with just one species which used to be included in *Boykinia*, but was removed from that genus because it has 10 stamens (not 5).

Telesonix jamesii (syn. *Boykinia jamesii*) ◗

This delightful plant is probably better known to gardeners under its synonym. It is a beautiful and much sought-after species which unfortunately does not always flower well in cultivation. The plants are tufted, 5–15cm (2–6in) tall. The stalked, kidney-shaped leaves are toothed, rather shiny green. The spikes of 5–25 cherry-red

241

or crimson flowers are borne on glandular-hairy stems which are often reddish towards the top. NW North America. May–June. In the wild it is found on limestone, but in the garden it will grow satisfactorily in a lime-free soil; perhaps at its best in a well-drained woodland soil. Propagation is by seed.

TEUCRIUM (Labiatae)

The germanders are an interesting group of Labiates widely scattered across the northern hemisphere. Many are aromatic, but all can be distinguished from most other genera in the family by the absence of a well-developed upper lip to the corolla—instead the upper lip is absent or reduced to one or two tiny scales. As a result of the absence of the upper lip the stamens protrude well beyond the corolla. The species listed here are reasonably easy to grow, and thrive in a well-drained soil in a sunny position. They are readily increased from seed, cuttings, or by division of the parent plant.

Teucrium chamaedrys ○☆
The Wall Germander is a variable species forming a small subshrub to 22cm (9in) tall. The oblong or oval leaves are dark green and shiny, blunt toothed. The pale to deep purple flowers form short leafy spikes. Widespread in C and S Europe and W Asia. June–September. A plant of dry habitats, banks and open woodland in its native haunts. Planted in too rich and moist a soil it will grow lank and leafy.

Teucrium montanum ○
The Mountain Germander is quite a different species, a spreading subshrub often forming an entangled mat. The leathery leaves are elliptical, deep green above, but whitish beneath, the leaf-margin generally rolled under. The yellowish-white flowers are borne in a flattened head, surrounded by a ruff of leaves. Mountains of C and S Europe. May–August. Becomes rather straggly unless clipped back at regular intervals.

Teucrium pyrenaicum ○
The Pyrenean Germander is a pretty species, less grown in gardens than it really deserves. Plants form a low creeping mat of slender stems with oval, toothed leaves. The flowers, like the former species, are borne in a flattened head and are cream or mauve, or more often bicoloured. Pyrenees. June–August.

Teucrium ackermanii ○
A Turkish species forming a spreading mat, like the two previous ones. The narrow grey-green leaves contrast well with the violet flowers. Reaches 80mm ($3\frac{1}{8}$in) in height. July–August.

Teucrium aroanum ○
An evergreen subshrub with spreading stems rooting at the leaf-joints, much-branched. The leaves are deep green, oblong, untoothed and densely hairy beneath. The purplish-grey flowers, 15–20mm ($\frac{3}{5}$–$\frac{4}{5}$in) long, are borne in dense heads. A plant of rocky mountain habitats in Greece where it is restricted to two mountains, Chelmos and Akhaia. August–September.

Teucrium polium ○☆
An extremely variable species. The forms usually cultivated make small bushy subshrubs with neat greyish- or whitish-green foliage and short whorled spikes of

Teucrium montanum

yellow or white flowers. Plants are generally 10–15cm (4–6in) tall. S Europe—particularly the Mediterranean region. Generally rather short lived in gardens.

Teucrium scordium ○◑☆
The Water Germander is common in rather wet places throughout much of Europe. The ordinary forms are not generally suitable for gardens, but the cultivar 'Crispum', with its fascinating crimped fleshy leaves, is worth obtaining. Plants grow to 25cm (10in) tall.

Teucrium subspinosum ○
A more unusual species which comes from W Asia where it inhabits the crevices of limestone cliffs. Plants form a small intricately branched spiny shrub to 20cm (4in) eventually. The tiny grey-green leaves are nicely crinkled. The bright pink flowers are borne during the summer, July and August. Rather rare in cultivation and generally grown in the alpine house; however it will succeed outdoors when wedged in a rock crevice and shielded from the worst of the winter weather.

THALICTRUM (Ranunculaceae)

The meadow-rues are not particularly showy plants on the whole, but they have a quiet and appealing charm that endears them to many. The flowers are generally rather smaller and consist of a showy bunch of stamens surrounded by 4 sepals which may be coloured like petals, but are often rather inconspicuous. The leaves are much divided, ferny and not unlike those of columbines, *Aquilegia*. Most meadow-rues require a moist, but well-drained leafy soil, and thrive best in semi-shaded positions.

Thalictrum alpinum ○◑

The Alpine Meadow-rue is a dainty little plant, often difficult to spot amongst its native meadows and rocks. Plants are small, to 15cm (6in) tall, with finely divided, neat foliage. The small flowers, borne in simple racemes, are violet with yellow anthers. Mountains of Europe, temperate Asia and North America. July–August. A species best grown on a gritty scree.

Thalictrum minus ○◑

The Lesser Meadow-rue is not unlike the previous species, but taller. The flowers are yellowish, drooping on branched stems. Mountains of Europe and Asia. May–July. Tolerates drier conditions than the other species included here.

Thalictrum chelidonii ◑☆

A coarser plant than *T. alpinum* with bluish-green foliage, but noted primarily for its graceful mauve or violet flowers, nodding gracefully on delicate stalks. More showy than most of the smaller meadow-rues. C and E Himalaya. July–September. The dwarfer forms in cultivation are well worth seeking out.

Thalictrum coreanum ◑

A Korean species with rose-pink flowers and bronzy foliage. Plants grow to 15cm (6in) tall. July–September.

Thalictrum kiusianum ◑☆

Perhaps the most appealing species, patch-forming, with greyish to bronzy, finely divided foliage and sprays of purple or pinkish-mauve flowers. Plants to 10cm (4in) tall. S Japan. June–July.

THERMOPSIS (Leguminosae)

The genus takes its name from the Greek for lupin-like and contains about 20 species native to Asia and North America, most coming from mountain areas between 1,500 and 5,000m (4,950–16,500ft). They are hardy, usually rhizomatous, perennials sending up annual, simple or branched, stems with trifoliate leaves. Most species prefer deep, well-drained soils and are best propagated by division, the seeds being generally slow to germinate.

Thermopsis montana ○

An erect perennial to about 45cm (18in) tall, the leaves with oval leaflets. The yellow pea-flowers are borne in racemes. The whole plant somewhat silky pubescent, the fruits straight and erect. W USA. May–June. An easy and useful plant for the larger rock garden.

THLASPI (Cruciferae)

A genus of 60 species widespread in Europe and Asia. Many are annuals and weedy, scarcely suitable for cultivation. However, there are a few little alpine species worthy of attention. They thrive best in rather poor well-drained soils and plenty of sunshine. Most are short lived, but can be propagated from seed or cuttings.

Thlaspi rotundifolium ○☆

Perhaps the loveliest species, which forms small tufts to 90mm (3½in) tall or oblong or rounded rather fleshy leaves, the lower in a lax rosette. The flowers are purple, beautifully honey-scented, borne in globular heads. Alps and Apennines. April–

July. A delightful plant—white forms are sometimes found. In the wild a plant of rocks and screes, to 3,000m (9,900ft).

Thlaspi stylosum ○
A very low cushion-forming plant to 50mm (2in), with fleshy leaves mostly in basal rosettes. The flowers are purplish with violet anthers. C and S Apennines. April–May.

THYMUS (Labiatae)

The thymes are well-loved garden plants used as much for their culinary characteristics and pleasing aromatic properties as for their decorative appeal. There are many cultivars grown in gardens. Most are fairly easy and tolerant plants, but prefer dry, well-drained soils and a sunny aspect. They are readily increased by seed, cuttings, or, the creeping kinds, by division of the parent plant.

Thymus serpyllum ○☆
The Wild Thyme of Europe is a matted carpeter with numerous non-flowering and rooting runners, bearing tiny elliptical deep-green leaves. The flowers, ranging from pale pink to deep rosy-purple, are borne in small globose heads; each flower is only 3–6mm ($\frac{1}{8}$–$\frac{1}{4}$in) long. April–July. A very variable species; many forms are known in cultivation including the following: 'Albus'—white flowers; 'Annie Hall'—soft pink flowers; 'Bressingham'—clear pink; 'Coccineus'—deep crimson flowers; 'Lanuginosus' (syn. *T. lanuginosus*)—a fine form with soft, hairy, greyish foliage; 'Minus'—a particularly small and compact form with pink flowers; 'Pink Chintz'—rich rose-pink flowers.

Thymus caespititius ○
Another caespitose species, forming woodier stems than the previous. The leaves are rather fleshy and spoon-shaped. The heads of purplish-pink flowers rise on leafy stems to 50mm (2in). NW Spain and the Azores. June–July. Unusual in cultivation.

Thymus doerfleri (syn. ***T. hirsutus***) ○☆
Like *T. serpyllum*, but forming carpets of hairy leaves and clusters of soft pink flowers. N Balkan Peninsula. June–July.

Thymus leucotrichus ○
A rare species in cultivation, not unlike the previous, but with narrow lanceolate leaves and clusters of pinkish-purple flowers. Mountains of C and S Greece. June–July.

Thymus membranaceus ○▲
A much-branched subshrub to 25cm (10in) bearing small linear leaves. The tubular whitish flowers, 14–15mm ($\frac{2}{3}$in) long, are borne in globose clusters surrounded by papery bracts. Mountains of SE Spain. June–August. A charming species with exceptionally large flowers for a thyme. Not easy in the open garden except in sunny, well-sheltered sites, given the very best of drainage. For this reason it is more often seen in the protection of an alpine house or frame.

Thymus cilicicus ○
Another bushy species, to 15cm (6in), with numerous deep green lanceolate leaves, forming 4-angled columns. The flowers are pale pink, borne in small globose heads. Turkey. July–August. A fine and attractive species, rather rare in cultivation.

Thymus × *citriodorus* ○☆

A hybrid between *T. pulegioides*, the commonest of the British thymes, and *T. vulgaris*, a W Mediterranean species. Plants form a neat bush to 24cm (10in) tall and eventually becoming woody below. The flowers are pale lilac, borne in small heads. The whole plant has a very pleasing lemon scent, especially when crushed. The best forms have variegated or coloured foliage: 'Aureus'—golden foliage; 'Silver Queen'—a fine form with green and silver variegated foliage.

TIARELLA (Saxifragaceae)

There are 6 species which come from Asia and North America, related to *Heuchera*. The leaves are both basal and on the flower-stems. The flowers have entire linear petals and 10 stamens. Tiarellas are for semi-shaded places, being woodland plants in the wild. They are propagated by division or by seed.

Tiarella cordifolia ○◐☆

The Foam Flower is stoloniferous plant which has softly hairy, 3- or 5-lobed leaves, which turn reddish brown in the autumn. The flower-stems, 20–30cm (8–12in) tall, carry fluffy, rather dense spikes of starry flowers; each flower is 2.5–5mm ($\frac{1}{8}$–$\frac{1}{5}$in) long with white petals. North America. May–July. The variant known as 'Purpurea' has bronze-purple leaves.

Tiarella wherryi ○◐☆

Another tufted plant, its leaves sharply lobed, often with darker blotches. The flowers can be white or pink and are produced in dense racemes on 30cm (12in) stems; the petals are narrower than in *T. cordifolia*. The species is not stoloniferous. North America. April–May.

TOLMIEA (Saxifragaceae)

This genus contains only one species which is often seen as a house plant, but it is perfectly hardy and can make a pretty green hummock in the rock garden. The calyx is narrowly bell-shaped with 5 sepals, (3 large and 2 smaller), but there are only 4 petals and 3 stamens. In the wild a woodlander and preferring similar conditions in cultivation. Propagation by division or seed.

Tolmiea menziesii ◐☆

The Pig-a-Back plant has hairy green leaves with 5 or 7 shallow lobes. Tall racemes of many greenish-yellow or brownish flowers are produced in early summer. A feature of this plant is the production of a daughter plant at the point where the leaf-blade joins its stalk—hence its vernacular name. The entire leaf can be removed and, when laid on soil, the new plantlets will quickly root. *T. menziesii* grows best in a cool shady position. NW North America. Late May–July. There are forms available with yellowish or pale green blotched variegations on the leaves.

TRACHELIUM (Campanulaceae)

A small primarily Mediterranean genus related to *Campanula*, but with deeply lobed flowers held in clusters at the shoot tips. Two species are included here; both are fine pan plants in the alpine house, but will succeed outdoors given some form of winter protection. A pane of glass placed overhead will probably suffice. In the wild both species are crevice plants in calcareous or conglomerate rocks. They are best propagated from seed.

Trachelium asperuloides ○
A dense cushion-forming plant to 50–60mm (2–2½in) tall. The numerous narrow leaves are pale green and stalkless. The small flowers are lilac-blue, borne in small clusters just above the foliage. S Greece. August–September. Best appreciated as a pan plant in the alpine house.

Trachelium jacquinii (including *T. rumelianum,* syn. *Diosphaera dubia*) ○
A more robust species to 15cm (6in), sometimes more, forming loose mounds. The slender, often arching, stems, bear numerous oval, toothed and pointed leaves. The dense flower-heads are blue or lilac-blue and are very attractive to butterflies. August–September. S Bulgaria and Greece. An interesting plant which will succeed in a tight sunny crevice on the rock garden or in a deep very well-drained scree or raised bed.

TREMACRON (Gesneriaceae)

A delightful little genus with only 2 species, native to SW China. In the wild they are plants of shady rocky habitats, similar to those favoured by the more familiar genus *Ramonda*; in cultivation they require similar conditions although they are most often seen in the alpine house.

Tremacron forrestii ◑▢
Plants form small rosettes of oblong or oval, coarsely toothed, rather thin, long-stalked leaves. The tubular bellflowers are yellowish-white, 12–14mm (½in) long and with protruding stamens; several flowers are borne on long hairy scapes. June–July. The second species, *T. mairei*, is very rare in cultivation and is distinguished by its thicker, more leathery, and broader leaves.

TRIFOLIUM (Leguminosae)

The clovers are hardy or half-hardy annual or perennial herbs with about 250 species in temperate and subtropical regions of both hemispheres, particularly in the E Mediterranean, W Asia and North America. The leaves are usually trifoliate and the leaflets tend to be toothed. The pea-like flowers are borne in spherical heads, short spikes or are occasionally solitary. The flower colour ranges from purple and red to white and less often yellow. The fruit-pods are mostly small, few-seeded, and hidden within the calyx. Propagation from seed or by division of the parent plant.

Trifolium repens ○
White Clover is a creeping perennial herb rooting at the nodes, and needs to be carefully excluded from any rock garden or scree, being far too invasive. The leaves are long-stalked, the leaflets often with a central, white crescent-shaped marking. The scented, white to pale pink (rarely purple) flowers, 8–13mm (⅓–½in) long, are borne in globose heads. The species is a common pasture plant and component of lawns. Widespread in Europe and W Asia. May–October. Although too invasive there are several fine cultivars prized for their ornamental foliage: 'Atropurpureum'—a dwarf form with bronze leaflets edged bright green; 'Pentaphyllum'—a creeping plant with bronze shiny leaflets; 'Purpurascens Quadriphyllum'—leaves with 3–6 green to purple leaflets.

Trifolium uniflorum ○
A creeping perennial to 60mm (2⅜in) in height, with a woody tap root and toothed, green leaflets, tinged with red. The flowers, about 15–20mm (⅜–⅘in) long, are white, cream or purple, sometimes bicoloured; they are solitary or 2–3 together in short-stalked heads. Greece and W Asia. June–July.

Trifolium alpinum ○☆
The Alpine Clover is a low tufted rather sprawling, hairless perennial with lanceolate leaflets. The pale to deep pink flowers, 18–25mm (⅘–1in) long, are borne in a dense, long-stalked cluster. Mountains of C and S Europe. June–July. The deeper coloured forms are the best for the rock garden.

TRILLIUM (Trilliaceae)

A genus of about 30 species often called Wake-Robins, native to North America and temperate E Asia. They are woodland plants with a rhizomatous rootstock. The stout fleshy stems bear a whorl of 3 unstalked or short-stalked leaves and a solitary 3-parted flower. The sepals are generally small, often recurved, but the 3 petals are large and conspicuous. Plants thrive best in a moist, well-drained, leafy or peaty soil, in dappled shade. Propagation by division or from seed. The smaller species make delightful pan plants.

Trillium erectum ◖☆
Plants to 30cm (12in) tall, patch forming, with deep green, sometimes mottled oval leaves. The erect flowers are reddish-purple, with narrow pointed petals and brownish sepals. E North America. May.

Trillium sessile ◖☆
A shorter plant than the previous, to 22cm (9in) tall with mottled green leaves and unstalked, erect purple flowers. USA. March–April.

Trillium luteum ◖
A rarer species, only 15cm (6in) tall, with mottled leaves and unstalked, erect flowers of a clear greenish-yellow. E USA. May–June.

Trillium grandiflorum ◖☆
Perhaps the loveliest of the larger species. Plants form clumps to 30cm (12in) tall with plain green broad leaves. The wide bell-shaped flowers are half nodding on short stalks, white but flushing with pink as they age, each 50–60mm (2–2⅜in) across. NE America. April–early June. 'Flore-plena'—a fine form with frilly double, camellia-like flowers.

Trillium ovatum ◖
Similar to *T. grandiflorum* but petals spreading out directly from the base (not erect in lower part). W North America. March–April.

Trillium nivale ◖
A small species, only 12–15cm (5–6in) tall with deep green leaves and white, short-stalked flowers which open fairly widely. SE USA. March–April.

Trillium rivale ◖
Similar to the previous, but smaller, the flowers spotted with pink within. E USA. April. Rare in cultivation.

Trillium cernuum ◑
A taller species, often reaching 45cm (18in) with broad rhombic-shaped leaves. The pendant, white, bell-shaped flowers arch on stems below the foliage; they are rather small with recurving petals. E North America. April–May.

TROLLIUS (Ranunculaceae)

A genus of fine buttercup-like plants with handsome palmately cut foliage. Most species are too coarse for the rock garden, except around water. They are easy to grow and tolerant perennials, easily increased by division of the parent clump. They thrive best in moist sunny situations. In *Trollius* the sepals are large, coloured and petal-like, whereas in *Ranunculus* normal small sepals and showy petals occur.

Trollius acaulis ○◑☆
A handsome small plant to 12cm (5in) with rather bright green, neatly lobed foliage. The golden flowers, 25–40mm (1–1⅝in) across, open to flat saucers. China and E Himalaya. June–July.

Trollius pumilus ◑
Very similar to the previous species, but generally larger and taller, to 15cm (6in). The leaf-segments are 3-lobed. N India and W China. June–July.

Trollius ranunculinus (syn. *T. patulus*) ○◑
A Caucasian species like a dwarf form of *T. pumilus*. The dwarfer forms may only be 80mm (3in) tall in flower. The golden-yellow flowers are about 30mm (1⅛in) across, sometimes larger. June–July.

TROPAEOLUM (Tropaeolaceae)

A genus which includes the cheerful garden Nasturtium, *Tropaeolum majus*, and most of whose members are climbers. Only one species is suitable for the rock garden.

Tropaeolum polyphyllum ○
The trailing stems to 40cm (16in) long, bear deeply lobed grey-green leaves and numerous yellow nasturtium flowers. After flowering, the stems die back and the plants survive the winter as a rhizome. Plants rarely set seed in cultivation. Chile and Argentina. June–July. This superb plant demands a sunny position and is most effective planted in a high place or at a top of a wall where its stems can hang downwards; the beautiful swags of flowers always attract comment.

UVULARIA (Convalariaceae)

A genus of attractive woodland plants from North America. They have the general apperance of a Solomon's Seal but the large long-petalled, rather twisted, flowers are very distinctive. Hardy and easily grown in a moist, well-drained cool, leafy or peaty soil. Propagation by division. The genus contains 2–3 species.

Uvularia grandiflora ○◑☆
A rhizomatous perennial with erect stems arching at the top when young. The basal leaves are small and sheathing the stem, but those above are heart-shaped, pointed and unstalked. The soft-yellow flowers droop close to the top of the stem, solitary or in pairs, each 25–40mm (1–1⅝in) long. April–May.

Uvularia perfoliata ○◐
Similar, but less vigorous and with smaller flowers. May. 'Flava'—deeper-coloured flowers.

VACCINIUM (Ericaceae)

A large genus widespread in both the New and Old Worlds, containing both deciduous and evergreen species. They are dwarf or large shrubs or small trees with alternate leaves. The 4–5-parted flowers are borne in axillary or terminal racemes, but are sometimes solitary, the corolla salver- to bell-shaped, the ovary inferior. The fruit is a berry. All the species need a cool peaty or leafy, lime-free soil. Propagation by cuttings or layers. Only a few are small enough to be considered here.

Vaccinium uliginosum ◐☐
The Bog Whortleberry grows wild in the northern hemisphere (including Scotland and N England). It forms an erect, much-branched, deciduous shrub to 75cm (30in) in height, with a creeping rhizome and attractive blue or grey-green leaves which become very colourful in autumn. Flowers 1–3, white tinged with pink, terminal, on short, scaly shoots. The berries, 8–10mm ($\frac{2}{5}$in) in diameter, are black with a waxy blue bloom; they are edible and sweet, but best used for jam or wine. May–June. Suitable only for the larger rock garden.

Vaccinium myrtillus ◐☐
The familiar Bilberry or Whortleberry of Brtitish and European moors and heaths, which also grows wild in N Asia and North America. Arising from a creeping rhizome, it forms an erect, freely-branched shrub with pink flowers which are produced singly or in pairs in the axils of the bright green, flat leaves, The edible berries, 7–9mm ($\frac{1}{3}$in) in diameter, are black with a bluish bloom and sweet to taste. April–July.

Vaccinium vitis-idaea ◐☐
The Cowberry is distributed over North America, N Asia and N and C Europe, also occurring further south in the mountains. It makes a good ground cover, being prostrate and evergreen with creeping rhizomes. The elliptical or oblong leaves are gland-dotted. The white or pink, urn-shaped flowers are borne in terminal racemes. The plentiful, acid-tasting red berries are much used for jam-making. May–June.

Vaccinium delavayi ◐☐
A neat, compact, evergreen shrub up to 1m (3ft) high, with small, crowded leathery, shiny leaves, sometimes stained with red. The pink, cream or white flowers are borne in terminal racemes and are followed by small, globose, purple fruits. May–June. A fine shrub, but only completely hardy in the mildest districts.

Vaccinium oxycoccos (syn. *Oxycoccos palustris*) ◐☐☆
The Cranberry of the moors of Scotland and N England, as well as N Europe, is a delightful creeping plant with stems up to 80cm (32in) long bearing tiny oval leaves, glossy green above, whitish beneath. The small long-stalked flowers are cyclamen-shaped, 4-petalled. The fruits are edible, red, globose to pear-shaped berries about 10mm ($\frac{2}{5}$in) in diameter. May–July.

Vaccinium macrocarpon ◑□☆
This is the American Cranberry, a taller and more robust version of *V. oxycoccos*, with berries up to 20mm (⅘in) in diameter. It is cultivated in some parts of Europe for its fruit and also grown for ground cover.

Vaccinium glaucoalbum ◑□
This Himalayan plant, although an alpine species, can become too tall for the alpine garden sometimes reaching over 1m (3ft) in height. It is an evergreen shrub with 50–60mm (2–2½in) long leaves which are green above and blue-white beneath. The racemes of white flowers are tinged with pink. The black, globose fruits are covered with a heavy white to blue bloom. June. This species needs a sheltered position to do well, not being reliably hardy except in milder localities.

VALERIANA (Valerianaceae)

A large temperate and tropical genus with around 150 species consisting of perennial herbs and shrubs, some of which have medicinal value. A few European species are suited to the rock garden and these are rhizomatous perennials with erect, unbranched flower-stems. The leaves can be entire or deeply cut and the flowers white or pink, borne in dense or lax flat-topped clusters. The seeds are topped by a long feathery appendage known as a pappus. All are sun loving and summer flowering, the larger species generally too coarse for the rock garden.

Valeriana montana ○◑
An erect, slighty hairy perennial to 15cm (6in) tall. The leaves are slightly lobed and shiny. Flowers variable, lilac, pink or nearly white, 5–7mm (¼in) in length. A native of the mountains of C and S Europe where it inhabits rocky places, generally on limestone. June–July. Prefers any well-drained soil.

VELLA (Cruciferae)

An unusual genus of much-branched subshrubs bearing typical crucifer flowers. Only one species is generally cultivated, although even this is rare in gardens. It requires a very well-drained sunny position, well sheltered, and is not reliably hardy in less mild districts. Propagation from seed or cuttings.

Vella spinosa ○
A spiny, spreading much-branched subshrub to 30cm (12in) tall. The thick fleshy leaves are narrow-lanceolate, bristly margined. The flowers are borne in long racemes, the petals yellow veined with violet. S and SE Spain and NW Africa, where it inhabits limestone rocks. May–June.

VERBASCUM (Scrophulariaceae)

A large and complicated genus containing some 360 species native to Europe, North Africa and Asia. Most Mulleins are characterized by having a branched or spike-like inflorescence of yellow flowers and grey-downy, often mealy, leaves, which usually form a basal rosette. The majority are tall, robust biennials or perennials only suitable for the herbaceous border. There are a few, however, which are small enough for the rock garden, enjoying well-drained soils in a sunny position. They are readily raised from seed.

251

Verbascum dumulosum ○☆

Forms a rigid plant up to 30cm (12in) tall bearing short spikes of clear yellow flowers, each with a rich purple eye. The leaves are rounded and covered in greyish-white, soft, woolly hairs. Asia Minor. July–August.

Verbascum spinosum ○

A shrubby species endemic to stony hillsides in Crete. Plants are intricately branched, up to 30cm (12in) tall, with each branch ending in a rigid spine. Flowers clear yellow, borne in short twiggy panicles. June–July.

Verbascum × letitia ○

A beautiful hybrid between *V. dumulosum* and *V. spinosum* forming a low, compact, twiggy shrub, 20cm (8in) high and 30cm (12in) wide, with grey-green leaves. Flower-spikes 7–10cm (2¾–4in) tall, clear primrose yellow. June–August. Perhaps the finest mullein for the rock garden. Plants are not always easy to please, requiring a sheltered warm site—a raised bed is ideal. In colder districts some winter protection is advisable.

VERONICA (Scrophulariaceae)

A very large genus of nearly 300 species which once included the woody relatives from New Zealand that are now separated as *Hebe*. The speedwells are hardy, spring and summer flowering herbs which are mostly native to north temperate regions of the world. Flowers are arranged in terminal or axillary racemes, or they may sometimes be solitary, arising from a leaf axil. Each flower is a shallow, bell- or star-shaped structure which is invariably blue and usually 4-lobed. The majority are sun lovers and thrive in most good garden soils. They are readily raised from seed or cuttings.

Veronica fruticans ○☆

A delightful British native 5–10cm (2–4in) high, which is found in mountainous regions throughout Europe. It forms a neat, prostrate evergreen, bearing oval, slightly toothed leaves and terminal racemes of deep blue flowers which have a conspicuous reddish eye in the centre. June–August.

Veronica nummularia ○◑

A procumbent, mat-forming alpine, about 14cm (5½in) tall in flower, which hails from the rocky screes in the mountainous areas of France and Spain. The leaves are small and rounded and the blue, occasionally pink, flowers are borne in a small cluster. Pyrenees. June–August. In the wild a plant of damp rocks and screes, often on schists, to 1,800 (5,950ft) altitude.

Veronica austriaca ○☆

A commonly cultivated species often represented in gardens by subsp. *teucrium*, which is very similar though taller. Both are procumbent with tufts of dark green, lanceolate foliage with short, dense, spikes of bright blue flowers. Mountains of C and S Europe. June–August. Several named forms are grown including 'Rosea'—pink flowers; 'Royal Blue'—taller racemes of bright blue flowers; 'Trehane'—yellow foliage and bright blue flowers.

Veronica prostrata (syn. V. rupestris) ○

A leafy mat-forming plant with flowering stems almost 25cm (10in) tall, bearing numerous deep blue flower-spikes. Mountains of Europe and W Asia. June–

August. An easy and showy species which has many forms. 'Spode Blue—pale blue flowers; 'Royal Blue'—a darker blue form; 'Alba'—pure white; 'Mrs Holt'—soft pink. Most are free-flowering, but often rather too invasive for the small rock garden. Very good amongst paving or along path edges.

Veronica pectinata ○☆
An E European and W Asian species, forming trailing mats. The foliage is small, grey and hairy. From the trailing stems arise short spikes of blue flowers. July–August. The most commonly grown form is the cultivar 'Rosea' which has rich pink flowers.

Veronica thymifolia ○
A native of the mountains of Greece and Crete where it forms carpets of matted woody stems covered in narrow, deep-green, thyme-like leaves. The flowers vary from blue and lilac to pink and grow in short racemes. June–July.

Veronica stelleri ○☆
A Speedwell from outside Europe, being a native of Japan. It is another mat-forming species with pubescent stems and oval, toothed leaves. The purple-blue flowers appear in long racemes on sturdy, short stems to 10cm (4in) high. July–August. One of the finest species for the average rock garden, though not seen as often as it deserves.

Veronica spicata ○
The Spiked Speedwell is one of the most distinctive in the genus. Plants form a creeping mat with oval or lanceolate, blunt-toothed, leaves. The deep blue flowers are borne in erect spikes up to 30cm (12in) tall, but often less. June–August. Widespread in Europe and W Asia. 'Alba'—white flowers; 'Nana'—a fine dwarf form ☆; 'Rosea'—purplish–pink flowers.

VIOLA (Violaceae)

The pansies and violets are amongst the most delightful of all the plants grown in our gardens. The genus is widespread with some 400 species scattered in temperate regions of the world, although some are to be found on tropical mountains. Many are easy and adaptable garden plants whilst others demand the most exacting conditions if they are to succeed. Some of the coarser species can prove troublesome weeds on rock gardens and screes. They can be raised from seed or from summer cuttings.

They are a very attractive group, mostly clump-forming perennials, although there are also some annual species. They have heart-shaped leaves, but again there are exceptions with divided leaves. The leaves are stalked; where they join the stem there are appendages known as stipules; the shape of these stipules is important in identification. Each flower-stem normally carries one flower with 5 petals, the lowest of which has a spur at the back; the 2 upper petals point upwards, whilst the lateral pair turn upwards (as in pansy-type flowers) or downwards (most violets).

Viola odoráta ◑
The old favourite Scented Violet which forms patches by producing plantlets at the tips of long runners. The leaves are heart-shaped and toothed, with their stipules oval and undivided. The very fragrant violet or white flowers are about 15mm (⅝in) across with a short spur, and the lateral petals are directed downwards. Widespread

253

Veronica spicata

in Europe. March–June. There are many named forms, the following being good rock garden plants. 'Alba'—the white-flowering form; 'Cœur d'Alsace'—rose-pink flowers; 'Sulphurea'—a creamy yellow-flowered form.

Viola rupestris ◗
A typcial violet with heart- or kidney-shaped leaves with stipules which are lance-shaped and entire or slightly toothed. The flowers are 10–15mm ($\frac{2}{5}$–$\frac{3}{5}$in) wide, violet-blue, reddish or white, with a very short spur 3mm ($\frac{1}{8}$in) long. Widespread in Europe. April–August. 'Rosea' has pinkish flowers. An easy and adaptable plant like the previous species.

Viola canina ◗
The common Dog Violet is a familiar species with spreading mats of deep green, heart-shaped leaves. The flower colour is variable, but in the best forms is a deep blue, 15–25mm ($\frac{5}{8}$–1in), with a greenish or whitish spur. Widespread in northern temperate regions. April–June. There is also an attractive, white-flowered form. Useful for a semi-shaded corner, but rather invasive.

Viola sagittata ◗
A coarse violet from E North America, with large arrow-shaped leaves and violet-blue flowers. Plants grow to 15cm (6in) tall. April–May. A useful woodland species.

Viola labradorica ○◗
This familiar violet comes from North America. Plants form spreading clumps of heart-shaped leaves, beset with bluish-purple or mauve flowers, held just above or amongst the foliage. May–June. The usual form seen in gardens has the leaves suffused with deep purplish-blue.—'Purpurea'. An accommodating and attractive plant for semi-shaded places, but not too close to more choice alpines. 'Purpurea' may not be a form of *V. labradorica;* however, this is the name under which it will be found in catalogues.

Viola yakusimana (syn. *Viola verecunda* 'Yakusimana') ◗☆
A tiny gem from Japan—certainly one of the smallest violets in cultivation. Plants scarcely reach 30mm (1⅕in) tall, bearing tiny heart-shaped leaves and equally miniature white flowers, 7–8mm (⅓in) across, the lip veined with bluish-purple. June–July. So small as to be overlooked on the rock garden, but a treasure for the alpine house or trough.

Viola jooi ○◗
Another gem, scarcely 80mm (3in) tall, usually with rather long heart-shaped leaves and pretty pinkish or mauve, sweetly fragrant flowers. Romania. May–July. Less often seen than it deserves.

Viola biflora ◗
This familiar species is widespread in Europe and Asia, particularly in damp and shaded mountain habitats. It is a rather fragile, creeping plant with pale green, heart- or kidney-shaped leaves. The small violet-flowers are bright yellow, 13–15mm (½–⅗in), solitary or paired; the lip has brownish veining. June–September.

Viola hederacea ◗
This creeping species is native to SE Asia, but it is only truly hardy in the open garden in mild districts. Elsewhere it is best confined to the alpine house. The trailing stems bear broad kidney-shaped leaves. The solitary long-stalked blooms, violet-mauve tipped with white, are held clear of the foliage. July–September.

Viola pedata ◗
A distinctive species known in its native North America as the Bird's-Foot Violet, from its palmately lobed leaves. Plants form tufts to 12cm (5in) tall, the flowers held amongst the maturing foliage, the lower petals pale purple with deeper veining, the upper 2 petals deep reddish-purple. April–May. Requires a rich leafy moist soil.

Viola pinnata ◗☆
The only European violet with palmately lobed leaves, and reminiscent of the previous species. The fragrant flowers are pale violet, 10–20mm (⅖–⅘in). Alps and W Asia. April–May, sometimes earlier. A delightful plant which thrives best in a moist leafy soil, though often short lived in cultivation. The early flowers, as in many Violets, are normal, but are later followed by smaller flowers which are held at the leaf-bases and fail to open; however, they often set copious seed.

Viola cornuta

Viola cornuta ○◑☆

The Horned Pansy is widely grown in gardens. The species is native to the Pyrenees, forming broad tufts, often with well-developed stems, and with deep green oval or lanceolate, slightly toothed leaves. The fragrant pansy flowers, 20–30mm ($\frac{4}{5}$–1$\frac{1}{5}$in), are violet or lilac with a whitish 'eye' and a characteristic long-pointed spur projecting behind. June–September. Plants grow to 20cm (8in) tall. An easy, accommodating and floriferous species deserving a place on every rock garden. There is a white-flowered form, 'Alba', as well as a dwarf form of the species 'Minor', which is a finer plant for rock gardens; 'Boughton Blue'—pale blue flowers; 'Jersey Gem'—rich blue-purple; 'Lilacina'—lilac-blue; 'Purpurea'—deep violet.

Viola calcarata ○

This is another long-spurred pansy, differing from the foregoing species in its more compact habit, less deeply lobed stipules and broader-petalled flowers of deep violet with a yellow, lined, centre. Plants grow to 8–10cm (3–4in) tall. Mountains of C and S Europe, excluding the Pyrenees. April–October. Less easy in gardens and often short lived; however, relatively easy from seed. Subsp. *zoysii* (syn. *V. zoysii*) has yellow flowers and is slightly more compact in habit. E Alps and Yugoslavia.

Viola lutea ○☆

The Mountain Pansy is a widespread species in the mountains of C and S Europe. Plants form tufts to 15cm (6in) tall, with oblong or lanceolate leaves. The pansy flowers, 15–30mm ($\frac{3}{8}$–1$\frac{1}{8}$in), vary in colour from yellow to violet or white, often bicoloured; the spur is short. June–September. An easy and charming species often sowing itself around freely. In the wild a whole range of colour forms can often be spotted in a single colony.

Viola tricolor ○◑

The common Heartsease is a familiar European native. Perhaps too invasive for the average rock garden, but none the less well worth having somewhere in the garden. A variable species, often annual, with flowers variable in size (8–16mm; $\frac{1}{3}$–$\frac{2}{3}$in) and colour with a range from violet to yellow, or more often bi- or tri-coloured. April–October. Will succeed on a wide variety of soils, except waterlogged ones. Together with *V. lutea* and other species, one of the parents of the garden pansy.

Viola gracilis ○

A dainty and variable species to 12cm (5in) tall, with oval, untoothed leaves in dense tufts, the uppermost leaves often toothed. The deep violet flowers have long, slender spurs and are rather elegant, often borne in profusion. Balkans and W Asia. The true species is rather scarce in cultivation, being generally superseded by coarser and less desirable hybrids; 'Alba'—white flowers; 'Moonlight'—creamy-yellow.

Viola bertolonii ○

A small tufted plant with very variable leaves from lanceolate to oval or rounded, with a few blunt teeth on the margin; the stipules are deeply cut into narrow lobes. The flowers are violet or yellow, 20–30mm ($\frac{4}{5}$–1$\frac{1}{8}$in) wide, with the lateral petals curved upwards. Alps and Apennines. July–August.

Viola altaica ○

A smallish plant with slender creeping rhizomes and large pansy flowers. The leaves are oval with a wedge-shaped base and the stipules are deeply lobed. The flowers, 25–40mm (1–1$\frac{3}{5}$in) across, may be yellow or violet with a spur some 5mm ($\frac{1}{5}$in) long. Turkey and S USSR. March–August. Subsp. *oreades* is occasionally offered by nurseries, but is scarcely any different.

Viola cenisia ○

One of the finest European Pansies, not unlike *V. calcarata*, but more refined, with small oval, untoothed leaves and similar stipules. The flowers, 20–25mm ($\frac{4}{5}$–1in), are bright violet or lavender, the petals delicately veined, the spur long and slender. SW and C Alps. June–September. In the wild a plant of limestone rocks and screes to 2,900m (9,500ft). Not particularly easy to establish in gardens and more often seen in the alpine house.

Viola saxatilis var. *aetolica* (syn. *V. aetolica*) ○☆

A tufted species with broad-oval leaves and spreading stems to 12cm (5in) bearing numerous small, bright yellow pansy flowers of great charm. E Europe and W Asia. June–September. One of the finest of the small-flowered pansies—well worth acquiring.

Viola macedonica ○
Not dissimilar to the previous species, but flowers a deep reddish violet. June–August.

Viola cucullata (syn. ***V. obliqua***) ○◑
Thick fleshy rhizomes produce heart-shaped, hairless, leaves which have narrow lanceolate stipules and rounded-toothed margins. The flowers are usually held above the leaves and are bluish-violet, darker in the centre, about 20–25mm (⅘–1in) wide with a very short fat spur; the 2 lateral petals are hairy at the base. E North America. April–July. Forma *albiflora* and 'Alba' are white-flowered variations, possibly the same.

Viola papilionacea ◑☆
A large leafy plant like a larger version of *V. cucullata*, with hairless, very broadly heart-shaped, leaves, 4–14cm (1½–5½in) across. North America. April–July. Forma *albiflora* (better known as 'Priceana') is the Confederate Violet, with white flowers veined with blue.

Viola septentrionalis ○◑☆
This is similar, and related, to *V. cucullata* and *V. papilionacea*, but its leaves are hairy on the undersides and less widely heart-shaped. The flowers are pale to dark violet and have hairs at the base of all the petals. It is widespread in North America. May–June. Forma *alba* is a white-flowered version. 'Freckles'—pale blue flowers speckled with darker purple.

Viola eizanensis (syn. ***V dissecta*** forma ***eizanensis***) ◑
A distinctive plant with the leaves deeply divided into several jagged lobes, and the stipules joined for most of their length to the leaf stalks. The rounded, pale pinkish-purple flowers are about 20–25mm (⅘–1in) long with a fat 5mm (⅕in) long spur. Japan. March–May.

Viola delphinatha ○
One of the gems of the genus, closely related to *V. cazorlensis*. Plants are subshrubby forming small tufts to 12cm tall. The slender stems are clothed in small deep green lanceolate leaves, long-lobed at the base. The small, long-spurred pansy flowers are pale to deep rosy-lilac and are borne on long slender stalks. June–July. Mountains of the Balkans. A beautiful and much sought-after species but by no means easy to establish. Best grown in a tufa block or sink, but most often seen in the alpine house.

VITALIANA (Primulaceae)

The one species used to be in the Genus *Douglasia*.

Vitaliana primuliflora (syn. ***Douglasia vitaliana***) ○☆
An attractive mat-forming dwarf species forming rosettes of greyish-green linear leaves, 5–10mm (⅕–⅖in) long. The solitary, almost stemless, flowers are borne 1–5 to each leaf-rosette. The bright yellow corolla, 15–20mm (⅗–⅘in) across, has a long tube and narrow, usually incurved, lobes. Mountains of C and S Europe. April–May. Care should be taken to select a floriferous clone, and preferably one in which the flower opens properly. Propagate plants from rooted fragments. Thrives in well-drained gritty soil. A nice plant for a trough garden.

WAHLENBERGIA (Campanulaceae)

A genus of ome 150 species widely scattered in Asia, Australia, New Zealand and Southern Africa. They are rather *Campanula*-like plants, differing primarily in details of the dehiscence of the fruit-capsule. *Edraianthus* is also often confused with *Wahlenbergia* but can be distinguished by the clusters of flowers with a ruff of bracts beneath, rather than by the long-stalked solitary flowers. Those included here are readily grown from seed or cuttings. They make attractive rock-garden plants.

Wahlenbergia albomarginata ○◑☆
A tufted perennial to 18cm tall. Leaves in basal rosettes, spoon-shaped with a reddish-brown margin. Flowers or long scapes, blue or white, bell-shaped, 16–18mm (⅗–¾in) long. June–July. New Zealand. Can be treated as an annual, or alternatively wintered under glass.

Wahlenbergia dinarica (syn. *Edraianthus dinaricus*) ○◑
A dwarf tufted perennial with linear leaves and large solitary violet flowers, each about 20mm (⅘in) long. Balkan Peninsula.

Wahlenbergia hederacea ◑☆
A dainty creeping perennial with thread-like stems and rounded leaves. The small pale blue, rarely white, flowers, 7–10mm (¼–⅖in) long are carried on slender stalks above the foliage. July–August. W Europe (including Britain). A charming plant for a moist peaty soil.

Wahlenbergia matthewsii
A New Zealand perennial species forming rather tough tufts of basal linear leaves. The erect flowers are pale lilac-blue, bell-shaped, about 15mm (⅗in) long. July–September.

Wahlenbergia saxicola ○◑
Another dwarf perennial, 2.5–10cm (1–4in) tall, with tufts of basal, spoon-shaped or lanceolate leaves, sometimes slightly toothed. The flowers are long-stalked, pale blue, about 10mm (⅖in) long. June–July. Plants sold under this name not infrequently prove to be *W. albomarginata*.

Wahlenbergia serpyllifolius (syn. *Campanula serpyllifolia* ○◑☆)
A dwarf mat-forming perennial with small oval leaves borne in basal rosettes, the leaves hairy along the margin. The flowers are deep red in bud but open a rich purple or violet-purple, bell-shaped, 15–20mm (⅗–⅘in) long, solitary on a leafy stem. June–July. Balkan Peninsula. A fine rock garden species. 'Major' is an especially large-flowered form.

WALDSTEINIA (Rosaceae)

A small genus with some 5 species native to northern temperate zones. They have the general habit of *Fragaria* and are equally easy to cultivate, succeeding readily on most average garden soils. Propagation generally by division of the parent plant.

Waldsteinia fragarioides ○◑
A mat-forming perennial with trifoliate leaves, the leaflets oval, variously lobed and toothed. The small yellow flowers are borne in branched sprays just above the

foliage. May–June. E USA. Useful for ground cover and generally too invasive for the smaller rock garden.

Waldsteinia ternata ○◑☆

Very similar to the preceding, but a rather lower plant with larger flowers which have an epicalyx (not present in *W. fragarioides*). April–May. E Europe to Asia. The commoner of the two in general cultivation.

WULFENIA (Scrophulariaceae)

A small genus of species scattered from SE Europe to the Himalaya. Propagation by division or from seed.

Wulfenia carinthiaca ○◑

A rather rare species native to the eastern Alps and the Balkan Peninsula. The deep green oblong, rather smooth leaves are borne in lax rosettes from a thick rhizome. The violet-blue, tubular 2-lipped flowers are each about 12mm long and are borne in dense spikes up to 30cm tall. June–August. A beautiful species requiring a moist but well-drained site. However, they are prone to winter wet so that some protection is desirable.

Conversion Table

mm	in		cm	in
1–2	$c.\frac{1}{16}$		10	4
3–4	$\frac{1}{8}$		11	$4\frac{2}{5}$
5	$\frac{1}{5}$		12	$4\frac{4}{5}$
6–7	$\frac{1}{4}$		13	$5\frac{1}{5}$
8	$\frac{1}{3}$		14	$5\frac{3}{5}$
9–10	$\frac{2}{5}$		15	6
11	$\frac{7}{16}$		16	$6\frac{1}{5}$
12–13	$\frac{1}{2}$		17	$6\frac{3}{5}$
14	$\frac{9}{16}$		18	$7\frac{1}{5}$
15–16	$\frac{3}{5}$		19	$7\frac{3}{5}$
17–18	$\frac{11}{16}$		20	8
19–20	$\frac{4}{5}$		21	$8\frac{2}{5}$
22	$\frac{7}{8}$		22	$8\frac{4}{5}$
25	1		23	$9\frac{1}{5}$
30	$1\frac{1}{5}$		24	$9\frac{3}{5}$
35	$1\frac{2}{5}$		25	
40	$1\frac{3}{5}$		26	$10\frac{2}{5}$
45	$1\frac{4}{5}$		27	$10\frac{4}{5}$
50	2		28	$11\frac{1}{5}$
55	$2\frac{1}{5}$		29	$11\frac{3}{5}$
60	$2\frac{2}{5}$		30	12
65	$2\frac{3}{5}$			
70	$2\frac{4}{5}$			
75	3			
80	$3\frac{1}{5}$			
85	$3\frac{2}{5}$			
90	$3\frac{3}{5}$			
95	$3\frac{4}{5}$			
100 = 10cm = 4				

Glossary

auricle an ear-like appendage, often at the base of a leaf.

bract small leaf- or scale-like organ at the base of a flower or flower-stalk.

bulbil small bulb-like organ found above ground, in the leaf-axils or amongst the flowers.

calyx the outer whorl of floral organs, the sepals. They are often small and greenish, but not always so.

corolla the coloured part of the flowers is generally the petals, collectively called the corolla.

epicalyx a calyx outside an existing calyx.

floret the individual flowers making up a cluster or flower-head.

flower-scape a leafless flower-stalk bearing one or more flowers, and with or without bracts.

inflorescence the whole structure bearing and including the flowers.

keel-petal the lowest petal of a pea flower, consisting of two petals joined together along the lower margin to resemble a keel.

lanceolate elliptical but broadest just below the middle.

moraine rocky detritus deposited at the sides and end of a glacier.

node the point on stems where leaves are attached.

panicle a branched raceme.

pedicel the flower-stalk.

perianth a collective name for corolla and calyx combined, especially when they are difficult to distinguish.

plicae small lobes between the main lobes, as in a gentian corolla.

raceme a simple type of inflorescence in which the axis is unbranched and the individual flowers are stalked.

rhizome a fleshy, swollen, underground stem bearing leaf-scars.

scree an accumulation of rock detritus below a cliff.

spike a simple type of inflorescence in which the axis is unbranched and the individual flowers unstalked.

stamen the male organ of a flower, consisting of a stalk or filament and the anther which bears pollen.

stipule a small bract-like or leaf-like structure found in some plants at the base of the leaf-stalk.

stolon a runner; a slender horizontal stem below or above ground which gives rise to new plants.

subshrub a plant with a woody base and an herbaceous upper part that dies back at the end of each year.

tufa a soft, often honeycombed, rock formed from deposits of calcium carbonate in limestone regions.

umbel an inflorescence in which all the main stalks arise from one point, like the spokes of an umbrella.

Index

Synonyms are in italics

264